Librarians Serving Disabled Children
and
Young People

Librarians Serving Disabled Children
and
Young People

Henry C. Dequin

Department of Library Science
Northern Illinois University
DeKalb, Illinois

1983

Libraries Unlimited, Inc.
Littleton, Colorado

LIBRARIES UNLIMITED, INC.
P.O. Box 263
Littleton, Colorado 80160-0263

Library of Congress Cataloging in Publication Data

Dequin, Henry C., 1925-
  Librarians serving disabled children and young
people.

  Bibliography: p. 255
  Includes index.
  1. Libraries and the handicapped. 2. Libraries,
Children's. 3. Libraries, Young people's. 4. Handi-
capped children--Education. 5. Handicapped youth--Educa-
tion. I. Title.
Z711.92.H3D47 1983   027.6'63   83-5381
ISBN 0-87287-364-1

Libraries Unlimited books are bound with Type II nonwoven material that meets and exceeds National Association of State Textbook Administrators' Type II nonwoven material specifications Class A through E.

To
ALBERTA

Preface

Books make their way into the world through a process analogous to human birth: first, conception; then, gestation; and finally, delivery. Attendant in both processes—human reproduction and book production—are eager anticipation and restless impatience, discomfort and pleasure, anguish and satisfaction, frustration and exhilaration, labor and ease, pain and joy. So it has been with this book. It has been conceived, nurtured, and born out of a felt need to provide material to assist those who serve the informational and educational needs of disabled children and young people.

In the title and throughout the following pages, I have directed this book toward librarians, primarily public librarians and school librarians who serve disabled children and young people from kindergarten age through high school. Although addressed to librarians, much of the material presented here can be informative and useful to others who work with disabled children and young people in this age span: special education teachers, regular classroom teachers, other professionals, and parents. Some of the material is also applicable to those who serve preschool children or college-age young people who are disabled.

Since persons who provide library and information services are the primary focus of this book, the term "librarians" is used in the title and throughout the book, rather than the impersonal phrase "library services," in order to emphasize the personal nature of these services. It is a *person, the librarian*, who gives service, and not an impersonal, inanimate library. For convenience and ease in expression, the term "librarian" is used to refer to those in library or media center settings who provide services to disabled children and young people. The word, therefore, is used generically for all those whose title may be librarian, library media specialist, library media director, learning center teacher, or any other such designation.

Librarians, as other people in society today, are feeling the impact of increased and wider attention toward disabled persons. Court cases and legislation during the seventies culminated in the widespread 1981 observance of the International Year of Disabled Persons, proclaimed by the United Nations, and the subsequent proclamation of the United States Congress which designated 1982 as the National Year of Disabled Persons. Librarians are responding to this increased concern for disabled persons by endeavoring to plan and implement library services and programs for all ages and types of disabled persons, and to provide materials for their information and educational needs. In order to do so, librarians need to broaden their knowledge of disabled persons; and they need to expand and update their professional expertise in serving the needs, interests, and abilities of disabled persons.

Because of the recency of the emphasis upon disabled persons, most library schools have not offered (and most still do not offer) formal course work in services and/or materials for disabled persons. Consequently, most librarians are trying to meet the library and information needs of disabled persons without having had any formal preparation and background in library school for this specialized area of library service. Some librarians, however, have been able to obtain some amount of information in recent years through institutes, seminars, workshops, conference sessions, and published material devoted to this subject.

To help bridge this information gap, I conducted a one-week institute at Northern Illinois University in 1979 for school library media professionals, "Services and Materials for the Handicapped." The institute was followed by a fellowship program, "Library and Information Services to the Handicapped" during 1981 and 1982, which included six persons, five of whom were professional librarians—a library educator, a college librarian, a public librarian, a school librarian, and a librarian from one of the regional libraries in the National Library Service for the Blind and Physically Handicapped network. Both the institute and the two-year fellowship program were funded by the United States Department of Education (formerly the United States Office of Education). The institute provided the conceptual stimulus for this book, and the fellowship program was the gestation period during which the book was written.

Many writings about the library and information needs of disabled persons are of recent vintage, principally since 1976. Most of the published material has been in the form of journal articles. Although several books have been published on this subject, the majority are collections of journal articles. Only a very few books have been written by single or joint authors, and these deal principally with library services for persons in general, without focusing specifically and exclusively on disabled children and young people. This book, therefore, emphasizes the services which librarians can provide for children and young people who are disabled.

My gratitude goes to many people who, in various ways, have contributed to the conception, writing, and publication of this book. Although they themselves may not be aware of it, I have been inspired and motivated by Kieth Wright, Ruth Velleman, Karen Harris, and Eliza Dresang, each of whom has contributed to the literature on disabled persons. My wife, Alberta, offered continuing support, understanding, and patience throughout the lengthy research and writing process. My graduate research assistants—Jennie Steinhebel Depke, Laura Rayburn, and Tina Birkholz—gathered and checked numerous bibliographic citations, withdrew materials from the university library and returned them again, typed some of the preliminary copy, and performed many other tasks. Margaret Jacob, secretary in the Department of Library Science, typed most of the final manuscript. Bohdan S. Wynar, editor-in-chief of Libraries Unlimited, was encouraging and patient throughout the entire process. Without these people, this book would never have seen the light of day.

Table of Contents

List of Tables

1_____ Assessing the Need for Library Services

"Not what we have, but what we use;
Not what we see, but what we choose—
These are the things that mar or bless
The sum of human happiness."
—Clarency Urmy
"The Things That Count"

INTRODUCTION

Just as other agencies and institutions in our society, libraries in the past have been largely oriented toward serving nondisabled users. This primary service to able-bodied persons has been reflected in the types of materials and the programs of service which librarians have provided.

Because of the increased national emphasis on the needs of disabled persons during the 1970s and the 1980s, more librarians now recognize that they have a responsibility to serve *all* people, including the information needs of disabled children, young people, and adults. This responsibility was underscored in the White House Conference on Library and Information Services held in Washington, D.C., November 15-19, 1979. One of the resolutions passed at the conference was a "call for the elimination of all barriers to library and information service whether the barriers be 'legal, fiscal, technical, attitudinal, environmental, cultural, geographic or other.' "[1]

Greater awareness of the need for library and information services for disabled persons, indicated at the national level in a meeting of representatives of the library profession and lay delegates from the entire country, is also reflected by concerns expressed at the state level. In Illinois, for instance, it was determined that library services should be provided to many previously unserved and underserved groups, including the blind, deaf, developmentally disabled, physically handicapped, mentally handicapped, and print handicapped.[2]

As disabled children and young people are brought more and more into the mainstream of education and of the general society, in increasing numbers they will require the services, programs, and materials of all types of libraries. Public, school, academic, and special librarians should therefore include this user group in library services and programs. Before embarking, however, on a wide-scale program to provide library services for every type of disabled person, librarians should assess the need for such service. Therefore, this chapter discusses 1) initiating an assessment of need and then suggests 2) steps in assessing the need for library services to disabled children and young people.

INITIATING AN ASSESSMENT OF NEED

Librarians may initiate services for disabled children and young people either as a result of external or internal action. A specific service may be inaugurated in response to a request from outside the library, either from a disabled individual, disabled groups in the community, or from advocates for disabled persons. Also, services may be instituted because failure to provide service to particular groups may jeopardize the library's federally funded programs. In both instances, librarians are being *re-active* to external requests or influences. It is far better for a librarian to assume a *pro-active* role by formulating an internal plan to determine the need for specific library services by disabled children and young people in the library's community.[3]

Even apart from the necessity to comply with federal legislation — notably in the mandate of Section 504 of the Rehabilitation Amendments of 1973 — library services for disabled children and young people should be provided in accord with the basic principles of librarianship. *Service* is in the very essence of the library profession, and librarians are dedicated to serving *all* the people, including those who have a disability. This service involves all of the basic principles, objectives, and activities that apply to library service for able-bodied individuals. Three aspects of service, however, should be underscored in relation to library services for disabled children and young people:

1. **Knowing yourself** is the first step in knowing others. A librarian must know what his or her reaction is toward disabled children and young people. The best library service will depend upon how positively the librarian can relate to disabled persons.

2. **Knowing your community** involves being aware of those services which are offered locally to disabled persons by other organizations and institutions.

3. **Knowing the various media** entails being familiar with the materials that can stimulate a disabled child's or young person's interest in books and learning.[4]

In the assessment process and in every phase of planning, implementation, and evaluation of services, the librarian should involve other people: disabled children and young people themselves, as much as possible; parents of disabled children; and other professional resource persons. Librarians in a school library media center should also consult with classroom teachers, the special education coordinator and teachers, resource teachers, principal, and curriculum director. An advisory council, including member-representatives chosen from various organizations for disabled persons, should be created at the very beginning of the assessment process. These representatives can supply valuable input at the various stages of the needs assessment and throughout the planning, implementation, and evaluation of the program of library services.

STEPS IN ASSESSING THE NEED

Several steps should be followed in assessing the need for library services to disabled children and young people:

Step One: *Identify the disabled population by gathering data on the incidence of disabling conditions.*

Before mounting a full-scale program of services for all disability groups, it would be well to determine how many disabled children and young people are within the library's community and what types of disabilities they have. It would be unwise to initiate an extensive program of library services for children with all the handicapping conditions which are defined in P.L. 94-142, The Education for All Handicapped Children Act, when, in fact, there may be no children in the library's community with certain types of disabling conditions. Further information regarding disabling conditions and their prevalence will be presented in chapter 2.

Data on the incidence of disabling conditions for the general population can be obtained by referring to statistics available from federal and state agencies. Community data are available from local school districts, regional and municipal planning agencies, rehabilitation and special service agencies (such as Easter Seals), and special institutions in the community. School librarians should be able to secure precise data from school officials and from district and state special education offices. Supplementary ways of identifying the population are the following:

—personal knowledge and contacts

—information from relatives and friends of disabled children and young people

—service organizations, charities, local chapters of organizations for disabled persons, community groups of disabled persons

—churches and synagogs

—community centers

—hospitals

—professionals working with disabled children and young people

Step Two: *Learn as much as possible about various disabilities, especially those disabilities which are present in the library's community.*

The extent of knowledge which a librarian should have about specific disabilities will vary according to the needs and interests of the individual librarian, as well as by the amount of involvement in working with disabled children and young people. Some librarians will need and want to learn as much as they can about the medical and psychological aspects of a wide variety of disabilities. For most librarians, however, extensive medical knowledge may not be necessary, and it may be sufficient to know only the basic characteristics of the primary handicapping conditions, such as hearing impairment, visual impairment, physical impairment, and mental retardation. All librarians, however, should be attuned to discreet recognition of disabled children and young people and how a particular disability affects their use of library materials and services.

Step Three: *Consider the age-group characteristics (needs, interests, abilities) and the educational levels of the disabled children and young people in the library's community.*

In this regard it is necessary to determine the answers to the following questions:

1. What information do disabled children and young people need?

2. What influences the need: age, school, abilities, interests?

3. How urgent is the need?

4. Is the need similar for all disabled children and young people with the same disability or different disabilities?

5. Do they have information needs which require special expertise, special materials, and/or special equipment?

6. What format(s) and method(s) of communication do disabled children and young people prefer to use?

7. What do they want to know about the library?

8. What do they already know about the library?

9. What do they need to have made accessible, e.g., card catalog for the vision impaired?

10. What ways would disabled children and young people suggest to make these library services accessible?

Step Four: *Learn as much as possible about the needs, interests, abilities, and learning styles of individual disabled children and young people in the library's community.*

The questions listed under step three should also be considered in regard to *individuals*. Although there may be some common characteristics which relate to age and/or disability, each child and young person is a unique individual with unique characteristics and should be treated as such. These individual characteristics will be discussed in chapter 5. By talking with the children and young people themselves, their parents, teachers, and other professionals who work with them, it can be determined what services the librarian should provide.

Step Five: *Consult recommended standards of library service for disabled persons.*

Various national standards contain useful guidelines which can be helpful in determining library services for disabled children and young people.

1. *Minimum Standards for Public Library Systems, 1966*[5] stresses the public library's aim to serve all people including individuals and groups regardless of age, education, or "human condition." The document

refers specifically to the provision of materials and services to groups and individuals with special needs. It includes consideration of the ease of access to the facilities and materials, the availability of specialized materials, and having the necessary personnel with special competence to serve persons with disabilities.[6]

2. *Standards for Library Services for the Blind and Visually Handicapped*[7] is a reprint of the standards for library services which first appeared in *The COMSTAC Report: Standards for Strengthened Services.*[8] Although these standards were developed for library services for those who are blind and visually handicapped, many aspects of the standards are applicable to all disabled persons. The report was prepared by the Commission on Standards and Accreditation of Services for the Blind and sets forth standards of service at the federal level and for state and regional libraries, community libraries, school libraries, and libraries of agencies serving blind and visually handicapped persons. It also indicates standards for equipment and physical facilities. Although formulated in 1966 and now superseded by other more recent documents, the standards offer some good basic guidelines and should be referred to by librarians who are planning library services for disabled children and young people. In addition to the section on library services, *The COMSTAC Report* contains five sets of standards for administration which are applicable to library services, namely, 1) agency function and structure, 2) financial accounting and service reporting, 3) personnel administration and volunteer service, 4) physical facilities, and 5) public relations and fund-raising. The report also presents standards for six other types of service programs for the blind and visually handicapped: 1) education, 2) orientation and mobility programs, 3) rehabilitation centers, 4) sheltered workshops, 5) social services, and 6) vocational services.

3. *Standards of Service for the Library of Congress Network of Libraries for the Blind and Physically Handicapped,*[9] published in 1979, has replaced *The COMSTAC Report* and focuses on standards for the regional and subregional libraries in the National Library Service for the Blind and Physically Handicapped network. The standards are presented in the areas of administration, resource development, service to users, and public education and information. A section on service to users contains guidelines regarding responsibility to users, circulation of equipment and materials, materials and information, referral for service, referral for production of requested materials, reader advisory service, special groups and agencies, temporary service, and measuring user satisfaction. Librarians who serve disabled children and young people in any way should be familiar with these standards and the services which are available through the National Library Service and its network of regional and subregional libraries. Utilization of these services should be included in plans for an individual library's services to disabled children and young people.

4. *Standards for Libraries at Institutions for the Mentally Retarded*[10] reflect several basic assumptions: 1) that mentally retarded individuals are able to profit from many library services and programs; 2) that

most institutions for the mentally retarded serve severely or profoundly retarded individuals or multiply handicapped individuals; and 3) that with the assistance of full library service, the staff of a mental retardation facility can provide better treatment and services to residents. The document provides the information which is needed in order to evaluate existing services or to plan new ones.

5. At the school level, the current national standards, *Media Programs: District and School*,[11] apply to media programs for all students in general but contain no specific statements regarding services for disabled children and young people or any other special groups. Reference is made, however, to the need for providing resources and guidance to all students in relation to their individual needs, interests, and learning styles as well as the need to adjust program requirements for children with handicaps and learning disabilities.[12]

Other statements, although not specifically in the nature of standards or guidelines, should also be considered when planning for library services for disabled children and young people. One of these is the statement prepared by the National Commission on Libraries and Information Science in 1975, *Toward a National Program for Library and Information Services: Goals for Action*.[13] Concern for library services for disabled children and young people is inherent in the commission's major goal:

> To eventually provide every individual in the United States with equal opportunity of access to that part of the total information resource which will satisfy the individual's educational, working, cultural and leisure-time needs and interests, regardless of the individual's location, social or physical condition or level of intellectual achievement.[14]

Specifically in regard to blind and physically handicapped persons, the document states:

> The more than six million blind and physically handicapped persons in the United States need materials in a special format. The National Commission commends the Library of Congress, Division for the Blind and Physically Handicapped, for its dedicated work in this area, and regards it as critical that its work be continued and expanded. Specifically, the Commission recommends that added efforts be made to seek out and serve those eligible for the service; utilize more effectively the limited resources available, considering the expense and time consumed in the production of embossed and recorded books and periodicals; increase the quantity and quality of available materials, taking advantage insofar as possible of new technological advances in the production of braille and music braille; and implement plans for the computerized National Union Catalog of embossed and recorded materials. Attention should also be directed toward the continued increase in the number of appropriate circulation outlets, so that handicapped persons may be served more adequately by their local libraries; further development of the multi-state service, centralized cataloging, storage and distribution centers,

development of more efficient interlibrary loan techniques; and the promotion of cooperation and communication among participating libraries and agencies.[15]

More recently, the White House Conference on Library and Information Services, held in 1979, passed two specific resolutions which attempt to identify needs and address various methods for meeting these needs in the areas of access-related issues and the special information needs of hearing-impaired persons. Although these resolutions were not formulated as national standards, they constitute far-reaching goals for action in library services for disabled persons. Consequently, they should be seriously considered by personnel, boards, and planning committees in all types of libraries.[16]

Step Six: *Determine the specific types of services, programs, and special materials which are needed by the disabled children and young people represented in the library's community.*

Consider, for example, whether deposit collections are needed in hospitals and other institutions, how many, and where they should be located; the number and routes of bookmobiles; and the number of disabled children who require home visits and how often. Special services will be further discussed in chapter 6, programs in chapter 7, and materials in chapters 8 and 9.

Step Seven: *Figure the cost of specific aspects of the service program in terms of personnel, materials, equipment, space, and ongoing costs.*

Every effort should be made and every avenue should be explored to obtain the necessary funds to support the program at the desired level. A proportion of the library budget should be allocated for services to disabled children and young people equivalent to the percentage of these individuals in the library's community. Frequently, additional funding may be available through local organizations, service groups, women's clubs, businesses, and industries as well as through governmental agencies at the local, state, and federal levels. Kieth C. Wright has given suggestions for obtaining additional funds and has listed a number of sources of information about grants. In particular, he has presented criteria and ideas regarding the preparation of foundation and government proposals.[17]

Realistically, however, it may not be immediately possible to implement all the services one would like because of financial constraints and limitations of personnel and facilities. Trade-offs may be necessary. A beginning can be made with the financial and human resources presently available, but a definite plan should be formulated to expand the service program each year.

NOTES

[1]"The WHCLIS Resolutions," *American Libraries* 11 (January 1980): 22.

[2]"Illinois White House Conference Recommendations," *Illinois Libraries* 61 (April 1979): 335.

[3]Helen Stough, " 'Let Me Hear Your Hand' — Library Service for Handicapped Children," *Illinois Libraries* 62 (December 1980): 878-81, has

emphasized such a pro-active role for the librarian in beginning a program of library service for disabled children.

[4]Moya Martin Duplica, "The Librarian and the Exceptional Child," *Rehabilitation Literature* 33 (July 1972): 198-203.

[5]American Library Association, Public Library Association, *Minimum Standards for Public Library Systems, 1966* (Chicago: American Library Association, 1967).

[6]Ibid., pp. 27, 33.

[7]*Standards for Library Services for the Blind and Visually Handicapped* (Chicago: American Library Association, 1967).

[8]Commission on Standards and Accreditation of Services for the Blind, *The COMSTAC Report: Standards for Strengthened Services* (New York: National Accreditation Council for Agencies Serving the Blind and Visually Handicapped, 1966), pp. 191-218.

[9]American Library Association, Association of Specialized and Cooperative Library Agencies, Standards for Library Service to the Blind and Physically Handicapped Subcommittee, *Standards of Service for the Library of Congress Network of Libraries for the Blind and Physically Handicapped* (Chicago: American Library Association, 1979).

[10]American Library Association, Association of Specialized and Cooperative Library Agencies, Standards for Libraries at Institutions for the Mentally Retarded Subcommittee, *Standards for Libraries at Institutions for the Mentally Retarded* (Chicago: American Library Association, 1981).

[11]American Association of School Librarians and Association for Educational Communications and Technology, *Media Programs: District and School* (Chicago: American Library Association; and Washington: Association for Educational Communications and Technology, 1975).

[12]Ibid., pp. 8, 12.

[13]National Commission on Libraries and Information Science, *Toward a National Program for Library and Information Services: Goals for Action* (Washington: U.S. Government Printing Office, 1975).

[14]Ibid., p. xi.

[15]Ibid., p. 41.

[16]National Commission on Libraries and Information Science, *Information for the 1980's: Final Report of the White House Conference on Library and Information Services, 1979* (Washington: U.S. Government Printing Office, 1980), pp. 72-74.

[17]Kieth C. Wright, "Funding Media Services for Handicapped Children," in *School Library Media Services to the Handicapped*, edited by Myra Macon (Westport, CT: Greenwood Press, 1982), pp. 117-29.

2 _____ Who Is Disabled?

"Of the maimed, of the halt and the
blind in the rain and the cold —
Of these shall my songs be fashioned,
my tales be told."
— John Masefield

INTRODUCTION

In order to provide optimum service to children or young people in school, public, or academic libraries, librarians need to know the characteristics of human growth and development for particular age groups. They should also learn as much as possible about an *individual* user's needs, interests, and abilities which combine to make each child or young person uniquely different from every other person.

Educational psychologists emphasize that distinctive patterns of human growth and development are characteristic of different age groups in the various stages of life. As each individual advances through life from infancy into childhood and adolescence and finally into adulthood, changes occur in the physical, mental, emotional, social, and spiritual development of that individual. Needs change, interests change, and abilities change as a person continues to grow. Yet, although these developmental changes are generally characteristic for all children and young people, they are not precisely the same for everyone. Each individual is uniquely different. While passing through the same periods of growth and development and subject to the same kinds of changes, each person is unique and different in the rate of growth and development as well as in the way the changes affect that individual.

Other factors need to be considered in regard to disabled children and young people. In addition to the general patterns of human growth and development at various age levels, there are unique characteristics for each type of disabling condition. Librarians need to be familiar with such disabling conditions and the distinctive characteristics of each disability. Yet each disabled child or young person is as uniquely different as those who are not disabled. The librarian who knows and recognizes the unique individuality of each library user who has a disability will be better able to serve those children and young people.

As a foundation for such understanding, this chapter focuses on four aspects in regard to disabled children and young people: 1) terminology, 2) definitions of disabling conditions, 3) labeling, and 4) prevalence of disabilities.

TERMINOLOGY

Greater concern about terminology has come with the increased emphasis in recent years upon individuals who are disabled. How should we refer to disabled individuals? What term or terms are the best to use to describe them? Are they "special," "exceptional," "disabled," "handicapped," "impaired," all of the above, or none of the above?

Much difference of opinion exists regarding the proper terminology. For each term, there are groups and individuals in favor of one term in preference to the others. Sometimes it is even insisted that only the preferred term is appropriate and that the other terms are inappropriate and should not be used. For each of the terms, however, there are advantages and disadvantages.

"Special" and "Exceptional"

The word "special" is widely used to describe that area of education which has come to be known since the beginning of this century as "special education." It designates an educational program which is different from the regular educational program arranged for the majority of children and young people. The premise behind the use of the term "special" is that most students are average or "regular" students and that some students are physically and/or mentally different from average students. The students who are different may have a physical disability (orthopedic, visual, or auditory) or their mental ability may be at either end of the intelligence scale, that is, either low intellectual ability or high intellectual ability (giftedness). Because of this difference from the "regular" and average students, these children are considered "special" and have "special" educational needs.

Some people and groups have adopted the term "exceptional" and use this word either in preference to "special" or as a synonym. The word designates the same kinds of individuals who are considered "special," that is, those with a physical disability and those who have either a lower or a higher mental ability. Some advocacy groups, such as the Council for Exceptional Children in Reston, Virginia, favor the word "exceptional." It is also used in the title of many books and a number of professional journals.

While both "special" and "exceptional" are useful words and can be properly understood in context, they also have certain disadvantages. By referring to some children and young people as "special" or "exceptional"—no matter for what reason—the impression may be given, especially to other children and possibly also to teachers and parents, that these children are more important, that they receive more consideration than the average "regular" child, and that the average child is not "special" or "exceptional." In actuality, each child and young person, as a unique individual, should be considered a "special" and "exceptional" person. Thus, in trying to offset past educational neglect of disabled and gifted children, care must be taken that other children and young people who are average and "regular," who are neither disabled nor gifted, are not neglected in the present.

Sarah McCracken, a special educator, pointed out another concern: the term "special" can be misconstrued by conveying the impression that special education has some "special" techniques or magical solutions in teaching these students. Because of this interpretation, she feels that many librarians and regular classroom teachers have been hesitant to work with "special" children and young people, believing that "they do not have that 'special' secret that opens up all the mysteries regarding how these children learn and exactly how to teach them. That is a myth...."[1]

"Handicapped" and "Disabled"

Similar to the synonymous meaning and usage of "special" and "exceptional," the words "handicapped" and "disabled" are closely associated to each other. Although the word "handicap" has been widely used for many years and is the term employed in federal legislation, it is a somewhat ambiguous concept, neither objective nor well defined nor understood very well. Research by Coet indicates that the definition of "handicap" differs significantly according to a person's sex, race, religion, and geographic location.[2] The dictionary states that the word "handicap" derives from "a game of forfeits and exchanges in which the players held forfeit money in a cap, alter. *hand in cap*." One definition of the word included in the dictionary is "a disadvantage that makes achievement unusually difficult, especially a physical disability that limits the capacity to work."[3]

Within recent years there has been a growing preference for the use of "disability" instead of "handicap." Some individuals and groups, such as the Disability Rights Movement, favor the terms "disability" and "disabled" and voice strong opposition to "handicap" and "handicapped."[4] The Educational Resources Information Center (ERIC) acknowledged in 1980 this growing preference by changing all the ERIC descriptors which used the words "handicapped" or "handicap" to "disabilities." Ruth Velleman, in her book *Serving Physically Disabled People*, makes a strong case for her preferred usage of "disabled" and its opposite "able-bodied."[5]

Velleman and other writers reason that "disability" and "disabled" describe a medical or biological condition, and therefore these terms are more acceptable than "handicap" and "handicapped," which denote a social condition and imply that an individual has limitations.[6] Thus, the reasoning in favor of "disability" and "disabled" goes this way: Disabled persons have impairments, such as missing or defective body parts or mental retardation. Because of the impairment, a disabled person is restricted or prevented from performing certain activities considered normal for humans. A disability, however, does not always present a handicap. The disability becomes a handicap only if it prevents a disabled person from overcoming the limitations of the disability. The word "handicapped," therefore, carries a negative connotation and implies that a disability prevents a person from being a fully functioning member of society. For example, children with hearing impairments are disabled because they need help in learning to communicate. These children are handicapped, however, only if their disability prevents them from participating in normal activities. If the disability does *not* prevent participation, then such children are not handicapped.

Frank Bowe's basic premise, reiterated throughout his excellent book *Handicapping America: Barriers to Disabled People*, is that a person may have a disability but need not be handicapped unless the society in which the individual lives imposes limitations, restrictions, obstacles, and barriers which are handicapping to that person.[7] The barriers may be real or artificial, tangible or intangible, but they are believed to be virtually insurmountable and to limit the person's total activities and lifestyle, making the person dependent upon others for assistance. Because of the focus on the barriers, this concept does indeed handicap and limit people.

Thus, a "disability" becomes a "handicap" only when the environment is full of attitudinal and physical barriers *and* when the disabled person accepts the limiting definition of himself or herself. In this limiting sense, the U.S. Department of Health, Education, and Welfare defined "handicapped" persons as those who have a physical impairment that limits one or more of their major life activities, such as "caring for one's self, performing manual tasks, walking, seeing, hearing, speaking, breathing, learning, and working."[8]

Some people reject the word "handicap" because of its historic associations and society's negative stereotypes. In bygone years those who were orthopedically or mentally handicapped, blind, or deaf were considered incompetent to help themselves and had to depend on the charity of others. Consequently, they were always poor beggars in society.[9] For this reason, some people feel that the word "handicapped" has a paternalistic tone and conjures up the stereotyped images of "helping the handicapped."[10] In line with this thought, Biklen and Bogdan stated that the word "handicap" derives from the practice of beggars holding "cap in hand" as they solicited alms.[11] However, dictionary definitions of the word do not include this derivation, as noted above.

Caution should be exercised also in the use of the terms "disability" and "disabled person." Both terms tend to accent the negative characteristics of an individual, what a person *cannot* do rather than what that person *can* do. Unfortunately, it is necessary to realize what an individual cannot do in order to concentrate on what that individual can do. However, when using the term "disabled person," it should be remembered that *the person is not disabled* but that the person has a particular disability. Further, a "disability" is only one aspect of an individual and not the sum of that person. It would be better to speak of the physical characteristics of a person rather than the disability or disabilities and to emphasize the *positive abilities* of that individual.

While both "disabled" and "handicapped" are used as acceptable adjectives in written and oral communication, their use as nouns in expressions such as "the disabled" or "the handicapped" is not considered good usage because such terms convey a separate and inferior status. "Individuals with handicaps" or "persons with disabilities" are positive alternatives which convey a sense of respect and equality. The preferred terms to describe the general public are "abled-bodied," "nondisabled," or "nonhandicapped" rather than the term "normal," which tends to demean persons with disabilities by suggesting that they are "abnormal" or "subnormal."

Other words and expressions have been suggested. The National Association of the Physically Handicapped has recommended the term "handicapper" in place of "cripple," "invalid," and "handicapped."[12] The term "handicapism" is advocated to designate the stereotyping, prejudice, and discrimination which society practices against the disabled.[13] Some people favor another new word, "physicalism," to denote discrimination on the basis of physical appearance.[14] A few years ago, Massachusetts passed a law prohibiting any kind of labeling. Henceforth, the law stated, handicapped children were to be identified only as "children with special needs." Yet this phrase, too, can be criticized because it seems to emphasize an individual's "neediness."[15]

The *Interracial Books for Children Bulletin*[16] presented a list of terms considered to be offensive and suggested some preferred substitutes:

Offensive	Preferred
handicap, handicapped persons	disability, disabled person
deaf and dumb, deaf-mute, the deaf	deaf, hearing disability, hearing impairment
mongoloid	Down's syndrome
cripple, crippled	orthopedic disability, mobility impaired, disabled person
the blind	blind person, sight disability, visually impaired
retard, retardate, idiot, imbecile, feeble-minded	retarded, mental impairment, mentally disabled
crazy, maniac, insane, mentally ill	emotional disability, emotional impairment, developmentally disabled

Librarians, as enlightened members of society, should take these suggestions seriously and make a conscious effort to employ the more preferred expressions in their own vocabulary.

Librarians also need to give attention to some of the outdated subject headings which have been used in library catalogs because they have been recommended in the *Library of Congress Subject Headings List* and *Sears' List of Subject Headings*. Some of these headings are "Abnormal children," "Abnormalities, Human," "Atypical children," "Children, Retarded," and "Children, Feebleminded." Other terms which are considered inappropriate today have been used as cross-references to "Mentally Handicapped Children," such as "Children, Backward," "Feebleminded," "Imbecility," and "Morons." In 1976 the Minnesota Conference on Handicapped Individuals proposed that inappropriate subject headings should be deleted from library catalogs and replaced with more appropriate headings.[17]

While recognizing the struggles and problems disabled persons have experienced, it must also be recognized that it is possible to be over-sensitive about terminology. The view taken in this book is that all of these terms—"special," "exceptional," "disabled," and "handicapped"—as well as the word "impaired" are valid terms. They can all be used if they are properly understood in a positive way in reference to those who may be defined by these terms. Although all the terms are used in this book in a synonymous sense, the words "disability" and "disabled" are used more frequently even though it is recognized that the terms "handicap" and "handicapped" are preferred by the federal government and are the terms used in legislation affecting the handicapped. It should be noted, however, that both "special" and "exceptional" are used in this book only in reference to children and young people who are disabled, not in reference to those who are gifted.

In the final analysis, the words themselves are not what is really important. More important are the ways in which the words are used and understood. Equally important are the attitudes of people toward disabled individuals (to be discussed in chapter 4), attitudes which lie behind the words that are used. If the attitudes are correct, the expression of those attitudes through words and terminology will be correct.

DEFINITIONS OF DISABLING CONDITIONS

There is a broad range of disabling conditions, encompassing many different types of disabilities and impairments. A disability may be mild or severe, temporary or permanent. It may be physical, intellectual, emotional, some other condition, or a combination of these. Many disabilities will affect learning, that is, the way the child acquires knowledge and processes information. Consequently, the child's use of learning materials and information resources will also be affected. Librarians should be aware of the types of disabling conditions in terms of library needs in order to serve those who have these disabilities.

The medical, sociological, psychological, and educational aspects of disabilities have been treated extensively in other sources. This section merely describes various disabling conditions on the basis of P.L. 94-142, The Education for All Handicapped Children Act, so that librarians may better understand these conditions and have a better base for providing library and information services to disabled children and youth.

P.L. 94-142 defines disabled children and young people from 0 to 21 years of age in terms of both physical and mental impairments. Eleven categories of disabilities are specifically mentioned and defined in the law: deaf, hard of hearing, visually handicapped, deaf-blind, orthopedically impaired, other health impaired, speech impaired, mentally retarded, specific learning disability, seriously emotionally disturbed, and multiply handicapped.[18] For discussion in this chapter, these eleven categories are grouped into the following six general categories:

1. sensory impairments

2. communication disorders

3. physical and orthopedic impairments

4. intellectual impairments

5. behavioral disorders

6. multiple and severe impairments

Sensory Impairments

Impairments related to the senses of seeing and hearing include persons who are deaf, hard of hearing, visually impaired, or both deaf and blind. Frequently these are invisible or "hidden" disabilities because they are not always obvious to others and are not easily detected unless the person wears a hearing aid, uses a white cane, or in some other way indicates an auditory or visual impairment.

VISUAL IMPAIRMENTS

Children and young people with visual impairments fall into one of several categories:

1.   Those who have no vision at all and are "totally blind." Associated with their blindness may be other factors, such as slower mobility, restricted interpersonal relations, and lowered school achievement.[19]

2.   Those who are partially sighted with various degrees of low vision. Their vision is quite defective even with correction. They can use their eyes but to a lesser degree than the average child. On the basis of medical standards they may be regarded as "legally blind" and therefore are visually impaired, but they are not considered "blind." Educational retardation may not be as great for these children as it is for those who are totally blind.[20] Although they may not see as sharply as an average person and may have to get very close in order to see an object or to read books in small print, legally blind children and young people are still able to function as sighted persons in the everyday routines of life.

3.   Those who have visual defects that can be corrected. They are able to function normally through the use of optical aids. Some may have a condition which can be remedied through medical treatment or through surgery, such as "lazy-eye."

4.   Those who are "color-blind." They do not see colors as the average person does and therefore have to adjust to the different way in which they perceive colors.

Children and young people in the third and fourth categories are usually not considered to be visually impaired to the extent that they require special library materials or educational arrangements, although some visually impaired children may be able to read only for short periods of time. Those who are partially sighted, low vision, or legally blind may require large-print books, magnification equipment, or talking books. It should be noted in this regard that it is not necessary for a child or youth to be legally blind in order to be visually impaired in regard to the educational process. Many are entitled to special educational services even though they are not legally blind.[21] Those who are totally blind, however, require communication through the senses of hearing and touch. In order to "read," they need books in braille, tactile devices, or talking books.

HEARING IMPAIRMENTS

Hearing impairments are divided into two broad categories:

1.   Those who are deaf, either totally or partially, in one or both ears. The hearing loss is so severe that the child cannot understand what is being said either with or without a hearing aid. For such children and young people, the sense of hearing is not functional for the usual activities of life.

2. Those who are hard of hearing and have difficulty hearing in one or both ears, but the difficulty is not as severe as deafness. For these children and young people there is at least a partial functioning of the sense of hearing either with or without a hearing aid.

There are two broad classes of deafness: 1) the *congenitally deaf* (*prelingual deafness*), which includes those who were born deaf or who lost their hearing before speech and language were developed; and 2) the *adventitiously deaf* (*postlingual deafness*), referring to those who were born with normal hearing but who lost their hearing after speech and language were developed either because of illness or accident.[22]

All children and young people who are deaf or hard of hearing have some degree of communication problem. As a result, many also have language and speech deficits, depending on when the hearing loss occurred, either before or after learning speech and language. Reading, spelling, and abstract concepts may be difficult for them. In order to process information they must use other sense channels either partially or totally and in a way that is different from children who have normal hearing. The manner and degree of such processing depend on the extent and type of hearing loss, the age when the loss occurred, the child's basic intelligence, the age of the child when remedial instruction was begun, and the quality of the instruction. Because of the difficulty with communication skills, the child may also have problems in relating to others and normal social maturity may have been slowed.[23]

Communication Disorders

Communication disorders are included in two of the eleven categories listed in P.L. 94-142, namely, "speech impaired" and "specific learning disabilities."

SPEECH IMPAIRMENT

"Speech impaired" is defined in the law as a communication disorder, such as stuttering, impaired articulation, a language impairment, or a voice impairment which adversely affects a child's educational performance. There are many forms of speech impairments, including, among others, disorders of articulation and voice which range from minor language difficulties to a total lack of speaking ability. The child's speech may deviate so far from the speech of other people that it calls attention to itself, interferes with the child's communication, or causes the child to become maladjusted. It may be unintelligible speaking or an unpleasant pitch and/or volume. There are also many causes for these disorders—developmental, functional, and/or organic—and speech impairments are sometimes related to deafness, mental retardation, or cerebral palsy. The speech impairment may be the only departure in a child who has an otherwise average and normal developmental pattern.[24]

LEARNING DISABILITIES

"Specific learning disabilities" are closely related to speech impairments but cover a much broader range of disorders. The law defines these as disorders affecting the child's understanding or use of spoken or written language, being manifested by an imperfect ability to listen, think, speak, read, write, spell, or do mathematical calculations. Conditions such as perceptual handicaps, brain injury, minimal brain dysfunction, dyslexia, and developmental aphasia are included in this category. The term does not include, however, children who have learning problems which are primarily the result of visual, hearing, or motor handicaps, mental retardation, or environmental, cultural, or economic disadvantage. Although those who are mentally retarded are not included in the category of learning disabilities, there may be some similarities between the two groups. Commenting on the definition of learning disabilities, Kieth Wright stated:

> This definition assumes that the child will have average or better I.Q. scores and that the performance of the child will not match what might be expected from the I.Q. level. This major discrepancy between what is expected and performance is usually found in some part of the language activity of the child, most typically in reading difficulties.[25]

Kirk and Gallagher also noted the frequent confusion among teachers, parents, and students surrounding the term "learning disability," and they attempted to make a differentiation by dividing learning disabilities into academic disabilities and developmental learning disabilities.[26]

Physical and Orthopedic Impairments

Physical and orthopedic impairments may be skeletal, neurological, or any loss of strength and stamina. Two categories listed in P.L. 94-142 fall into these areas, "orthopedically impaired" and "other health impaired."

"Orthopedically impaired" refers to those children having a severe physical disability that adversely affects educational performance. The term includes impairments such as club foot, absence of a limb, cerebral palsy, poliomyelitis, bone tuberculosis, and so forth. These are physical handicaps or motor disabilities which are not visual, hearing, or speech impairments.

In the category of "other health impaired" are children who have limited strength, vitality, or alertness due to chronic or acute health problems, such as a heart condition, tuberculosis, rheumatic fever, nephritis, asthma, sickle cell anemia, hemophilia, epilepsy, lead poisoning, leukemia, or diabetes, which adversely affects a child's educational performance. These health problems are relatively long-term physical conditions which involve the blood, heart, digestion, or respiration. Velleman describes 19 physical disabilities, many of which are specifically named in the law.[27]

In order to receive special educational services, the orthopedic or other health impairment must be severe enough that it affects the child's educational performance. While this may be the case for some children and young people who are impaired in these ways, physical impairments do not necessarily affect intellectual and mental ability. Depending on the age at which the impairment occurred and the nature and severity of the impairment, a child may learn to read, write, spell, do arithmetic, and progress educationally just as well as other children. The motor coordination and mobility of the child may be affected to the extent that the use of crutches, a walker, a cane, or a wheelchair is required.

Emotional problems may result because of the disability, however, as well as deficiencies in social age and relationships with others. In addition to the motor handicap, there may also be other complications which affect mental ability, speech, or the senses of seeing and hearing.[28]

Intellectual Impairments

Children and young people who have intellectual impairments are referred to as "mentally retarded" in general usage as well as in P.L. 94-142. As was pointed out previously, mentally retarded and learning disabled children are not the same, even though there are some similarities between the two groups. The law defines "mentally retarded" to include those who have significant subaverage general intellectual functioning together with deficits in adaptive behavior or functional proficiency, that is, behavior which meets the standards of independence and social responsibility that are expected of a person's age and cultural group. These behavioral deficits should have been observable throughout the child's development and, as a result, have affected the child's educational performance adversely.

This definition is basically identical to those adopted by the American Association on Mental Deficiency and by the American Psychiatric Association.[29] The definition emphasizes that intelligence quotient (I.Q.) scores alone should not be considered in determining mental retardation. It is necessary to consider also when these characteristics of subaverage intellectual functioning appeared as well as how the individual has adapted and is able to function in his or her own social environment. Even though a person may have subaverage intelligence, it is possible for the person to function with good social adjustment as a productive member of society.

Behavioral Disorders

Emotional disturbance in children and young people was contained in P.L. 94-142 in the category "seriously emotionally disturbed." This category includes schizophrenic or autistic children and others who have a marked degree of one or more of the following characteristics, displayed over a long period of time:

1. an inability to learn which cannot be explained by intellectual, sensory, or health factors

2. an inability to build or maintain satisfactory interpersonal relationships

3. inappropriate types of behavior or feelings under normal circumstances

4. a general pervasive mood of unhappiness or depression

5. a tendency to develop physical symptoms or fears associated with personal or school problems

The term does not include children who are socially maladjusted, unless they are also seriously emotionally disturbed.

While emotionally disturbed children experience difficulty in coping with some situations, they may be either high or low in intelligence. Academically they may even be a success, but more frequently they fail in school in at least some subjects.[30] Although some of these children may appear to be like retarded children in many ways, particularly because their reading level is low, emotionally disturbed children are different from retarded children. Some may have a very good reading ability, while others may have difficulty understanding both written and spoken language.

Multiple and Severe Impairments

The final category of impairments listed in P.L. 94-142 is the "multiply handicapped." Children and young people in this category may have a combination of impairments, other than deaf-blind, that causes such severe problems that the child cannot be accommodated in a special education program for any one of the impairments. In the past, many multiply and severely handicapped children and young people were excluded from a public school education and were sometimes placed in a residential school instead. P.L. 94-142 now makes it mandatory to educate all children in the least restrictive environment, and public schools must therefore organize to serve these children within the public school system.

LABELING

Disabling conditions were discussed in the preceding section in terms of the eleven categories listed in P.L. 94-142. Although these categories are used in the law as well as in this book, it should be remembered that categories, classifications, or labels are used here only for the sake of convenience and discussion.

In the past, labels and classifications were used as a means of placing a child in a particular educational program which separated the child from nonhandicapped children and the regular school program. The classification of a child as retarded, a slow learner, dumb, emotionally disturbed, bad, or any other label constituted a stigma which was just as great as being labeled a drunkard.[31] As a result of such a stigma, a child who was labeled "mentally retarded," for instance, would frequently be teased by other children for being in the "dummy" class.

Instead of contributing to a child's educational growth, the label often served only to hold the child back. Several research studies have indicated that labeling has had a negative influence on the attitudes of educators toward disabled children.[32] A child who was labeled "retarded" was viewed and treated differently by administrators, teachers, counselors, parents, and others and was expected to behave in certain stereotyped patterns. As a result of the label, a child who had previously been considered on the basis of positive and individual characteristics became a child characterized by a disability.[33] The label often became a self-fulfilling prophecy. Less was expected of the child by teachers, parents, and other adults. The child, too, would frequently behave according to that image, adopting the behavioral patterns of the other "retarded" children.[34]

In past practice many children were misclassified and placed in an inappropriate educational setting. Smith and Greenberg found that decisions to label children as mentally retarded often tended to be biased against the lower socioeconomic levels and thus contributed to the inappropriate labeling of these children.[35] In 1973 Dimond extensively traced some of the court cases in which children were labeled and classified wrongly and thus were denied the right to an equal and appropriate education.[36] The case of the *Pennsylvania Association for Retarded Children v. the Commonwealth of Pennsylvania*, which will be discussed in the next chapter, is only one example out of many which presented abundant evidence of misclassification and denial of educational opportunity.[37] In many instances a child who may have been labeled wrongly was stuck for life with that classification. When labels were once applied to a child, they were very difficult to remove, and only one child in ten who was labeled as disabled was ever returned to a regular classroom. Bowe criticizes the practice in education of finding something wrong with a child who did not progress adequately in school rather than finding something wrong with the instruction the child received.[38]

Although labels can have negative effects on children and should be eliminated as much as possible, it is not possible to avoid some form of labeling or classification. Whether the labels are formal or informal, whether they are regarded as negative or positive, they will undoubtedly continue to exist in some form.[39] Kirk and Gallagher listed both the supposed advantages and disadvantages of labeling and suggested a middle ground, recommending that precautions should be taken if labeling is used.[40] Even the contemporary use of the terms "special," "exceptional," "disabled," "handicapped," and "impaired" can be a form of labeling.[41] Although these terms are generally used with positive motivations and intentions, they, too, might inadvertently result in negative effects. It is necessary to try to retain the usefulness of the terminology while endeavoring to minimize any negative and harmful effects of labels. The procedural due process guarantees in P.L. 94-142 are aimed at assuring that the classification is accurate and that the proposed treatment is appropriate.[42]

Within recent years, largely as a result of P.L. 94-142 and a general effort to consider each handicapped child and young person as an individual, there has been a trend away from the use of categorical and diagnostic labels. It is recognized that special children do not always fit into neat categories with equable and consistently homogeneous characteristics. Special educators, for instance, are considering the functioning level of the child and are attempting to meet the child's educational needs on the basis of the individual's current functioning level. If everyone in society, including librarians, would view each child as a learner rather than trying to pin a label on the child, greater optimism and a more favorable atmosphere would exist for all disabled persons.[43]

PREVALENCE OF DISABILITIES

Statistics which report the number of disabled children and young people in the United States differ to some extent, depending on how the categories are grouped and how the figures are reported. In P.L. 94-142 the Congress concluded that in 1975 there were about 8 million handicapped children and young people, approximately 12% of the total school population. Brewer and Kakalik reported varying prevalence estimates from eleven different sources and noted that the estimates were generally in the range of 9 to 12% or above. They also indicated that in 1970 the number of handicapped youth aged 0-21 stood at 9.5 million.[44]

The difference in reporting methods and statistics can be seen by comparing Tables 1-4. Table 1 contains the 1975 estimates (by type of disabling condition) that were used by the Congress as a basis for its findings as reported in P.L. 94-142. At that time it was estimated that there was a total of 7,887,000 disabled children and young people from birth to 19 years old, of whom approximately 50% were receiving educational services. The estimated number of handicapped children who were served or unserved in 1975-1976 is reported in table 2 (page 38) by type of handicap. The totals in table 2 correspond to those given in table 1, but the percentages of those served and unserved are different. For almost every type of handicap recorded in table 2 the percentage served is greater than in table 1. This difference may be because the U.S. Office of Education was projecting greater services as a result of the passage of P.L. 94-142. More recent figures for the school year 1977-1978 show that 3,777,106 children (7.36% of school-age children) received educational services (see table 3, page 39), while there was a potential number of 2,380,950 unserved children (see table 4, page 39).

Table 1
Education of the Handicapped[45]

Type of Handicap	Total Number	Percent Served
Speech impaired	2,293,000	81%
Mentally retarded	1,507,000	83
Learning disabilities	1,966,000	12
Emotionally disturbed	1,310,000	18
Crippled and other health impaired	328,000	'72
Deaf	49,000	71
Hard of hearing	328,000	18
Visually handicapped	66,000	59
Deaf-blind, other multiple handicapped	40,000	33
Total	7,887,000	50% (Average)

Source: U.S. Office of Education

(Text continues on page 40)

Table 2
Estimated Number of Handicapped Children
Served and Unserved by Type of Handicap[46]

Category	1975-76 Served (Projected)	1975-76 Unserved	Total Hand. Children Served & Unserved	% Served	% Un-served
Total Age 0-19	4,310,000	3,577,000	7,887,000	55%	45%
Total Age 6-19	3,860,000	2,840,000	6,700,000	58%	42%
Total Age 0-5	450,000	737,000	1,187,000	38%	62%
Speech Impaired	2,020,000	273,000	2,293,000	88%	12%
Mentally Retarded	1,350,000	157,000	1,507,000	90%	10%
Learning Disabilities	260,000	1,706,000	1,966,000	13%	87%
Emotionally Disturbed	255,000	1,055,000	1,310,000	19%	81%
Crippled & Other Health Impaired	255,000	73,000	328,000	78%	22%
Deaf	45,000	4,000	49,000	92%	8%
Hard of Hearing	66,000	262,000	328,000	20%	80%
Visually Handicapped	43,000	23,000	66,000	65%	35%
Deaf-Blind & Other Multi-Handicapped	16,000	24,000	40,000	40%	60%

Source: U.S. Office of Education

Table 3
Children Served by Handicapping Condition,
School Year 1977-78[47]

Category	Total	Percent of Total	Percentage of School-Aged Children
Speech Impaired	1,226,957	32.5	2.39
Learning Disabled	969,368	25.7	1.89
Mentally Retarded	944,909	25.0	1.84
Emotionally Disturbed	288,626	7.6	0.56
Other Health Impaired	136,164	3.6	0.27
Orthopedically Impaired	88,070	2.3	0.17
Deaf and Hard of Hearing	87,144	2.3	0.17
Visually Handicapped	35,688	0.9	0.07
Total	3,777,106	100.0	7.36

Source: U.S. Office of Education

Table 4
Potential Number of Unserved Children by
Handicapping Condition, School Year 1977-78[48]

Speech Impaired	569,138
Learning Disabled	570,142
Mentally Retarded	235,385
Emotionally Disturbed	737,714
Other	268,570
Total	2,380,950

Source: U.S. Office of Education

Summarizing the data in table 2 for 1975-1976 (which is more clearly presented than for 1977-1978 in tables 3 and 4), the following points can be noted about disabled children and young people whose educational needs were served or unserved in 1975-1976:

1. For the total age group of 0-19 more than 4 million (4,310,000 — 55%) were served.

2. Fewer children in the 0-5 age group (450,000 — 38%) were served.

3. The great majority of disabled children who were served (4,140,000 — 96%) had speech impairments, mental retardation, learning disabilities, emotional disturbances, and other health impairments.

4. Children with sensory impairments involving vision and hearing constituted a much smaller number (170,000 — 4%) of the total served handicapped population.

5. The largest percentages of served children in comparison to the unserved were those in the categories of speech impaired (88%), mentally retarded (90%), crippled and other health impaired (78%), and deaf (92%).

6. The children served the least were those who had learning disabilities (13%), emotional disturbances (19%), or were hard of hearing (20%).

7. The children in the mid-range who were served were the visually handicapped (65%) and the multiply handicapped (40%).[49]

Comparing tables 2 and 3, there was a smaller number of served school-aged children in 1977-1978 (3,777,106) than in 1975-1976 (projected 3,860,000). Correspondingly, a comparison of the unserved children in tables 2 and 4 indicates a smaller number in 1977-1978 (2,380,950) than in 1975-1976 (2,840,000).

The above data indicate the large number of disabled children and young people who require the services of school and public libraries, many of whom will ultimately be drawing also upon the services of academic libraries. Many school, public, and academic libraries are presently providing services, materials, and programs to children and young people with various types of disabilities. It may be assumed, however, that libraries and librarians have not yet reached their fullest potential in such services. Just as educational services have not yet been fully provided to all disabled children and young people, library services to this segment of our population also need to be expanded and increased.

NOTES

[1]Sarah McCracken, "Selecting Materials for Individual Handicapped Learners," in *Services and Materials for the Handicapped: Proceedings of an Institute for School Library Media Professionals, August 12-17, 1979*, ed. Henry C. Dequin (DeKalb, IL: Northern Illinois University, 1979), p. 111.

[2]Larry J. Coet, "Defining the Term 'Handicap': A Function of Sex, Race, Religion, and Geographic Location," *Psychological Reports* 41 (1977): 783-87.

[3]*Webster's Third New International Dictionary of the English Language Unabridged* (Chicago: Encyclopaedia Britannica, 1976), p. 1027.

[4]Frieda Zames, "The Disability Rights Movement—A Progress Report," *Interracial Books for Children Bulletin* 8 (Numbers 6 and 7, 1977): 16-18.

[5]Ruth A. Velleman, *Serving Physically Disabled People: An Information Handbook for All Libraries* (New York: R. R. Bowker, 1979), p. 4.

[6]Ibid. See also John Gliedman and William Roth for the Carnegie Council on Children, *The Unexpected Minority: Handicapped Children in America* (New York: Harcourt Brace Jovanovich, 1980), p. 9.

[7]Frank Bowe, *Handicapping America: Barriers to Disabled People* (New York: Harper and Row, 1978), pp. vii-xiii and passim.

[8]U.S. Department of Health, Education, and Welfare, "Nondiscrimination on the Basis of Handicap," *Federal Register* 42 (May 4, 1977): 22678.

[9]Jacobus ten Broek and Floyd W. Matson, "The Disabled and the Law of Welfare," *California Law Review* 54 (May 1966): 809-810.

[10]Joan Tollifson, "An Open Letter ...," *Interracial Books for Children Bulletin* 8 (Numbers 6 and 7, 1977): 19.

[11]Douglas Biklen and Robert Bogdan, "Media Portrayals of Disabled People: A Study in Stereotypes," *Interracial Books for Children Bulletin* 8 (Numbers 6 and 7, 1977): 4.

[12]Kieth C. Wright, *Library and Information Services for Handicapped Individuals* (Littleton, CO: Libraries Unlimited, 1979), p. 13.

[13]Biklen and Bogdan, "Media Portrayals," p. 4.

[14]"Disabled—Yes; Handicapped—No: The Language of Disability," *Interracial Books for Children Bulletin* 8 (Numbers 6 and 7, 1977): 5.

[15]Ibid.

[16]Ibid.

[17]Ibid. See also Emmett A. Davis and Catherine M. Davis, *Mainstreaming Library Service for Disabled People* (Metuchen, NJ: Scarecrow Press, 1980), pp. 15-19. Davis and Davis, pp. 108-154, present a list of subject headings related to disabilities based on the Hennepin County Library, *Library of Congress Subject Headings List, Sears' List of Subject Headings*, and their own suggestions.

[18]U.S. Department of Health, Education, and Welfare, Office of Education, "Education of Handicapped Children: Implementation of Part B of the Education of the Handicapped Act," *Federal Register* 42, no. 163, August 23, 1977, 42478-79.

[19]Samuel A. Kirk and James J. Gallagher, *Educating Exceptional Children*, 3rd ed. (Boston: Houghton Mifflin, 1979), p. 37.

[20]Ibid.

[21]Garry D. Brewer and James S. Kakalik, *Handicapped Children: Strategies for Improving Services* (New York: McGraw-Hill, 1979), p. 84.

[22]See Kirk and Gallagher, *Educating Exceptional Children*, pp. 181-82; and Brewer and Kakalik, *Handicapped Children*, pp. 85-86.

[23]Kirk and Gallagher, *Educating Exceptional Children*, pp. 35 and 181.

[24]Ibid., pp. 38-39. See also pp. 349-52.

[25]Kieth C. Wright, "Handicapping Conditions and the Needs of Handicapped Children," in *Services and Materials for the Handicapped; Proceedings of an Institute for School Library Media Professionals, August 12-17, 1979*, ed. Henry C. Dequin (DeKalb, IL: Northern Illinois University, 1979), p. 27.

[26]Kirk and Gallagher, *Educating Exceptional Children*, pp. 290-91.

[27]Velleman, *Serving Physically Disabled People*, pp. 25-50.

[28]Kirk and Gallagher, *Educating Exceptional Children*, pp. 40-41.

[29]Ibid., p. 104; Brewer and Kakalik, *Handicapped Children*, pp. 88-89; and Wright, *Library and Information Services*, p. 80.

[30]Kirk and Gallagher, *Educating Exceptional Children*, p. 41.

[31]Paul R. Dimond, "The Constitutional Right to Education: The Quiet Revolution," *The Hastings Law Journal* 24 (May 1973): 1111.

[32]Ronald H. Coombs and Jerry L. Harper, "Effects of Labels on Attitudes of Educators toward Handicapped Children," *Exceptional Children* 33 (February 1967): 399-403. Tom B. Gillung and Chauncy N. Rucker, "Labels and Teacher Expectations," *Exceptional Children* 43 (April 1977): 464-65; and William R. Jacobs, "The Effect of the Learning Disability Label on Classroom Teacher's Ability Objectively to Observe and Interpret Child Behaviors," *Learning Disability Quarterly* 1 (Winter 1978): 50-55.

[33]Bowe, *Handicapping America*, pp. 137-38; Kieth C. Wright, "Introduction to and Interpretation of PL 94-142," in *Services and Materials for the Handicapped; Proceedings of an Institute for School Library Media Professionals, August 12-17, 1979*, ed. Henry C. Dequin (DeKalb, IL: Northern Illinois University, 1979), p. 5; Alan Abeson and Jeffrey Zettel, "The End of the Quiet Revolution: The Education for All Handicapped Children Act of 1975," *Exceptional Children* 44 (October 1977): 116; and Jeffrey J. Zettel and Alan Abeson, "Litigation, Law, and the Handicapped," *School Media Quarterly* 6 (Summer 1978): 237-38.

[34]Bowe, *Handicapping America*, pp. 137-39.

[35]I. Leon Smith and Sandra Greenberg, "Teacher Attitudes and the Labeling Process," *Exceptional Children* 41 (February 1975): 319-24.

[36]Dimond, "The Constitutional Right to Education," pp. 1087-1127.

[37]*Pennsylvania Association for Retarded Children v. Commonwealth of Pennsylvania*, 334 F. Supp. 1257 (E.D. Pa. 1971). See also Leopold Lippman and I. Ignacy Goldberg, *Right to Education: Anatomy of the Pennsylvania Case and Its Implications for Exceptional Children*, Teachers College Series in Special Education (New York: Teachers College Press, Teachers College, Columbia University, 1973); and H. Rutherford Turnbull III, "The Past and Future Impact of Court Decisions in Special Education," *Phi Delta Kappan* 59 (April 1978): 525.

[38]Bowe, *Handicapping America*, pp. 137-38.

[39]Brewer and Kakalik, *Handicapped Children*, p. 27.

[40]Kirk and Gallagher, *Educating Exceptional Children*, pp. 488-90.

[41]Dimond, "The Constitutional Right to Education," p. 1093.

[42]Brewer and Kakalik, *Handicapped Children*, pp. 77, 165-66.

[43]Wright, *Library and Information Services*, pp. 75-77.

[44]Brewer and Kakalik, *Handicapped Children*, pp. 78-81.

[45]*Congressional Quarterly Almanac; 94th Congress, 1st Session ... 1975*, vol. 31 (Washington, DC: Congressional Quarterly, 1976), p. 652.

[46]U.S. Department of Health, Education, and Welfare, Office of Education, National Advisory Committee on the Handicapped, *The Unfinished Revolution: Education for the Handicapped; 1976 Annual Report* (Washington, DC: Government Printing Office, 1976), p. 2.

[47]U.S. Department of Health, Education, and Welfare, Office of Education, Bureau of Education for the Handicapped, *Progress toward a Free Appropriate Public Education; A Report to Congress on the Implementation of Public Law 94-142: The Education for All Handicapped Children Act*, prepared by the State Program Implementation Studies Branch, HEW Publication No. (OE) 79-05003, January 1979, pp. 159, 162.

[48]Ibid., p. 163.

[49]Cf. Kirk and Gallagher, *Educating Exceptional Children*, p. 9.

3 _____ The Right to Library and Educational Services

> "No authority is needed for the fundamental
> American principle that a public school
> education through high school is a basic right
> of all citizens."
> — *Cook v. Edwards*, 1972

INTRODUCTION

When President Gerald R. Ford signed Public Law 94-142, The Education for All Handicapped Children Act, on November 29, 1975, it was the culmination of a long and hard struggle. Many people — parents, lawyers, legislators, educators, and other advocates — had been involved in the effort to secure equal education for all children and young people who are disabled. The years preceding the passage of this law have been described as a period of "quiet revolution"[1] and of "quiet evolution,"[2] a time during which the "battle cry" for the advance of public policy in the United States changed from solicitations for charity to a declaration of rights.[3] Responses to that "battle cry" came in the form of state and federal court decisions and legislation which served to shape the current public policy guaranteeing the right to public education to all children and young people from age three to twenty-one. P.L. 94-142 was the capstone to all the court cases and legislation that had been enacted in the preceding years.

All segments of society in the United States have been affected by the requirements and implications of this national law. Librarians in all types of libraries — school, public, academic, and special — have felt the effects of P.L. 94-142 because the right to an education also implies the right to library services since libraries are educational institutions. As disabled children and young people are incorporated more completely into the mainstream of education and of society, they will also use the resources and services of all types of libraries to a greater extent.

In order to provide improved library services to disabled children and young people, it is well to know where we have been and where we are now in regard to the legal and educational status of those who have disabilities. Therefore, in this chapter the following topics will be considered: 1) the past treatment of disabled persons; 2) court cases dealing with the educational rights of the handicapped; 3) federal legislation, especially P.L. 93-112 and P.L. 94-142; 4) a declaration of rights for disabled children and young people; and 5) the situation since 1975.

45

PAST TREATMENT OF DISABLED PERSONS

In past history throughout the world, individuals with a disability were regarded as second-class citizens. Frequently they were objects to be scorned, ridiculed, shunned, or pitied. Some societies excluded them completely; in other societies, such as that of the ancient Spartans, a child born with a deformity was killed. The treatment of disabled persons in the past has been summarized in this way:

> With minor exceptions, mankind's attitudes toward its handicapped population can be characterized by overwhelming prejudice. [The handicapped are systematically isolated from] the mainstream of society. From ancient to modern times, the physically, mentally or emotionally disabled have been alternatively viewed by the majority as dangers to be destroyed, as nuisances to be driven out, or as burdens to be confined.[4]

The treatment of disabled persons in Europe has been chronicled in four stages. The first stage was during the pre-Christian era when disabled persons were neglected and often mistreated. The second stage occurred during the expansion of Christianity when persons with a disability were pitied and protected. During the third stage in the eighteenth and nineteenth centuries, education and care were provided in separate institutions. In the fourth stage, the latter part of the twentieth century, there has been greater acceptance of handicapped individuals and attempts to integrate them into the mainstream of society as fully as possible.[5]

These stages have had their parallels in the history of the United States. In the first stage, during the years after 1776, disabled persons were generally neglected. Society made no provision for their education, and they were "stored away" in charitable institutions or poorhouses. Frequently they just remained at home without any education or special training. As late as 1850, 60% of the persons in poorhouses may have been the blind, the deaf, the insane, and "idiots."[6]

During the second stage, from 1817 to 1869, concern for the education of persons with disabilities, notably the visually and hearing impaired, began to be displayed in the United States. Residential schools or asylums were established in many states for the blind, deaf, and mentally retarded. The first residential school for the hearing impaired, the American Asylum for the Education and Instruction of Deaf and Dumb Persons (now the American School for the Deaf), was opened in 1817 by the Reverend Thomas Hopkins Gallaudet in Hartford, Connecticut. The purpose of the school was to teach deaf children to communicate by spelling and gesturing with their fingers. Dr. Samuel Gridley Howe, a physician, established the first residential school for the blind in 1829 in Watertown, Massachusetts, and called it the New England Asylum for the Blind (afterwards named the Perkins Institute for the Blind). Howe believed that handicapped children are able to learn and that, in addition to compassionate care, they should have an organized education. Thirty years later, in 1859, Howe was instrumental in establishing in South Boston, Massachusetts, the Massachusetts School for Idiotic and Feebleminded Youth, the nation's first residential school for the mentally retarded. Each of these initial residential schools was followed by the establishment of similar schools in other states, but with an emphasis on custodial care rather than education. These institutions were primarily the responsibility of the state department of health or social welfare rather than the public school system, since charity and not education was still the primary motivation during that period.[7]

During the third stage of development in the United States, beginning in 1869, in addition to the continuation of the residential schools, special day classes were instituted within the public schools. In 1869 the first public day school class for the deaf was begun in Boston. In 1896 a special class for the mentally retarded was initiated in Providence, Rhode Island. At the beginning of the twentieth century, special education programs for handicapped children began to be established in many public schools throughout the country. In Chicago in 1899 a class was begun for children with physical handicaps, and in 1900 a special classroom for blind children was opened in a regular school. A program for children with speech defects was begun in New York City in 1908.[8]

Although such day classes for handicapped children in the public schools began to be an accepted alternative to residential schools, relatively few disabled children benefited in this way. Even when compulsory attendance laws were passed in the latter part of the nineteenth century and education became virtually universal for nonhandicapped children, children with disabilities were not included. Reflecting the view of the larger society at that time, education systems felt that handicapped children "would be out of place in regular classrooms and therefore should be excluded."[9] The idea was thus conveyed that disabled children were inherently inferior to nondisabled children.

In the fourth stage, in more recent years there have been numerous provisions for handicapped individuals as a result of state and federal legislation and the appropriation of funds. Such legislation was stimulated by both World War I and World War II because of the many persons injured in those wars. The period following World War II also witnessed greater growth in special education classes, although there was still an uneven pattern of service. While special education programs were mandated by state legislation in many states, in other states only permissive or selective programs were legislated.[10] Some states also began to provide subsidies to public schools for special education classes. By 1950, thirty-four states had established such subsidizing laws for children with most types of handicaps.[11]

In spite of the advances in the development of special education programs, the freedoms and rights of exceptional children were largely ignored. Some disabled children benefited through the development of sound programs, while others suffered because of imposed restrictions, segregation, and the refusal by school officials to serve them.[12] In some instances children with disabilities were excluded completely. Some were classified, labeled, or placed incorrectly or inappropriately, or their educational programs were not appropriate for their needs. Some education decision making was "arbitrary and capricious." Under certain circumstances and in some jurisdictions, denial of service to disabled children by way of transportation and/or education was considered to be legitimate.[13]

According to traditional practice, the school administrator had the responsibility to make all the important decisions regarding the education of a disabled child. The administrator decided whether or not the child could be admitted to the public school, what diagnostic label to give the child, and the kind of educational program that would meet the child's special needs. In many instances these decisions were a matter of administrative convenience rather than what was best for the education of the child.[14]

The U.S. Office of Education conducted studies which documented the extent of the educational neglect of disabled children and young people. In 1948 only 12% of the disabled children in the United States were receiving a special education. This figure increased to 21% in 1963 and to 33% in 1967. During the 1968-1969 school year, 19 states served less than 31% of their disabled youth, 11 states served 20% or less, only 7 states provided special education for over 51% of their disabled children, and 30 states served less than 11% of their children of school age who were emotionally disturbed.[15] The National Advisory Committee on the Handicapped reported that the education of 90% of disabled children and youth was being neglected in 1950 but decreased to 60% in 1970 and to 45% in 1976.[16]

Edwin W. Martin, Jr., Deputy Commissioner of the Bureau of Education for the Handicapped (BEH), recounted several instances of educational neglect of disabled children. When an Ad Hoc Subcommittee on the Handicapped of the U.S. House of Representatives was holding hearings in 1966, parents reported that their disabled children had been refused admission to school or were placed in substandard facilities either in basements, in buildings that were not schools, or in old churches. One day an employee at the BEH asked Martin to help her find a school for her son who had multiple disabilities because none of the schools in the Washington, D.C., area would admit him. They finally found a school that would accept the child, but the tuition was $9,000 a year ($4,000 more than the woman earned) and the school district would pay only $1,500 toward the tuition. Another mother related the story of her adolescent daughter. Although mentally retarded, the girl would stand every day at a window in her home watching the school bus go up the road without her. Repeatedly she asked her mother why she could not go to school with the other children.[17]

Disabled children could be excluded from school because existing laws in many states made it legally possible to do so. On the basis of these laws, children could be excluded if they had certain physical or mental conditions, or if their attitudes were considered to interfere with their attendance at school and their application to their studies. Children were often excluded who were blind, "dumb," or "feebleminded" and for whom no other instructional program was provided. They could be excluded if they lived more than a certain distance from a public school in a location where transportation was not provided by the school officials.[18]

Such instances of neglect, exclusion, discrimination, and segregation caused educators to awaken to the responsibilities that public schools should assume for the education of those who are disabled. They led also to numerous court cases and legislative mandates regarding the education of disabled children and young people.

COURT CASES

In an attempt to remedy the abuses of the past, disabled citizens and their advocates went to the courts and achieved much success. Between 1971 and 1976 over forty cases were argued successfully in the courts in favor of disabled persons.[19] The decisions of the courts over the past decade reflect a change from the previous custodial view of disabled persons to one of full participation in the mainstream of society.[20]

The basic rationale for litigation in both state and federal judicial systems was the equal protection clause of the Fourteenth Amendment of the U.S.

Constitution. Although the Constitution does not specifically establish the right of every child to an education, it does guarantee the individual's right to equal protection under the law and insures that all persons who are under the same circumstances and conditions should receive the same treatment. This constitutional right became the basis for appeals to the courts on behalf of disabled persons.

In addition to the equal protection rights of the Fourteenth Amendment, court cases involving the educational rights of handicapped individuals have been based on arguments regarding the value of education. These arguments were used in 1954 in the classic court case of *Brown v. the Board of Education* of Topeka, Kansas. Although this was a school desegregation suit involving the educational rights of minority black children, it had bearing on the educational rights of handicapped children. The U.S. Supreme Court ruled that education in separate facilities was inherently unequal. It also established the principle that the opportunity of an education, "where the state has undertaken to provide it, is a right which must be made available to all on equal terms."[21]

Two landmark federal court cases in the early 1970s set the "quiet revolution" in motion by establishing the precedent for the right of disabled children and young people to education. In both cases the courts decided where handicapped children should receive their education in relation to nonhandicapped children.

Pennsylvania Association for Retarded Children v. Commonwealth of Pennsylvania

The first of these two court cases has become the "cornerstone" of the revolution to obtain equal educational rights for all disabled children. In January 1971 the Pennsylvania Association for Retarded Children (PARC, now the Pennsylvania Association for Retarded Citizens) brought a suit against the Commonwealth of Pennsylvania. As a class action suit it was filed on behalf of thirteen mentally retarded children who represented all other retarded children of school age in the state, including the severely and profoundly retarded. The suit maintained that the Commonwealth of Pennsylvania had failed to provide access to a free public education for all retarded children.[22] According to Thomas K. Gilhool, the attorney who represented the plaintiffs, at least 14,267 retarded children had been denied an appropriate education in Pennsylvania.[23]

The PARC case was resolved by consent agreement in which the following points were declared by the court:

1. All mentally retarded persons are capable of benefiting from a program of education and training. No child is uneducable or untrainable.

2. Since the Commonwealth of Pennsylvania had undertaken to provide a free public education to all of its children between the ages of six and twenty-one years, including its exceptional children, the Commonwealth of Pennsylvania may not postpone, terminate, or deny any mentally retarded child access to a free public program of education and training.

3. The Commonwealth was obligated to place each mentally retarded child in a free public program of education and training appropriate to the child's capacity by September 1972. The presumption was made that placement in a regular public school was preferable to placement in a special public school class

and that placement in a special public school class was preferable to placement in any other type of program of education and training.[24]

Mills v. Board of Education

The second landmark court case was *Mills v. Board of Education of the District of Columbia* in 1972. This, too, was a class action suit brought by the parents and guardians of seven District of Columbia children on behalf of all disabled children who were not in school. Several disability classes were represented: behavioral problems, mentally retarded, emotionally disturbed, and hyperactive. The court ordered that an appropriate free public education should be provided to all school-age children, regardless of the severity of their disability. Among the stipulations of the decree are the following:

1. No child could be excluded from a regular public school assignment unless adequate alternative educational services suited to the child's needs were provided (which could include special education or tuition grants).

2. Each child of school age shall be provided a free and suitable publicly supported education regardless of the degree of the child's mental, physical, or emotional disability or impairment.

3. The educational needs of all identified exceptional children shall be evaluated and a proposal for each individual placement in a suitable educational program shall be filed.[25]

U.S. District Judge Joseph Waddy summed up the court's view when he said that all children have the right to "suitable publicly supported education, regardless of the degree of the child's mental, physical, or emotional disability or impairment."[26]

Both *PARC* and *Mills* also contained other provisions regarding an individualized education plan for each disabled child, involvement of parents in educational decisions, due process procedures, and other aspects. These two cases and other court decisions[27] can be linked to both state and federal legislation relating to handicapped individuals. Many of the regulations in *PARC* and *Mills*, as well as in other court decisions, were also incorporated into P.L. 93-380 and P.L. 94-142.

The right to education was strengthened further by the passage of state statutes and regulations in response to continuing advocacy and pressures from parents, groups, and other interested persons during the late 1960s and early 1970s prior to the passage of P.L. 94-142. By 1972, 70% of the states had enacted mandatory legislation regarding the education of handicapped children.[28] By 1975 all state legislatures except two, Ohio and Mississippi, had adopted some mandatory legislation requiring the education of the majority of disabled children in the state.[29]

Gilhool summarized these actions in this way:

And so it is. It is a new language that suggests a new conception of the handicapped citizen, a new conception of that citizen's place in our society, a new conception of those obligations owed to him by those who act in place of the society, a conception that suggests that handicapped citizens no longer have what they may have by the grace or by the good will of any other person but that they have what they must have by right. It is now a question of justice.[30]

FEDERAL LEGISLATION:
PUBLIC LAWS 93-112 AND 94-142

From the discussion in the preceding section, it is obvious that efforts on behalf of disabled persons began with the states rather than with the federal government, particularly in regard to education. Federal law, however, is more far-reaching and takes priority over state laws if a state wishes to receive federal funds for programs that are regulated by specific federal laws.

Since 1827, 195 federal laws relating to handicapped individuals have been passed.[31] Many of the earlier laws reflected the custodial view of handicapped persons and their welfare. Disabled persons were then regarded as wards of the state to be protected, isolated, and institutionalized rather than to be given full and equal rights with the rest of the citizenry.

Some of the past federal actions are particularly noteworthy. The first federal law pertaining to the education of handicapped individuals was in 1857 with An Act to Incorporate the Columbian Institution for the Deaf and Dumb and the Blind in Washington, D.C. (renamed Gallaudet College in 1954).[32] In 1879 the American Printing House for the Blind was created in Lexington, Kentucky, by an act of Congress. In the 1930s the U.S. Office of Education first assigned a staff member to monitor special education. These actions, however, did not yet signify a national commitment to the needs of disabled persons.[33]

It was not until the 1970s that greater activity took place at the national level. Sixty-one (almost one-third) of the total 195 federal bills were passed during the first five years of the 1970s, from January 1970 to November 1975. In 1974 thirty-six bills which directly or indirectly affected handicapped individuals, both children and adults, were passed by Congress and signed by the president.[34]

Two federal laws stand out with great significance regarding the educational rights of disabled children and young people: P.L. 93-112, The Rehabilitation Amendments of 1973, and P.L. 94-142, The Education for All Handicapped Children Act of 1975. Each of these laws has achieved the stature of a "Bill of Rights for the Handicapped." P.L. 93-112, particularly Section 504, contains the most notable *overall* policy for all disabled persons regardless of age, while P.L. 94-142 is the foremost declaration of educational rights for all disabled children and young people.[35]

Coupled with P.L. 94-142 must also be considered P.L. 93-380, The Education Amendments of 1974, which laid some of the groundwork for P.L. 94-142. P.L. 93-380 amended the Elementary and Secondary Education Act of 1965 by 1) broadening the commitment to handicapped children, 2) authorizing massive increases in funds to help states meet the "right to education" mandates of the courts, and 3) specifying due process requirements protecting the rights of such children by placing them in "the least restrictive environment." While P.L. 94-142 is a complete revision of Part B of P.L. 93-380, the latter had already provided for the guarantee of due process procedures and the assurance of education in the least restrictive environment.[36]

Previous amendments to the Elementary and Secondary Education Act had also benefited handicapped individuals. P.L. 89-313 provided federal assistance to state-operated and -supported schools for disabled children and young people. P.L. 89-750 enacted a grant program for the support of approved programs at the local district level and also established the Bureau of Education for the Handicapped to handle all federal programs designed to meet the needs of persons with disabilities. The same law also created the National Advisory Committee on the Handicapped.[37]

P.L. 93-112,
The Rehabilitation Amendments of 1973

Although P.L. 93-112 was passed in 1973, its regulations did not go into effect until June 1977. It is now a mandatory civil rights law for disabled persons, enforced by the Office of Civil Rights.

The law contains four sections:

Section 501 requires that federal departments and agencies may not discriminate against qualified applicants for employment solely on the basis of disability and must take affirmative action to employ and promote qualified disabled individuals.

Section 502 established the Federal Architectural and Transportation Barriers Compliance Board.

Section 503 requires any federal contractor of at least $2,500 to take affirmative action in hiring qualified handicapped persons.

Section 504 requires the removal of physical barriers;

requires the hiring of qualified handicapped persons;

requires the provision of needed auxiliary aids, such as readers for the blind and interpreters for the deaf in educational institutions;

requires specified deadline dates for implementation.

When Section 504 became law in 1973, it applied specifically only to discrimination in employment. The Rehabilitation Act Amendments of 1974 (P.L. 93-516) extended coverage of Section 504 to all areas of civil rights for disabled persons, including education. Consequently, it is the one section of the law that applies specifically to the educational rights of disabled children and young people.

Section 504 provides that:

No ... qualified handicapped individual in the United States ... shall, solely by reason of his handicap, be denied the benefits of, or be subjected to discrimination under any program or activity receiving federal financial assistance.[38]

In this law a handicapped person is defined as any person who:

— has a physical or mental impairment which substantially limits one or more major life activities, such as caring for one's self, performing manual tasks, walking, seeing, hearing, speaking, breathing, learning, and working;

— has a record of such an impairment;

— is regarded as having such an impairment.[39]

This definition includes such diseases or conditions as speech, hearing, visual and orthopedic impairments, cerebral palsy, epilepsy, muscular dystrophy, multiple sclerosis, cancer, diabetes, heart disease, mental retardation, emotional illness, and specific learning disabilities such as perceptual handicaps, dyslexia, minimal brain dysfunction, and developmental aphasia.

In accordance with a formal opinion of the Attorney General of the United States, alcohol and drug addicts are also considered handicapped individuals. Physical or mental impairments do not constitute a handicap, however, unless they are severe enough to substantially limit one or more of the major life functions.

In regard to education, Section 504 refers to "public elementary and secondary education," that is, the traditional school-age population, and not to specific age groups (as in P.L. 94-142 which specifies ages three to twenty-one). It states simply that all education programs from preschool through adult education will not discriminate on the basis of handicap. The basic requirements of Section 504 in regard to preschool, elementary, secondary, and adult education are:

1. No handicapped child can be excluded from a public education because of disability.

2. Every handicapped child is entitled to a free appropriate education, regardless of the nature or severity of the handicap.

3. Handicapped students must not be segregated in public schools but must be educated with nonhandicapped students to the maximum extent appropriate to their needs.

4. Evaluation procedures must be improved in order to avoid the inappropriate education that results from misclassification.

5. Procedural safeguards must be established so parents and guardians can object to evaluation and placement decisions made with respect to their children.

6. State or local educational agencies must locate and identify unserved handicapped children.[40]

P.L. 94-142, The Education for All Handicapped Children Act of 1975

The signing of P.L. 94-142 on November 29, 1975, was the beginning of the conclusion of the quiet revolution to achieve basic educational rights for all disabled children and young people. "Representing a major new commitment by the federal government, [P.L. 94-142] was regarded by its chief sponsor, Sen. Harrison A. Williams Jr. (D N.J.), as the most important education legislation enacted since the landmark Elementary and Secondary Education Act was enacted in 1965."[41] This law came about because of the convergence of several factors: parental awareness, advocacy efforts, court decisions regarding handicapped individuals, and also trends at that time in school financing.[42]

The provisions of P.L. 94-142 are closely coordinated with the education provisions of Section 504, both of which became effective September 1, 1978. P.L. 94-142 is a federal education funding law which has the binding force of national public policy. It is mandatory, however, only if a state wishes to receive federal funds for the education of disabled children. When fully operational in fiscal 1982, the federal government will provide up to 20% of the extra cost of educating a disabled child.

P.L. 94-142 does not stand alone in the history of the declaration of educational rights for all handicapped children. Many of the mandates contained in this law at the national level were already expressed by court decisions, such as *PARC* and *Mills*, as well as by similar statutes, rules and regulations, bylaws, and other guidelines passed at both the state and federal levels even before the passage of P.L. 94-142, especially in P.L. 93-380.[43] The Education for All Handicapped Children Act of 1975, however, embraced as national public policy some of the standards and policies that had been established since 1969 by state and federal courts, legislatures, and other policy-making bodies in the United States. It was a partial response by Congress to the inappropriate and illegal practices that had taken place and represents a continued evolution on the part of the federal government in the education of all handicapped children and young people.[44]

P.L. 94-142 signified a federal commitment to all disabled children and established as national policy that education is a fundamental right which must be extended to all handicapped persons. Although most of the principles and concepts contained in the law were not new, they became requirements through this law. It is a significant law because, unlike other federal education laws, it has no expiration date and is regarded as permanent. It is a unique piece of legislation because of its detail and specificity regarding the implementation of its requirements. It also specified a number of the processes in order to assure that the educational program will be provided. First priority was to be given to handicapped children who were not receiving an education; second priority to the most severely handicapped children whose education was inadequate.[45]

The law has implications also for nonhandicapped children and young people in the specification of the Individualized Education Program (IEP) tailored to the individual's particular needs and capacities. Since an IEP is now required for each handicapped child, it is conjectured that such an individualized plan may soon be required also for nonhandicapped children and youth. The law also has implications for preschool education. By making educational service a standard part of the elementary school operation for all handicapped children beginning at the age of three, this may be a step in the direction of placing all preschool programs within the province of the elementary school system.[46]

The key elements of P.L. 94-142 are:

Section 3 (b)   lists nine reasons why the needs of handicapped children are not being met, and what should be done to meet their needs.

Section 3 (c)   states the purpose of the act.

Section 4 (a)   includes definitions of terms, such as "special education," "free appropriate public education," "individualized education program," "excess costs," "native language," and "intermediate educational unit."

Section 611   states the maximum amount of the grant to which a state is entitled.

Section 612   states what a state must do to qualify for assistance.

Section 612 (B)   states when the states must comply with P.L. 94-142.

The law was passed because Congress found that:

(1)   there are more than eight million handicapped children in the United States today;

(2)   the special educational needs of such children are not being fully met;

(3)   more than half of the handicapped children in the United States do not receive appropriate educational services which would enable them to have full equality of opportunity;

(4)   one million of the handicapped children in the United States are excluded entirely from the public school system and will not go through the educational process with their peers;

(5)   there are many handicapped children throughout the United States participating in regular school programs whose handicaps prevent them from having a successful educational experience because their handicaps are undetected;

(6)   because of the lack of adequate services within the public school system, families are often forced to find services outside the public school system, often at great distance from their residence and at their own expense;

(7)   developments in the training of teachers and in diagnostic and instructional procedures and methods have advanced to the point that, given appropriate funding, State and local educational agencies can and will provide effective special education and related services to meet the needs of handicapped children;

(8)   State and local educational agencies have a responsibility to provide education for all handicapped children, but present financial resources are inadequate to meet the special educational needs of handicapped children; and

(9)   it is in the national interest that the Federal Government assist State and local efforts to provide programs to meet the educational needs of handicapped children in order to assure equal protection of the law.[47]

Both P.L. 94-142 and Section 504 set forth these basic requirements:

1. Disabled children and young people must be provided a free appropriate public education.

2. Disabled children and young people must be educated with nondisabled peers to the maximum extent appropriate.

3. Education agencies must identify and locate all unserved disabled children and young people.

4. Evaluation procedures must be adopted to ensure appropriate classification and educational services.

5. Procedural safeguards must be established.

The two laws differ along these dimensions:

1. P.L. 94-142 provides money, while Section 504, a civil rights statute, does not.

2. P.L. 94-142 specifies certain age requirements, but Section 504 applies to all ages.

3. It is not necessary for a state to comply with P.L. 94-142 unless it wishes to receive federal funds for the education of disabled children and young people. It is, however, necessary for all areas of society to comply with Section 504.

A DECLARATION OF RIGHTS

On the basis of national law and policy as embodied in P.L. 94-142 and Section 504 of P.L. 93-112, education today is recognized as the right of all disabled children and young people. They have a right to an education that is suited to their particular needs. Specifically, the rights and protections accorded by law are the following:

—the right to an education

—the right to a free public education at no cost to parents or guardian

—the right to an appropriate education

—the right to be educated in the least restrictive environment

—the right to an individualized education program

—the right to nondiscriminatory testing and evaluation procedures

—the right to access of records and confidentiality of data and information

—the right to regular parent or guardian consultation

—the right to a surrogate

—the right to due process of law, including:
  —the right to notice
  —the right to a hearing
  —the right to personal presence
  —the right to counsel
  —the right to raise issues
  —the right to protection against arbitrary rulings and the right to fairness and impartiality
  —the right to a hearing time
  —the right to proof of damages
  —the right to introduce evidence
  —the right to a hearing before a tribunal of jurisdiction[48]

The rights of those who have disabilities are the essential rights of all other people: 1) physical access to transportation and to buildings, 2) the opportunity to be employed, and 3) the right to equal education. In regard to libraries and library services, handicapped individuals have the right to receive the same services as those who are not handicapped, namely: 1) access to library buildings and facilities, 2) appropriate materials which they can use depending on the nature of their disability, 3) participation in the regular programs sponsored by the library as well as special programs directed toward disabled persons, and 4) any other services which the nonhandicapped receive. Librarians have an obligation to assure that these rights are accorded to all who have a disability, including disabled children and young people.

THE SITUATION SINCE 1975

It seems that people naturally expect that something will be done as a result of court decisions and legal enactments. While this is generally true, there is no absolute guarantee that implementation will follow. Court decisions that are rendered have to be carried out. Laws that are passed have to be enforced. Money that is authorized and promised has to be appropriated and funded. History shows that class action suits which affect large numbers of people have been fulfilled very slowly.[49]

This is equally true in regard to state and federal legislation related to disabled children and young people. Although The Rehabilitation Amendments of 1973 and The Education for All Handicapped Children Act of 1975 have become national law, much still remains to be done to bring about the full implementation of these laws. Since 1975 numerous court cases have been filed in state appellate and federal courts under Section 504 and P.L. 94-142 involving the rights of disabled children and youth.[50] These cases have concerned the areas of identification and placement, range of services, payment for tuition, discipline and procedural and jurisdictional questions. In the future, the courts may face increased litigation revolving around zero reject, nondiscriminatory evaluation, appropriate education, program quality, least restrictive placement, and procedural due process.[51] It has also been suggested that litigation may revolve around the lack of suitable materials and equipment, such as braille materials or hearing devices.[52]

Although, as reported by the National Advisory Committee on the Handicapped in 1976, "the condition of education of the handicapped has never been better,"[53] some aspects of the two laws still remain to be resolved and put into full effect. This was pointed out in a rather disconcerting and negative report by Gliedman and Roth prepared for the Carnegie Council on Children. The report expresses serious reservations about P.L. 94-142 for these reasons:

1. P.L. 94-142 does not take a clear position against the traditional medical view of the needs of disabled children. This view has been part of the traditional school vision and, consequently, educators look upon disabled children as "perpetual patients" confined to a limited world.

2. P.L. 94-142 does not make a clear break with the past philosophy of special education.

3. The participation of parents in educational decisions has not been completely resolved and schools can overrule the rights of parents by assuming the typical doctor-patient relationship.[54]

Other issues which require clarification relate to the Individualized Education Program (IEP). If the IEP is regarded as a constitutional right of disabled children, then all nondisabled children are entitled to an IEP too. If, however, the IEP is considered as an educational procedure whose aim is to facilitate the achievement of the learner, then the question has been raised whether Congress has overstepped its authority by mandating an educational procedure which has implicit accountability requirements for the schools. Also, since the law requires parental input and approval of the child's IEP, there is an implication that all parents have the right to be involved in designing their child's educational program.[55]

Another factor upon which implementation of P.L. 94-142 depends is the involvement of the classroom teacher in the process of planning and creating change, including the decision-making stage. As Roubinek pointed out, the classroom teacher's guidance and support are crucial because the power and force of the law alone will not bring about the basic desired educational change for the benefit of the children.[56] Concern has also been expressed about being forced to go too fast too soon, the modification of facilities, the lack of proper funding, and the necessity for proper training of teachers.[57] Administrative problems will concern the identification of disabled children and young people, placement, training teacher personnel, individualized education programs, adopting procedural safeguards, and awaiting lawsuits.[58]

Thus the "quiet revolution" is really not ended but has now become the "unfinished revolution."[59] The declaration of educational rights in P.L. 94-142 marked the beginning of the implementation of the law and the full granting of these declared rights to *all* disabled children and young people, but the years since 1975 have shown that the implementation process has not yet been fully accomplished. Although September 1, 1978, was designated in the law as the date for full implementation, the right to a public education has not yet been fully accorded to all children and youth who are disabled. In schools throughout the country, much still remains to be done to provide full educational opportunity to all disabled children and young people. In libraries, too, as contributing citadels to the educational process, more consideration needs to be given to expanded services and programs which will assist those who are disabled in their pursuit of education and information.

Summing up, the momentum that has been gathering during the past decade will gather further force, and major inroads will be made in the unfinished elements of the revolution in education of the handicapped. Neglect and pity will give way to respect for individual rights, and one day the handicapped will be regarded not in terms of their limitations but on the basis of their qualities as human beings.[60]

NOTES

[1]Paul R. Dimond, "The Constitutional Right to Education: The Quiet Revolution," *The Hastings Law Journal* 24 (May 1973): 1087-1127; Frederick J. Weintraub and Alan Abeson, "New Education Policies for the Handicapped: The Quiet Revolution," *Phi Delta Kappan* 55 (April 1974): 526-29, 659 (reprinted in *Public Policy and the Education of Exceptional Children*, ed. Frederick J. Weintraub, Alan Abeson, Joseph Ballard, and Martin L. LaVor (Reston, VA: The Council for Exceptional Children, 1976), pp. 7-13; and Alan Abeson and Jeffrey Zettel, "The End of the Quiet Revolution: The Education for All Handicapped Children Act of 1975," *Exceptional Children* 44 (October 1977): 114-28.

[2]Samuel C. Ashcroft, "Learning Resources in Special Education: The Quiet Evolution," *Education and Training of the Mentally Retarded* 12 (April 1977): 132-36.

[3]Alan Abeson, "Section I: The Educational Rights of Exceptional Children — Overview," in *Public Policy and the Education of Exceptional Children*, ed. Frederick J. Weintraub, Alan Abeson, Joseph Ballard, and Martin L. LaVor (Reston, VA: The Council for Exceptional Children, 1976), pp. 5-6. See also the references in footnote 1.

[4]*Case v. State of California*, Civil No. 13127, Court of Appeals, Fourth District, California, filed December 14, 1973.

[5]Samuel A. Kirk and James J. Gallagher, *Educating Exceptional Children*, 3rd ed. (Boston: Houghton Mifflin, 1979), p. 5. See also the discussion of the historical treatment of disabled persons in Frank Bowe, *Handicapping America: Barriers to Disabled People* (New York: Harper and Row, 1978), pp. 2-8.

[6]Kirk and Gallagher, *Educating Exceptional Children*, pp. 5-6; and U.S. Department of Health, Education, and Welfare, Office of Education, National Advisory Committee on the Handicapped, *The Unfinished Revolution: Education for the Handicapped; 1976 Annual Report* (Washington, DC: Government Printing Office, 1976), p. 8.

[7]U.S. Department of Health, Education, and Welfare, *The Unfinished Revolution*, p. 9. See also Bowe, *Handicapping America*, p. 11; Kirk and Gallagher, *Educating Exceptional Children*, pp. 5-6; Wayne D. Lance, "Who Are *All* the Children?," *Exceptional Children* 43 (October 1976): 66-67; and Martin L. LaVor, "Federal Legislation for Exceptional Persons: A History," in *Public Policy and the Education of Exceptional Children*, ed. Frederick J. Weintraub, Alan Abeson, Joseph Ballard, and Martin L. LaVor (Reston, VA: The Council for Exceptional Children, 1976), p. 96.

[8]Kirk and Gallagher, *Educating Exceptional Children*, pp. 5-6; Lance, "Who Are *All* the Children?," p. 67; and LaVor, "Federal Legislation," pp. 96-97.

[9]U.S. Department of Health, Education, and Welfare, *The Unfinished Revolution*, p. 10.

[10]Gloria Calovini, "Implications of Public Law 94-142," *Illinois Libraries* 59 (September 1977): 468. See also the table of state statutory responsibilities in Alan Abeson and Joseph Ballard, "State and Federal Policy for Exceptional Children," in *Public Policy and the Education of Exceptional Children*, ed. Frederick J. Weintraub, Alan Abeson, Joseph Ballard, and Martin L. LaVor (Reston, VA: The Council for Exceptional Children, 1976), pp. 84-87, in which the following are listed for each state: the type of mandation, date of passage, compliance date, ages of eligibility, and categories excluded. This table is reprinted in U.S. Department of Health, Education, and Welfare, Office of Education, Bureau of Education for the Handicapped, *Progress toward a Free Appropriate Public Education; A Report to Congress on the Implementation of Public Law 94-142: The Education for All Handicapped Children Act*, prepared by the State Program Implementation Studies Branch, HEW Publication No. (OE) 79-05003, January 1979, pp. 20-21.

[11]U.S. Department of Health, Education, and Welfare, *The Unfinished Revolution*, p. 12.

[12]L. James Stowell and Cindy Terry, "Mainstreaming—Present Shock," *Illinois Libraries* 59 (September 1977): 475.

[13]Abeson and Zettel, "The End of the Quiet Revolution," p. 117. See also the extensive treatment of exclusionary practices and misclassification in Dimond, "The Constitutional Right to Education," pp. 1087-1127.

[14]John Gliedman and William Roth for the Carnegie Council on Children, *The Unexpected Minority: Handicapped Children in America* (New York: Harcourt Brace Jovanovich, 1980), pp. 177-78.

[15]Frederick J. Weintraub, Alan R. Abeson, and David L. Braddock, *State Law and Education of Handicapped Children: Issues and Recommendations* (Arlington, VA: The Council for Exceptional Children, 1971), pp. 14-15, cited in Jeffrey J. Zettel and Alan Abeson, "Litigation, Law, and the Handicapped," *School Media Quarterly* 6 (Summer 1978): 234-35.

[16]U.S. Department of Health, Education, and Welfare, *The Unfinished Revolution*, p. 1.

[17]Edwin W. Martin, Jr., "Education of All Handicapped Children and Public Law 94-142," in *Education of All Handicapped Children and PL 94-142; Report of the Sixteenth National Conference on Human and Civil Rights in Education, March 17-19, 1978, Sheraton Park Hotel, Washington, D.C.* (Washington, DC: National Education Association, 1978), p. 5.

[18]Alan Abeson, Nancy Bolick, and Jayne Hass, "Due Process of Law: Background and Intent," in *Public Policy and the Education of Exceptional Children*, ed. Frederick J. Weintraub, Alan Abeson, Joseph Ballard, and Martin L. LaVor (Reston, VA: The Council for Exceptional Children, 1976), p. 23.

[19]U.S. Department of Health, Education, and Welfare, *The Unfinished Revolution*, p. 4.

[20]Kieth C. Wright, *Library and Information Services for Handicapped Individuals* (Littleton, CO: Libraries Unlimited, 1979), p. 28.

[21]*Brown v. Board of Education*, 347 U.S. 483, 74 S. Ct. 686, 98 L, Ed. 873 (1954).

[22]*Pennsylvania Association for Retarded Children v. Commonwealth of Pennsylvania*, 334 F. Supp. 1257 (E.D. Pa. 1971).

[23]Thomas J. Gilhool, "Education: An Inalienable Right," in *Public Policy and the Education of Exceptional Children*, ed. Frederick J. Weintraub, Alan Abeson, Joseph Ballard, and Martin L. LaVor (Reston, VA: The Council for Exceptional Children, 1976), p. 17.

[24]*PARC v. Commonwealth of Pennsylvania*. Discussions of this case and the consent agreement are contained in the following: Leopold Lippman and I. Ignacy Goldberg, *Right to Education: Anatomy of the Pennsylvania Case and Its Implications for Exceptional Children*, Teachers College Series in Special Education (New York: Teachers College Press, Teachers College, Columbia University, 1973); Gilhool, "Education," pp. 14-21; Abeson and Zettel, "The End of the Quiet Revolution," p. 117; Zettel and Abeson, "Litigation, Law, and the Handicapped," pp. 235-36; Weintraub and Abeson, "New Education Policies for the Handicapped," pp. 8-9; Abeson, Bolick, and Hass, "Due Process of Law," pp. 25-27; Dimond, "The Constitutional Right to Education," pp. 1115 ff.; Peter Kuriloff and others, "Legal Reform and Educational Change: The Pennsylvania Case," *Exceptional Children* 41 (September 1974): 35-42; and other sources.

[25]*Mills v. Board of Education of the District of Columbia*, 348 F. Supp. 866 (D.D.C., 1972). Discussions of this suit and the court decision are contained in the following: Abeson and Zettel, "The End of the Quiet Revolution," p. 118; Zettel and Abeson, "Litigation, Law, and the Handicapped," p. 236; Weintraub and Abeson, "New Education Policies for the Handicapped," pp. 9-10; Dimond, "The Constitutional Right to Education," pp. 1115 ff.; and other sources.

[26]Quoted in U.S. Department of Health, Education, and Welfare, *The Unfinished Revolution*, p. 4.

[27]Dimond, "The Constitutional Right to Education," pp. 1087-1127, discusses some of these cases.

[28]Alan Abeson, "Movement and Momentum: Government and the Education of Handicapped Children," *Exceptional Children* 39 (September 1972): 63; and Abeson and Ballard, "State and Federal Policy for Exceptional Children," p. 83.

29U.S. Congress, Senate, *Education for All Handicapped Children Act*, S.6., 94th Congress, 1st Session, June 2, 1975, Report No. 94-168, referred to in Abeson and Zettel, "The End of the Quiet Revolution," p. 118; and in Zettel and Abeson, "Litigation, Law, and the Handicapped," p. 236. See also Abeson and Ballard, "State and Federal Policy for Exceptional Children," pp. 83-87, especially the table of state statutory responsibilities as of July 1, 1975 (reprinted in U.S. Department of Health, Education, and Welfare, *Progress toward a Free Appropriate Public Education*, pp. 20-21).

30Gilhool, "Education: An Inalienable Right," p. 21.

31See the list of "Federal Laws for the Handicapped" in LaVor, "Federal Legislation for Exceptional Persons: A History," pp. 103-111.

32LaVor, "Federal Legislation for Exceptional Persons: A History," pp. 97, 103, 106.

33U.S. Department of Health, Education, and Welfare, *The Unfinished Revolution*, p. 5.

34LaVor, "Federal Legislation for Exceptional Persons: A History," p. 76.

35Abeson and Zettel, "The End of the Quiet Revolution," p. 127; Zettel and Abeson, "Litigation, Law, and the Handicapped," p. 244.

36Abeson, Bolick, and Hass, "Due Process of Law," pp. 30-31.

37U.S. Department of Health, Education, and Welfare, *The Unfinished Revolution*, p. 5. See also LaVor, "Federal Legislation for Exceptional Persons: A History," p. 100.

38Section 504 of the Rehabilitation Act of 1973, 29 U.S.C., 706 (S. 84.4).

39Ibid., (S. 84.3).

40Ibid., (S. 84.33-84.37).

41*Congressional Quarterly Almanac; 94th Congress, 1st Session ...* 1975, vol. 31 (Washington, DC: Congressional Quarterly, 1976), p. 651.

42Lisa Walker, "Public Law 94-142: Legislative Development and Intent of Congress," in *Education of All Handicapped Children and PL 94-142; Report of the Sixteenth National Conference on Human and Civil Rights in Education, March 17-19, 1978, Sheraton Park Hotel, Washington, D.C.* (Washington, DC: National Education Association, 1978), pp. 10-11.

43Abeson and Zettel, "The End of the Quiet Revolution," p. 116.

44Frederick J. Weintraub, Editorial Comment to "The End of the Quiet Revolution: The Education for All Handicapped Children Act of 1975," by Alan Abeson and Jeffrey Zettel, *Exceptional Children* 44 (October 1977): 114.

[45]*Congressional Quarterly Almanac ... 1975*, p. 651; L. F. Beatty, "Impact of Public Law 94-142 on the Preparation of School Media Coordinators," *Educational Technology* 18 (November 1978): 44.

[46]Leroy V. Goodman, "A Bill of Rights for the Handicapped," *American Education* 12 (July 1976): 6.

[47]*Education for All Handicapped Children Act, Statutes at Large* 89, Sec. 3, 774-775 (1975).

[48]*Education for All Handicapped Children Act, Statutes at Large* 89 (1975); *Vocational Rehabilitation Act, Statutes at Large* 87 (1973); Abeson and Zettel, "The End of the Quiet Revolution," pp. 122-26; Zettel and Abeson, "Litigation, Law, and the Handicapped," pp. 234-45; and Don R. Barbacovi and Richard W. Clelland, *Public Law 94-142: Special Education in Transition* (Arlington, VA: American Association of School Administrators, n.d.), pp. 6-7, 34-36. See also the references in footnote 1.

[49]Kirk and Gallagher, *Educating Exceptional Children*, p. 479.

[50]One of these cases is discussed by Jean Postlewaite, "*Mattie T. v. Holladay*: Denial of Equal Education," *Amicus* 2 (April 1977): 38-44. This case was filed under P.L. 94-142 to require the enforcement of procedural safeguards in evaluating children, the establishment of a program to identify handicapped children, the use of nondiscriminatory tests in evaluating children, and the development of integrated programs for the handicapped.

[51]H. Rutherford Turnbull III, "The Past and Future Impact of Court Decisions in Special Education," *Phi Delta Kappan* 59 (April 1978): 523-27; and John W. Melcher, "Law, Litigation, and Handicapped Children," *Exceptional Children* 43 (November 1976): 129-30.

[52]Turnbull, "The Past and Future Impact," p. 525.

[53]U.S. Department of Health, Education, and Welfare, *The Unfinished Revolution*, p. 1.

[54]Gliedman and Roth, *The Unexpected Minority*, pp. 174-90.

[55]Melvyn I. Semmel and Joseph L. Heinmiller, "The Education for All Handicapped Children Act of 1975: National Perspectives and Long Range Implications," *Viewpoints; Bulletin of the School of Education, Indiana University* 53 (March 1977): 15.

[56]Darrell L. Roubinek, "Will Mainstreaming Fit?," *Educational Leadership* 35 (February 1978): 410-12.

[57]"Latest in Dealing with Handicapped Pupils," *U.S. News and World Report*, February 27, 1978, pp. 49-50; and Semmel and Heinmiller, "The Education for All Handicapped Children Act," p. 14.

[58]Fred P. Orelove, "Administering Education for the Severely Handicapped after P.L. 94-142," *Phi Delta Kappan* 59 (June 1978): 699-702.

[59]U.S. Department of Health, Education, and Welfare, *The Unfinished Revolution.*

[60]Ibid., p. 17.

4 _____Attitudes:
A Basic Element of Service

"Not blindness, but the attitude of the seeing
to the blind is the hardest burden to bear."
— Helen Keller

INTRODUCTION

In the above statement, Helen Keller focused with perceptive insight on a basic and crucial issue: the attitudes of the total society and of individuals in the society toward disabilities and disabled persons are of the utmost importance. Itzhak Perlman, the virtuoso violinist who triumphed over a childhood impairment, recently stated: "For a handicapped youngster, the number one barrier to overcome is attitudinal."[1] In a similar vein the 1976 report of the National Advisory Committee on the Handicapped declared: "... the single most important requirement for significant advances ... is an affirmative public attitude toward handicapped people and their rights and capabilities."[2]

The difficult and slow process of implementing court decisions and public laws is transcended only by the greater difficulty and slowness in influencing and changing the attitudes of the public toward disabled children, young people, and adults. Enforcement of laws can ultimately effect change in public practices and the treatment of disabled persons. Public policy, therefore, influences to a great extent the outward behavior of the general society toward its disabled population as well as the attitudes that those who are disabled have toward themselves.[3] The internal attitudes of *individuals* in society, however, cannot be legislated nor enforced. Ideas, beliefs, and feelings which have been molded within an individual toward disabled persons can be affected and changed only through a slow, snail-like process of growth and development.

This chapter considers attitudes toward disabled children and young people, under the following headings: 1) definition of attitudes; 2) the attitudes of society toward disabled persons; 3) the attitudes of society as reflected in books and other media; 4) research on attitudes toward disabled persons; 5) the modification of attitudes; and 6) what librarians and educators can do to effect attitudinal changes.

DEFINITION OF ATTITUDES

Among the dictionary definitions of the word "attitude" is this meaning: "a position or bearing as indicating action, feeling, or mood; the feeling or mood itself."[4] This definition indicates that attitudes lie in the complex and abstract area of each individual's internal mechanisms and consequently are changeable, often elusive, and sometimes revealed and expressed differently in varying circumstances and situations.

Social psychology has identified three components of attitudes: cognitive, affective, and behavioral. The *cognitive component* forms the foundation of an attitude and is the basic *idea*, the *belief/disbelief*, which a person has regarding animate or inanimate objects or situations. The *affective component* constitutes the cognitive idea as it is expressed in a *feeling* or *emotion*, a *like/dislike*, which a person has toward another person, object, or situation. The *behavioral component* is the way a person acts and responds to another person or to an inanimate object as a result of the inner idea and feeling.[5] Thus, basic *beliefs* develop into *feelings* and find their outlet in the *actions and behavior* of an individual and of the general society.

Attitudes can be compared to icebergs. Two-thirds of an iceberg lie unexposed below the surface of the water, while only one-third is exposed above the water line. So also, two of the components of an attitude — belief and feeling — often remain unexposed, unrevealed, and unexpressed below the surface of an individual's personality. It is frequently only the third component — behavior and action — which is exposed and revealed to the view and observation of other people.

Although beliefs, feelings, and actions are basically either positive or negative, favorable or unfavorable, there may be some discrepancies and inconsistencies. The behavior of a person does not always correspond to the beliefs and feelings of that person; beliefs may not be the same as feelings and behavior; and feelings may be different from the beliefs and behavior. In other words, what people think and feel is not always what they say and do, and vice versa. Social and environmental factors which are present when the attitude is expressed or the action is performed influence the behavioral and verbal expression of that attitude.[6]

ATTITUDES OF SOCIETY TOWARD DISABLED PERSONS

An analysis of the attitudes toward disabled persons reveals the three basic components of all attitudes: beliefs, feelings, and actions. These three components are frequently inextricably intertwined, making it difficult to consider one component in isolation from the other two. Like the tip of an iceberg, the publicly exposed actions and behavior of the general society and of individuals within the society toward disabled persons may conform to the public policy as laid down in P.L. 94-142 and Section 504. It is not always possible, however, to ascertain the basic underlying beliefs and feelings which may be submerged\ in an individual, in the collective society, or in groups within the society.

Historical Attitudes

Negative ideas and wrong beliefs regarding disabled persons have existed throughout the history of civilization. These ideas and beliefs affected the feelings of people toward those who were handicapped and, in turn, affected societal actions and treatment of disabled persons. In ancient days when the Spartans murdered their own disabled children and when all disabled people were generally regarded as social outcasts to be spurned, ridiculed, or left to fend for themselves, such external actions and behavior reflected the primitive inner beliefs and feelings of society. Ignorance, misconceptions, and misinformation regarding disabled persons resulted in insensitivity, discomfort, dislike, and fear. These beliefs and feelings produced, in turn, the actions of mistreatment, intolerance, neglect, and isolation of handicapped individuals.

In the United States the generally negative attitudes of society in the past were nurtured by public policies. Those policies, for example, excluded disabled children from education in the public schools, placed them in separate institutions, and denied them access to school buildings and transportation. On a broader scale, the policies hindered disabled persons, including children and young people, from accessing public buildings and from participating in services and programs designed for the general public. Consequently, able-bodied children and adults generally did not have much contact with disabled persons either in school, in the world of work, or in general social situations. Thus, there was little opportunity for able-bodied persons to observe or associate with handicapped individuals in situations other than those in which disabled persons were treated as second-class citizens.

Through the years the treatment of disabled persons has improved throughout the world and in the United States. Today, "more than 50% of the people in the United States express slightly positive attitudes toward disabled people and indicate that they have sympathetic feelings for them."[7] Yet there still exist many negative ideas, false beliefs, wrong feelings, and inappropriate and inconsiderate actions toward disabled children, young people, and adults. While the Rehabilitation Amendments of 1973 seek to eliminate architectural and physical barriers to disabled persons, attitudinal barriers which are the result of wrong beliefs, negative feelings, and unfavorable actions cannot be eliminated by legislation. Consequently, although attitudinal barriers are just as real as physical barriers, they are much more difficult to change and remove. They are also more difficult to detect since attitudes lie within the affective domain and are more subtle and frequently invisible. Such attitudinal barriers nevertheless exist in our society, in institutions, and in individuals as well as in the minds of disabled persons themselves; and they impose severe limitations and restrictions on disabled individuals.

Beliefs Regarding Disabled Persons

Distorted and stereotyped images of disabled persons are still current. Sometimes they are stereotyped as subhuman, as people who are incapable, passive, weak, overly sensitive, fragile, easily hurt, childlike, unable to make decisions, without sexuality, and in need of the protection of others. In contrast to this stereotype is the "super-crip trip," which views disabled persons as more courageous because of their disability or as having superhuman powers and qualities.

Romanticized ideas are held regarding certain disabled individuals who have made impressive achievements, and many people believe that a person with a disability is compensated in some other way.[8] The opposite of that belief is the concept of "spread," which assumes that a person's disability extends to other physical or mental areas and that the disabled person is also incapacitated in other ways.[9] There is also the belief that a disabled person is less than a complete human being and is therefore totally depersonalized by nondisabled people.[10]

Feelings toward Disabled Persons

Such mistaken ideas and beliefs affect the feelings and emotions that people have about disabled persons. The most common feeling is fear. Since the behavior of disabled persons does not always follow predictable patterns which we have come to expect in other people, we are afraid of handicapped individuals because they are different from our expectations, values, ideals, and what we consider "normal." Disabled persons make us aware that we, too, are vulnerable. We are afraid that they are contagious, afraid of "catching handicap germs," afraid of becoming handicapped ourselves.[11] Edwin W. Martin, Jr., Deputy Commissioner of the Bureau of Education for the Handicapped, expressed such fear in this way:

> I think that we discriminate against the handicapped because we are finite: we all live and die, and we are all subject to illness and disability. I think we are unconsciously affected when we see people who have disabilities for our own security and well being are threatened. For many years, people didn't want to use the word "cancer" because it was a risk. Yet, as a risk it is part of life—something that might happen to us. Unfortunately, disabled people have had to bear our unconscious anxiety about our own finiteness.
>
> As we move forward, however, we need to understand why we are uncomfortable and accept the reasons. It is okay to feel uncomfortable. The feelings are normal. School children may have them. We may have them as teachers. Everybody I know who has worked in special education has had them and gone through them in some form or another. We should not deny them.[12]

The discomfort which most able-bodied persons feel when they meet a disabled person comes from a feeling of insecurity and not knowing exactly how to act with disabled people. Nondisabled individuals are afraid of saying the wrong thing, of doing something they should not do, or of not doing something they should. In such contacts it frequently happens that a person will almost totally ignore the disabled individual, acting as if the person is not really there or is not able to speak for himself or herself. In some instances, emotions toward disabled persons may take the form of insensitivity toward their situation, of dislike, and even of repulsion.

Another common feeling is that disabled persons are to be pitied because of their condition. Telethons and public service announcements on television on behalf of disabled persons have frequently been appeals to pity as well as for money. Although the intentions have been good, the result has often been a negative stereotyping.

Actions toward Disabled Persons

Shaped by misinformed beliefs and misguided feelings, attitudes toward disabled persons are visibly displayed in the outward actions and behavior of individuals and of the general society. Neglect and mistreatment of disabled persons in the distant past later changed to a condescending attitude in providing protection and custodial care as wards of society. While such attitudes are still displayed to some extent, more frequently the behavioral aspects of attitudes are more subtly expressed. A frequent reaction is to maintain a social distance from disabled persons, to avoid them through different patterns of behavior, or to withdraw completely from their presence and environment. Sometimes the attitude becomes patronizing and condescending, and disabled persons are treated like children. In some instances, disabilities and disabled persons become the objects of humor, disparaging jokes, and figurative language.[13]

As a result of the changed public policy expressed in such laws as P.L. 94-142 and Section 504, there is now greater and more sincere concern regarding those who are disabled. The attitudes of people in the United States toward disabled persons, as reflected in the external actions and behavior of the society, have progressed through the years from neglect and mistreatment to pity and protection, to education and care in separate institutions, to a greater acceptance and integration of disabled individuals into the mainstream of the society. People with disabilities are now being treated more as *persons*. A more realistic view of disabled persons was evident during 1981 with the emphasis on the International Year of Disabled Persons, proclaimed by the United Nations. But there is still a long way to go!

ATTITUDES OF SOCIETY AS REFLECTED IN BOOKS AND OTHER MEDIA

Literature, films, television shows, and other media forms which were produced in the past are replete with negative stereotypes of disabled persons, including disabled children and young people. Biklen and Bogdan deplore the "handicapist stereotypes" which have been presented in media portrayals of disabled people. After surveying a sample of classic literature and popular contemporary media, Biklen and Bogdan concluded in 1977 that there were few books and films which treated disabilities with sensitivity and accuracy.[14]

Schwartz agreed with this conclusion on the basis of his examination of a number of children's books. Disabilities have been treated accurately and without evasion, however, in some children's books, for example, Judy Blume's *Deenie*, Florence Parry Heide's *Sound of Sunshine, Sound of Rain*, and Beverly Butler's *Gift of Gold*.[15]

Literature and other media forms have stereotypically portrayed disabled persons as:

- —unable and pathetic
- —objects of violence
- —sinister and/or evil
- —"atmosphere"
- —"super-crip"
- —laughable
- —his/her own worst—and only—enemy
- —a burden
- —nonsexual
- —incapable of fully participating in everyday life
- —possessing sinister magical powers
- —objects of fear
- —terribly lonely
- —having bad dispositions

In addition, disabilities have sometimes been depicted as a form of divine punishment, and disabled characters have been named according to their disability, for example, Captain Hook and Pegleg Pete.[16]

Portrayals of deafness and hearing impairment in a large number of adult and children's books have reflected handicapist attitudes and stereotypes. In children's books which have a deaf character, the following negative portrayals have been found:

- —hearing aids are emphasized
- —deaf people are in isolation, with no contact with other deaf people
- —the deaf person is blamed for his or her deafness
- —deafness is ridiculed
- —deaf people are frightening
- —deaf children try to hide their deafness[17]
- —the deaf child has personality traits which are repugnant to society and which bring out society's baser instincts of hatred and rejection[18]

Authors have endeavored through such portrayals to create sympathy for the deaf character, with the intention of causing a hearing child who reads the book to accept deaf peers.

Historically, the fictional presentation of deaf persons shows inaccuracies, distortions, and misrepresentations. In the eighteenth and nineteenth centuries, deaf persons were portrayed in fiction as either curiosities or as saints, not accepted as a part of the regular society and, indeed, could never be accepted as long as they remained deaf. In the first part of the twentieth century, deaf characters were depicted as very lonely and in isolation. Authors of the 1960s and

1970s displayed a greater interest in deaf characters but still did not write with real understanding about the experience of being deaf.[19]

Although the foregoing discussion has emphasized the portrayal of deaf persons in fiction, the major emphasis, at least in adolescent fiction, has been and still is upon characters who are blind or physically impaired. Within recent years, however, the disabling conditions portrayed in contemporary adolescent fiction have been expanded to include characters who have cerebral palsy, a mental disability, or who are emotionally disturbed.[20]

More recent portrayals of disabled persons in newspapers, magazines, television shows, movies, and books have been more realistic and favorable. It is to be hoped that this outward expression of more positive attitudes in various media forms and in societal behavior is the result of more enlightened beliefs and ideas, as well as more sensitive feelings on the part of the peoples of the world and of the United States regarding the disabled. It is also to be hoped that more and more individuals within society will express an attitude of genuine concern and acceptance in their actions and behavior toward disabled persons, based on correct beliefs and positive feelings.

RESEARCH ON ATTITUDES TOWARD DISABLED PERSONS

Extensive research on attitudes toward disabled persons has been conducted for the past fifty years. The initial work was done in 1930 by Schaefer,[21] the first person to study attitudes toward a specific disability group, and in 1931 by Strong,[22] the first to investigate comparative attitudes toward different disabilities and toward other groups.

Many different instruments and techniques have been used to measure attitudes toward disabled persons: simple unstructured interview schedules, questionnaires, Likert scales, nonprojective social distance scales, sentence completion, adjective checklists, Q-sorts, sociometric choice devices, and picture story projectives.[23] Perhaps the most frequently used instrument has been the Attitudes Toward Disabled Persons (ATDP) scale developed in 1959 by Yuker, Block, and Campbell. The ATDP was constructed to measure attitudes toward disabled persons in general, rather than attitudes toward specific disability groups, as well as to measure the attitudes of both disabled persons and nondisabled persons.[24] In 1966 it was reported that various investigators had administered the ATDP to approximately 15,000 persons in numerous studies.[25] Since that time it has been used in many additional studies and is regarded as an adequate instrument for research purposes.[26]

Hierarchy of Preferences

Researchers have found that a hierarchy or hierarchies of preferences toward disability groups exist which establish the relative position of a specific disability in the hierarchy. For example, professionals and students in the areas of education, medicine, psychology, and social work ranked exceptional children in the following hierarchical order: 1) academically talented, 2) antisocial, 3) sight handicapped, 4) mildly retarded, 5) hearing handicapped, 6) brain injured, and 7) severely retarded.[27] Another hierarchy placed the attitudes of regular classroom teachers in this order: 1) more positive toward learning-disabled children, 2) less positive toward emotionally disturbed children, and 3) least positive toward educable mentally retarded children.[28]

Yuker, in summarizing the research on attitudes toward disabled persons, presented a hierarchy consisting of five classes:

1.   People who have comparatively minor disabilities, such as those who are partially sighted, speech impaired, or hard of hearing, or who have heart disease or an ulcer;

2.   People who have lost one or more extremities;

3.   People who have completely lost a major sense, that is, vision or hearing;

4.   People who are mentally ill;

5.   People who have acute and chronic brain injuries, such as cerebral palsy, epilepsy, or mental retardation.

Attitudes of nondisabled people are more favorable and positive toward persons with the disabilities at the top of the list and decrease toward persons as the list continues. Attitudes toward disabled persons at the top of the list are also easier to change than attitudes toward persons at the bottom of the list.[29]

Factors Which Influence Attitudes

Several factors have been studied to determine their influence on attitudes toward disabled persons: 1) age, 2) sex, 3) level of information about disabled persons, and 4) degree of contact with disabled individuals.

AGE

Since attitudes are learned and acquired as one progresses through life, they do not always stay the same but change as a person advances in years. Unfortunately, however, changes in attitudes may not necessarily be on the positive side of more acceptance of disabled persons but, in some cases, may become more negative and less accepting.[30]

Although the relationship of age to attitude is complex and there is an interrelationship with other factors, such as degree of contact and amount of information, the findings of research studies are contradictory. Yuker, Block, and Younng examined the research data and made the conclusion that, in general, there is little or no correlation between age and attitudes toward disabled persons.[31]

SEX

Research indicates that women usually have more favorable attitudes toward disabled individuals than men do.[32]

LEVEL OF INFORMATION

Most people assume that positive and favorable attitudes toward disabled persons can be formed by providing accurate information and knowledge regarding disabilities and disabled persons. While there are studies which have concluded that attitudes do become more positive as the level of information increases,[33] Yuker has reported that "most social scientists are skeptical of this view" because increased information is not always effective. Data from research studies indicate that only about 50% of the time does an increased level of information bring about a positive change in attitude and greater acceptance of disabled persons. Information by itself, therefore, does not automatically affect a person's attitudes.[34]

DEGREE OF CONTACT

Similarly, contact of nondisabled persons with disabled individuals can have varying effects—sometimes positive, sometimes negative, and sometimes no effect at all. Some studies have found that attitudes become more positive as the degree of contact with disabled persons increases.[35] In other studies, however, closer contact with disabled persons, such as mentally retarded children, was associated with greater rejection by their peers.[36] The effect on attitudes of contact with disabled persons depends on a number of variables:

1. *Frequency of contact.* In general, the more frequent the contact between two individuals, the more positive the attitudes that result....

2. *Status.* The relative status of the persons who interact with one another has also been found to be important. The most positive attitudes result when the two persons have equal status....

3. *Type of interaction.* If the interaction is friendly, positive attitudes tend to result. If it is unfriendly or hostile, the resulting attitudes tend to be negative....

4. *Intimacy.* The closer the contact and the more that each individual gets to know the other, the more favorable the attitudes that result....

5. *Societal and institutional norms.* When the laws and regulations of a society and its leaders view integration of disabled persons with favor, it is carried out without much difficulty and has positive effects....

6. *Setting.* The setting will influence the norms that prevail, the type of interaction that occurs, and the amount of intimacy that occurs....

7. *Perceived normality.* ... disabled persons are frequently perceived as different from non-disabled people. This perception often results in rejection ... a major goal of contact and integration should be to have disabled persons perceived as similar to everyone else....[37]

Both level of information and degree of contact appear to be the important factors in developing positive attitudes toward disabled individuals, possibly more important than the factors of age and sex. Yet both information and contact can have either positive or negative effects. In order to bring about positive attitude changes, it is essential to have an appropriate presentation of the right kind of information together with the proper kind of contact under the right conditions. Research data indicate that such a combination is effective for all types of disabilities, but Yuker has concluded that attitudes depend to a greater extent on the amount and type of contact with disabled persons and, to a lesser extent, on the information that people have about disabilities.[38]

Attitudes of Educators

During the past ten to fifteen years there has been increased research activity on attitudes toward disabled persons. The attitudes of all ages of both disabled and nondisabled persons — adults, young people, school-age and preschool children — have been studied in relation to all types of disabling conditions, as well as in relation to disability in general. Such research has focused on the attitudes of many different groups in society: professionals in education, medicine, psychology, social work, and other disciplines; employers; parents; and students at all educational levels.

Particularly extensive is the research literature involving educators, which reveals varied and inconclusive findings. Some studies of educators have indicated favorable attitudes on the part of teachers,[39] but on the basis of other research studies it was concluded in 1958 that educators accepted disabled persons to a lesser degree than nondisabled persons.[40] This conclusion has been corroborated by more recent research, including studies which have revealed that the use of labels has a negative effect on the attitudes and expectations of teachers regarding disabled children.[41] Similarly, eighty-four administrators of special education programs for educable mentally retarded students listed the attitudes of nonacceptance on the part of both teachers and students among their four greatest administrative concerns.[42]

In a study in which the ATDP scale was used, Conine found that elementary school teachers were neither accepting nor rejecting of disabled children and that their attitudes appeared to be similar to those of the general public. This study concluded that the unfavorable attitudes of the public toward disabled persons may reflect, at least in part, the prejudicial attitudes of teachers. In other words, since everyone in society has gone through the school system and has been influenced by teachers, the negative attitudes of teachers have contributed to the unfavorable attitudes of the general public. Another conclusion of this study was that understanding on the cognitive level does not necessarily reflect upon the feelings of individuals; therefore any attempts to change the attitudes of teachers need to go beyond cognitive dimensions and be directed toward a change in feelings.[43]

The attitudes of educators toward disabled children and young people can be summarized in Yuker's remarks regarding professionals in general:

... it is difficult to draw conclusions about the attitudes and behavior of professional personnel and staff members. Personality factors and institutional norms will play as important a role as professional status so that it is impossible to generalize about the attitudes of any professional group, or to predict differences among professional groups with any degree of confidence.[44]

Attitudes of Nondisabled Children

As in other areas of life, attitudes and practices are transmitted from one generation to the next. Thus, the attitudes of young children are largely influenced by the actions, as well as by the expressed and unexpressed beliefs and feelings, of their parents and other elders. By the age of four or five most children begin to discriminate against disabled persons and have developed their own attitudes which include basic beliefs, feelings, and behavioral tendencies toward disabled persons.[45]

Data from research studies which have investigated the attitudes of nondisabled children toward disabled children are just as inconclusive as the findings in studies of the attitudes of adults. Disabled children were *less accepted* by their peers in many studies which focused on physically handicapped children,[46] learning-disabled children,[47] and mentally retarded children.[48] Some studies, however, have found that disabled children were *not less favorably accepted* by their peers.[49] Still other investigations have found that, while *some disabled children were rejected* by their peers, *others were quite popular.*[50]

Attitudes of Librarians

In the large body of research on attitudes toward disabled persons, no past studies have been located which have investigated the attitudes of professional librarians, supportive library staff members, library school faculty and administrators, or library science students. Even apart from research studies, there is very little literature which pertinently and specifically discusses the attitudes of librarians toward disabled persons and which offers suggestions specifically for the improvement of librarians' attitudes. By contrast, there has been an abundance of material written about architectural barriers in libraries, perhaps because libraries, as public institutions, must comply with the requirements of Section 504 of the Rehabilitation Amendments of 1973 if they wish to receive public funds.

On the basis of previous research on attitudes toward disabled persons, it might be expected that the attitudes of librarians, if measured in a research study, would be very similar and reveal the following:

—that more than 50% of librarians have slightly positive attitudes, since it appears that over 50% of the people in the United States have slightly positive attitudes toward disabled persons[51];

—that the attitudes of librarians would be similar to other professional groups, especially educators, and that research would reveal the same varied and inconclusive results;

—that the degree of contact, both personal and professional, which librarians have with disabled persons would be the most influential factor;

—that the type and level of information which a librarian has about disabilities and disabled persons would be the second most important factor, bringing about greater acceptance of disabled persons about 50% of the time;

—that female librarians would have more favorable attitudes than male librarians and, since the majority of professional librarians are women, that librarians as a group would have highly favorable attitudes;

—that the age of librarians would not indicate a significant correlating effect upon their attitudes toward disabled persons.

A beginning was made recently in the investigation of the attitudes of librarians toward disabled people in regard to age, sex, level of information, and amount of contact. Two studies were completed, both of which used the ATDP scale.

In a 1981 study by Dequin and Faibisoff it was found that the Illinois public librarians who responded had highly favorable attitudes, with a mean score of 80.598 out of a possible ATDP score of 120. When measured on a t-test, the respondents scored significantly higher in the following comparisons: 1) ages 30-39 versus ages 40-49, ages 50-59, and ages 60-69; 2) those who had a library science degree versus those who did not have a library science degree; 3) those who had received information about disabled persons through an entire course versus those who had received information through an entire course and an institute/workshop; and 4) those who had received information through part of a course and an institute/workshop versus those who had received information through part of a course. Each of the comparisons of information in which significance was indicated was small in number of respondents, which may have affected the results. No significant difference was found in the areas of sex or contact.[52]

Also in 1981, Schilling conducted a similar study among Illinois academic librarians. This study, too, showed highly favorable attitudes toward disabled persons. Respondents had a mean score of 83.75 on the ATDP scale. Results were slightly different from the study of public librarians, however, in regard to age and contact. Significance was indicated on a t-test by the following groups of academic librarians: 1) ages 20-29 versus ages 40-49, 2) ages 20-29 versus ages 50-59, and 3) those who had at least one type of contact with disabled persons versus those who had no contact with a disabled person. Contact was also shown to be significant 1) for those who had a disabled immediate family member and 2) for those who had a disabled family member *and* a disabled friend. No significant difference was indicated in regard to sex, experience in libraries, education and information, and whether the respondent was disabled.[53]

Both of these studies, therefore, indicated that over 50% of the public and academic librarians who responded had favorable attitudes toward disabled persons and that there was no significant difference between the sexes. The two studies present slightly different results, however, in regard to age, level of information, and amount of contact.

Another study was conducted by Dequin in 1982 among Illinois school librarians. The results of this study, however, remain to be tabulated and analyzed.

MODIFICATION OF ATTITUDES

Attitudes are not an innate part of human personality but are learned and acquired throughout life. Once learned, however, they have a tendency to persist, although they are always subject to the influences of later experiences. Consequently, a person's feelings and actions toward someone else or toward an inanimate object can be modified, but such change will come about only if the person's basic beliefs and ideas are changed.[54] Attitude changes can be either in a positive or negative direction, but it is only when the change of beliefs is positive and favorable that the feelings and actions will be improved in a positive and favorable direction.

It is possible, therefore, to transform negative attitudes toward disabled persons into positive ones. To do so requires changes in the three components of attitudes: 1) the cognitive component can be changed by supplying accurate information and knowledge through books and other forms of media, 2) the affective component can be changed by fostering greater empathy and understanding through direct contact or vicarious experiences with disabled persons, and 3) the behavioral component can be changed when the cognitive and affective components are altered.[55]

In the past, there were few research studies which investigated altering attitudes toward disabled persons and the manner of preparing nondisabled persons to accept persons with a disability.[56] This situation has changed within recent years as more research and literature have become available regarding the modification of attitudes toward disabled persons.

While some kinds of negative attitudes are rather difficult to change, other kinds are easier to alter. Yuker has summarized the conclusions of research data regarding the difficulty of changing attitudes in this way:

1. Extreme attitudes are more difficult to change than moderate ones....

2. Attitudes that are based on many beliefs and much information will be very hard to change, even if the "original" information was incorrect. It is much more difficult to counteract negative beliefs than to provide information that will lead to positive beliefs.

3. Attitudes that are part of an interrelated system of consistent beliefs will be difficult to change....

4. Attitudes that are similar to those held by the members of a person's reference (i.e., peer) groups will be difficult to change.

5. Attitudes that fit in with a person's needs or his view of himself are more difficult to change than attitudes that are unrelated to motivational factors....

6. Motivation to change is the final important factor....[57]

Research studies (as well as other literature) related to the modification of attitudes fall into two categories: 1) those that have provided increased *knowledge and information* about disabilities and disabled persons, and 2) those that have provided increased *direct contact* with disabled persons.[58] Although both increased information and direct contact have been found effective, the best approach to fostering positive attitudes is a combination of direct contact with disabled persons and accurate information regarding them and their disabilities.[59]

Information

Investigations of the effectiveness of increased information in developing positive attitudes have found that instructors can change the attitudes of their students by using a special instructional program. For example, the attitudes of university students in special education were changed through a carefully planned and sequenced instructional program.[60] Also, the attitudes of young mentally gifted children were altered through a special unit on creative Americans, including some who were disabled.[61] In a study in which the traditional lecture approach was compared with an innovative active learning approach (which included role playing, simulation of disabling conditions, problem-solving activities, and open-ended discussions), it was found that the active learning approach tended to exert a generally more positive effect upon the attitudes of fifty undergraduate subjects.[62]

In a 1977 study by Donaldson and Martinson, a nondisabled group of students listened to a live panel discussion by a group of individuals who had visible disabling conditions and who presented their views and perceptions of physical disability. A second group viewed the same discussion by means of videotape; a third group listened to an audio presentation, and a fourth group served as the control group. After the presentations, the subjects in each group responded to the ATDP scale. The effectiveness of the panel discussion was assessed on the basis of this measure. Both the live and videotaped presentations were effective in modifying stereotypic attitudes toward physically disabled persons. Since the audio presentation was not significant in modifying attitudes, Donaldson and Martinson concluded that the visual information indicating that the panel members were physically disabled may have been a significant factor in the modification of attitudes in the live and videotaped groups. The study suggests that such a presentation can be effective in improving attitudes toward physically disabled persons.[63]

Workshops and discussion groups on disabilities have been found to have the greatest potential for affective change.[64] Haring conducted a workshop experiment which consisted of fifteen two-hour sessions over a period of thirty weeks. During the first hour of each session, a lecture was presented on one of eight areas of exceptionality, and in the second hour participants divided into small groups to discuss the exceptionality. Films, demonstrations, and visitations were included throughout the experiment. Among other things, it was concluded that the workshop 1) highly increased the information and understanding of the participants regarding disabled children, 2) was effective in modifying the attitudes of the participants toward greater acceptance of disabled children, 3) effected positive changes in the responses of the participants to disabled children, and 4) had a strong positive influence on participants' attitudes, philosophy, and teaching methods, which was reflected in their teaching relationships with disabled children.[65]

The effectiveness of the workshop concept was supported by a follow-up study of school library media professionals who participated in an institute on services and materials for the handicapped, conducted at Northern Illinois University, DeKalb, Illinois. In the eight months following the institute, the number of participants who offered services to disabled children and young people increased by 300%, from six to twenty-four participants. In addition, the total number of services offered by the participants increased by 1300%, from 24 to 338 services.[66] Such increased activity can be attributed to heightened attitudinal awareness and response.

A step-by-step account of how to conduct an attitudinal workshop was presented by Fix and Rohrbacher. They described planning, presenting, evaluating, and following up on the workshop, in which participants are sensitized through simulation of disabilities and self-examination to the attitudinal barriers facing those who are physically disabled. Timing, participants, and the types of disabilities on which to focus are important factors to consider. Also discussed were facilities and equipment, selection and criteria for helpers, training of helpers, stage setting, group discussion, and the evaluation process.[67] The involvement of parents of disabled children as participants, presenters, and group leaders, as well as the participation of disabled individuals, can be very effective in producing attitudinal change.[68]

Conferences are also effective ways of improving attitudes toward disabled persons, although not as beneficial as workshops and discussion groups. Formal courses, however, do not appear to do much to change the affective component of attitudes but may influence the behavioral tendencies of the participants.[69]

Contact with Disabled Persons

Some studies have investigated the effect on attitudes of contact and interaction between nondisabled and disabled persons. On the basis of an experimental study involving interaction between nondisabled and disabled persons as measured by the ATDP scale, Evans concluded that disabled persons can affect the attitudes of nondisabled persons with whom they interact socially.[70] Role-playing activities, such as traveling for an extended period of time in a wheelchair or with a blindfold on, have been found to affect interpersonal attitudes toward disabled persons and lead to more positive responses.[71]

Velleman reported on a program conducted by Ronald Friedman at the Human Resources School in Albertson, New York. Called the Peer-Peer Program, it successfully integrated elementary and junior high school physically disabled students with nondisabled peers to whom they were matched. The program has also served to develop positive social attitudes toward disabled children and young people.[72]

Information and Direct Contact Combined

A combined methodology of increased information and direct contact has been found to be the best approach to fostering positive attitudes. Higgs found that attitudes change as a result of age, experience, and education. Individuals who had higher degrees of contact also tended to possess more information about physical disabilities and had more positive attitudes toward physically disabled persons. Higgs concluded that the general public lacked both exposure to physically disabled people and quality information about them.[73]

Rusalem studied junior and senior high school students who had initial negative attitudes toward deaf-blind persons. These students tended to develop a more favorable attitude toward deaf-blindness as a result of a brief exposure to deaf-blind individuals, the manual alphabet, and information concerning the disability. The improved attitude was evidenced on both verbal and behavioral levels.[74]

Harasymiw and Horne conducted an experiment in which an in-service program to provide teachers with new knowledge about disabled children was combined with classroom experiences in working with special children. They concluded that in-service education could make teachers less anxious in working with disabled children but that a much longer procedure of familiarization with various disabilities may be required to modify the underlying social distance attitudes.[75]

The workshop experiment conducted by Haring and referred to earlier in this chapter was a combination of increased information and direct contact, designed to influence teacher attitudes toward disabled children. The workshop proved highly effective in increasing teachers' information and understanding of exceptional children. In addition, classroom experience with exceptional children concurrent with the workshop seemed to play a crucial role in the effectiveness of the workshop program.[76]

WHAT LIBRARIANS CAN DO TO
EFFECT ATTITUDINAL CHANGES

Librarians have a multilevel responsibility toward themselves, their colleagues, children and young people, and parents and other adults to foster positive attitudes toward disabled children and young people as well as toward disabled adults. There are several things librarians can and should do:

First, librarians should examine and assess their own personal attitudes toward those who are disabled and make changes wherever necessary to achieve more positive personal attitudes. Only when one's own feelings are recognized and resolved can a librarian move on to recognize the feelings of other people.

Second, librarians should increase their knowledge of and information about disabilities, disabled persons, and the myriad possibilities of library service for those who are disabled. They should read about disabilities. They should talk with disabled persons. They should attend workshops, institutes, seminars, and conferences on this subject, and perhaps also take a formal course in a library school on library services for disabled persons.

Third, librarians should interact with disabled people in the community, the library, and the profession. As librarians associate more with disabled persons in the right setting, they will be better able to understand disabled children and young people, recognize them as persons, and serve their library needs.

Fourth, librarians should be agents of the common good by working to change the attitudes of nondisabled children, young people, and adults by disseminating information and knowledge regarding disabled persons to the entire community. Librarians can be effective in fostering positive attitudes toward disabilities and disabled persons. Many excellent lists of books and audiovisual materials are available which can be helpful in influencing the attitudes of other librarians and media people, teachers, parents, children, and young people as well as disabled persons themselves. Among these materials are the following:

Baskin, Barbara H., and Harris, Karen H. *Notes from a Different Drummer: A Guide to Juvenile Fiction Portraying the Handicapped.* New York: R. R. Bowker, 1977.

An annotated guide to 311 books of juvenile fiction portraying disabled persons, published between 1940 and 1975, with extensive annotations. Reading levels are indicated. Title and subject indexes are included.

Cohen, Shirley, and Koehler, Nancy. *Fostering Positive Attitudes toward the Handicapped: A Selected Bibliography of Multimedia Materials.* New York: City University of New York, Graduate School and University Center, 1975. (ED 140515, EC 100852).

A bibliography of thirty-four multimedia materials — 16mm films, filmstrips and audiotapes, videocassettes, videotapes, slides, audiotapes, and records — including information on title, length, distributor, cost, and content.

Cohen, Shirley, and Koehler, Nancy. *A Selected Bibliography on Attitudes toward the Handicapped.* New York: City University of New York, Graduate School and University Center, 1975. (ED 140517, EC 100855).

A list of eighty-five references (1962-1975) for professionals and children. Grade level is given for the children's books which will foster positive attitudes toward disabled children.

Hanley, Robert J., Jr. "The Special Student: Selected Media." *Previews* 7 (January 1979): 2-6.

A list of eighteen audiovisual materials is included which can be useful in modifying the attitudes of adults — librarians, teachers, and parents — toward disabled children and young people.

Hazard, Marilynn. "A Bibliography — Subject: The Handicapped." *Ohio Media Spectrum* 31 (Fall 1979): 54-57.

An annotated bibliography of forty-five books to help nondisabled children at various age levels to understand the disabled better and know what they are like.

Monson, Dianne, and Shurtleff, Cynthia. "Altering Attitudes toward the Physically Handicapped through Print and Non-Print Media." *Language Arts* 56 (February 1979): 163-70.

A bibliography of fifty-five fiction, nonfiction, and biography/auto-biography books which includes types of disability and recommended grade levels.

Fifth, librarians should endeavor to influence the attitudes of other professional librarians, library support staff, and nondisabled children, young people, and adults in the community. In-service workshops for all library staff members and programs for the able-bodied in the community can be arranged. The workshops and programs should include information about disabilities and disabled persons, coupled with direct contact and interaction with disabled children, young people, and adults. As indicated earlier in this chapter, the effectiveness of an instructional approach can be increased through direct contact with disabled persons as resource people. Such information and contact will help library staff members and people in the community know how to relate to persons with disabilities and to remove unfounded fears.

In order to change attitudes through in-service workshops and library programs for the community, the participants need to *do* something. Some of the activities that are highly effective in bringing about attitude change are: 1) self-examination, 2) role playing or role reversal, 3) public commitment by a person to a specific attitude or action, and 4) counter-attitudinal advocacy.[77] Experiential simulation exercises can deal with 1) motor disability, 2) sensory disability, and 3) learning and emotional disabilities.[78] In addition, library programs which emphasize materials and devices for disabled persons can be successfully designed and implemented for nondisabled children, young people, and adults. Program participants should be given the opportunity to see and examine special materials, such as large-print books, braille books, cassette recordings, and high-interest/low-vocabulary books. They should also be able to see and operate special devices, such as braille writers, telecommunication devices for the deaf, the Visualtek®, the Optacon®, the Kurzweil Reading Machine®, and equipment used by physically disabled persons.

Many topics can be pursued in staff workshops and community programs. Among them are the following:

1. An introduction to the subject of disability

2. An analysis of literature for stereotypes

3. An investigation of stereotypes in television programs, cartoons, and comic books

4. A discussion of societal discrimination against disabled people

5. An introduction to the Disability Rights Movement

6. A discussion of ways in which to combat handicapism

7. An analysis of specific books about disabled persons

These topics can be effective in detecting and combatting negative attitudes. They are adaptable for all age levels and can involve activity on the part of the participants.[79]

Specifically in regard to the elimination of the fears that children have about disabled people, several positive approaches are possible:

1. Talk openly about physical and mental limitations. Emphasize what disabled persons *can* do rather than what they cannot do.

2. Borrow wheelchairs and crutches so children can become familiar with them.

3. Play games that give the idea of physical limitations.

4. Use books and films for more understanding.

5. Invite disabled individuals to talk to children.

6. Have a physical therapist demonstrate techniques and equipment.

7. Use a child with a temporary disability as the basis for a discussion of children's feelings toward disabled children and their difficulties.

8. Invite disabled children to programs, sports exhibitions, and concerts.

9. Try a creative exchange with a school for disabled children, using swimming or vocational programs.[80]

The combined use of print and nonprint media has been found to be effective in altering attitudes. Monson and Shurtleff presented two filmstrips ("Julie" and "Spanish Dancer") to nonhandicapped children and then discussed the two shows. The results suggested that the use of audiovisual media can influence children's attitudes toward people with physical handicaps, particularly when cooperating teachers provide good models and encourage positive attitudes. Children who also read several of the books on a bibliography of fiction, nonfiction, and biography/autobiography dealing with various handicaps showed the greatest positive changes.[81]

Sixth, librarians should work to foster positive attitudes on the part of disabled persons toward themselves and toward other disabled persons. The primary way this can be done is to accept them as persons who have a legitimate right to library services and materials. Library programs can also be developed specifically for disabled children and young people which will help them better to accept themselves and other disabled persons.

If librarians pursue these suggestions, the ideas/beliefs, feelings, and actions of professional librarians, library staff members, and the general public can become more favorably disposed toward disabled children and young people, as well as toward all disabled persons.

NOTES

[1]U.S. Committee for UNICEF, *News of the World's Children* 28 (December 1980): 1-2.

[2]U.S. Department of Health, Education, and Welfare, Office of Education, National Advisory Committee on the Handicapped, *The Unfinished Revolution: Education for the Handicapped; 1976 Annual Report* (Washington, DC: Government Printing Office, 1976), p. 15.

[3]Frederick J. Weintraub and Alan Abeson, "New Education Policies for the Handicapped: The Quiet Revolution," *Phi Delta Kappan* 55 (April 1974): 529.

[4]*Webster's Third New International Dictionary of the English Language Unabridged* (Chicago: Encyclopaedia Britannica, 1976), p. 141.

[5]H. C. Triandis, *Attitude and Attitude Change* (New York: John Wiley, 1971), pp. 2-4; Edwin P. Hollander, *Principles and Methods of Social Psychology* (New York: Oxford University Press, 1967), p. 121. See also John M. Crandell, Jr., "The Genesis and Modification of Attitudes toward the Child Who

Is Different," *Training School Bulletin* 66 (1969): 72-79; and Harold E. Yuker, "Attitudes of the General Public toward Handicapped Individuals," in *The White House Conference on Handicapped Individuals*, Vol. 1: *Awareness Papers*, pp. 89-105 (Washington, DC: Government Printing Office, 1977), pp. 93-94. Frank Bowe, *Handicapping America: Barriers to Disabled People* (New York: Harper and Rowe, 1978), pp. 114-17, labeled the three components "information, conation, and action." Beatrice A. Wright, "An Analysis of Attitudes—Dynamics and Effects," *New Outlook for the Blind* 68 (March 1974): 108-118, discussed two of the components, namely, the cognitive and affective factors.

6Yuker, "Attitudes of the General Public," p. 93.

7Ibid., p. 94.

8Barbara H. Baskin and Karen H. Harris, *Notes from a Different Drummer: A Guide to Juvenile Fiction Portraying the Handicapped* (New York: R. R. Bowker, 1977), p. 4.

9Ibid., pp. 4-5; Ruth A. Velleman, *Serving Physically Disabled People: An Information Handbook for All Libraries* (New York: R. R. Bowker, 1979), p. 5; Wright, "An Analysis of Attitudes," p. 109.

10Velleman, *Serving Physically Disabled People*, p. 5.

11Shirley Cohen, *Special People: A Bright Future for Everyone with Physical, Mental, and Emotional Disabilities* (Englewood Cliffs, NJ: Prentice-Hall, 1977), pp. 3-7; Velleman, *Serving Physically Disabled People*, p. 6.

12National Conference on Human and Civil Rights in Education, *Education of All Handicapped Children and PL 94-142; Report of the Sixteenth National Conference on Human and Civil Rights in Education, March 17-19, 1978, Sheraton Park Hotel, Washington, D.C.* (Washington, DC: National Education Association, 1978), p. 6.

13Baskin and Harris, *Notes from a Different Drummer*, pp. 3-11.

14Douglas Biklen and Robert Bogdan, "Media Portrayals of Disabled People: A Study in Stereotypes," *Interracial Books for Children Bulletin* 8 (Numbers 6 and 7, 1977): 4-9.

15Albert V. Schwartz, "Disability in Children's Books: Is Visibility Enough?," *Interracial Books for Children Bulletin* 8 (Numbers 6 and 7, 1977): 10-15.

16Biklen and Bogdan, "Media Portrayals," pp. 4-9; Schwartz, "Disability in Children's Books," pp. 10-15.

17Albert V. Schwartz, "Books Mirror Society: A Study of Children's Materials," *Interracial Books for Children Bulletin* 11 (Numbers 1 and 2, 1980): 19-24, analyzed 70 children's books, including over 50 titles in signed English.

[18]Patrick Groff, "The Child's World of the Fictional Deaf," *Top of the News* 32 (April 1976): 261-67, critiqued six books, all written since 1962, which have a deaf child as the main character or subcharacter: *Into the Forest* by Rosamund Essex, *David in Silence* by Veronica Robinson, *Dead before Docking* by Scott Corbett, *Child of the Arctic* by Hubert Woods, *A Single Light* by Maia Wojciechowska, and *The Nothing Place* by Eleanor Spence.

[19]Trenton Batson, "The Deaf Person in Fiction—From Sainthood to Rorschach Blot," *Interracial Books for Children Bulletin* 11 (Numbers 1 and 2, 1980): 16-18 analyzed both negative and positive portrayals of deaf characters in several contemporary novels, namely, *The Heart Is a Lonely Hunter* by Carson McCullers, *Silent Witness* by Susan Yankowitz, and *Rites of Passage* and *In This Sign* by Paul West.

[20]In three articles, Janet Stroud analyzed adolescent novels for their treatment of characters with various types of disabilities: "Treatment of the Mentally Handicapped in Young Adult Fiction," *Top of the News* 36 (Winter 1980): 208-212 (13 books which have mentally disabled characters); "Portrayal of Physically Handicapped Characters in Adolescent Fiction," *Top of the News* 36 (Summer 1980): 363-67 (12 novels depicting blindness, physical disabilities, and cerebral palsy); and "Characterization of the Emotionally Disturbed in Current Adolescent Fiction," *Top of the News* 37 (Spring 1981): 290-95 (11 books which have emotionally disturbed characters).

[21]F. M. Schaefer, "The Social Traits of the Blind," (Master's thesis, Loyola University, 1930).

[22]Edward K. Strong, Jr., *Change of Interests with Age; Based on Examination of More Than Two Thousand Men between the Ages of Twenty and Sixty Representing Eight Occupations* (Palo Alto, CA: Stanford University Press, 1931), pp. 188-89, 222. Using three response categories (liking, disliking, and indifferent), Strong examined the interests of 2,340 men for 53 "peculiarities of people," some of whom were listed as "unfortunate" and included "cripples," "side-show freaks," "people with protruding jaws," "people with hooked noses," "blind people," and "deaf mutes."

[23]Harold E. Yuker, J. R. Block, and Janet Younng, *The Measurement of Attitudes toward Disabled Persons* (Albertson, NY: Human Resources Center, 1966), pp. 4-17, reviewed the studies in which these techniques were used from 1930 to 1965.

[24]Ibid., p. 18.

[25]Ibid., p. 3.

[26]Marvin E. Shaw and Jack M. Wright, *Scales for the Measurement of Attitudes* (New York: McGraw-Hill, 1967), p. 481.

[27]Sue Allen Warren and Dale Robert Turner, "Attitudes of Professionals and Students toward Exceptional Children," *Training School Bulletin* 62 (February 1966): 136-44.

[28]Jay R. Shotel, Richard P. Iano, and James F. McGettigan, "Teacher Attitudes Associated with the Integration of Handicapped Children," *Exceptional Children* 38 (May 1972): 677-83.

[29]Yuker, "Attitudes of the General Public," pp. 96-97.

[30]Ibid., p. 95.

[31]Yuker, Block, and Younng, *The Measurement of Attitudes*, pp. 44-48.

[32]Yuker, "Attitudes of the General Public," p. 95. Cf. Yuker, Block, and Younng, *The Measurement of Attitudes*, pp. 48-50.

[33]Reginald W. Higgs, "Attitude Formation — Contact or Information?," *Exceptional Children* 47 (April 1975): 496-97.

[34]Yuker, "Attitudes of the General Public," p. 97.

[35]Higgs, "Attitude Formation," pp. 496-97.

[36]Jay Gottlieb and M. Budoff, "Social Acceptability of Retarded Children in Non-graded Schools Differing in Architecture," *Studies in Learning Potential* 2 (1972): 1-17.

[37]Yuker, "Attitudes of the General Public," p. 100. Cf. Shirley Cohen, "Improving Attitudes toward the Handicapped," *Educational Forum* 42 (November 1977): 16.

[38]Yuker, "Attitudes of the General Public," pp. 95, 101.

[39]Stefan J. Harasymiw and Marcia D. Horne, "Integration of Handicapped Children: Its Effects on Teacher Attitudes," *Education* 96 (Winter 1975): 153-58; and J. Newman, "Faculty Attitudes toward Handicapped Students," *Rehabilitation Literature* 37 (July 1976): 194-97.

[40]Norris G. Haring, George G. Stern, and William M. Cruickshank, *Attitudes of Educators toward Exceptional Children* (Syracuse, NY: Syracuse University Press, 1958), p. 14.

[41]Ronald H. Coombs and Jerry L. Harper, "Effects of Labels on Attitudes of Educators toward Handicapped Children," *Exceptional Children* 33 (February 1967): 399-403; Tom B. Gillung and Chauncy N. Rucker, "Labels and Teacher Expectations," *Exceptional Children* 43 (April 1977): 464-65; William R. Jacobs, "The Effect of the Learning Disability Label on Classroom Teacher's Ability Objectively to Observe and Interpret Child Behavior," *Learning Disability Quarterly* 1 (Winter 1978): 50-55; and Leon I. Smith and Sandra Greenberg, "Teacher Attitudes and the Labeling Process," *Exceptional Children* 41 (February 1975): 319-24.

[42]Nancy J. Warnock, "Making General Education 'Special'," *Education and Training of the Mentally Retarded* 11 (December 1976): 304-308.

[43]Tali A. Conine, "Acceptance or Rejection of Disabled Persons by Teachers," *Journal of School Health* 39 (April 1969): 278-81.

[44]Yuker, "Attitudes of the General Public," pp. 101-102.

[45]Reginald L. Jones and Dorothy D. Sisk, "Early Perceptions of Orthopedic Disability: A Developmental Study," *Rehabilitation Literature* 31 (February 1970): 34-38; and Cohen, "Improving Attitudes," pp. 11-13.

[46]See, for example, Helen K. Billings, "An Exploratory Study of the Attitudes of Noncrippled Children toward Crippled Children in Three Selected Elementary Schools," *Journal of Experimental Education* 31 (Summer 1963): 381-87; Louise Centers and Richard Centers, "Peer Group Attitudes toward the Amputee Child," *Journal of Social Psychology* 61 (October 1963): 127-32; and Jones and Sisk, "Early Perceptions of Orthopedic Disability," pp. 34-38.

[47]See, for example, Virginia L. Bruininks, "Actual and Perceived Peer Status of Learning-Disabled Students in Mainstream Programs," *Journal of Special Education* 12 (Spring 1978): 51-58; Tanis H. Bryan, "Peer Popularity of Learning Disabled Children," *Journal of Learning Disabilities* 7 (December 1974): 621-25; and Tanis H. Bryan and James H. Bryan, "Social Interactions of Learning Disabled Children," *Learning Disability Quarterly* 1 (Winter 1978): 33-38.

[48]See, for example, Willie Kate Baldwin, "The Social Position of the Educable Mentally Retarded Child in the Regular Grades in the Public Schools," *Exceptional Children* 25 (November 1958): 106-108, 112; Hollace Goodman, Jay Gottlieb, and Robert H. Harrison, "Social Acceptance of EMRs Integrated into a Nongraded Elementary School," *American Journal of Mental Deficiency* 76 (January 1972): 412-17; Gottlieb and Budoff, "Social Acceptability of Retarded Children," pp. 1-17; Richard P. Iano and others, "Sociometric Status of Retarded Children in an Integrative Program," *Exceptional Children* 40 (January 1974): 267-71; Donald J. Monroe and Clifford E. Howe, "The Effects of Integration and Social Class on the Acceptance of Retarded Adolescents," *Education and Training of the Mentally Retarded* 6 (February 1971): 20-24; James L. Mosley, "Integration: The Need for a Systematic Evaluation of the Socio-Adaptive Aspect," *Education and Training of the Mentally Retarded* 13 (February 1978): 4-8; and Chauncy N. Rucker, Clifford E. Howe, and Bill Snider, "The Participation of Retarded Children in Junior High Academic and Nonacademic Regular Classes," *Exceptional Children* 35 (April 1969): 617-23.

[49]Patricia Kennedy and Robert H. Bruininks, "Social Status of Hearing Impaired Children in Regular Classrooms," *Exceptional Children* 40 (February 1974): 336-42; and Richard M. McCarthy and Robert A. Stodden, "Mainstreaming Secondary Students: A Peer Tutoring Model," *Teaching Exceptional Children* 11 (Summer 1979): 162-63.

[50]Jay Gottlieb and Barbara W. Gottlieb, "Stereotypic Attitudes and Behavioral Intentions toward Handicapped Children," *American Journal of Mental Deficiency* 82 (July 1977): 65-71; and Reginald L. Jones, Karen Lavine, and Joan Shell, "Blind Children Integrated in Classrooms with Sighted Children: A Sociometric Study," *New Outlook for the Blind* 66 (March 1972): 75-80.

51Yuker, "Attitudes of the General Public," p. 94.

52Henry C. Dequin and Sylvia G. Faibisoff, "Results of an Attitudinal Survey," in *Summary Proceedings of a Symposium on Educating Librarians and Information Scientists to Provide Information and Library Services to Blind and Physically Handicapped Individuals, San Francisco, California, July 2-4, 1981* (Washington, DC: The Library of Congress, National Library Service for the Blind and Physically Handicapped, 1981), pp. 6-9.

53Irene Normark Schilling, "A Survey of the Attitudes of Academic Librarians in Illinois toward Disabled Persons" (Study conducted in the Department of Library Science, Northern Illinois University, DeKalb, Illinois, December 1981).

54Hollander, *Principles and Methods of Social Psychology*, p. 121.

55Dianne Monson and Cynthia Shurtleff, "Altering Attitudes toward the Physically Handicapped through Print and Non-Print Media," *Language Arts* 56 (February 1979): 163-64. Cf. Crandell, "The Genesis and Modification of Attitudes," pp. 72-77.

56Cohen, "Improving Attitudes," p. 10; and Joseph H. Evans, "Changing Attitudes toward Disabled Persons," *Rehabilitative Counseling Bulletin* 19 (June 1976): 472.

57Yuker, "Attitudes of the General Public," p. 99.

58Evans, "Changing Attitudes," p. 572.

59Cohen, "Improving Attitudes," p. 18.

60Alfred L. Lazar, Russell Orpet, and George Demos, "The Impact of Class Instruction on Changing Student Attitudes," *Rehabilitation Counseling Bulletin* 20 (September 1976): 66-68.

61Alfred L. Lazar, Juliana T. Gensley, and Russel E. Orpet, "Changing Attitudes of Young Mentally Gifted Children toward Handicapped Persons," *Exceptional Children* 37 (April 1971): 600-602.

62Michael D. Orlansky, "Active Learning and Student Attitudes toward Exceptional Children," *Exceptional Children* 46 (September 1979): 49-52.

63Joy Donaldson and Melton C. Martinson, "Modifying Attitudes toward Physically Disabled Persons," *Exceptional Children* 43 (March 1977): 337-41.

64Cohen, "Improving Attitudes," p. 17.

65Norris Grover Haring, "A Study of Classroom Teachers' Attitudes toward Exceptional Children" (Ed.D. dissertation, Syracuse University, 1956). Cf. Haring, Stern, and Cruickshank, *Attitudes of Educators*.

66Jennie Pamela Steinhebel, "An Evaluation of Institute Participants in Providing Library Media Services for the Handicapped" (DeKalb, Illinois: Northern Illinois University, Department of Library Science, 1980).

67Colleen Fix and Jo Anne Rohrbacher, "What Is a Handicap? The Impact of Attitudes," *Personnel and Guidance Journal* 56 (November 1977): 176-78.

68Cohen, "Improving Attitudes," p. 17.

69Ibid., p. 16.

70Evans, "Changing Attitudes," pp. 572-79.

71Gerald L. Clore and Katharine McMillam Jeffery, "Emotional Role Playing, Attitude Change, and Attraction toward a Disabled Person," *Journal of Personality and Social Psychology* 23 (July 1972): 105-111; and Velma March and Robert Friedman, "Changing Public Attitudes toward Blindness," *Exceptional Children* 38 (January 1972): 426-28.

72Velleman, *Serving Physically Disabled People*, pp. 7-8.

73Higgs, "Attitude Formation," pp. 496-97; and Reginald W. Higgs, "Attitudes toward Persons with Physical Disabilities as a Function of Information Level and Degree of Contact," *Dissertation Abstracts International* 32 (8-A) (February 1972): 4450.

74Herbert Rusalem, "Engineering Changes in Public Attitudes toward a Severely Disabled Group," *Journal of Rehabilitation* 33 (June 1967): 26-27.

75Harasymiw and Horne, "Integration of Handicapped Children," pp. 153-58.

76Haring, "A Study of Classroom Teachers' Attitudes." Cf. Haring, Stern, and Cruickshank, *Attitudes of Educators*.

77Yuker, "Attitudes of the General Public," pp. 99-100.

78"Teaching about Handicapism," *Interracial Books for Children Bulletin* 8 (Numbers 6 and 7, 1977): 22-26.

79See "Teaching about Handicapism," pp. 22-26, for a further discussion of these topics and suggested activities.

80Elizabeth J. Pieper, "Preparing Children for a Handicapped Classmate," *The Instructor* 84 (August 1974): 128-29.

81Monson and Shurtleff, "Altering Attitudes," pp. 163-70.

5 _____ Serving Individual Abilities, Needs, and Interests

"The same heart beats
in every human breast."
— Matthew Arnold
"The Buried Life"

"Like, — but oh how different!"
— William Wordsworth
"Yes, It Was the Mountain Echo"

INTRODUCTION

School, public, academic, and special librarians have much in common —
they are all involved in the educational process. Melvil Dewey believed that, in the
highest sense, every librarian is a teacher.[1] Every librarian is therefore, in effect,
an educator, perhaps not in a formal way but certainly in bringing knowledge and
information together with the user. Every librarian is (or ought to be) concerned
about the entire body of knowledge and information as it is contained in various
formats, print and nonprint. And every librarian is (or ought to be) concerned
about the individual user who requires and desires knowledge and information
either for educational or for recreational purposes.

Librarians need to consider the ways in which disabled children and young
people are the same and yet different from other children and young people,
either disabled or able-bodied. This chapter therefore discusses 1) disabled
children and young people as unique individuals; 2) the concept of learning style
in relation to abilities, needs, and interests; and 3) the Individualized Education
Program set forth in P.L. 94-142 which involves the diagnosis of distinctive
abilities, needs, and interests and the prescription of library services and materials
for the individual.

DISABLED CHILDREN AND YOUNG PEOPLE AS UNIQUE INDIVIDUALS

Similarities

In one way, disabled children and young people are the same as able-bodied children and young people. The National Advisory Committee on the Handicapped stated that "handicapped children are far more like their nonhandicapped peers than they are unlike them."[2] In making this statement, the committee was pointing out that disabled children and young people should be considered as part of the mainstream of humanity. Instead of setting them apart from other people, even to the extent of not regarding them as persons or as human beings, as has frequently been done in the past, they should be treated as human beings and as persons.

There is, of course, a basic truth to this view. Disabled children and young people are human beings the same as all other human beings. They are living, breathing, thinking, acting persons like all other persons. They have the human physical properties — mouth, nose, lips, eyes, ears, arms, legs. In varying degrees they have the ability to hear, see, speak, and think. One or more of these properties and abilities may be lacking either totally or partially, but in the aggregate they are fellow human beings.

Any disability which an individual has should be de-emphasized in the minds and actions of us all. Instead, the individual should be thought of and treated as a person, as a human being. Children and young people who have a disability are *persons* first of all, and they are "disabled," "handicapped," "special," or "exceptional" secondarily. When we are in contact with these children and young people, we should not consider them as *disabled* children and young people but as *persons* who have a handicapping or disabling condition. A librarian, therefore, does not serve a disability but a person. The disability is just one part of a whole person. Instead of the disability, we need to concentrate on the *abilities* of the person.

Differences

It is also a truism that each disabled child and young person is different, just as every human being is different from all other human beings. There are differences between those who are disabled and able-bodied, as well as differences among those who are disabled. Disabled children and young people are not all the same, and these differences are normal. The range of differences includes physical appearance, physical growth, social maturity, abilities, interests, needs, and experiences. Even disabilities are different because no two medical cases are exactly alike. It just happens that some persons have individual differences and unique characteristics that are greater than others.

Individual differences have been a subject of discussion in education for a long time. Yet, even though educators may talk a lot about individual differences, these differences are not totally recognized in our schools, libraries, and society at large. We frequently expect people, including children and young people, to be the same, and especially the same as ourselves: in the way they look, think, act, learn, read, hear, and see. Many people feel that any departure from this sameness makes a person unusually different instead of interestingly or challengingly different.

Kirk and Gallagher have discussed two concepts of individual differences: interindividual differences and intraindividual differences. They have defined *interindividual differences* as the variability *between people*, those differences which exist among and between members of a group. People differ in regard to height, weight, reading ability, writing ability, spelling ability, and many other characteristics. When these individual differences are measured by psychological and educational tests and the distribution is plotted on the theoretical normal curve, most people fall into the middle range, and smaller percentages normally fall into the upper and lower ranges. Children and young people have been classified and grouped in special classes or ability groups on the basis of this concept of interindividual differences.[3]

By contrast, the concept of *intraindividual differences* recognizes that there are differences in abilities *within an individual*. Each child or young person has unique assets and deficits, and it is more important to be aware of these differences within the individual than to compare the individual with other children or young people. This concept has become dominant in special education and forms the basis for developing an instructional program for a particular child which conforms to the individual's abilities and disabilities rather than a comparison of the individual disabled child with other children, either disabled or able-bodied.[4]

THE CONCEPT OF LEARNING STYLE IN RELATION TO ABILITIES, NEEDS, AND INTERESTS

The concept of learning style has also emerged more and more within recent years and has thrust itself upon the consciousness of today's educators and other professionals. Also emphasizing the uniqueness of the individual, the concept has received increasing recognition by researchers and scholars. In varying phraseology, reference has been made to this concept in professional literature. In its 1977 annual report, the National Advisory Committee on the Handicapped acknowledged the concept of learning style in relation to the Individualized Education Program (IEP), stating that the IEP "implies accommodation to each child's learning style, with the student proceeding at his or her own pace, using materials that emphasize his or her particular strengths."[5]

At present, however, learning style is not a well-defined concept. The term is sometimes used as an implied alternative to "cognitive style," a term which is understood in a variety of dimensions and which has no single universally accepted definition. Cognitive style represents different ways of categorizing the inner activities of an individual whose mind and person are engaged in the learning process.[6] There is a distinct differentiation, however, between the definitions of cognitive style and learning style.[7] Unfortunately, many who use the term "learning style" do not precisely define their usage.

Rita and Kenneth Dunn have developed a clear and precise definition and construct of learning style. On the basis of their research, they have identified four categories which suggest that learners are affected by eighteen elements: 1) immediate environmental elements (sound, light, temperature, and design); 2) their own emotional elements (motivation, persistence, responsibility, and need for structure or flexibility); 3) sociological elements or needs (self, pair, peers, team, adult, or varied); and 4) physical elements or needs (perceptual strengths, intake, time, and mobility).[8] These elements assist in determining the learning style of all learners — children, young people, and adults — whether able-bodied or disabled.

Regardless of the exact construct of learning style, the concept in general recognizes that learning is an individual process which is different in some ways for each person. Each individual learns in light of several factors: 1) ability to read printed materials, ability to listen to verbal presentations, and ability to view pictorial materials with understanding; 2) content and subject interests; 3) background knowledge; 4) previous experience; 5) the personal physical condition which is brought to the act of learning; and 6) the environmental factors of setting and surroundings. In light of these factors, as a librarian endeavors to serve children and young people who have a disability (as well as those who do not have a disability), it is important to identify an individual's preferred learning style by considering the *abilities, needs*, and *interests* of the individual. Furthermore, librarians should provide materials for a child or young person by matching the individual's learning strengths to the characteristics of various materials. This importance has been underscored by the Library Service to Children with Special Needs Committee of the Association for Library Service to Children in its publication, *Selecting Materials for Children with Special Needs.*[9]

Abilities

In services for disabled children and young people, both in libraries and in schools, emphasis should be on the *abilities* of the individual rather than on the *disability(ies)*, on what the person is *able* to do rather than *not able* to do, on what the child *can* do rather than what the child *cannot* do. While in some situations and circumstances it is necessary to consider the disability, the disability should not be over-emphasized to the neglect of the person's *intellectual, physical*, and *emotional abilities*. For instance, a librarian must accept the fact that a child who is blind cannot see and therefore cannot use regular printed materials, but the child can hear and thus use spoken materials or can touch and use braille materials. Again, a young person who is totally deaf will not be able to benefit from spoken materials but will be able to use printed and pictorial materials through the sense of sight. At the Southwest School for the Deaf in Lawndale, California, the educational program was designed to develop fully the communication modality which deaf students do have, that is, vision; and visuals are used extensively in order to capitalize on students' ability to see.[10]

Librarians need to build on the positive characteristics of each individual rather than on the negative ones, that is, how well a child or young person can see, read, hear, talk, and so forth, and how that child or young person can be helped to see, read, hear, and talk even better. Children and young people who are disabled have many of the same capabilities as persons who are not disabled and, with some training and education, those capabilities can be developed to their full potential. Every disabled child or young person deserves the opportunity to develop abilities, overcome weaknesses, and be a productive member of society, living with dignity and self-respect. Access to library and information services appropriate to individual abilities affords them that opportunity.

Examples abound of individuals who have overcome a disability and have developed their positive abilities to the fullest extent. For example:

— Sir Walter Scott had a physical disability but became a world-famous novelist.

— Franklin Delano Roosevelt was paralyzed in both legs as a result of poliomyelitis but went on to become president of the United States for four terms.

— Ludwig von Beethoven became partially deaf at the age of thirty-two and totally deaf at forty-six but composed some of the world's most beautiful music during the years of his deafness.

— Glenn Cunningham was burned so severely in a schoolhouse fire when he was eight years old that the doctors said he would never walk again, but he set the world's record in 1934 for running a mile in four minutes and 6.7 seconds.

— Itzhak Perlman became paralyzed when he was four years old but today is an incomparable concert violinist.

— Albert Einstein, considered retarded and uneducable in his childhood, did not talk until he was four years old nor read until he was nine and had great difficulty learning math under traditional instructional methods but became one of the world's greatest mathematicians and theoretical physicists and developed the theory of relativity.

— Thomas Edison was labeled in the public schools as "too stupid to learn" and had to be taught at home by his mother the three R's and other basic academic subject matter but became one of the world's greatest inventors.

— Winston Churchill was called dull and hopeless and failed in the sixth grade but became prime minister of England and one of the world's greatest statesmen.

— John Milton became blind at the age of forty-four but later wrote his greatest works, including "Paradise Lost."

— James Thurber lost one eye in childhood and the sight of his other one in adulthood but continued to produce stories and cartoons of delicacy, wit, and highly individualized humor.

— Helen Keller was deaf and blind as a result of a childhood illness but became an author, lecturer, stateswoman, world figure, and a symbol to the world of the power of will in overcoming disabilities.

— Sarah Bernhardt, the immortal French actress, had her leg amputated but continued to reign supreme on the stage.

— Amy Lowell had learning problems but became a world-renowned poetess.

— Christy Brown was born with cerebral palsy, was eighteen years old before he could communicate in the slurred, gasping language he used throughout adulthood, had the use of neither hand and of the left foot only, but with his toes he wrote on an electric typewriter his first novel, *Down All the Days*, which became a best-seller.

—George Gordon, Lord Byron, was lame from birth, his right leg and foot (possibly both feet) contracted by poliomyelitis, but he became one of England's greatest and most passionate poets.

—Ray Charles was blind from birth but became one of the best-loved jazz/soul singers and musicians in the United States.

—Bill Cullen was crippled by poliomyelitis as a youngster but became a popular television program host.

In citing the above examples of individuals with a disability who have become world-prominent and famous, it is not intended to depict an image of "super-crip" for disabled persons. Not all disabled children and young people can attain such heights, nor can all those who have no disability. Yet, examples of individuals who have not let their disabilities hold them back, but who have instead overcome their disabilities and achieved their highest potential, serve as an inspiration to all who have disabilities. Even though a child or young person may not become world-famous, that person can still capitalize on his or her abilities and endeavor to fulfill his or her greatest potential. Probably everyone knows some examples of ordinary people who have never become famous but have not let their disabilities hold them back and have accomplished much in a profitable life. There are also many examples of persons who have achieved what they could within the range of the limitations and restrictions of their disability. For this reason librarians, teachers, and others who work with disabled children and young people must be more concerned about each person's *abilities* rather than the disabilities, helping the child to utilize and develop his or her abilities to the fullest.

Needs

Disabled children and young people have all the basic and universal needs of mankind—physical, intellectual, emotional, social, and spiritual. Abraham Maslow has classified these universal human needs in a five-step hierarchy:

1. Physiological—the need for shelter and the satisfaction of hunger and thirst;

2. Safety—the need for protection against physical danger, and release from anxiety which may be aroused by various kinds of threats;

3. Love—the need for love, affection, acceptance, and a feeling of belonging in relationships with parents, friends, teachers, and other social groups; to love and be loved; to have friends;

4. Esteem—the need for self-esteem which comes through mastery of various tasks and confidence in one's own worth, adequacy, and capacities; the need for recognition and approval from others;

5. Self-actualization—the need to fulfill one's highest potential as a human being through creative self-expression in personal and social

achievements; the need to feel free to act (within the limits of general and social needs), to satisfy one's curiosity, and to understand one's world.[11]

Although there is little research evidence to support Maslow's theory, it is widely accepted because it makes much sense. Librarians who work with disabled children and young people need to be aware of these universal human needs because the attempts people make to satisfy their needs are the motivating factors in their lives.

In addition to these universal needs of human beings in general, disabled children and young people basically have the same needs which other children in their age group have, needs which are special to their particular age group. Each disabled child and young person also has unique *individual* needs. Some of their individual needs will relate to subject matter and information content, while others will have to do with the format and the manner in which the material is presented.

Writers in standard library literature have emphasized for many years that librarians should give personal service to children and young people and provide for their individual needs. While some of these allusions have been vague and veiled, others have been more clearly explicated. Most of the writers, however, have restricted their concern to personal services related to books and reading. With the increasing acceptance of new technological advances and nonprint materials into the library program, attention to personal and individual needs has been expanded to include viewing and listening services.[12]

While the basic need of disabled children and young people for information, knowledge, education, learning, and training is the same as for all other children and young people, they have unique and different needs as individual persons. The librarian should endeavor to identify these needs in relation to the individual's abilities and interests, as well as in relation to the type of materials which are best suited to meet the needs and abilities of the individual. Their specific needs will also be influenced by their disabilities. For example, assuming that a disabled child is able to read, listen, or view pictorial formats, the child's reading needs, listening needs, and pictorial viewing needs will be similar to other children's, both disabled and non-disabled, and will be as general as the child's age level. Yet these reading, listening, and pictorial viewing needs will also be as individual and as special as the individual child or young person. If, however, the child is not able to use either reading, listening, or pictorial viewing materials because of his or her disability, the child's need for that type of material will be eliminated but the need for the types of materials the child is able to use will be the same as for other children. Both the strengths and weaknesses of a child in modality reception and expression must be considered in meeting the informational and materials needs of the individual child.

Other library needs of disabled children and young people should also be considered:

1. A library atmosphere which will give all users a feeling of respect and acceptance for their own individual self-esteem and worth.

2. Adequate space for each individual.

3. Quiet study areas as well as areas for quiet discussion with other individuals.

4. Adequate supervision.

5. A variety of activities which the individual can pursue.[13]

6. Materials that are simple to manipulate, are reliable and flexible, and give the opportunity to interact actively rather than to accept passively what is directed at them.[14]

Interests

As in the case of needs, disabled children and young people usually share the universal interests of their age group. Generally, they are interested in the same subjects as their peers—fantasy, animals, music, cars, science fiction, sports, mystery, romances, etc.—no matter in which format that subject is presented, verbal or visual (print or pictorial), as long as they have the ability to use the medium. However, in the case of some hearing-impaired children whose maturity levels may be lower than their age group, their interests may be much lower than the norm for their age levels.[15]

As with all individuals, disabled children and young people have individual and unique interests and do not share all the generally common subject interests of their age group, anymore than their nondisabled peers do. Each person develops special subject interests which are particular to him or her as an individual. In regard to the format or medium through which the subject is presented, the individual's particular learning style may also indicate an interest in one medium more than others. One child may be more interested in reading materials, another in auditory materials, another in pictorial viewing materials. Consequently, the individual may be able to learn and acquire knowledge better through the medium which is of greater interest. If the individual's disability prevents the use of any format, that person will naturally be more interested in those formats which he or she has the ability to use.[16]

THE INDIVIDUALIZED EDUCATION PROGRAM

Recognizing the uniqueness of learning styles based on individual abilities, needs, and interests, an Individualized Education Program (IEP) for each disabled child and young person aged three to twenty-one has been mandated in P.L. 94-142. In its 1977 report, the National Advisory Committee on the Handicapped stated: "Enforcing a view of handicapped children as individuals rather than as faceless members of a category is but one of a number of potential advantages of the IEP."[17] The report goes on to say:

> In its call for an "individualized education program" (IEP) for each handicapped child, P.L. 94-142 can be credited with having codified what has long been recognized as superior teaching practice. In doing so it may very well speed the use of the approach for all children. In any case, the IEP is for several reasons of particular importance in the education of children with handicaps. Not the least of these reasons is the fact that it provides a natural point of departure from the conventional tendency to see handicapped children primarily in terms of their disabilities rather than as individuals—of viewing them as

homogeneous, failing to recognize the wide variations that they, no less than nonhandicapped children, display. Another is lowered expectations, of demanding (and thereby usually getting) far less of the handicapped child than of his or her "normal" peer.[18]

In summary, the report states: "... the IEP is the quintessential expression of P.L. 94-142's fundamental purpose."[19]

The IEP must be developed consistent with P.L. 94-142 guidelines,[20] the dictates of Section 504 of the Rehabilitation Amendments of 1973,[21] and the rules and regulations governing the operation of special education of each state agency. Only two aspects of the guidelines will be discussed here in relation to librarians and library service: 1) the components of the IEP, and 2) the participants in the IEP meetings.

The law specifies that the written statement of the IEP must include the following components:

— A statement of present levels of educational performance;

— Annual goals, including short term instructional objectives;

— Specific special education and related services to be provided;

— Extent to which the child will be able to participate in regular educational programs;

— Projected dates for initiation of services and the anticipated duration of the services;

— Appropriate objective criteria, evaluation procedures, and schedules for determining at least annually whether the short term instructional objectives are being achieved.[22]

The IEP is both a diagnostic and prescriptive process for an individual child or young person. It encompasses diagnosis of a child's specific educational needs based on what the individual has accomplished and is able to do, as well as what the child needs to learn. It is a statement of the child's strengths, abilities, and special problems, identifying the specific services that will be provided to meet the child's learning needs. It also prescribes appropriate learning tasks in the form of instructional objectives which are relative to the child's developmental age and grade placement and which focus on learning style, modality functions, and skills in specific areas which are relevant to the individual.

Diagnostic and prescriptive procedures are certainly not new with P.L. 94-142 because they have long been advocated by many educators, especially those who have emphasized individualized learning. However, the mandate in P.L. 94-142 (within the context of the IEP) for diagnosis and prescription regarding disabled children is a recognition of the value of such procedures and may well signal the use of this approach for all school children. Disabled children and young people (as well as all others) should be diagnosed on the basis of academic achievement, potential, perceptual strengths, and interests. Prescriptions can then be made for their use of the media to which they can most easily relate and through which they will learn most successfully.[23] It is this relationship to the use of media with which librarians need to be concerned in the diagnosis and prescription. Librarians, together with other professionals, should diagnose the *abilities, interests, and needs* of disabled children and young people in order to *prescribe materials* which they can use to fill their needs and satisfy their interests according to their abilities.

Although P.L. 94-142 refers to "related services to be provided," there is no specific mention of library services or of library materials and equipment in the prescribed requirements for the IEP. Yet it is reasonable to conclude that materials and equipment are vital and necessary to the implementation of the IEP and that a child's IEP should contain a description of any special software and hardware, as well as of library services which are required to accomplish the instructional objectives. Materials should be matched to the child and the instructional objectives on the basis of the child's characteristics and the characteristics of the media. Specifically listed in the IEP should be those resources and devices which are not typically used in regular classrooms, such as braille books and braille writers, and any materials and equipment used because of and in reference to specific instructional objectives of the child, such as Language Masters. Such special materials and equipment should be listed on the IEP next to the short-term instructional objectives for which they are to be used. This procedure presumes, of course, that appropriate learning materials and technological equipment and devices will be identified for each objective after the objectives have been drafted.

In order to accomplish this, librarians and teachers need to know the characteristics of all materials and equipment in relation to the instructional objectives and the abilities of each child. Consideration must be given to both input and output modes. Is the input medium presented through auditory, visual, or haptic (that is, the presentation of information through touch and body position) channels? What output modes are required: vocal (speech), written (writing or making responses), or gestural (gesture, pantomime, making choices, sorting, pointing)? Which materials and equipment can be used by the child to receive the information and make the necessary responses in spite of his or her disability? Which materials and equipment will therefore coincide with the instructional objectives? What can be used effectively to teach the concepts of each objective? The overall goal for both librarians and teachers is to help disabled children and young people succeed in those areas in which they are able. Success depends on a carefully planned program that meets the individual's needs and which uses appropriate materials.

P.L. 94-142 also requires that participants in the IEP meetings should include:

—A representative of the public agency, other than the child's teacher, who is qualified to provide or supervise the provision of special education;

—The child's teacher;

—One or both parents;

—The child, where appropriate;

—Other individuals at the discretion of the parent or agency;

—Evaluation personnel.[24]

Librarians are not included in the list of required participants in the IEP meeting designated by P.L. 94-142. This does not mean, however, that librarians should *not* be involved because there is provision in the law for "other individuals" and personnel. The spirit of the law, as interpreted by the National Advisory Committee on the Handicapped, is to include those persons who are able to make a contribution to the development of the child's IEP: "... the preparation of each IEP should be an interdisciplinary effort, with appropriate participation by every member of the staff who can make a substantial contribution."[25]

Librarians can indeed make a "substantial contribution," and therefore appropriate professional practice should include librarians in the IEP process. The IEP concept presumes close involvement of school librarians working with and for regular classroom teachers and special educators. Ideally, the librarian should be a member of the curriculum team which develops the IEP but, if not included in the actual IEP meeting, the librarian can be a valuable consultant. Most school librarians have been professionally educated as teachers and are therefore able to assist in the diagnosis of a child's learning style, abilities, needs, and interests. In addition, professional librarians, through their education in library school, are aware of the value of various approaches in learning through the visual and auditory modes or recordings, talking books, pictures, slides, films, filmstrips, and other media. They can therefore contribute in the prescriptive decisions regarding the materials and equipment which will meet the instructional objectives of the IEP in relation to the child's abilities, needs, interests, and learning style. They are also able to suggest ways in which various media might best be utilized or adapted to accomplish the instructional objectives. In some instances, a public librarian can also contribute in an advisory capacity, especially when some appropriate materials are housed in the public library.

School librarians will also know which materials are readily available in the building library media center. Some resources may have to be borrowed from other sources, such as the school district library media center, the public library, a library system, or through community, state, and national agencies; and the librarian will know how to obtain these resources. If it is necessary and desirable to purchase some materials, the librarian's knowledge of selection tools and ability in evaluating materials will be invaluable. Similarly, the librarian will be able to determine and obtain the necessary hardware and technology for the transmission of the software.

Designed to meet the unique needs of the individual learner, the IEP is now a reality for disabled children and young people and may be the vanguard for *all* children and young people.[26] The IEP is but another form of Individually Prescribed Instruction (IPI), Individually Guided Education (IGE), and other programs which have been advocated by many educators for some time. It embodies the application of the basic principles of instructional technology, which has been defined in this way:

> It is a systematic way of designing, carrying out, and evaluating the total process of learning and teaching in terms of specific objectives, based on research in human learning and communication, and employing a combination of human and nonhuman resources to bring about more effective instruction.[27]

In the IEP, consideration can be given to a diagnosis of the individual's learning style, abilities, needs, and interests, and to an appropriate prescription of behavioral and instructional objectives which incorporate the utilization of appropriate instructional materials. Librarians involved in this process become participants in the diagnosis of learning tasks, the prescription of resources, and the effective utilization of technology.

One school system implemented a program which included:

a diagnostic teacher—to evaluate individual students and help plan appropriate educational programs

a learning facilitator—to expedite diagnostic teaching practices planned for the student

a librarian—to help guide the activities of the students, evaluate progress, and help design innovative instructional activities of the student. The librarian was thus placed in the position of being an integral part of individualized programs.[28]

School librarians might well consider a number of activities in order to provide individualized library services for each disabled child or young person:

1. Maintain a folder for each child. Include (a) testing information on reading, listening, and viewing abilities; (b) subject and media interests; (c) dated library media center observations; (d) dated notes from conferences with teachers, parents, counselors, students themselves, agencies working with the student; and (e) objectives for the child in the library media center.

2. Order any additional materials necessary for remediation and students' needs (either classroom or library use).

3. Discuss library media center objectives and activities with each student.

4. Establish and maintain intermittent contact with the classroom teachers of each student. Together, build a workable plan for each student involving activities in the library media center.

5. Continually re-evaluate the student's progress and attitude regarding library media center objectives, activities, and use of materials.[29]

NOTES

[1]Melvil Dewey, "The Profession," *American Library Journal* 1 (September 30, 1876): 6.

[2]U.S. Department of Health, Education, and Welfare, Office of Education, National Advisory Committee on the Handicapped, *The Individualized Education Program: Key to an Appropriate Education for the Handicapped Child; 1977 Annual Report* (Washington, DC: Government Printing Office, 1977), p. 13.

[3]Samuel A. Kirk and James J. Gallagher, *Educating Exceptional Children*, 3rd ed. (Boston: Houghton Mifflin, 1979), pp. 27-31.

[4]Ibid.

[5]U.S. Department of Health, Education, and Welfare, *The Individualized Education Program*, p. 13.

[6]Definitions of "cognitive style" have emanated largely from the field of psychology and describe the perceptual and personality characteristics within an individual as the person seeks to "know" and to "learn." Ausubel stated that each individual is different in his "cognitive organization and functioning" (David P. Ausubel, *Educational Psychology; A Cognitive View* [New York: Holt, Rinehart and Winston, 1968], p. 170). Individuals were referred to by McCain and Brown as "analytical" and "nonanalytical" (Floyd McCain, Jr. and Laurence D. Brown, *The Effect of Cognitive Style in Verbal and Pictorial Concept Formation Tasks* [Bloomington, IN: Indiana University, 1969], p. 1). Kagan, Moss, and Sigel used the terms "descriptive, categorical-inferential, or relational-contextual" (referred to by McCain and Brown, *The Effect*, p. 1). Taba, Levine, and Elzey considered cognitive styles to be "modes of thought" (Hilda Taba, Samuel Levine, and Freeman F. Elzey, *Thinking in Elementary School Children* [San Francisco: San Francisco State College, 1964], p. 8). Messick, departing slightly from the usual psychological sense, looked upon cognitive style as "information processing habits" (referred to by Wayne C. Fredrick and Herbert J. Klausmeier, "Cognitive Styles: A Description," *Educational Leadership* 27 [April 1970]: 669). Hill conceived of cognitive style in terms of the meaning of symbols, their cultural determinants, and modalities of inference (Joseph E. Hill, *The Educational Sciences* [Detroit: Wayne State University, 1968], pp. 14-15). While each of these definitions is somewhat different, all of them reflect a concern for categorizing or diagnosing the inner mental processes of an individual.

[7]John A. Connolly and Mary L. Hoaglund, "Adapting Instruction to School Objectives and Student Needs," *Educational Technology* 12 (April 1972): 32. Connolly and Hoaglund defined learning style "as the profile of a student's relative ability to learn via visual, auditory or kinesthetic-tactile sensory pathways," based on Gary M. Ingersoll, "The Effects of Presentation of Modalities and Modality Preferences on Learning and Recall," (unpublished doctoral dissertation, Pennsylvania State University, 1970). Their definition of cognitive style as "mental processes ... especially suited to learning either concrete or abstract relationships" was based on J. P. Guilford, *Personality* (New York: McGraw-Hill, 1959) and Arthur R. Jensen, "How Much Can We Boost IQ and Scholastic Achievement?," *Harvard Educational Review* 39 (Winter 1969): 1-123.

[8]Rita Dunn and Kenneth Dunn, *Teaching Students through Their Individual Learning Styles: A Practical Approach* (Reston, VA: Reston, 1978), pp. 2-17.

[9]American Library Association, Association for Library Service to Children, Library Service to Children with Special Needs Committee, *Selecting Materials for Children with Special Needs* (Chicago: American Library Association, 1980), p. 1.

[10]Frances Wood and Alfred Hirshoren, "The Hearing Impaired in the Mainstream: The Problem and Some Successful Practices," *Journal for Special Educators* 17 (Spring 1981): 297-98.

[11]A. H. Maslow, "A Theory of Human Motivation," *Psychological Review* 50 (July 1943): 370-96.

[12]American Association of School Librarians, *Standards for School Library Programs* (Chicago: American Library Association, 1960), p. 15; American Association of School Librarians and Department of Audiovisual Instruction, *Standards for School Media Programs* (Chicago: American Library Association; and Washington, DC: National Education Association, 1969), pp. 2, 20; and American Association of School Librarians and Association for Educational Communications and Technology, *Media Programs: District and School* (Chicago: American Library Association; and Washington, DC: Association for Educational Communications and Technology, 1975), pp. 8, 15. In 1965 the AASL adopted an official statement declaring the need to consider individual differences in the selection and use of materials; see 1960 *Standards*, pp. 11-12. The 1960 *Standards* (pp. 15-17), the 1969 *Standards* (pp. 1, 2, 3, 8, 20), and the 1975 *Media Programs* (pp. 8, 15) reflect a concern for personal and individual service to students in regard to reading, viewing, and listening materials.

[13]Patricia Robertson, "Impact of the Physical Environment on the Emotionally Disturbed and Socially Maladjusted Student," in *The Special Child in the Library*, ed. Barbara Holland Baskin and Karen H. Harris (Chicago: American Library Association, 1976), p. 8.

[14]Harold Stolovich, "A Pocket Calculator Never Loses Patience," *Audiovisual Instruction* 21 (December 1976): 19-20.

[15]Mary Jane Metcalf, "Helping Hearing Impaired Students," *School Library Journal* 25 (January 1979): 27.

[16]A brief discussion of the interests and needs of disabled children in relation to materials is given in *Selecting Materials for Children with Special Needs*, which was prepared by the Library Service to Children with Special Needs Committee of the Association for Library Service to Children.

[17]U.S., Department of Health, Education, and Welfare, *The Individualized Education Program*, p. 6.

[18]Ibid.

[19]Ibid., p. 13.

[20]U.S., Department of Health, Education, and Welfare, Office of Education, "Education of Handicapped Children: Implementation of Part B of the Education of the Handicapped Act," *Federal Register* 42, no. 163, August 23, 1977, 42490 ff. In addition to the primary source of P.L. 94-142 itself, discussions of the IEP and its requirements are given in other sources, such as: Ann P. Turnbull, Bonnie Strickland, and John C. Brantley, *Developing and Implementing Individualized Education Programs* (Columbus, OH: Charles E.

Merrill, 1978); U.S., Department of Health, Education, and Welfare, *The Individualized Education Program*, pp. 1-37; Alan Abeson and Jeffrey Zettel, "The End of the Quiet Revolution: The Education for All Handicapped Children Act of 1975," *Exceptional Children* 44 (October 1977): 123-25; Jeffrey Zettel and Alan Abeson, "Litigation, Law, and the Handicapped," *School Media Quarterly* 6 (Summer 1978): 242-43; Colleen S. Blankenship, "The Role of the Library Media Specialist in the IEP Process," in *Services and Materials for the Handicapped; Proceedings of an Institute for School Library Media Professionals, August 12-17, 1979*, ed. Henry C. Dequin (DeKalb, IL: Northern Illinois University, 1979), pp. 35-42; Don R. Barbacovi and Richard W. Clelland, *Public Law 94-142: Special Education in Transition* (Arlington, VA: American Association of School Administrators, n.d.), pp. 45-66; Frederick J. Weintraub, "Understanding the Individualized Education Program (IEP)," *Amicus* 2 (April 1977): 26-30; Joseph Ballard and Jeffrey Zettel, "Public Law 94-142 and Section 504; What They Say about Rights and Protections," *Exceptional Children* 44 (November 1977): 180-82.

[21] *Vocational Rehabilitation Act. Statutes at Large.* vol. 87 (1973), #84.33 (b) (2) cited the IEP as "one means" of meeting the standard of a free appropriate public education.

[22]U.S., Department of Health, Education, and Welfare, "Education of Handicapped Children," p. 42491.

[23]Rita Stafford Dunn, "Individualizing Instruction—Teaming Teachers and Media Specialists to Meet Individual Needs," *Audiovisual Instruction* 16 (May 1971): 28; Dunn and Dunn, *Teaching Students through Their Individual Learning Styles*, p. 2. See also Barbara D. Bateman, "Prescriptive Teaching and Individualized Education Programs," in *Educating All Handicapped Children*, ed. Robert Heinich (Englewood Cliffs, NJ: Educational Technology Publications, 1979), pp. 39-61.

[24]U.S., Department of Health, Education, and Welfare, "Education of Handicapped Children," p. 42490.

[25]U.S., Department of Health, Education, and Welfare, *The Individualized Education Program*, p. 9; see also p. 7.

[26]Cf. Garry D. Brewer and James S. Kakalik, *Handicapped Children: Strategies for Improving Services* (New York: McGraw-Hill, 1979), p. 76.

[27]Sidney G. Tickton, ed., *To Improve Learning: An Evaluation of Instructional Technology*, 2 vols. (New York: R. R. Bowker, 1970), vol. 1, pp. 7, 21.

[28]Elnora Alexander, "All Students Are Exceptional," *Learning Today* 6 (Spring 1973): 30-35.

[29]Adapted from Jo Anne Paroz, Loy Sue Siegenthaler, and Verlene H. Tatum, "A Model for a Middle-School Resource Room," *Journal of Learning Disabilities* 10 (January 1977): 10; Sue Diehl, "Making the Media Center Special to the Special Child," *School Media Quarterly* 6 (Summer 1978): 273; and Loyce Stracener, "The Library/Media Center in Adaptive Education," *School Media Quarterly* 6 (Summer 1978): 277.

6 General and Special Library Services

"In these days it is doubtful that any child
may reasonably be expected to succeed in life,
if he is denied the opportunity for education.
Such an opportunity ... is a right which must
be made available to all on equal terms."
— *Brown v. Board of Education*

INTRODUCTION

Librarians customarily provide a wide range of services for the intellectual, cultural, vocational, and recreational needs and interests of their users. Some of these services directly involve the individual user, such as reference, reader's advisory or reading guidance, referral, circulation of materials, viewing of audiovisual materials, listening to recordings, and services to the homebound. Behind the scenes are many other library services about which the user may be totally unaware but which indirectly benefit the individual user nevertheless: the evaluation and selection of materials, acquisitions, technical processing of materials, and many other activities. Both direct and indirect services are intended for all, young and old alike, who are capable of entering a library and who have the ability to make use of the services as they have been established. It is the basic thesis of this and the next chapter (as well as this entire book) that library services and programs, as so many other areas of social and public life, have traditionally been arranged with able-bodied persons in mind and that it is necessary to consider also the special needs, interests, and abilities of disabled persons in relation to the entire range of library services and programs.

The decision of the U.S. Supreme Court in the case of *Brown v. the Board of Education* underscored a fundamental democratic principle when the court concluded that the opportunity of an education, "where the state has undertaken to provide it, is a right which must be made available to all on equal terms."[1] This principle has ramifications and implications also for libraries as well as for other social institutions, that is, the programs and services which a library provides are a right which should be made available on equal terms to everyone, including disabled children, young people, and adults. Any library service or program which is provided to able-bodied persons should also be provided to disabled persons. The emphasis in this book is on those library services and programs which relate to children and young people who are disabled.

105

After a needs assessment has been made and the population of disabled children and young people has been identified, it is possible to plan a program of services which will benefit the types of disabled persons who are in the library's community, that is, those who are visually impaired, hearing impaired, learning disabled, physically impaired, mentally retarded, or emotionally disturbed. Children and young people with these disabilities require the same basic kinds of library and information services as children and young people who are able-bodied, although the services may vary somewhat, according to the individual and the type of disability which each individual has, just as they vary with every individual nondisabled library user. This chapter discusses 1) general library services for all disabled children and young people, and 2) special library services for various types of disabled children and young people.

GENERAL LIBRARY SERVICES FOR
ALL DISABLED CHILDREN AND YOUNG PEOPLE

Before discussing guidance, instruction, and reference services, some general suggestions about services which a librarian can provide are in order:

— Determine what books and other materials about various disabilities the library already owns.

— Purchase additional nonfiction and fiction materials which discuss disabling conditions and disabled persons.

— Contact sources of free materials.

— Make library resources about disabilities known in the community through printed literature, newspapers, radio, and television.

— Prepare bibliographies and mediagraphies on various disabilities.

— Seek out disabled children and young people and inform them of the library's services.

— Invite clubs or groups of disabled children and young people to meet in the library.

— Publish a newsletter for disabled children and young people.

— Encourage other staff members to learn more about disabled children and young people.

— Set up a professional library for library personnel and teachers.[2]

— Prepare kits for different types of disabled children and young people and their parents, including books and pamphlets, a directory of agencies, bibliographies for parents, and bibliographies of appropriate books and toys for the children.

— Provide a collection of educational games for disabled children and young people.

— Begin a club for disabled children and young people and have them meet monthly in the library for crafts, games, listening to records, and other activities.

— Circulate a monthly tape-a-letter to blind and visually impaired children and young people.[3]

These kinds of activities are in the nature of regular, ongoing services which the librarian can pursue for the benefit of all children and young people who are disabled.

Guidance in Reading, Viewing, and Listening

Reading guidance has long been considered one of the essential services of a professional librarian, and much has been written on this subject. During the past twenty-five years, because of the increased production of audiovisual materials and the development of new audio and video technologies, the librarian's role has expanded to include viewing and listening guidance. This role of the librarian in guiding the viewing and listening of children and young people has probably been written about in the literature of librarianship more than it has been a reality in the actual practice of librarians, whether they are in school library media centers, public libraries, or academic libraries. Many librarians continue to place more emphasis in their daily activities upon books and reading guidance than upon audiovisual materials and guidance in listening and viewing. The age-old adage, "The right *book* for the right child at the right time," should now be, "The right *material* for the right child or young person at the right time." There are several reasons why librarians should include audiovisual materials in the library's collection and in guidance activities: 1) research has shown that audiovisual materials are effective avenues of learning; 2) audiovisual materials are particularly effective for those individuals who process information and knowledge more readily through audiovisual means than through reading; 3) audiovisual materials are essential vehicles for those who, because of their disability are not able to use traditional printed materials; and 4) many more quality audiovisual materials are now available. Therefore, children's and young adult librarians should be committed to bringing children and young people together with books *and* audiovisual materials.

To the extent possible and necessary, the library's collection should include 1) printed materials in the form of books, magazines, newspapers, and pamphlets; 2) audiovisual materials, such as filmstrips, films, filmloops, slides, pictures, transparencies, cassette recordings, and disc recordings; and 3) the newer technologies: videocassette recordings, videodisc recordings, and appropriate microcomputer software programs. Some disabled children and young people will be able to use these materials directly, while others will require the help of aids and devices. All materials, the equipment to use audiovisual materials, and special aids and devices should be arranged in the library or media center for ready and easy location and access by disabled children and young people on their own, by librarians who may be helping them, and by teachers who are endeavoring to match materials to specific learning objectives and learner characteristics.

A librarian provides guidance in reading, viewing, and listening in group situations and on an individual basis. Indirectly, guidance is given to all disabled children and young people when free physical access to the library and the use of its facilities are made possible and when the shelving and various areas of the library or media center are suitably labeled in large lettering for easy and ready movement to the areas and materials desired. More directly, lists of recommended materials, both print and audiovisual, which are suitable for general use by disabled children and young people can be developed and made available. The librarian may need to generate an individualized list of materials for some children. The time-honored practice of presenting book talks as a means of guidance should be extended to the presentation of talks about audiovisual materials and mass media which are of interest to disabled children and young people. Discussions of books, audiovisual materials, and mass media are effective with small groups of children and young people. These talks or discussions about books and audiovisual materials can be either with groups of disabled children by themselves or with disabled and nondisabled children together. Other guidance activities for groups can be in the form of story hours, puppet shows, reading aloud, film programs, other audio or visual or audiovisual programs, and interest centers. In addition, guidance is given by drawing attention to materials and mass media programs through bulletin boards, exhibits, displays, and posting information about appropriate television programs or movies.

Individually, the librarian's guidance in reading, viewing, and listening extends beyond merely making materials available and helping disabled children and young people locate the materials they want. It also includes assistance in selecting materials and determining which materials will be most suitable to the child's needs, interests, and abilities. In some instances, the librarian will need to guide the disabled user in developing competency in reading printed materials, in visual literacy, in listening skills, and in using the necessary aids, devices, and equipment. Librarians can also assist disabled children and young people in developing the ability to evaluate print and audiovisual materials critically.

A librarian's professional guidance activities should include gathering as much information as possible about the abilities and interests of individual disabled children and young people. If possible, each child should be tested for reading ability, listening ability, and pictorial viewing ability. Interests should be assessed in regard to subject areas and also in regard to preference for the format of materials. Together with test scores on ability in reading, listening, and pictorial viewing, knowledge of individual interests regarding both subject content and materials format can be helpful to the librarian in guiding the disabled child or young person. Additional information about the child's needs and interests regarding materials can be garnered through personal conversations and conferences with the child as well as through conferences with the child's parents, school teachers, and counselors.

All information regarding abilities and interests should be kept on file in the library or media center for use in future contacts with the individual. While this suggestion may be more feasible in the setting of a school library media center where the library media professional has closer and more frequent contacts with students, certain aspects of such an arrangement are also possible in a public library. It must be remembered, however, that information from tests and interest inventories is only a guide because both abilities and interests are dynamic rather than static. Abilities will change and hopefully improve over a period of time. Interests always fluctuate and vary according to age, experience, and other outside influences. Therefore, librarians should not be slavishly bound to the record of ability tests and interest inventories but consider them only as a point of reference. Such tests and inventories should be administered periodically so the data can be kept up to date.

Most individual guidance in reading, viewing, and listening is probably given by the librarian spontaneously as the need arises and in relation to specific questions and concerns. In response to these expressed needs, the librarian can help the disabled child or young person locate suitable print and/or audiovisual materials at the appropriate level of reading, listening, or viewing. At the same time, it is also important for disabled children and young people to pick whatever they want sometimes, not just what their ability levels indicate, whether the material chosen happens to be above or below their ability level.

Every contact with a disabled child or young person gives the librarian an opportunity to learn more about the information needs of that individual. A record of such contacts, together with a notation on the kind of help that was given, can be placed in the child's file for future reference. If possible, it would also be helpful to keep an ongoing record of the titles and types of all materials which the child checks out of the library. Such information can give the librarian a composite picture of the child's use of materials and provide further insight in future guidance contacts with the child.

BIBLIOTHERAPY

While reading guidance and bibliotherapy are not the same, there are aspects of the two which are similar, and bibliotherapy may be considered a more technical and more systematic form of reading guidance. There is much confusion, however, over what bibliotherapy really is, how it works, and even whether it works at all. Some people aver that librarians can practice bibliotherapy effectively with disabled children and young people (as well as with those who are able-bodied),[4] while others question its value in general practice and maintain that it should be forgotten and not attempted at all.[5] Rubin distinguishes between institutional, clinical, and developmental bibliotherapy and states that school and public librarians who provide bibliotherapy approach the matter in a developmental sense.[6]

As practiced by librarians, bibliotherapy is more an *art* which involves the use of books, poetry,[7] and other materials for therapeutic purposes rather than a *science* which requires expert medical counsel and direction.[8] Two aspects are necessary if bibliotherapy is to be effective: books or audiovisual materials must be both *experienced* and *discussed* either individually or in groups with the assistance of a facilitator. In other words, there must be discussion in order for therapy to occur because it is this aspect of discussion which distinguishes bibliotherapy from reading guidance. Discussion is not necessarily an essential part of all reading guidance services, and there are no planned supplementary activities in reading guidance, as in bibliotherapy, to determine what the effect of the recommended material has been on the user.[9]

Simply stated, then, a librarian, in functioning as a bibliotherapist, recognizes that a disabled child or young person has an actual physical, social, mental, or emotional problem. In some instances, the problem may be one with which the child may have to deal in the future. The librarian therefore recommends that the child read a certain book or use certain audiovisual material which deals with a similar situation and which may help the individual face and overcome the problem. The child's experience with the material may take place either individually or in groups or with the librarian. Following the experience, there should be discussion with the librarian/bibliotherapist so the child gains insight into the problem and can be helped to overcome it.

If a librarian is inclined to practice bibliotherapy with disabled children and young people, it should be with a great amount of caution and discretion. Most librarians are not trained as professional psychiatrists, psychologists, therapists, or counselors; and very few library schools offer a course in bibliotherapy. Librarians should be very careful not to attempt to probe an individual's psyche and possibly, as a result, do more harm than good. If, however, it is readily apparent that a disabled child or young person has an emotional or social problem or that the child's mental or physical disability is causing problems, the librarian may tactfully suggest a book or audiovisual material which may have therapeutic results. Many lists of helpful books and audiovisual materials on various disabilities are available.[10] In some instances, a disabled child or young person may express concern and anxiety regarding a specific problem, and in such cases the librarian can recommend a helpful book or audiovisual material and then discuss the material with the child. It cannot always be assumed, however, that a child or young person with a certain disability wants or needs material about persons with the same disability. A person's disability does not always cause problems which need to be resolved by therapeutic reading, listening, or viewing.

Instruction in Library Media Skills

The objective of library media skills instruction is to prepare disabled children and young people to use the library with a minimum amount of assistance. Although such instruction can be accomplished more systematically in the teaching environment of a school library media center, a certain amount of instruction can and should also be given in public and academic libraries, especially to individuals. Some aspects of library media skills may need to be taught especially to children and young people with specific types of disabilities. While scheduled times for formal instruction should be arranged for groups of disabled children and young people, the librarian will also need to spend much time in giving informal instruction to individual disabled children and young people.

The kinds of skills that are taught to disabled children and young people are the same as those taught to able-bodied children and young people. They need to be oriented to the library or media center and its facilities, services, materials, equipment, and personnel. They need to know:

—how to use the card catalog

—how to locate materials in the library

—how to use materials

—how to operate equipment

—how to check out materials

They also need to develop patterns of independent learning, good study habits, and the ability to evaluate print and audiovisual materials critically.

Although the methodologies for teaching library media skills to disabled children and young people are essentially the same as for able-bodied individuals, there are some special considerations. Children with sensory, mental, or learning disabilities may require a slower-paced instruction. One skill at a time should be taught, followed by review exercises which will vary in number depending upon the complexity of the skill and the capabilities of the learners.[11] Visuals, such as overhead transparencies, should be used heavily because many children with disabilities learn visually, especially those who are deaf, hearing impaired, or mentally retarded. With a minimum amount of direction, many disabled children and young people, including those who are mentally retarded, can learn to locate library materials.

The card catalog presents a problem for children and young people with certain types of disabilities. Visually impaired children may not be able to read the small type which is used in the traditional card catalog. For those who can read large print, an alternative is to type the catalog cards on a ¼-inch primary typewriter using 5x8-inch cards, or to hand letter the catalog cards in larger print. Catalog cards can also be typed in braille form, if there is a sufficient number of visually impaired library users who can read braille.[12] Since many deaf, hearing-impaired, and retarded children are frequently retarded in language development, they may experience difficulty in using the card catalog. Therefore, they need simplified subject headings with few subdivisions and many "see" references directing them from simple terms to more difficult headings used in the catalog.[13] If these adaptations cannot be made to accommodate disabled users, the librarian will have to give much more assistance to these individuals. A possible solution to these problems is to acquire a microcomputer and automate the entire catalog, using larger print, simpler headings, and the necessary "see" references.

The entire task of instruction in library media skills need not only fall upon librarians. Disabled children and young people can also assist in teaching these skills to other children. In a study reported by Dequin and Smith it was concluded that 1) learning-disabled elementary school students can be trained to perform basic library media skills with a significant increase in ability, and 2) learning-disabled students who are trained in library media skills can be effective tutors of younger nondisabled students in performing the same skills. While this study showed that disabled children can be tutors of able-bodied children, it would also be possible for disabled children and young people to teach library media skills to other disabled individuals.[14]

Reference Services

Reference services for disabled and nondisabled children and young people are very much the same. The difference is not so much in the kinds of reference services provided as in the kinds of materials, resources, and equipment which are used to satisfy the reference needs of disabled children and young people. Reference services for them include the usual services of providing the necessary reference materials and making them accessible; referring them to appropriate references when they are needed; providing facilities such as carrels for individual study; answering questions; giving reader's advisory, referral, and current awareness services; helping to develop study skills and the ability to compare and evaluate sources; obtaining materials through interlibrary loan; preparing bibliographies and literature searches; maintaining a community resource file which includes resources for disabled persons; and photoduplicating needed materials. The librarian should be aware of the services available from the state library and the state board of education which will help disabled children and young people. A register of local individuals and service organizations which are available to meet the more extensive requirements of those who are disabled should be maintained and should include persons available for service as transcribers, personal readers, braillists, interpreters, etc. Another resource file can include current reference materials which describe library services available to disabled persons from state and national library agencies.

Disabled children and young people need reference materials appropriate to their abilities in reading, viewing, and listening. Some may need reference materials in special formats, such as the *Talking World Book Encyclopedia* for those who are visually impaired, and the special equipment or devices to utilize the special formats. They may also need more individual assistance from the librarian in locating and using reference materials.

SPECIAL SERVICES FOR VARIOUS TYPES OF DISABLED CHILDREN AND YOUNG PEOPLE

In addition to the general services discussed in the preceding section, disabled children and young people require special services from the librarian, both in groups and on an individual basis. These services naturally fall into the categories of the general services: guidance in reading, viewing, and listening; instruction in library media skills; and reference services. The extent of such special services depends upon two factors: 1) the type of disability and the way in which the disability affects the use of library services and materials, and 2) the abilities which the child or young person has in using library services and materials. The following pages briefly present some of the special services according to the type of disabling condition.

Visually Impaired

Blind and visually impaired children and young people require special library services and materials depending on the extent of their impairment — whether they are totally blind, legally blind, or visually impaired. A visual impairment may not always be readily obvious, and frequently the visually impaired child will not tell the librarian about the disability. Sometimes even the child may not be aware of a visual problem. In school settings, the librarian will probably be informed about the visually impaired children who are in the school, but in public libraries such information may not be available. Librarians should train themselves to recognize visual problems and thus detect children and young people who may need special library materials and services. Indications of visual problems can be observed when a child is reading if the child turns or tilts the head, if one eye turns in or out, if there is marked redness, or if the child squints or frowns.[15]

Librarians should consider the amount of visual ability which individuals have and the extent to which they can move about in the library on their own, use the card catalog, locate the materials they need, and use the printed word. All children and young people who have a visual impairment do not require braille materials or talking books or even large print materials. In fact, only a small number of visually impaired persons are totally blind, and only about 5% of the entire totally blind population is able to read braille materials. The majority of those who are visually impaired, including many who are "legally blind," use vision as their principal sense modality and are usually readers of print rather than braille materials. Legally blind children and young people should therefore not automatically be considered blind. Many of them can function as sighted persons through the use of low-vision aids and visual training, and many who have borderline vision are able to read standard-sized print and even small print better and faster than large print. By conferring with the individual, the librarian can determine whether to use regular-print, large-print, braille, or recorded materials. Large-print materials have a type size of sixteen points or larger, that is, the lower case "o" is slightly less than one-eighth inch high. The print should have good contrast and be free from glare. Illustrations should have good color contrast and a minimum of background clutter in order to be enjoyed by low-vision children and young people.[16] Candace Catlin Hall has suggested the use of an overlay transparency for quick identification and labeling of books with large print. The system would permit both students and teachers to identify suitable books for those who are visually impaired and make it possible for librarians to prepare special bibliographies of large-print books.[17]

The librarian should provide specialized materials in recorded, large-print, or braille forms appropriate to the requirements of the visually impaired users of the library. Fiction and nonfiction books, reference books such as dictionaries and encyclopedias, magazines, and newspapers are available in braille, large-print, or recorded form. Twin vision books, tactual maps, and braille globes can be obtained. Kits are available which have both a print copy and a cassette of a book and can be used by the visually impaired child, either alone or with a sighted friend. Science and other models which are accompanied by tapes can also be purchased. Materials for the visually impaired can be obtained from a variety of sources which will be further discussed in chapter 8. Some of the main sources are the National Library Service for the Blind and Physically Handicapped (NLS), the American Printing House for the Blind (APHB), and Recording for the Blind (RFB). Some publishers are producing many books in large print, such as the following companies:

John Curley and Associates
P.O. Box 37
South Yarmouth, MA 02664

Thorndike Press
One Mile Road
Thorndike, ME 04986

Ulverscroft Large Print Books Ltd.
P.O. Box 3055
Stamford, CT 06905

If the required materials cannot be obtained from other sources, they can often be provided locally. Materials can also be brailled or recorded by library staff members and/or volunteers who have been properly trained for these tasks.

For those interested in music, the Music Section of the NLS provides braille music, braille books about music, music instruction on cassettes and disc recordings, large-print music, periodicals in various formats, and reference services in all areas of music.

In addition to the materials themselves, appropriate equipment and devices are needed to utilize the materials. These may include various optical aids, the Optacon®, the Visualtek®, the Kurzweil Reading Machine®, and cassette tape players. These will be discussed in chapter 10.

Visually impaired children and young people may need more assistance from the librarian in learning how to make the best use of the library and its materials and services. They should be thoroughly familiarized with the arrangement of the library and the location of furniture, materials, and equipment. They may need personal attention and guidance in performing some of the routine library tasks, such as locating and retrieving materials from the shelves. They may require help in using the card catalog. Because catalog cards are printed in elite type, use of the card catalog is usually a frustrating chore for those who are visually impaired, and they require assistance in this task. As mentioned earlier, this situation could be alleviated for many visually impaired children by typing the catalog cards in ¼-inch primary type, by hand-lettering the cards in larger print, or by automating the catalog. Braille books, talking books, and recorded material can be cataloged on 5x8-inch cards, with large type on the front of the card and the same information in braille on the back. To accommodate the braille imprint without having it come through the front typed portion, the cards can be made from folded 8x10-inch card stock, with the fold at the top and punched at the bottom center so they are held together by a rod in each drawer.[18]

Radio reading is a growing service throughout the country and is a logical and beneficial extension of a library's total service to children and young people who are print-handicapped. It is the best way to meet their need for immediacy of information. Through the reading of the most important newspaper articles and selected magazine articles, information which would not otherwise be available is transmitted to those who are visually impaired and provides them with more in-depth coverage than regular news programs on television and radio.[19] Other types of programs, such as the reading of stories and poems and dramatizations, can also be geared to their needs and interests. The National Library Service for the Blind and Physically Handicapped, Library of Congress, Washington, DC 20542, has produced a circular, *Directory of Local Radio Services for the Blind and Physically Handicapped*, which gives basic information on such services throughout the United States and lists public (noncommercial) radio stations offering reading or informational program services.

In providing library service to visually impaired children and young people, other factors should be considered:

1. The level of illumination should be appropriate for the child. Some require higher levels for reading, a minimum of 50 footcandles, while a few may require reduced lighting.

2. They should be seated next to a window or provided with a portable reading lamp which has a number of levels of intensity. Glare and shadows should be eliminated.

3. The quality of print should be clear and attractive.

4. The posture of the child is important for the elimination of visual fatigue.

5. A reading stand, optical aids, and magnifying devices should be available for those who require them.[20]

6. They should not be given excessive or unnecessary reading.

7. Nonverbal communication should be avoided when communicating with a visually impaired child.

8. If visuals are used, the librarian should determine where the child can best see the overhead projection, film, filmstrip, or slides. Visuals should be explained if they are used.

Hearing Impaired

Library services and materials for hearing-impaired children and young people depend upon two factors. First, the extent of the hearing impairment may range from total deafness to hard of hearing or slight hearing loss and will determine the amount of spoken communication they are able to receive. Secondly, because of their hearing impairment, they may have difficulty in speaking and expressing themselves in verbal communication. These receptive and expressive language problems pose a dual problem for librarians in the two-way street of communication: *to* and *from* the hearing impaired individual. In order to know the needs, interests, and abilities of deaf children in relation to library services and materials, the librarian must surmount the problem of communication and be able to *communicate to the child* and to *receive communication from the child.*

Alice Hagemeyer, librarian for the deaf at the District of Columbia Public Library who is herself deaf, has discussed the communication problems of deaf persons as one reason why they do not use a library. As a child, one individual had a bad experience in a public library when a teacher took the school class there. The teacher had previously told the children a little about the library. When they got to the library, the teacher left them there so they could learn more about the library and get some books. However, the librarians did not know what to do with the children. They could not communicate with the children or listen to them, and the children felt isolated because they did not know how to express their needs to the librarians. As a result, this deaf person never went back to the library again.[21]

The burden of communication between deaf and hearing persons has long been placed on the person who is deaf. Hearing people have expected that a deaf person should be able to read lips and speak or exchange written messages. Many now feel, however, that hearing professionals, including librarians, must assume responsibility for knowing how to communicate with hearing-impaired people. Suggestions are sometimes made that librarians should know sign language so they can serve hearing-impaired people better.[22] While it would certainly be beneficial for more librarians to have a knowledge of sign language, it is highly unrealistic to expect that all librarians are going to learn sign language. In certain situations, such as in schools which have a large number of deaf students, this may be a necessary requirement for the librarian. All librarians, however, will not have much contact with deaf library users, if indeed they have any contact at all; and all librarians cannot be expected to know sign language for a few possible deaf persons, any more than a librarian should know all foreign languages in order to serve an occasional library user who speaks another language.

There are a few techniques which can be helpful when communicating with deaf persons:

1. Before speaking, get the deaf person's attention by a tap on the shoulder, a wave, or other visual signals.

2. Face the light so the mouth and face can be easily seen.

3. Speak slowly and clearly without exaggerating or overemphasizing words because this tends to distort lip movements and make speechreading more difficult. It should not be assumed that all deaf children and young people are able to read lips because lipreading is a very difficult skill to master. Only 26% of speech is visible on the lips, and even the best lipreaders cannot read everything. Consequently, all deaf children are not adept speech or lip readers.

4. When speaking, look directly at the person. Even a slight turn of the head can obscure the deaf person's view. Moustaches, pencil-chewing, putting hands in front of one's face, and other distracting factors affect communication.

5. If necessary, communicate by means of paper and pencil, without feeling embarrassed. Sometimes a telecommunication device can be used.

6. Maintain eye contact with the person to help convey the feeling of direct communication. When an interpreter is present, talk directly to the deaf person, who can then turn to the interpreter if necessary.

7. If there is difficulty getting an idea across, rephrase a thought, or restate a sentence, rather than repeating exactly the same words. Sometimes a particular group of lip movements is difficult to speechread.

8. Use body language, facial expression, and pantomime to help communicate.

Librarians should always be alert for children who may be deaf or hard of hearing. If a hearing aid is visible, it is obvious that the child has a hearing problem. Without such visible evidence, however, a hearing impairment may not be readily recognized since it is a hidden disability. Indications of a possible hearing impairment are the following: 1) if a child asks to have statements repeated, 2) if a child has trouble understanding when a person is not facing him or her, 3) if a child understands only when a speaker is close, 4) if a child talks loudly, and 5) if a child has unusual voice quality.[23] Hearing-impaired children may also have problems in communication skills.

Frequently, deaf and other hearing-impaired children and young people are retarded in other language arts, especially reading. While the amount of such retardation varies according to the degree of hearing loss, it is not uncommon for deaf adults to be reading at the second- or third-grade level. Because of language retardation, hearing-impaired children have reading problems which include a limited vocabulary and difficulty with syntax, idioms, and multiple meanings.[24] Therefore, even though they may be able to see perfectly well with the eyes, they may not be able to read at their age or grade level.

Librarians have to teach hearing-impaired children how to use the library and the appropriate materials to the fullest extent. They need to know how to locate the materials and how to operate the necessary equipment. It may also be necessary for the librarian to help them understand the language in periodicals and reference books.[25] Reference service can be provided by means of a teletypewriter. Interpreters should be available for any library programs, such as story hours.

Another service librarians should provide for hearing-impaired individuals is the right kind of materials for their abilities, interests, and needs. Since many deaf and hard-of-hearing children and young people are deficient in verbal communication skills through spoken and written words, they must learn primarily through the sense of sight, utilizing their visual ability to the fullest extent. Therefore, librarians should use visual elements to convey ideas and concepts, because hearing-impaired children require materials in which pictorial presentations are prominent and well depicted. It cannot be assumed, however, that pictures in themselves are sufficient. Hearing impaired children may still have difficulty interpreting some illustrations. Therefore, pictures should be used simultaneously with spoken and manual communication.[26]

Hearing-impaired children and young people need printed materials at their reading level and which meet their interest and maturity levels. Their interests may not be the same as those of their hearing peers, and the extent of the difference or similarity in interests is open to debate. Some hearing-impaired children have interest and maturity levels which are practically the same as those of their hearing counterparts, while others have interest and maturity levels much lower than what is regarded as the norm for their particular age levels.[27] Wordless picture books, signed picture books, and appropriate magazines can be useful. Comic books — either educational, classics, or popular comics from newsstands — can be used effectively with deaf children.[28] High-interest/low-reading-level books can be helpful to many hearing-impaired children and young people, although the child who is profoundly deaf is a poor reader of high/low books.[29] Also, many high/low books have too many difficult sentence structures and language patterns and not enough illustrations.[30]

For both learning and entertainment, the visual media are the best form for use with deaf and hearing-impaired children and young people. Although many nonverbal films are available and can be effectively used, other visual media — pictures, slides, filmstrips, films, videocassettes, and videodiscs — can also be used. The effectiveness of these materials can be increased if they are captioned. If the materials are not captioned, it is possible to combine the use of films, filmstrips, slides, or other video presentations which have an audio track with the use of overhead transparencies. Captions to accompany the visual presentation can be printed on a transparency. By using two screens, the visual can be projected on one screen and the captions on the other. As the visual portion progresses, a mask can be moved down on the transparency and the caption displayed on the overhead screen, thus coordinating the captions with the visual.[31] Another possibility is to prepare captions on 2x2-inch slides and project them simultaneously with the film image. For maximum effectiveness, the reading rate of subtitles or captions should be twenty words a minute, there should not be more than two lines per caption, and there should be a maximum of six words per line.[32]

It is not always possible to subtitle or caption films satisfactorily for use with deaf children and young people, even though the films may be intrinsically good in themselves and highly suitable for use with hearing persons. Difficulties sometimes arise in trying to attach a print supplement to a sound-oriented medium because 1) the rate of narration may be too fast, 2) the vocabulary level may be too complex, 3) the background sound may be essential to the action of the film, 4) the editing or scene changes may be too fast, or 5) vocal inflections or regional dialects may become lost or distorted. Other problems can occur in the areas of dialog, sound effects, or visual noise. The dialog in the film may include 1) commentary of on-screen personalities, 2) puns or idioms which rely on the context for interpretation, 3) poetry or lyrics which depend on rhythm, or 4) well-known speeches which cannot be rephrased without changing their original meaning. Problems related to sound effects can include 1) music which is used as the subject or a very integral part of the film, or 2) sounds that cannot be reproduced in print, for example, the roar of a jet. Captioning may not be possible because of visual noise, such as 1) scenes which would obscure the legibility of captions, or 2) pre-existing captions that would interfere with new captions.[33]

CLOSED-CAPTIONED TELEVISION PROGRAMS

Librarians might well consider making it possible for hearing-impaired children and young people to watch closed-captioned television programs in the library. Closed-captioning is a process by which the audio portion of a television program is translated into captions or subtitles which appear on the screen. Hearing-impaired viewers can then read what they cannot hear. Closed captions can only be seen on a television set equipped with a special decoding device available from Sears, Roebuck and Company or from the National Captioning Institute under the product name TeleCaption.® Two types of units are sold: a captioning adapter that can be attached to an ordinary television set and a 19-inch portable color set with built-in decoding circuitry, called a captioning TV receiver. The nonprofit National Captioning Institute (NCI), established in 1979, captions the television programs and has a captioning center in the suburbs of Washington, DC, and another in Los Angeles.

NCI began in March 1980 to closed-caption selected television programs of the American Broadcasting Company (ABC), the National Broadcasting Company (NBC), the Public Broadcasting Service (PBS), and numerous independent producers and syndicators. In April 1982, it was reported that there were about thirty-five hours of closed-captioning programs available from these three networks, although NBC had stated that they were considering curtailment or elimination of this service.[34] The Columbia Broadcasting System (CBS) declined to participate in NCI's closed-captioning service because it is experimenting with a "teletext" system which CBS believes could provide captioned programs.

The number of programs that are captioned has been increasing steadily. Among the regular children's programs are "Sesame Street," "3-2-1 Contact," "Disney's Wonderful World," and "Little House on the Prairie." NCI has also contracted with the U.S. Department of Education to caption 600 hours of educational programs which are available to schools. Further information about these educational programs can be obtained from:

Dr. Frank Withrow
Chief, Educational Technology Development Branch
U.S. Department of Education
400 Maryland Avenue, SW
R.O.B. #3, Room 3116
Washington, DC 20202

Since closed-captioning is relatively new and requires special equipment which most hearing-impaired persons do not yet have in their homes, it would be an excellent service for librarians to provide a television set with decoding capabilities. In this way, hearing-impaired children and young people, as well as adults, would be able to view television programs in the library. For more information about NCI, closed-captioning, and TeleCaption® decoders, phone or write:

National Captioning Institute
Suite 1500
5203 Leesburg Pike
Falls Church, VA 22041
(703) 998-2400

    or

National Captioning Institute
1443 Beachwood Drive
Hollywood, CA 90028
(213) 469-7000

Communication Disorders

As with deaf and hearing-impaired children, librarians who serve children and young people with any type of communication disorder should be concerned primarily about communication. All people, of course, have a basic need to communicate, but those who are disabled in this way often require inventive ways of communication. Every possible approach, including body language, should be used in an effort to communicate with the child and ascertain the child's abilities in relation to materials and distinctive library needs and interests.

In the case of learning-disabled children and young people, many library materials and resources will be difficult and perhaps impossible for them to use. A librarian faces a real challenge in finding materials that are interesting enough and at the appropriate ability level of the child. They may require high-interest/low-reading-level books, easy-to-read paperbacks, sports and humorous magazines, newspapers, and even comic books. It may also be necessary to give these children individual instruction in how to use the card catalog and reference books, such as dictionaries, encyclopedias, and atlases, and how to locate materials in the library. They may need special help in learning how to operate equipment. Films and television programs can be beneficial in reaching them and reducing anxiety because these media are associated with recreation and fun. The librarian should also arrange for learning-disabled children to utilize the materials of the National Library Service for the Blind and Physically Handicapped, since these children are now eligible for this service.

Physically and Orthopedically Impaired

The first consideration in providing library services to physically and orthopedically impaired children and young people is getting them into the library. Many of them are intellectually, emotionally, and socially the same as physically able children and young people, and a librarian can accommodate them simply by making the library facilities accessible. Children who use a wheelchair should not be isolated from other library users. Furniture and shelving should be arranged so there is enough space for a wheelchair to move around. A table should be available which is high enough for the arms of a wheelchair to fit under. Some temporary modifications in the library arrangement may have to be made to accommodate a child on crutches.

In many instances, the abilities, needs, and interests of physically disabled children in relation to library services and materials are the same as their able-bodied peers. For library programs and services, such as skills instruction, storytelling, and puppet theater, they can participate with other children. Because of their physical disability, however, they may have lower energy levels and, when physically tired, may regress to lower levels of mental functioning. In some cases, because of poor muscle control, there may be difficulty in handling certain formats, sizes, and weights of materials and equipment. A child who is not able to use either one or both hands or arms may require adaptive devices in order to turn the pages of a book or to operate equipment. Such children, although they may have the ability to read, are considered print-handicapped and are therefore eligible to receive talking books, equipment, and devices from the National Library Service for the Blind and Physically Handicapped. Formats that are highly automated, such as audiocassettes and videocassettes, and equipment that can be operated easily, should be used.

In addition to the categories described above, librarians are frequently in contact with children and young people who have a temporary handicap. They may be wearing a cast or an eyepatch, using crutches, a walker, or a wheelchair, have temporary blindness, and perhaps temporary but total immobilization. These children, too, need library services and materials and the help of an understanding librarian.

Intellectual Impairments

Intellectually impaired children and young people need library materials and services as much as those with other types of disabling conditions. In some instances, small groups of these children can be invited to the library. However, since many who are mentally retarded cannot get to the library, it is important for the librarian to go to them.

In providing services for intellectually impaired children and young people, the mental ability and capacity of the individual child must be considered. Mental ability determines the level of books and other materials which the child can profitably use. It also affects the individual's needs and interests related to library services and materials. However, although abilities vary among children who are retarded, it cannot be assumed that mentally retarded children are necessarily limited to the ability level which may be indicated by their achievement test scores.[35] They are frequently able to function above the level of their test scores, and their interests may be comparable to other children or young people of the same age.

As librarians endeavor to satisfy the library needs of intellectually impaired children and young people, they should get to know the children individually and try to ascertain their ability in reading, viewing, and listening as well as their interests in regard to fiction, nonfiction, and other media formats. All library services – guidance, reference, and instruction – should be at their intellectual level. Since a multisensory approach is the most effective method for teaching mentally retarded and learning-disabled children, a wide variety of materials should be available in the library: conventional print materials, high-interest/low-vocabulary books and magazines, recordings, films, filmstrips, filmloops, slides, multimedia kits, large-print materials, tactile learning aids, toys, games, puzzles, puppets, musical instruments, and braille playing cards.

All books and audiovisual materials should be suitable to the child's mental ability. The material should move from that which is familiar to that which is less well known. Books should be written in a simple structure, with simple sentences and vocabulary that can be understood by the child. They should be short books because mentally retarded children have a short attention span. Pictures should be used whenever possible. Audiovisual materials – films, filmstrips, audio-recordings – can be effective if they are at the child's ability level. At the secondary level, popular magazines are very important. Although magazines contain easy materials, they are not obviously easy. Nevertheless, magazines are highly suitable because the articles are short, sentences and vocabulary are simple, and pictures convey a large part of the message.[36]

The Altoona Area Public Library in Pennsylvania developed a program of services for the mentally retarded called L.I.F.E. (Learning Is For Everyone), which had three major objectives: 1) to serve mentally retarded persons of all ages and ability levels; 2) to serve the parents, teachers, and advocates of retarded citizens; and 3) to serve the general public. A collection of multimedia materials appropriate to the needs of retarded persons was developed and integrated with the regular collection in order to encourage mainstreaming.[37]

Behavioral Disorders

Children and young people who have behavioral disorders (also referred to as "emotionally disturbed children") must be individually assessed in order to provide appropriate library services for them. Since children in this category span such a wide range, including schizophrenic and autistic children, they also have a wide range of abilities, interests, and needs in regard to library services. Some are very low in native intelligence and others are at the genius level, although the latter may function at a much lower level than their innate abilities would indicate is possible. They may have short attention spans, experience difficulty in concentrating on a task, and be easily distracted.[38]

Librarians need to have a great amount of patience and understanding in working with emotionally disturbed children. Kieth Wright has listed several ways in which a librarian can assist emotionally disturbed children:

1. by helping children who come to the media center to develop their own self-concepts and positive mental health attitudes;

2. by dealing with positive behavior when it occurs and ignoring negative behavior so long as it is not self- or other- destructive;

3. by creating an environment where people can be isolated, protected, or in which they can safely act out feelings;

4. by not underestimating the potential good which media center resources can do.[39]

Children and young people with emotional disturbances have a basic inner need to achieve success and therefore require materials that will be minimally frustrating. Books and audiovisual materials should depict nonthreatening situations and provide models of coping behavior which are socially acceptable. They should present social and family problems and all kinds of interpersonal relationships, showing a satisfactory resolution of disputes and differences. Since many of these children have difficulty accepting themselves, they need materials which show them not only how to come to terms with their own limitations but how to accept other people's strengths and enjoy them.[40]

NOTES

[1]*Brown v. Board of Education*, 347 U.S. 483, 74 S.Ct. 686, 98 L, Ed. 873 (1954).

[2]Adapted in part from John Barrow, "Library Service for the Deaf," *Wisconsin Library Bulletin* 74 (September-October 1978): 216.

[3]Carol C. Iffland, "Mainstreaming," *Illinois Libraries* 58 (December 1976): 807-808. See Helen Stough, " 'Let Me Hear Your Hand'—Library Service for Handicapped Children," *Illinois Libraries* 62 (December 1980): 880, for additional suggestions a librarian can pursue in providing service for disabled children.

[4]See, for example, Mary Rita Stoneburg, "Bibliotherapy and Its Use with Exceptional Children," *Illinois Libraries* 62 (October 1980): 665-71; and Barbara E. Lenkowsky and Ronald S. Lenkowsky, "Bibliotherapy for the LD Adolescent," *Academic Therapy* 14 (November 1978): 179-85, reprinted in *Meeting the Needs of the Handicapped: A Resource for Teachers and Librarians*, ed. Carol H. Thomas and James L. Thomas (Phoenix: Oryx Press, 1980), pp. 122-27.

[5]Lucy Warner, "The Myth of Bibliotherapy," *School Library Journal* 27 (October 1980): 107-111, indicated that she examined twenty-eight studies on bibliotherapy and found that 1) ten were not successful, 2) four showed short-term gains which were not maintained, 3) two showed theoretical improvement but did not change behavior, 4) four showed results only with subjects who wanted to change, 5) four found other techniques more successful, 6) two endorsed it in conjunction with other techniques, and 7) only two claimed unqualified success.

[6]Rhea J. Rubin, "Uses of Bibliotherapy in Response to the 1970s," *Library Trends* 28 (Fall 1979): 243-44.

[7]Dorothy Kobax and Estelle Nisenson, "Poetry Therapy," in *Meeting the Needs of the Handicapped: A Resource for Teachers and Librarians*, ed. Carol H. Thomas and James L. Thomas (Phoenix: Oryx Press, 1980), pp. 169-71.

[8]Stoneburg, "Bibliotherapy and Its Use with Exceptional Children," p. 665.

[9]Joni Bodart, "Bibliotherapy: The Right Book for the Right Person at the Right Time—and More!" *Top of the News* 36 (Winter 1980): 183.

[10]See, for example, Stoneburg, "Bibliotherapy and Its Use with Exceptional Children," pp. 665-71; and Henry C. Dequin, "Services and Materials for Disabled Children," *Illinois Libraries* 63 (September 1981): 546-54.

[11]Mary Jane Metcalf, "Helping Hearing Impaired Students," *School Library Journal* 25 (January 1979): 28, reprinted in *Meeting the Needs of the Handicapped: A Resource for Teachers and Librarians*, ed. Carol H. Thomas and James L. Thomas (Phoenix: Oryx Press, 1980), pp. 197-203.

[12]For a description of how braille catalog cards can be made, see Sally M. Mahoney and Lisslotte Z. Stokes, "A School Library Program for the Blind," *Wilson Library Bulletin* 40 (May 1966): 829+.

[13]Metcalf, "Helping Hearing Impaired Students," p. 28.

[14]Henry C. Dequin and Jane Smith, "Learning Disabled Students Can Be Tutors in Library Media Skills," *Top of the News* 36 (Summer 1980): 352-56.

[15]Russell H. Mattern, "Detecting Visual Problems," *Ohio Media Spectrum* 30 (January 1978): 35-36.

[16]Winifred G. Daniell, "School Library Service to the Visually Handicapped," *School Media Quarterly* 3 (Summer 1975): 347.

[17]Candace Catlin Hall, "Use of a Type Size Transparency in School Libraries and Media Centers," *Education of the Visually Handicapped* 11 (Winter 1979-80): 112-17.

[18]Beverly Kessler, "Books at Your Finger Tips," *Ohio Media Spectrum* 30 (January 1978): 28.

[19]Sharon Hammer, "Radio Reading—A Logical Form of Library Service," *Health and Rehabilitative Library Services Division Journal* 2 (Fall 1976): 17-19.

[20]K. C. Sykes, "Print Reading for Visually Handicapped Children," *Education of the Visually Handicapped* 4 (October 1972): 71-72. Cf. Martha Rosemeyer and Marian Sundheimer, "Canton City Works with Visually Impaired Students," *Ohio Media Spectrum* 30 (January 1978): 30-31.

[21]Ruth A. Velleman, *Serving Physically Disabled People: An Information Handbook for All Libraries* (New York: R. R. Bowker, 1979), p. 148.

[22]See, for example, Pedro Acevedo, "It's Hearing People Who Make Problems for Deaf People," *Interracial Books for Children Bulletin* 11 (Numbers 1 and 2, 1980): 11; Elsa Z. Posell, "Libraries and the Deaf Patron," *Wilson Library Bulletin* 51 (January 1977): 402-404; and Kieth C. Wright, *Library and Information Services for Handicapped Individuals* (Littleton, CO: Libraries Unlimited, 1979), p. 60.

[23]*Special People, Special Needs, Special Services* (Athens: University of Georgia, Bureau of Educational Studies and Department of Educational Media and Librarianship, 1978), p. 16.

[24]Metcalf, "Helping Hearing Impaired Students," p. 27; and Mary Jane Metcalf, "Library Services for the Hearing Impaired," *Illinois Libraries* 63 (October 1981): 617.

[25]Metcalf, "Helping Hearing Impaired Students," p. 29.

[26]Ibid., p. 27.

[27]Ibid.

[28]Bill Stark, " 'Meanwhile ...': A Look at Comic Books at Illinois School for the Deaf," *American Annals of the Deaf* 121 (October 1976): 470-77, reprinted in *Meeting the Needs of the Handicapped: A Resource for Teachers and Librarians*, ed. Carol H. Thomas and James L. Thomas (Phoenix: Oryx Press, 1980), pp. 208-213.

[29]Michael J. Sadoski and Doris C. Sadoski, "Sign Language Films for Library Users," *California Librarian* 39 (April 1978): 56.

[30]Metcalf, "Helping Hearing Impaired Students," p. 29.

[31]Louise M. Wright, "Library at Ohio School for the Deaf," *Ohio Media Spectrum* 30 (January 1978): 42.

[32]Salvatore J. Parlato, Jr., "Read Any Good Films Lately?," *Audiovisual Instruction* 22 (September 1977): 30-31.

[33]Ibid.

[34]*ECT Network*, April 1982, p. 3.

35Karen H. Harris, "Selecting Library Materials for Exceptional Children," *School Media Quarterly* 8 (Fall 1979): 24.

36Ibid., pp. 24-25.

37Mary Zajac, "Learning Is for Everyone," *RQ* 18 (Spring 1979): 248-50; and Anne-Marie Forer and Mary Zajac in cooperation with the Altoona Area Public Library, "Library Services to the Mentally Retarded," Report on the L.I.F.E. Project (Altoona, PA: Altoona Area Public Library, n.d.).

38Harris, "Selecting Library Materials for Exceptional Children," p. 25.

39Kieth C. Wright, "Handicapping Conditions and the Needs of Handicapped Children," in *Services and Materials for the Handicapped; Proceedings of an Institute for School Library Media Professionals, August 12-17, 1979*, ed. Henry C. Dequin (DeKalb: Northern Illinois University, 1979), p. 30. See also Wright, *Library and Information Services for Handicapped Individuals*, pp. 92-93.

40Harris, "Selecting Library Materials for Exceptional Children," pp. 25-26.

7 _____Library Programs

"No ... otherwise qualified handicapped individual ... in the United States shall, solely by
reason of his handicap, be excluded from the
participation in, be denied the benefits of, or
be subjected to discrimination under any
program or activity receiving federal financial
assistance."
     —P.L. 93-112, The Rehabilitation
     Amendments of 1973.
     Section 504.

INTRODUCTION

As indicated in the above quotation, Section 504 of the Rehabilitation
Amendments of 1973 requires that programs which are provided for the general
public must also be accessible to disabled persons. The intent of this requirement
is to make all benefits, services, or programs available to disabled persons just as
they are to nondisabled persons.

In meeting this requirement, the emphasis is on "integration," not in
providing "separate but equal" programs. Public librarians and school librarians
must integrate disabled children and young people into the regular programs and
services which are provided for nondisabled children and young people. In doing
so, care must be taken that those who are disabled are not isolated from
nondisabled program participants, although it may sometimes be desirable to
arrange some programs particularly for children with specific types of disabling
conditions. This should be the exception, however, depending upon the type of
program which is arranged.

With this thought of integration in mind, this chapter offers 1) general
programming suggestions, and then discusses 2) types of programs, both in
relation to the abilities, needs, and interests of disabled children and young
people.

GENERAL PROGRAMMING SUGGESTIONS

Library programs which are aimed at integrating disabled children and
young people must be well planned before being implemented. Resource persons
both inside and outside the institution should be consulted and include the library

staff, parents of the disabled children, and the children themselves to the extent possible. In school library media programming, the resource persons should also include classroom teachers, special education teachers and coordinator, curriculum coordinator, and principal.

The Library Service to Children with Special Needs Committee of the Association for Library Service to Children has prepared a helpful pamphlet, *Programming for Children with Special Needs.* The pamphlet discusses basic aspects of programming, such as criteria, procedures (goals, objectives, resources, program outline, and evaluation), personnel, facilities, and costs. Characteristics of disabled children, the implications of the characteristics for library programming, and examples of programs are given for physically disabled children, blind and partially sighted children, deaf and hearing-impaired children, emotionally disturbed children, learning disabled children, mentally disabled children, and multiply disabled children.[1]

All programming should be based upon the needs, interests, and abilities of the children or young people who will be involved in the program. Just as it is wise to determine the number of disabled persons in the library's community and to make an assessment of their library needs before initiating library services for disabled persons on a broad scale, it is also necessary to ascertain the kinds of programs and the subjects which interest the children and meet their needs. This can best be learned by talking with the children themselves, their parents, their teachers, and others who are closely associated with them. The abilities of the children must also be considered in planning a program.

General objectives for the overall program, as well as specific objectives for each subprogram, should be formulated, and the ways of accomplishing the objectives should be determined. The general objectives of library programming for disabled children and young people should state what the children and young people will be able to do as a result of the library's program, such as:

— To relate to and identify with the librarian, other disabled children and young people, and the library;

— To develop healthy mental attitudes toward themselves and others;

— To be active, contributing members of their own peer group;

— To read the same books and use the same materials that other children read and use;

— To derive pleasure from reading books and using other materials;

— To gain knowledge, through all media sources, of opportunities available to them;

— To communicate ideas from the materials they use;

— To demonstrate ability in using the library by selecting, withdrawing, and returning materials;

— To recognize that the expectations which librarians have for them are the same as for other children and young people.[2]

Similarly, specific objectives should be formulated for each aspect of the program, such as story hours, audiovisual programs, or any other type of program.

Evaluation of the overall program and of specific aspects of the program should be determined in the initial planning and be made on the basis of the objectives. Various evaluation measures can be employed: conferences with individual children, with teachers, and with parents; observation of the children while a program is being presented; and follow-up activities intended to measure the behavioral change in the children as a result of the program.[3]

Although library programs are usually planned for large groups, other programming structures are also possible, such as small groups, tutoring, pairing, and solitary activity. The programs which are discussed in the following pages are mostly for groups, either for only disabled children or groups in which the disabled and nondisabled are together. Some of the programs can also easily be arranged for smaller groups or for individuals.

Publicity and Outreach

A well-planned program of publicity and outreach, carefully implemented, is vital to the success of any library program. It is one thing to arrange a good program which will be of interest and benefit to children and young people who are disabled. It is another to "get the word out" about the programs that are arranged. Librarians need to let the what, where, when, why, and how of library programs be known, both to disabled children and young people and to their parents.

Suggestions on how to reach specific disabled children and young people and their parents might be obtained from advocacy groups, institutions, or organizations of disabled persons in the community. Invitations can be mailed directly to the children and young people, with an accompanying letter to parents explaining the program. Announcements can also be distributed to children in school classes. The invitations and announcements should be printed in large type and simply worded for the benefit of visually impaired and language-impaired children. Posters can be strategically placed in stores and businesses in the community as well as in the library itself. Announcements should be included in the library newsletter. Press releases and photographs can be sent to local newspapers and shoppers. Public service announcements and guest spots can be arranged for radio and television stations. Flyers and bookmarks can be distributed from the library circulation desk. Word-of-mouth communication chains should also be zealously pursued. All publicity should include information regarding special accommodations, that is, whether an interpreter for the deaf will be present at the program and whether the building is accessible to children in wheelchairs.

The following checklist might be used as a "publicity countdown":

_____ At least eight weeks before the program:
Collect all relevant information regarding the needs, interests, and abilities of the children or young people

Plan the program in detail

Begin word-of-mouth promotion among the public and the library staff

_____ Six weeks before the program:
Write an announcement for the library newsletter

Design all graphics, invitations, and announcements and arrange to have them printed

_____ Four weeks before the program:
Mail press releases, photographs, and public service announcements to newspapers, radio stations, and television stations. (Determine the deadlines in advance.)

_____ Three weeks before the program:
Contact radio and television stations for guest appearances

Mail invitations and announcements to children, young people, and their parents

_____ Two weeks before the program:
Place posters in the library, business places, and other strategic locations

Distribute announcements in school classes

Distribute flyers and bookmarks at the circulation desk

Post a sign-up sheet, if necessary

_____ One week before the program:
Intensify word-of-mouth campaign with library users

The National Library Service for the Blind and Physically Handicapped has produced a booklet, *Reaching People*, which is a manual on public education for libraries serving blind and physically handicapped individuals. The suggestions in the manual can very easily be adapted to library programs for disabled children and young people. Individual sections cover the following topics which should be considered when planning a program:

— Guidelines for contacting the mass media

— How to get the names and addresses of the right people at mass media agencies

— How to prepare, organize, and distribute a news release for newspapers, radio, and television

— How to use photographs in print and on the air

— How to deal with the print media

- How to deal with the electronic media

- How to prepare short public service announcements

- How to take advantage of nationally prepared information

- Basic information on brochures, newsletters, fact sheets, and bibliographies

- How to make and use posters

- How to display exhibits and what to include

- How to write, photograph, and assemble slide shows

- How to choose and use a telephone answering machine

- How to mail to specific target audiences

- How to find, contact, and cooperate with community organizations and agencies

- How to recruit and use an advisory committee

- How to organize programs that bring people together to learn about your services

- How to plan and run an awards program

- How to coordinate a speakers' bureau

- How to prepare an informal or formal speech[4]

A copy of *Reaching People* may be obtained from the National Library Service for the Blind and Physically Handicapped, Library of Congress, 1291 Taylor Street, NW, Washington, DC 20542.

Facilities

Suitable facilities and physical arrangements are essential to the success of the library's programs and services for disabled children and young people. First of all, the library itself and the room where the program is held or the services are provided should be easily accessible to physically disabled and blind children and young people. Floors should be smooth, hard, and slip-resistant. They should be free of all obstacles, such as door stops or raised outlets. Thresholds should be covered so they can be negotiated smoothly. Carpeting should be tightly fastened to the floor, smooth and tightly woven without a high pile. Electrical cords should not tangle on the floor or dangle from tables or study carrels.

Directional signs should be posted in strategic locations and printed in letters which are large enough to be seen easily from a distance by visually impaired children. The signs should be positioned low enough to be read by those in wheelchairs and be adequately lighted so they can be read by the visually impaired.

The card catalog and other files should be easily accessible to wheelchair users. If the catalog cannot be low enough for use from a wheelchair, service should be provided to take drawers to a table for use by the person in a wheelchair. Drawers should not be packed so tightly that the user of a magnifying glass cannot read the cards.

Aisles between stack areas should be wide enough to allow wheelchair passage. At least thirty inches is essential, although a minimum of three to four feet is the recommended standard width between shelves. Within space limitations and practical considerations, shelving should not go higher than five feet. Three-foot (counter height) shelving is the most preferable. Where shelving is higher, reachers should be available so disabled persons can reach books on the upper shelves, or service should be provided to bring material from the stacks for those who cannot reach all the shelves.

Tables and study carrels should be accessible by wheelchair users. There should be a clear height of 28½ inches from the underside of the work surface of a table or carrel to the floor. Chairs should be built for ease of use and ease of emergence.

Other seating areas should be easily accessible. In a large room setting, wheelchair users should have access to a seating area other than the back row.

A soundproof booth, carrel, or room should be available for the use of tape recorders or talking-book machines.

Several sources can be consulted for detailed specifications regarding recommended standards for facilities to accommodate disabled persons:

American Library Association. Association of Specialized and Cooperative Library Agencies. Standards for Library Service to the Blind and Physically Handicapped Subcommittee. *Standards of Service for the Library of Congress Network of Libraries for the Blind and Physically Handicapped.* Chicago: American Library Association, 1979.

American National Standards Institute. *Specifications for Making Buildings and Facilities Accessible to and Usable by Physically Handicapped People, ANSI A117.1 (1980).* New York: American National Standards Institute, 1980.

Jones, Michael A. *Accessibility Standards Illustrated.* Chicago: Capital Development Board, State of Illinois, 1978.

National Library Service for the Blind and Physically Handicapped. *Planning Barrier Free Libraries: A Guide for Renovation and Construction of Libraries Serving Blind and Physically Handicapped Readers.* Washington, DC: The Library of Congress, 1981.

TYPES OF PROGRAMS

Awareness Programs

In spite of the increased emphasis within recent years on disabled persons, many able-bodied people are unaware of the ramifications of various disabilities for those who have them. Librarians can help to increase awareness by offering library programs on disabling conditions and disabled persons. The programs can be arranged for various groups of nondisabled persons—children, young people, and adults. Among the many types of possible programs are the following:

—Disabled children, young people, or adults can present a talk to able-bodied individuals;

—A physical therapist can demonstrate techniques and equipment;

—Children with a temporary disability can discuss the difficulties they experience and the feelings of other nondisabled children toward them;

—A resource person can make a presentation and lead a discussion on societal discrimination against disabled people;

—Books, television programs, cartoons, or comic books can be analyzed for stereotypes;

—Books, films, and other audiovisual materials can be presented for more understanding;

—Participants can simulate the experience of disabled persons: 1) the hearing impaired by wearing ear plugs for several hours; 2) the visually impaired by wearing a blindfold while eating and doing other things; 3) the physically impaired by maneuvering a wheelchair or using crutches and doing various things.[5]

A program to broaden the experiences of disabled children and to sharpen their awareness of their environment through library services was carried out by Elwyn Institute, a private institution which offers day and resident programs for children who are disabled by reason of mental retardation, learning disabilities, visual and/or auditory impairment, or emotional disturbances. The program began with a library orientation course in which seventy-five children, ages six to twelve, were taught library manners, the means of finding books, and the use of audiovisual equipment. They had a tour of a local public library and were able to practice correct behavior in the library. They quickly came to view the library as a place of quiet enjoyment. Various methods were used to bring library services to the children, and a film was made showing what the children had learned about library procedures. The report of the program included a bibliography of library materials for institutional developmentally disabled children divided into early childhood, K-4; biographies, grades 3-7 and 4-9; histories of the United States, grades 4-8; and careers.[6]

The Howard Whittemore Memorial Library in Naugatuck, Connecticut, conducted an awareness program related to visual handicaps, which could easily be repeated in other public libraries or in school libraries. Extending over a period of several months and involving both children and adults, the project pursued eight specific aims. Special materials were borrowed, including braille and large-print materials, twin-vision books, various aids and devices such as abacuses, brailled and tactile numbered clock faces, textured cylinders of varying weights, deeply etched dissimilar blocks, a braillewriter, a slate, and a stylus. A talking-book machine was demonstrated, and catalogs and examples of special materials from the National Library Service for the Blind and Physically Handicapped were on display. These special materials were integrated rather than segregated into the audiovisual listening center. Media coverage was a vital part of the project. Although one aspect of the program did not happen as expected, that is, having visually impaired children use the public library, sighted children did become more aware of blindness and blind persons.[7]

Handicapped Awareness Day was held at the Crofton branch of the Annapolis and Anne Arundel County (Maryland) Public Library. Library users were asked to complete regular activities using a wheelchair, crutches, a neck brace, a walker, and so forth. For the more adventurous persons there were obstacle course activities, such as pushing a stroller or shopping cart, or attempting to use the restroom. Movies about disabilities were shown continuously, and speakers from various organizations representing disabled persons gave presentations.[8]

Story Hour and Storytelling Programs

Librarians and society in general highly value books and reading, both for educational purposes as well as for recreation and enjoyment. Many disabled children and young people, however, are poor readers and do not read at their age or grade level. This is particularly true for those with language and communication problems as a result of deafness, hearing impairment, speech impairment, mental retardation, and some learning disabilities. Blind children and many visually impaired children are unable to use books which are printed in conventional type-size. Consequently, these children and young people are frequently reluctant readers, and many just look at pictures in a book without trying to read the story. Librarians constantly need to encourage and stimulate these children to read.

One way to provide encouragement to reluctant readers and to give enjoyment through books and stories is through a story hour, probably the most frequent program activity offered to children by librarians in school and public libraries. All children, whether they are able-bodied or disabled in some way, enjoy the presentation of stories. Stories have both recreational and educational value. They give children knowledge of their own and other cultures, expand the experience of children beyond their own immediate environment, and stimulate their interest in books and other media forms. Disabled children and young people, too, whether their disability is visual, auditory, physical, intellectual, or emotional, can receive these benefits from story hours and storytelling sessions. For those who are homebound and cannot come to the library, librarians can arrange to visit them in their homes to tell them stories.

Storytelling is restricted almost entirely to younger children as a formal program activity. "Story hours" and "storytelling programs" are usually not arranged for adults and young people. This is unfortunate because adolescents and adults can enjoy hearing stories and can benefit in this way. The telling of stories has its roots in the very beginning of the history of mankind as a means of preserving the heritage of civilizations and as a form of entertainment. Through the years, adults as well as children have loved to tell stories and to hear stories told; this is still true, in an informal way today, for adults and teenagers. Librarians seriously need to consider offering some type of story programs to young people and adults, not only to those with a disability but to the able-bodied as well.

Stories can be presented in a variety of ways. They can be read aloud directly from a book. They can be told from memory, without reading, either by the librarian or by another person who has ability in storytelling. Original stories can be told by those who have some creative and imaginative ability. Stories can be told while the storyteller draws pictures on a chalkboard or overhead projector. They can also be accompanied with the use of puppets, flat pictures, flannelgraphs, realia, arts, crafts, or other appropriate materials. Two helpful resources are: *Tell and Draw Stories*, by Margaret J. Oldfield (Creative Storytime Press, Arts and Crafts Unlimited, Box 572, Minneapolis, MN 55440), and *Storytelling with the Flannel Board*, by Paul S. Anderson (T. S. Denison and Company, 9601 Newton Avenue S., Minneapolis, MN 55437). Many stories are also now available in other media forms and can be presented on recordings or shown by means of films, captioned films, filmstrips, and slides.

When preparing for a story hour or storytelling program, a number of aspects should be considered:

1. Learn beforehand as much as possible about the children who will be present, both as a group and as individuals—their home and school interests, their chronological and mental ages, their learning characteristics, their ability to understand, their limitations because of their individual disabilities, their learning problems and other needs, and their approximate attention span.

2. Develop a theme or several themes for the story session, such as adventure stories, realistic stories in some way related to the children's experiences, books on shapes and colors, animal stories, nature books, easy and brief biographies, fiction and nonfiction books about racing cars or motorcycles, and mystery stories.

3. Select suitable books on the theme. For language-impaired children (deaf and mentally retarded), it is best to choose books and stories which have large and bright pictures, simple plots with which they can identify, and no lengthy descriptions or phrases which may be confusing.

4. Read the story several times. Commit it to memory, although not necessarily verbatim (except, perhaps, for classic stories).

5. Outline the key incidents in the story and review them frequently.

6. Practice telling the story aloud. Use a tape recorder, if possible, in order to listen to the practiced presentation.

7. Time the story. Children generally, and many disabled children especially, have a short attention span. Therefore, each story and the entire storytelling session should not be too long. It is better to begin with one short story or several short stories rather than one long story, and then gradually expand to longer stories and longer sessions as the attention span of the children increases. Children need to learn to listen and have something worth listening to.

8. Speak in a pleasant voice, with interest and enthusiasm. Make voice changes for the different characters and animals.

9. Act out the story, using body movements, gestures, and facial expressions.

10. Plan for the participation of the children. Have them act out parts of the story, imitate animals, point to something in a picture, or guess what is going to happen. Pose questions to be answered; for nonverbal children the questions should require only simple responses, such as descriptive sounds or gestures which indicate "yes" or "no." Involve them in creative activities. Discuss the story with them.

11. Use realia, such as natural things, stuffed animals, mechanical things, bird exhibits, scratch and sniff materials, and tactile objects.[9]

For the benefit of all the children, but especially for those who are deaf, the person presenting the story should face the light and speak clearly and distinctly. Hearing-impaired children should sit where they can hear. An interpreter should be present for deaf children if the storyteller does not know sign language, although it is preferable for the person who tells the story to sign the story at the same time. Visually impaired children should sit close to the storyteller in order to see pictures in the book and any other visuals that are used.
. The story should move in clearly defined steps:

1. Introduce the story by setting the scene for the children. Show the book to the children. Write the title of the story and the names of the characters on the chalkboard or overhead. Explain parts of the story which may be difficult for the children to understand. For deaf and mentally disabled children particularly, it is important to use vocabulary and sentence structure that are familiar to the children. Deaf children need this introductory time in order to adjust to the storyteller's face and unique lip patterns.

2. Build up the story toward the projected action by preparing the children for what will happen in the story.

3. Introduce action which lives up to the expectations of the children and catches their imagination.

4. Describe the reaction to the action.

5. Bring the story to a climax which will definitely indicate to the children that it is the conclusion of the story.[10]

The storyteller should watch the children during the presentation to make sure they understand the words and concepts which are used. If there is any indication of puzzlement in the faces of the children, it may be necessary to repeat a word, a sentence, or explain a word or concept. Sometimes the storyteller may have to stop and ask if the children understand. If the children seem to be losing interest, the storyteller should try to enliven the story and renew their interest or draw the story to a close as quickly as possible.

Pictorial presentations—flat pictures, flannelgraphs, films, filmstrips, slides, overhead transparencies, visual objects—should be utilized in story hours as much as possible. Visuals are effective with all persons, but especially for the deaf, hearing impaired, or mentally retarded. For the benefit of visually impaired children, visuals should be large drawings which can be clearly and easily seen. If some children are blind, the visuals should be explained, or raised line drawings can be used. Illustrations should interpret, clarify, and amplify the story; they should not be impressionistic but representational and precise.[11] Stories told with slides and flannelboard, however, are better than those told on filmstrips or film for several reasons: 1) hearing-impaired children can understand slide and flannelboard stories better; 2) the storyteller can actively involve the children in the story as it is told; and 3) both slides and flannelboard can be produced locally, and the storyteller can therefore control the content of the story.[12]

Several considerations should be kept in mind when using books and stories with mentally retarded children. Many of the following suggestions in regard to intellectually impaired children are also applicable to other disabled children, especially those who are language impaired:

—the story should be simple with simple sentence structure;

—the plot should be active and relate situations with which the children can identify;

—the story should move from what is familiar to what is less well known;

—illustrations should be realistic and easily recognizable, with only a few objects on each page;

—new words should be introduced and be within the range of the children;

—manipulations of time and flashbacks should not occur;

—narrators should not change within the story;

—devices such as irony should be avoided;

—concepts should be developed logically, completely, and sequentially without any gaps;

—repetition should be used;

—children who can speak should be brought into the story by asking them to imitate animals, locate objects on a page, or guess what is going to happen next;

—nonverbal children should be asked questions that can be answered by gestures which indicate "yes" or "no."[13]

For blind children the storyteller's voice is the only way in which to describe the actions and incidents of the story and to convey moods and tones. Therefore, the storyteller must appeal to the auditory sense as well as to the senses of touch, taste, smell, and general awareness. Blind children respond to a story differently than sighted children do, and the storyteller needs to pay keen attention to the way in which blind children are responding.[14]

Stories for mentally retarded children should be very concrete and literal rather than abstract and figurative because they tend to have poor ability to make associations, generalize, predict, and interpret. Since their reaction time is slow, the stories should be very specific and call for a definite response from the children. Furthermore, since the language ability of mentally retarded children tends to be limited, the stories should be an opportunity for them to expand their language experience. The storyteller should examine the language of the story for level of difficulty, for words which are obsolete, obscure, or obtuse in meaning, and for localisms, unusual idioms, and foreign words or phrases. Any unfamiliar concepts in the story should be illustrated through pictures, posters, models, or toys. Humor in a story should be obvious and direct in order to be appreciated by mentally retarded children.[15]

The storyteller-signer for deaf children should be one person who acts out the story through a special kind of sign language. Each character's words and personality should be conveyed by distinct signs. The signs should move smoothly, rapidly, or slowly according to the action of the story. Signs should describe the location of the story, as though setting a stage for the action, with the placement of houses, trees, and other objects remaining constant. The storyteller should use facial expression, body action, and mime.[16]

Materials which combine signs and stories and which can be useful to storytellers in telling stories to deaf children are available from:

Gallaudet College Bookstore
Gallaudet College
Kendall Green
7th and Florida Avenue, NE
Washington, DC 20002

Joyce Motion Picture Company
8613 Yolanda Avenue
P.O. Box 458
Northridge, CA 91324

Comic Books

Although comic books are not usually highly regarded by librarians and teachers, they can be effective with deaf children and other children who have language problems. The sequential presentation of pictures is a visual form of language and, combined with the simple and colloquial language in the overhead balloons, makes comic books very suitable for use by deaf and language-impaired children. They can be used to introduce children to the classics, nursery rhymes, fairy tales, and Aesop's fables. Deaf children like to read comic books, and very often the reading of the classics in comic book format leads the children to read simply written adaptations of the classics themselves. Captioned slide stories based on the comics can also be produced, presenting the caption first in simple language, followed by the visual.[17] For information on comics, an excellent source is Comics Code Authority, 41 East 42nd Street, New York, NY 10017.

Audiovisual Programs

Many types of programs can utilize the audio and/or visual formats which are now plentifully available and include a wide variety of educational and recreational subjects of interest to disabled children and young people according to their ages and abilities. All types of formats—moving pictorial, still pictorial, recordings of the spoken word and music, talking books, art prints, sculpture—can be used with disabled children and young people. The use of audiovisual materials can help to increase the listening and viewing skills of the children and, if captions are included, also their reading skills. Studies indicate that disabled children have shown improvement in their attitude toward school when they are in classes in which the overhead projector is used.[18] Audio and/or visual programs—videotape, audiotape, and slides—can also be produced in which the children themselves are involved and participate.

Moving pictorial materials—16mm films, 8mm films, videocassettes, videodiscs, and television programs—can be utilized in programs for children and young people of various ages, interests, and abilities. The showing of films helps to reduce anxiety, especially for learning-disabled and emotionally disturbed children. Since films and television programs are usually associated with entertainment and recreation, children regard them as fun. With no obligation to perform, they can just relax and enjoy the presentation. In schools, film programs can be incorporated into the regular course of the school day. A combination of films and illustrated books can be effective. Family film programs can be presented in the evening.[19]

Sonya Abbye has prepared a list of 16mm films, divided into three areas: 1) social and emotional needs, 2) language and development, and 3) films for five senses. The films were evaluated for quality of language, visual appeal, and narrative strength. Although suggested for use with five- to fourteen-year-old children who are learning disabled, the films can be used effectively with various types of disabled children and young people who are either in school library or public library programming.[20]

Nonverbal or non-narrated films are effective with deaf and language-impaired children and young people as well as with those who have other disabilities. Nonverbal films tell a story or convey a message pictorially, through visual content, without relying upon words. Although some of these films may be silent, they are not the same as silent films. They usually have soundtracks that suggest mood through music and may also have sound effects and even small amounts of conversation. Since intelligence is not really correlated with an ability to understand the English language, children with aural or language impairments may be able to comprehend nonverbal films just as well as their hearing peers. However, they should always be prepared for the film's intended message before they view the film. Such preparation may be a brief introduction to certain concepts or questions without detailed explanations. Furthermore, a film should not be dismissed for possible use with those who are deaf simply because it may contain *some* language.[21] Parlato has listed some useful nonverbal films in a number of categories, including deafness, romance, insights into other subcultures, Indians, poverty, friendship versus property rights, personal health, sex-related subjects, ecology, and humor.[22]

Children and young people who are deaf, hearing impaired, blind, or visually impaired should have the opportunity to participate in all the library audiovisual programs and activities together with nondisabled children. Special arrangements, however, may have to be made for these children in order to capitalize on their abilities and compensate for their disabilities. Deaf children can view the visual portion on the screen while an interpreter presents the verbal portion through sign language. Captioned films can be shown to those who are deaf and hearing impaired together with their hearing peers. Blind children can enjoy films and other visually presented programs with sighted children when someone describes the visuals which are projected on the screen. Most visually impaired children will be able to see the projected visuals sufficiently well without assistance if they are permitted to sit close enough to the screen. If rear projection can be used, visually impaired children can get as close to the screen as necessary without blocking the picture.[23]

Modern video technology offers unique possibilities for library programs arranged for deaf and hearing-impaired children and young people, which allow for the inclusion of hearing children at the same time. Since 1976 the Federal Communications Commission has allocated line 21 of the 525-line United States television screen for captioning which can be viewed with special decoders. In 1980 Sears Roebuck began selling decoding devices at a modest cost. The National Captioning Institute now produces about forty hours of "closed-captioned" programming which is aired on the Public Broadcasting Service (PBS), National Broadcasting Company (NBC), or American Broadcasting Company (ABC). Television program listings now indicate which programs are closed-captioned. Librarians can obtain a video recorder and a decoder in order to tape programs for off-air viewing by those who are hearing impaired and their hearing peers, to be used either in the library or else borrowed for home use. Copyright regulations, of course, must be observed. Portable video players and decoders can also be circulated to borrowers for home use.[24] Information about closed-captioned television programs may be obtained from:

National Captioning Institute
5203 Leesburg Pike
Falls Church, VA 22041

Sign language videotapes can also be used with those who are deaf and hearing impaired. Various groups and institutions are now combining sign language with video. D.E.A.F. Media, an organization operated by deaf persons, has produced *Rainbow's End*, a series of children's sign language programs similar to *Sesame Street*. Commercially produced sign language study videotapes, which teach various competency levels of American Sign Language (ASL) and other manual sign language systems, are now available. These programs can be shown to deaf children and young people, their parents, and those who are learning to interpret.[25]

In San Diego, California, Project Video Language has been a successful experiment in the use of television. The project was begun in 1975 in answer to the need for organized visual stimulation in motivating and teaching deaf students. Videotapes were created as an essential part of a comprehensive language instruction curriculum, drawing upon the resources within the San

Diego area. Actors, puppets, clowns, and hearing-impaired students have participated as performers, while the taping locations have included such areas as the San Diego Zoo, Sea World, and the beach. Each skit emphasizes the total communication concept through a spoken narration, signing, and captioning.[26]

Toys and Games

Although it is an established fact that the contemporary library goes beyond the domain of printed materials, most libraries have limited quantities of materials, such as developmental toys and games, for disabled children and young people. While it might be presumed that the provision of toys and games lies in the province of parents, such materials, however, are not generally accessible to parents, either because parents are not aware of educational publishers or because it may not be convenient or even possible for parents to purchase from such companies. This is therefore an opportunity for librarians to build and maintain collections of toys, games, and simulations. These materials can be used profitably with children and young people who are impaired aurally, visually, physically, intellectually, and emotionally. The effectiveness of games and simulations in the education of the deaf, for example, has been noted by Smith.[27] Such materials can help children to develop skills in motor tasks, reading, math, auditory discrimination, visual discrimination, and language development.

The Nebraska Department of Education has established Toybrary, a toy-lending program available to parents of disabled children. Toybrary collections are located at most regional libraries and at some education facilities throughout the state. An illustrated Toybrary catalog contains extensive descriptions of the available toys. The catalog is divided into sections that indicate the learned skills, such as "Toys for Developing Muscle Control," "... That Encourage Exploring," "... That Challenge the Mind," "... That Appeal to the Senses," and a section that offers additional "Resource Materials for Parents." Most Toybrary toys are commercially manufactured, but several catalog entries provide instruction for the homemade variety. Brochures accompany each toy and offer specific game and activity suggestions. Further information can be obtained from:

Special Education Branch
Nebraska Department of Education
301 Centennial Mall South
Lincoln, NE 68509

Public libraries have also developed toy or game collections. In Oak Park, Illinois, the local chapter of the Council for Exceptional Children established a Game Lending Library in cooperation with the Oak Park Public Library. Although the collection is located at one of the branch libraries, materials may be borrowed by any adult residing in surrounding suburbs. To obtain further information, contact:

Children's Services
Oak Park Public Library
834 Lake Street
Oak Park, IL 60301
(312) 383-8200

A list of games that children with physical disabilities can play and enjoy with or without adaptations was prepared by Katherine Bissell Croke and Betty Jacinto Fairchild and titled, *Let's Play Games*. It is available from the National Easter Seal Society, Department WD, 2923 West Ogden Avenue, Chicago, IL 60612. Write first in order to get the current price.

Toys and games in a library provide opportunities for both parents and children. Parents can check out toys and manipulative equipment which will be useful in the therapy of their disabled children, while the children can also use the toys and games in the library. If the children are in a school library setting, they might use the toys in free-time play, or as extra reinforcement for class work, or as reward time for good behavior.[28]

Toys should be available in the library because they can be used for the educational and therapeutic needs of children as well as for enjoyment and pleasure. They can help children to develop imagination, motor skills, and social skills. The toys should be of good quality and which parents would be least likely to purchase themselves. Shirley Johnson has suggested six categories of toys: balls, blocks, colors, noisemakers, shapes, and wheels. She also suggested that toys can be combined with an activity card which gives ideas on how the toy might be used to help a child develop coordination or some other skills.[29] Fay McClanahan, however, has categorized toys into eight groups:

1. Puzzles—sturdy wooden puzzles, including knob puzzles

2. Building—wooden and rubber blocks, Tinkertoys,® Lincoln Logs,® assorted easy and difficult construction sets

3. Creative Play—puppets, flannelboards and cutouts, art materials

4. Games—any and all

5. Language—Viewmasters,® chalkboards, telephones, books

6. Manipulatives—pegboards, lacing beads and cubes, stacking and nesting toys

7. Music—tambourines, bells, cymbals, etc.; records

8. Toys—Nerf® balls, tactile balls, sandbox toys[30]

McClanahan also recommended an organization system for the toys:

1. Determine an abbreviation for each category, such as: T for toys, G for games, P for puzzles, CP for creative play

2. Give each group a color code

3. Give each toy its own accession number

4. Mark the accession number on each piece of the toy, game, or puzzle

5. Store the toys in clear plastic boxes or zip-lock bags

6. Label each toy with a color coded self-adhesive label on which is the name of the toy or game, the number of parts, and the toy's accession number code

7. Store the toys in a cupboard in the library where they can be easily accessed by students, teachers, and parents

8. Shelve the toys in the cupboard according to categories.[31]

In order to keep the toy library functioning properly, it is necessary to establish strong circulation policies and a good record-keeping system, since toys or parts of the toy can be damaged or lost. In McClanahan's library a contract was developed which had to be signed by each parent, the therapist, the teacher, and the student when the first withdrawal from the toy library was made. The contract included time limitations and check-out and check-in procedures indicating that the user was responsible for replacement if an item was lost or damaged or parts were missing. Check-out privileges would be suspended until the item was replaced by the user. Contracts were kept in a notebook, together with a check-out sheet for each individual. The user was required to sign each time an item was checked out. Returned items had to be given directly to the librarian, who would check the condition of the material and determine that it was complete. Materials that were intact were returned to the proper shelf. If an item was damaged or a part was missing, the librarian would decide the amount of the parent's reimbursement on the basis of the cost of the entire item, the part lost or damaged, and the work needed to repair or replace the part. This information was kept in the toy library notebook for future reference.[32]

Creative Dramatics

Creative dramatics, improvisational drama, or role playing enable children to act out situations without any formal or strict guidelines. They are able to express their own feelings and at the same time work cooperatively with others. The emphasis is on participation rather than a finished product. The activities could also be videotaped so the participants can view them later. Various creative drama activities are possible:

1. Warm-up games and exercises include listening for sounds, looking around and listing everything that is seen, studying what a partner is wearing, touching objects and naming the feeling, feeling unseen objects and identifying them, identifying sounds, using the whole body and pretending to be someone or something, and using only fingers and hands and pretending something.

2. Pantomime involves all participants simultaneously, without using words, and is especially suitable for children and young people who are withdrawn or speech impaired.

3. Orff-Schulwerk is a process that has been used successfully with mentally impaired teenagers and adults in a variety of settings. The process begins with an idea and expands on it through improvisation, selectivity, fulfillment, and closure.

4. Acting out a story read by a leader, especially a story with a lot of action, is a nonthreatening activity and a great deal of fun.

5. Role playing is similar to improvisation, and participants are able to select the situations, occupations, and people they wish to characterize.[33]

Other Programs

Librarians can arrange many other types of programs which will be beneficial and enjoyable to disabled children and young people and stimulate their experience. Among these programs are the following:

— Programs in which models, puzzles, toys, and games (educational and recreational) are used

— Puppet programs[34]

— Music programs, such as sing-alongs and rhythm bands

— Arts and crafts programs

— Hobby clubs

— Special holiday events

— Pet programs

— Magic shows

— Dial-a-story programs for the homebound

— Talent shows

— Tongue-twister contests

— Family night programs

— Family reading groups

— Dancing or pantomime programs (especially helpful for nonverbal communication with deaf and hearing impaired children)

A joint program can be arranged by school and public librarians in which disabled children and young people are taken on a field trip to the library. The public librarian can present a brief program about the library and take the children on a tour of the facility. The librarian can show the location of various materials and demonstrate how to ask for and use equipment. Library cards can be issued to the children at the end of the visit, and the librarian can help them select something to borrow.

A party at the public library during the summer can provide an enjoyable experience for children in meeting the librarians who serve them and learning more about their library. The party can include a program of live entertainment, a puppet show, or any other suitable type of program. The event can conclude with a tour of the library and refreshments.[35]

Very Special Arts Festivals have been growing in popularity and can be sponsored either by a school library or a public library or by both. Such festivals give disabled children and young people an opportunity for involvement in the arts and help to increase their learning, self-esteem, and feelings of accomplishment. Entries might include film and media productions; live vocal and instrumental music; dance, drama, puppets, and readings; painting, drawing, sculpture, and crafts; and other presentations, such as workshops, demonstrations, and exhibits.[36]

Information about Very Special Arts Festivals can be obtained from the following:

The National Committee—Arts for the Handicapped
1825 Connecticut Avenue, NW
Suite 418
Washington, DC 20009

Alan Short Center
521 East Acacia Street
Stockton, CA 95202

Gene Maillard
New York State Department of Education
Albany, NY 12234

Jim Blanchard
Clover Park Schools
5214 Steilacom Boulevard
Lakewood Center, WA 98499

NOTES

[1]American Library Association, Association for Library Service to Children, Library Service to Children with Special Needs Committee, *Programming for Children with Special Needs* (Chicago: American Library Association, 1981).

[2]Elizabeth Johnson and Thelma Merriweather, "Blind Children Learn to Relate," *American Libraries* 1 (February 1970): 168-69.

[3]Ibid., p. 169.

[4]National Library Service for the Blind and Physically Handicapped, *Reaching People: A Manual on Public Education for Libraries Serving Blind and Physically Handicapped Individuals* (Washington, DC: Library of Congress, 1980).

[5]Adapted from Elizabeth J. Pieper, "Preparing Children for a Handicapped Classmate," *Instructor* 84 (August 1974): 128-29; and Peggy H. Glazzard, "Simulation of Handicaps as a Teaching Strategy for Preservice and Inservice Training," *Teaching Exceptional Children* 11 (Spring 1979): 101-104.

[6]Elwyn Institute, "Using the Library to Enhance Awareness of Life's Realities in Handicapped Children Residing in an Institution" (Harrisburg: Pennsylvania State Library, 1978). (ED 167 140).

[7]Candace Catlin Hall and Ann Yarmal, "Libraries and P.L. 94-142; Awareness Planning Makes a Difference," *Top of the News* 35 (Fall 1978): 67-73.

[8]Diane Johnson, "Handicapped Awareness Day," *Library Journal* 105 (February 1, 1980): 360.

[9]Adapted from Jean D. Brown, "Storytelling and the Blind Child," *The New Outlook* 66 (December 1972): 356-60, reprinted in *The Special Child in the Library*, ed. Barbara Holland Baskin and Karen H. Harris (Chicago: American Library Association, 1976), pp. 109-112; Jane Biehl, "Storyhours for the Deaf," *Ohio Media Spectrum* 30 (January 1978): 43-46; Hilda K. Limper, "Serving Mentally Retarded Children in Our Libraries," *Catholic Library World* 45 (April 1974): 423-25, reprinted in *Library Services to the Blind and Physically Handicapped*, ed. Maryalls G. Strom (Metuchen, NJ: Scarecrow Press, 1977), pp. 91-95; and Coy Kate Hunsucker, "Public Library Service to Blind and Physically Handicapped Children," *Health and Rehabilitative Library Services Division Journal* 2 (Fall 1976): 3-5.

[10]Adapted largely from Patrick Huston, "Storytelling," *The Volta Review* 74 (February 1972): 200-204, reprinted in *The Special Child in the Library*, ed. Barbara Holland Baskin and Karen H. Harris (Chicago: American Library Association, 1976), pp. 112-14.

[11]Barbara H. Baskin and Karen H. Harris, "Storytelling for the Young Mentally Retarded Child," in *The Special Child in the Library*, ed. Barbara Holland Baskin and Karen H. Harris (Chicago: American Library Association, 1976), p. 115.

[12]Mary Jane Metcalf, "Helping Hearing Impaired Students," *School Library Journal* 25 (January 1979): 28, reprinted in *Meeting the Needs of the Handicapped: A Resource for Teachers and Librarians*, ed. Carol H. Thomas and James L. Thomas (Phoenix: Oryx Press, 1980), pp. 197-203.

[13]Karen H. Harris, "Selecting Library Materials for Exceptional Children," *School Media Quarterly* 8 (Fall 1979): 24; and Hunsucker, "Public Library Service to Blind and Physically Handicapped Children," p. 5.

[14]Brown, "Storytelling and the Blind Child," p. 357.

[15]Baskin and Harris, "Storytelling for the Young Mentally Retarded Child," pp. 114-17.

[16]Ruth A. Velleman, *Serving Physically Disabled People: An Information Handbook for All Libraries* (New York: R. R. Bowker, 1979), p. 148.

[17]Bill Stark, " 'Meanwhile ...': A Look at Comic Books at Illinois School for the Deaf," *American Annals of the Deaf* 121 (October 1976): 470-77, reprinted in *Meeting the Needs of the Handicapped: A Resource for Teachers and Librarians*, ed. Carol H. Thomas and James L. Thomas (Phoenix: Oryx Press, 1980), pp. 208-213.

[18]Richard J. McKay, Linda Schwartz, and Kathy Willis, "The Instructional Media Center's Function in Programs for Special Needs of Children at the Middle School Level," *International Journal of Instructional Media* 4 (No. 1, 1976-1977): 2.

[19]Sonya Abbye, "The Learning-Disabled Child ... Films for Social, Emotional, Language and Sensory Needs," *Film Library Quarterly* 9 (No. 3, 1976): 37, reprinted in *Meeting the Needs of the Handicapped: A Resource for Teachers and Librarians*, ed. Carol H. Thomas and James L. Thomas (Phoenix: Oryx Press, 1980), pp. 128-35.

[20]Ibid., pp. 37-43.

[21]Salvatore J. Parlato, Jr., "Films without Words: Benefits and Caveats," *International Development Review* 17 (Winter 1975): 34.

[22]Salvatore J. Parlato, Jr., "Using Non-Verbal Films with the Deaf and Language-Impaired," *Sightlines* 10 (Winter 1976/77): 10-11, reprinted in *Meeting the Needs of the Handicapped: A Resource for Teachers and Librarians*, ed. Carol H. Thomas and James L. Thomas (Phoenix: Oryx Press, 1980), pp. 223-27; and Salvatore J. Parlato, Jr., "Captioned and Nonverbal Films for the Hearing-Impaired," *Library Trends* 27 (Summer 1978): 61-62. See also Salvatore J. Parlato, Jr., *Films—Too Good for Words; A Directory of Nonnarrated 16mm Films* (New York: R. R. Bowker, 1973).

[23]John F. Henne, "Serving Visually Handicapped Children," *School Library Journal* 25 (December 1978): 364, reprinted in *Meeting the Needs of the Handicapped: A Resource for Teachers and Librarians*, ed. Carol H. Thomas and James L. Thomas (Phoenix: Oryx Press, 1980), pp. 234-37.

[24]Roberto Esteves, "Video Opens Libraries to the Deaf," *American Libraries* 13 (January 1982): 36.

[25]Ibid.

[26]Max Kreis, "Project Video Language: A Successful Experiment," *American Annals of the Deaf* 124 (September 1979): 542-48.

[27]Harry Smith, "Games and Simulation Studies for the Deaf," *American Annals of the Deaf* 124 (September 1979): 611-15.

[28]Fay D. McClanahan, "Toys for Learning," in *The Value of Toys in Institutional Libraries* (Pierre: South Dakota State Library, 1980), p. 15.

[29]Shirley A. Johnson, "A Toy Library for Developmentally Disabled Children," *Teaching Exceptional Children* 11 (Fall 1978): 27, reprinted in *Meeting the Needs of the Handicapped: A Resource for Teachers and Librarians*, ed. Carol H. Thomas and James L. Thomas (Phoenix: Oryx Press, 1980), pp. 66-72.

[30]McClanahan, "Toys for Learning," p. 17.

[31]Ibid., pp. 17-18.

[32]Ibid., pp. 18-19.

[33]American Alliance for Health, Physical Education, Recreation, and Dance, "Creative Dramatics," *Practical Pointers* 1 (September 1977): 1-9, reprinted in *Meeting the Needs of the Handicapped: A Resource for Teachers and Librarians*, ed. Carol H. Thomas and James L. Thomas (Phoenix: Oryx Press, 1980), pp. 73-80. See also J. Paul Marcoux, "Helping Emotionally Disturbed Children through Creative Dramatics," *Communication Education* 25 (March 1976): 174-77, reprinted in *Meeting the Needs of the Handicapped: A Resource for Teachers and Librarians*, ed. Carol H. Thomas and James L. Thomas (Phoenix: Oryx Press, 1980), pp. 164-68.

[34]For a discussion of the use of puppets and the involvement of multiply handicapped children, see Bette Claire Uldrich, "The Little Red Hen," *Ohio Media Spectrum* 30 (January 1978): 54-56.

[35]Hunsucker, "Public Library Service to Blind and Physically Handicapped Children," p. 5.

[36]E. C. Maillard, M. Barkin, and E. Brathwaite, "A Very Special Arts Festival," *Instructor* 86 (March 1977): 134-38. See also Michael Irwin, "Media, the Arts, and the Handicapped," *Audiovisual Instruction* 24 (November 1979): 33-36.

8 _____Locating Materials

"Knowledge is of two kinds:
we know a subject ourselves,
or we know where we can
find information about it."
— James Boswell
Life of Dr. Johnson

INTRODUCTION

Materials of all kinds are a librarian's stock-in-trade. They are necessary to help disabled children and young people achieve their basic right to education, to satisfy the informational and recreational needs and interests of each person according to individual abilities and learning styles, and to provide appropriate library services and offer beneficial programs.

Library and information services for disabled children and young people have been influenced by a tremendous growth in the number and complexity of materials now available. Not only has there been an abundant production of general materials that are useful with nondisabled and disabled children and young people, but there has also been a marked increase in specialized materials prepared specifically with disabled persons in mind. These general and specialized materials can assist in meeting the informational and recreational needs and interests of disabled children and young people.

Through education in library school and experience on the job, librarians are knowledgeable in regard to the standard selection tools for locating materials. They may not yet be acquainted, however, with the abundant specialized sources which now exist for obtaining information about suitable materials for those who are disabled physically, cognitively, or emotionally. Because of the recency of these sources, most librarians have not become familiar with them through formal course work in library schools. These sources of information about materials for disabled persons take a variety of forms. It is the purpose of this chapter to familiarize the reader with some of the 1) general lists of materials, 2) retrieval systems, 3) other sources of information, and 4) specialized bibliographies and mediagraphies.

GENERAL LISTS OF MATERIALS

Before searching for new materials to purchase, the librarian should consider the materials which are already in the collection of the library or media center. Many of these materials can be used with and by disabled children and young people, even though they may have been acquired originally with nondisabled persons in mind. Disabled children and young people do not always need new and highly specialized materials nor modified versions of materials used by nondisabled children. In many instances, those who are disabled can utilize regular materials,[1] and standard selection tools can be used for locating such materials and for reading evaluative reviews. For example, the following standard selection tools can be examined for locating general materials which disabled children and young people can use, as well as for locating some materials about disabilities and disabled persons:

Children's Catalog
Junior High School Library Catalog
Senior High School Library Catalog
National Council of Teachers of English publications
  Adventuring with Books (for pre-kindergarten through grade eight)
  Your Reading (for junior high students)
  Books for You (for senior high students)
  High Interest-Easy Reading for Junior and Senior High School Students
Elementary School Library Collection
Core Media Collection for Elementary Schools
Core Media Collection for Secondary Schools
Free and Inexpensive Materials for Preschool and Early Childhood
Reading Ladders for Human Relations
Good Reading for Poor Readers, by George Spache
Gateways to Readable Books: An Annotated Graded List of Books in Many
  Fields for Adolescents Who Are Reluctant to Read or Find Reading
  Difficult
Periodicals for School Media Programs
Start Early for an Early Start: You and the Young Child

Frequently, other colleagues — librarians in school and/or public libraries, special education teachers, or regular classroom teachers — can supply information about materials which they have used and which have been beneficial to disabled children and young people. Recent research has indicated that teachers, for example, value person-to-person contact the most as a way in which to obtain information about existing materials.[2]

Any search for materials, either for individuals or for groups or for the general library collection, is a painstaking endeavor. This is also true in locating appropriate materials for disabled children and young people. Therefore, a number of cautions should be regarded in seeking out and using any list of materials, such as those described in this chapter. For instance, a list may be out of date in comparison with more recent listings, or it may have been expanded and superseded. Many of the items in a bibliography or mediagraphy may not be usable, either because the materials are inappropriate for the intended purpose or because they are no longer available for purchase. A large number of lists contain only bibliographic citations, without any evaluative comments or recommendation, and frequently also without a descriptive annotation.

In addition to standard selection tools and person-to-person contact, it is also advisable to be aware of specialized bibliographic sources and to use them wisely and knowledgeably as circumstances warrant because different disability conditions also require different and special types of materials, both in content and format.[3] In the recent past, the number of specialized bibliographic tools for locating and selecting materials for disabled persons has burgeoned. A major forward thrust came in 1978 with the publication of a number of indexes by the National Information Center for Special Education Materials (NICSEM).

National Information Center for
Special Education Materials (NICSEM)

In Public Law 91-61, the United States Congress in 1969 authorized the establishment of the National Center on Educational Media and Materials for the Handicapped (NCEMMH) at Ohio State University.[4] Among other services and activities, NCEMMH began in 1972 to develop and generate the National Instructional Materials Information System (NIMIS), a national computer-based information retrieval system specifically designed to provide assistance in locating information about instructional materials used in the education of disabled children and young people. During the time of the existence of NCEMMH, the NIMIS data base grew to nearly 36,000 child-use, nonprint instructional materials. On October 1, 1977, the Bureau of Education for the Handicapped, U.S. Office of Education, contracted with the University of Southern California to continue the development of a national, computer-based, prescriptive information system for special education materials; and the National Information Center for Special Education Materials (NICSEM) was established to publish the NIMIS data base in printed form and to continue its development.

NICSEM is the only national system charged with the task of gathering information on learner, assessment, training, and parent materials for disabled persons, organizing that information in a structure useful to special education and librarians, and making it conveniently available in a variety of formats. The NICSEM system permits retrieval of materials based upon the instructional goal and the discrete learner skill or content area targeted by an Individualized Education Program (IEP). The system is therefore prescriptive because it enables educators to select materials in accordance with the learner's IEP.

The NICSEM system consists of two subsystems: 1) the data base subsystem which stores and retrieves bibliographic, thesaurus, and source information; and 2) the product generation subsystem which selects appropriate entries based upon specified criteria and formats. The data base subsystem consists of three interrelated data bases. The *bibliographic data base* contains information on instructional and parent/professional materials designed to enhance the education of disabled learners. The *thesaurus data base* contains the vocabulary used to index and access materials in the bibliographic file and organizes these terms in hierarchical, alphabetical, and permuted formats. The file also contains cross-references and clarifying definitions of terminology used. The *source data base* contains information on the location of publishers, producers, and distributors of materials in the bibliographic file. The three data bases are interactive in that both the source and thesaurus files serve as check-points for new bibliographic input in a step that ensures the validity of source and thesaurus codes.

Librarians and educators will most frequently use the bibliographic file which offers a flexible structure for indexing and accessing materials. The system permits the individualized matching of materials with learner style, level, and objective. Specific information on the physical format of a material and the individual characteristics of the intended learner are provided for each material entered. Materials can thus be retrieved on the basis of any combination of these variables. Specific information provided in the entries includes: 1) title, 2) media, 3) series reference, 4) author/editor/production credit, 5) publisher/producer, 6) distributor, 7) copyright/release/production year, 8) cost/cost units/cost year, 9) Library of Congress/ISBN numbers, 10) physical description (including adapted format), 11) thesaurus terms, 12) academic/reading/interest levels, 13) exceptionality codes, 14) presentation/response mode codes, 15) descriptive statement, 16) table of contents, and 17) titles within series.

The product generation subsystem provides the capability of reproducing selected segments of the three data bases in a wide variety of product formats. Included is the capability of producing print indexes from one or a combination of the data bases, machine-readable tapes for establishment of on-line search services or stand-alone versions of the data base, batch searches of the bibliographic data base, and custom catalogs.

Initially, in the latter half of 1978, NICSEM published the total NIMIS data base of 36,000 abstracts under the title *Master Catalog of NIMIS/NICSEM Special Education Information Volumes I and II.* Four additional indexes, divided according to the type of disability, were also published as subsets of the information contained in the *Master Catalog.* Subsequently, other volumes, as indicated below, were produced, and the entire series now provides an extensive bibliographic guide to information on materials for all kinds of disabled persons.

The current edition of the *Master Catalog* is published under the title *NICSEM Master Index to Special Education Materials* and contains 40,000 entries which constitute the original NIMIS data base and the materials which have been added since NICSEM was established. The *Master Index* is divided into five major sections: 1) Subject Heading Outline, 2) Index to Major Category Headings, 3) Subject Section, 4) Alphabetical Title Section, and 5) Source Directory. The Alphabetical Title Section constitutes the major portion of the index and includes a descriptive nonevaluative abstract of each item.

At the present time, NICSEM has produced six additional volumes:

NICSEM Special Education Thesaurus

Contains over 2,500 terms structured in a six-level hierarchy corresponding to instructional objectives commonly found in the Individualized Education Programs of disabled children and young people. Term categories cover learner characteristics (disabling conditions), motor skills, independent living skills, communication skills, cognitive skills, mathematics, curriculum content areas, personal and social development, career education, legislation, learner evaluation, learner programming, learner instruction, and special education administration

Special Education Index to Assessment Materials

Contains 1) information on assessment instruments appropriate for different age levels and exceptionalities, and 2) information about professional materials dealing with the assessment of disabled individuals

Special Education Index to In-Service Training Materials
Contains descriptions of approximately 500 materials useful to professional administrators, agencies, and organizations in planning and conducting in-service training on such topics as disabling conditions, mainstreaming, learner instruction, and training procedures

Special Education Index to Parent Materials
Contains information on approximately 2,500 materials usable by parents of disabled children and young people, or by professionals who work with parents of those who are disabled. Covers such areas as home instruction, parents' rights, due process procedures, parent effectiveness, and child development

Special Education Index to Learner Materials
Contains information on 10,000 materials designed or selected for use with disabled learners

NICSEM Source Directory
Contains the names and addresses of the publishers, producers, and distributors of the materials indexed on the NICSEM data base

In addition to the above volumes, NICSEM has also published a number of mini-indexes to special education materials. These are:

Family Life and Sex Education
Contains information on such topics as sex education, premarital counseling, marriage, family planning, and child care

Functional Communication Skills
Includes information on materials useful in teaching functional reading and writing skills. Covers such topics as reading labels, signs, and menus; using a newspaper; filling out forms; and writing letters and taking messages

High Interest, Controlled Vocabulary Supplementary Reading Materials for Adolescents and Young Adults
Includes titles of adapted classics, adventure stories, animal stories, biographies, ethnic stories, historical stories, humor, science fiction, and stories about friendship or contemporary problems

Independent Living Skills for Moderately and Severely Handicapped Students
Includes materials about feeding and eating, sleep behaviors, toilet training, personal care, travel and mobility, functional communication, homemaking, health care and safety, consumer skills, personal financial management, leisure activities, and civic responsibilities

Personal and Social Development for Moderately and Severely Handicapped Students
Contains information about materials dealing with the personal, affective, and social development of moderately, severely, and multiply handicapped students. Features materials covering self-concept, emotions and feelings, attitudes, socially appropriate behavior, and interpersonal relations

Two volumes have been produced by NICSEM using the National Information Center for Educational Media (NICEM) data base:

NICEM Index to Nonprint Special Education Materials—Multimedia (Learner Volume)
   Contains 33,558 titles that are appropriate for use with disabled learners. Title selection was based on appropriate media formats (silent films, filmstrips with captions or scripts, silent motion cartridges, records and tapes) and grade levels (preschool, kindergarten, intermediate, and junior high school)

NICEM Index to Nonprint Special Education Materials—Multimedia (Professional Volume)
   Contains 5,192 titles relevant to the interests and needs of parents, teachers, and other persons working with disabled children and young people

Both of these volumes highlight only nonprint materials that are suitable for direct use with disabled children and young people (in the *Learner Volume*) or that were selected for use by parents, teachers, and other professionals (in the *Professional Volume*).

The NICEM/NICSEM publications include information on all media formats: audiorecordings, talking books, motion pictures, filmstrips, videorecordings, slides, materials with special requirements, display materials, manipulative materials, three-dimensional materials, transparencies, kits, and print materials. Entries in the indexes provide information on: 1) title, 2) author, 3) material format, 4) publisher/producer/distributor, 5) cost, 6) contents, 7) academic level, 8) reading level, 9) interest level, 10) specialized formats (i.e., braille, large print, captions, talking books), 11) thesaurus term assignments, and 12) exceptionality codes.

Since the NICSEM publications are expensive, especially the *Master Index*, few libraries will be able to afford to purchase all of them, and some libraries may not have the funds to purchase any of them. Careful selection should be made in obtaining those volumes which will be the most helpful in a particular library. Librarians should ascertain where the indexes are available—in large public libraries, school district special education offices, state departments, and universities—so they may be able to refer to them whenever necessary.

Additional information about the NICSEM publications can be obtained by calling or writing:

NICSEM
University of Southern California
University Park
Los Angeles, CA 90007
(800) 421-8711

RETRIEVAL SYSTEMS

Modern technology is aiding the cause of searching for materials for disabled persons. Librarians whose library; school, or district has a computer installation can access a number of data banks by means of cathode ray tube or hardcopy terminals for immediate on-line computer searches. If computer terminals are not locally available, searches may be requested from various service bureaus.

NIMIS and NICEM

The NIMIS and NICEM data banks are available for on-line computer searches, either through NICSEM at the address mentioned above or through two other service bureaus:

Lockheed Information Systems
3251 Hanover Street
Palo Alto, CA 94302
(800) 982-5838

Bibliographic Retrieval Service
Corporation Park, Building 702
Scotia, NY 12302
(518) 374-5011

If desired, it is also possible to purchase the NIMIS data tapes for 24-hour use of this data base.

Educational Resources Information Center (ERIC)

Librarians and other educators are readily familiar with the Educational Resources Information Center (ERIC) and its services in providing abstracts from an extensive data bank of educational materials. The complete text of a citation can be read either in microfiche or hardcopy. The ERIC system can be searched either manually or by computer by using the appropriate descriptors and arranging a Boolean search technique. Through this system, it is possible to retrieve information about ERIC documents through ED numbers and about ERIC journals through EJ numbers. In the area of materials for those who are disabled, many bibliographies can be retrieved through the ERIC system.

ERIC computer searches are available from many universities, research centers, commercial organizations, state departments of education, and educational information centers, as well as from some of the ERIC Clearinghouses, including the Clearinghouse on Handicapped and Gifted Children. A list of the ERIC data base search services may be obtained from:

User Services Coordinator
ERIC Processing and Reference Facility
4833 Rugby Avenue, Suite 303
Bethesda, MD 20014
(301) 656-9723

Council for Exceptional Children (CEC)

The Council for Exceptional Children (CEC), which is also the location of the ERIC Clearinghouse on Handicapped and Gifted Children, acquires selected professional materials related to or concerned with the education of handicapped and gifted children and young people. It does not, however, include instructional materials for use by children.[5] CEC offers custom computer searches as a quick and easy access to the *Exceptional Child Education Resources* (ECER) data base (formerly *Exceptional Child Education Abstracts*) and/or the ERIC data base. It is possible, therefore, to access both the ERIC and the ECER data banks by contacting the CEC. Bibliographic Retrieval Service, mentioned above, can also supply printouts from the ERIC and ECER systems.

CEC provides a computer printout which contains citations that include document identification or order number (ED, EJ, or EC), title, author, publication date, source or publisher, number of pages, and an abstract averaging 200 words. Four basic types of references may appear in the search: 1) journal articles, 2) documents available from the ERIC system, 3) commercially published materials, and 4) doctoral dissertations. CEC Information Services/ERIC Clearinghouse on Handicapped and Gifted Children, however, does not provide copies of any of the documents or articles in the search except those published by CEC. Searches may be requested by calling CEC toll free or by writing to the following address:

The Council for Exceptional Children
Information Services
1920 Association Drive
Reston, VA 22091
(800) 336-3728

Besides providing computer searches, CEC also publishes *Exceptional Child Education Resources* (ECER), a quarterly print presentation of all citations in the ECER data base. Computer Search Reprints, printouts of searches that have already been completed, are also available. These topical bibliographies on specific areas of concern contain selected abstracts of significant references taken from recent volumes of ECER. Selection can be made from significant categories which include current issues and topics on exceptional child education. Each bibliography averages fifty to one hundred citations and includes publication date, author, title, source, availability, descriptors, and an abstract or descriptive summary. A current list of the available reprints may be received from CEC.

State Retrieval Systems

Many state departments of education have established their own information retrieval system. Such is the case in Illinois, for example, with the Illinois Resource and Dissemination Network (IRDN). IRDN has computer access to approximately sixty data bases of Lockheed's Dialog Information System. Retrieval is possible from the data files of ERIC, NIMIS, ECER, NICEM, and others. IRDN provides a search printout of document and journal article abstracts and will copy a reasonable quantity of documents and articles upon request. For more information about IRDN, Illinois school library media professionals should contact:

Illinois Resource and Dissemination Network (IRDN)
Illinois State Board of Education
100 North First Street
Springfield, IL 62777

Residents of other states should contact state education departments to inquire about similar services.

Educational Patterns, Inc.

The Educational Patterns, Inc. (EPI) Retrieval System[6] is a card sorting process. Each card contains detailed information on a specific piece of instructional material. Material from twenty-four subject areas can be coded into the system and accessed by format, grade level, interest level, types, stimulus, response, and interaction. The unique aspect of this system is that it is custom designed, based on a library's inventory of its own materials. Consequently, materials are readily available in the local collection, and the system can be updated on a continual basis. It is quick to use and can be learned in approximately one hour. The system includes 1) an ordering component of over 2,000 cards representing approximately 8,000-10,000 materials, 2) a prescriptive component of 800 cards designed specifically for the local institution based on that institution's collection, and 3) a teacher-made component of over 400 cards representing creative teacher-designed ideas in vocabulary development, readiness, phonics, and perceptual skills. The high cost of the entire system (almost $4,000) may make it too expensive for an individual library or school building; and, if purchased for wider use at the system or district level, librarians and teachers may not want to travel to a central location to select appropriate materials. A less expensive Do-It-Yourself Retrieval System is also available at about $100 for small libraries or institutions which need a coding system for prescriptive purposes. EPI also provides an update service and duplicate retrieval systems. Information on this retrieval system is available from:

Educational Patterns, Inc.
63-110 Woodhaven Boulevard
Rego Park, NY 11374
(212) 894-7217

System FORE

System FORE (Fundamentals, Operations, Resources, Environment)[7] is an inexpensive retrieval system which correlates materials to specific learning objectives in three skill areas: language, reading, and mathematics. This system can assist in developing and implementing Individualized Education Programs because it helps in assessing a student's needs and abilities and identifies available materials to be prescribed for that student. Materials to match each objective are selected from a list of over 8,000 references. Each reference is keyed to learning center use, type of material, and the sensory modalities required of the student. Just about any materials can be coded into the system, which is flexible and can be changed as necessary. Updates can be performed personally and easily. However, it takes a lot of time to code all available materials. Users also need to be oriented to the system through workshops and in-service training, and it requires much space for setting up and storing. Available books include *System FORE Handbook, FORE Mathematics, FORE Language, FORE Reading*, and *FORE Secondary*, which is a continuation of the System FORE Language, Reading, and Mathematics programs through the next five years of skills development. Contact the following address for more information:

FOREWORKS
7112 Teesdale Avenue
North Hollywood, CA 91605
(213) 982-0467

Other retrieval systems, ranging from inexpensive to expensive are also available. Information about them is included in *Guide to Finding Appropriate Instructional Materials: Existing Retrieval Systems*, by McCormack, Doyle, and Blieberg, and in *Instructional Materials for Exceptional Children: Selection, Management, and Adaptation*, by Stowitschek, Gable, and Hendrickson.

OTHER SOURCES OF INFORMATION

Numerous agencies and organizations provide informational materials about disabilities and disabled persons. It is not our purpose to list and describe all of them in this chapter. Their names and addresses can be obtained from state libraries, special education offices within school districts, state education departments, and books such as the following: *Meeting the Needs of the Handicapped*, edited by Thomas and Thomas; *Serving Physically Disabled People*, by Velleman; and *Library and Information Services for Handicapped Individuals*, by Kieth C. Wright. The *Directory of National Information Sources on Handicapping Conditions and Related Services* lists 285 national organizations and gives for each an abstract which includes handicapping conditions served, a description of the organization, and information services.[8] The following section discusses only a few organizations which may be especially useful to librarians working with disabled children and young people.

National Library Service for the Blind and Physically Handicapped (NLS)

Through the enactment of the Pratt-Smoot Act of 1931, the U.S. Congress authorized the Library of Congress to produce books for adult blind persons and to distribute these books through regional or local centers. In 1934 the services were expanded to include talking books, and in 1952 the service was extended to children by deleting the word "adult." Music instruction materials were added in 1962. Later, in 1966, the service was again expanded to include not only blind persons but also those who are partially sighted or physically handicapped, both adults and children. More recently, those who are learning disabled became eligible for services.

Formerly called the Library of Congress Division for the Blind and Physically Handicapped, the National Library Service for the Blind and Physically Handicapped (NLS)[9] includes a network of over 160 cooperating libraries—fifty-six regional and more than 100 subregional (local) libraries—in the United States, Puerto Rico, the Virgin Islands, and Guam. In 1979 the Association of Specialized and Cooperative Library Agencies of the American Library Association produced updated standards of service for the NLS network of libraries. It is hoped that additional standards will be formulated in the near future for public libraries, elementary and secondary school libraries, and other types of libraries.[10]

The NLS is one of the foremost suppliers of materials for those who are blind or partially sighted, physically disabled, and who, either temporarily or permanently, are not able to use standard printed materials. The service provides braille publications, large-print materials, talking books on cassette and disc recordings, and the special equipment—cassette recorder or phonograph—to use with the talking books. Materials and equipment are distributed to the regional and subregional libraries and are then sent from the libraries to borrowers and returned to the libraries by postage-free mail.

Currently, the NLS book collection contains over 30,000 titles, including many children's books. Because the NLS philosophy holds that disabled children are entitled to the same range of materials which nondisabled children and young people enjoy, picture books are produced as well as fiction and nonfiction books at different interest and ability levels for children of preschool age through junior high school. Included are picture books that stimulate other senses than vision, such as "scratch and sniff" books and books with special inserts to touch. The picture books cover a broad range of stories, songs, and rhymes as well as presenting the alphabet, counting, and simple information.[11] Textbooks and curriculum materials, however, are not produced or distributed by NLS.

Seventy magazines on disc and in braille are offered by NLS. Users may request free subscriptions to such magazines as *U.S. News, National Geographic, Consumer Reports, Good Housekeeping, Sports Illustrated, Jack and Jill,* and many other popular magazines. Current issues are mailed to readers at the same time the print issues appear or shortly thereafter.

Talking-book machines are designed to play disc-recorded books and magazines at 8rpm and 16rpm. Cassette-book machines are designed for cassettes recorded at 15/16ips and the standard speed of 1⅞ips as well as on two tracks and four tracks. Available accessories for playback equipment include earphones and pillowphones. An auxiliary amplifier for hearing-impaired persons is available on special request.

The music collection consists of scores in braille and large type; textbooks and books about music in braille, large type, and in recorded form; elementary instruction for piano, organ, and guitar on cassette; and other instructional materials in recorded form.[12]

Although NLS materials and equipment are provided primarily for the personal use of qualified children and young people at home, a teacher or school librarian may register an eligible child or young person to use materials and equipment at school. NLS also loans deposit collections and the necessary equipment to institutions that serve ten or more eligible users. Librarians who do not have the required number of eligible readers may request a small set of demonstration materials which can be used to explain the service to potential users.

Catalogs of braille and recorded books are available under the following titles:

"For Younger Readers"
"Cassette Books"
"Talking Books Adult"
"Press Braille Adult"

Subject bibliographies of braille and recorded books are also produced on "Bestsellers," "Freedom," "Health," "Home Management," "I Went to the Animal Fair," "Magazines," "Religion," "Science," "Science Fiction," and "Sports."

Users also receive bimonthly publications, *Talking Book Topics* or *Braille Book Review*, which list the latest books and magazines produced by NLS. A separate publication, *Magazines*, lists selected periodicals available in special media, including magazines produced in a variety of formats: braille, disc, cassette, large type, Moon type, and open reel. In addition, NLS publishes many bibliographies that can be helpful to librarians in selecting materials for disabled children and young people. Examples of recent publications of the NLS are the following:

"Magazines in Special Media"

"Reading, Writing, and Other Communication Aids for Visually and Handicapped Persons"

"Reading Materials in Large Type"

"Building a Library Collection on Blindness and Physical Handicaps; Basic Materials and Resources"

"National Organizations Concerned with Visually and Physically Handicapped Persons"

"Information for Handicapped Travelers"

"Sports and Games for Handicapped Persons"

"Bibles and Other Scripture in Special Media"

"Subject Guide to Spoken Word Recordings"

These free publications and information about the NLS may be obtained from the national headquarters:

The National Library Service for the Blind and Physically Handicapped
Library of Congress
Washington, DC 20542

Librarians can make arrangements for qualified persons to use the services and materials of the NLS by contacting the nearest regional or subregional library in the NLS system. A free directory of all the cooperating libraries is also available from the above address.

NLS is a very valuable service, but it should be remembered that it is primarily a book and magazine mailing service. Other types of materials are not produced, and the printed materials which NLS does produce in other forms represent only a small portion of the publishing output. NLS is therefore not a substitute for local library service in school and public libraries and for the individual attention of librarians to disabled children and young people.

Two additional national agencies supply textbooks and other materials for blind and visually impaired persons. They are the American Printing House for the Blind and Recording for the Blind.

American Printing House for the Blind (APHB)

The American Printing House for the Blind (APHB),[13] founded in 1858, is the oldest public or private nonprofit national agency for the blind in the United States. It is the largest independent publishing house for the blind in the world, devoted solely to producing material for the visually impaired, along with the development and manufacture of tangible aids for their use. Although anyone may purchase their products, certain materials are restricted solely to use by the legally blind. Under the federal quota system, eligible persons are entitled to certain materials free.

APHB publishes braille books in both hardcover and pamphlet bindings, printing approximately fifty million braille pages each year. It also prints and distributes over sixty braille magazines, mostly for other nonprofit agencies for the blind, including *Boy's Life, Current Events, My Weekly Reader, National Geographic, Reader's Digest, General Rehabilitation,* and *Blind Data Processor.* Large-type textbooks are published for visually impaired children and young people below college level who have sufficient vision to read larger-than-average type but cannot read ordinary-size type. Talking books are produced in three forms: rigid long-play phonograph records, flexible throw-away records intended for the use of one person, and special long-play cassettes. The records play at a speed of 8rpm and contain three hours of reading on a 10-inch rigid record, and two hours on a 9-inch flexible record. Cassettes have a playing time of six hours on four tracks and a speed of 15/16ips. APHB produces over eight million Talking Book records a year, comprising full-length books and twenty-nine nationally known magazines such as *Newsweek, Reader's Digest, Atlantic, Harper's, Jack and Jill, Sports Illustrated, Ellery Queen, Farm Journal, American Heritage, Saturday Review, Junior Scholastic, Senior Scholastic,* and *Changing Times.* In addition, APHB also manufactures a large variety of special educational aids for the blind, including braille slates and styluses, braillewriters, special notebook covers and binders, embossed and bold-line writing paper, relief globes and maps, braille atlases, an abacus, arithmetic slates, geometrical forms (solids, planes, and wire outlines), an appliance for illustrating algebraic equations or geometrical problems, embossed and bold-line graph sheets, a large wooden erector set for small children, and other items. Catalogs of the materials in the various formats, a catalog of educational and other aids, and promotional materials are available from the APHB. The catalogs list materials in such categories as textbooks, high-interest/low-vocabulary, fiction, nonfiction, supplementary reading, and music. For information, write to:

American Printing House for the Blind
1839 Frankfort Avenue
P.O. Box 6085
Louisville, KY 40206
(502) 895-2405

The Instructional Materials Reference Center for the Visually Handicapped at the APHB accumulates, evaluates, and disseminates instructional materials related to the education of the visually impaired. The center is national in scope, serving as the National Reference Center for Visually Handicapped, and is a clearing house for educational materials for the visually impaired. Consultative services are available on a limited basis from the APHB staff members. The center maintains a Central Catalog of Volunteer Produced Textbooks, done in braille, large type, and recorded form. When requested, lists of these with their sources and costs are supplied, if known. Production and distribution of manuals and descriptive instructions on the use of special materials, along with a model shop for developing and evaluating aids, are a part of the center's continuing efforts. The center's professional staff provides exhibits, demonstrations, and lectures for professional meetings, teacher-training programs, and school in-service programs, if funds are available. The center also maintains a central registry of educational aids manufactured for the visually impaired and another registry of commercially available items that may be used or adapted for use with the visually impaired. The center's catalog may be purchased, if desired.

Recording for the Blind (RFB)

Recording for the Blind (RFB) is a national, nonprofit, voluntary organization which supplies recorded educational books on a free loan basis to individuals who cannot read standard-print material because of visual, physical, or perceptual disabilities, including persons with properly certified learning disabilities. RFB provides its services directly to qualified individuals who register by submitting an application for service. Schools, agencies, or their representatives are not eligible as borrowers, but librarians should be aware of this source of materials so they can inform disabled children and young people who are qualified.

RFB has a Master Tape Library which contains over 50,000 titles and records new books at the rate of approximately 4,000 each year. When a needed book is not available, RFB will record it for a borrower if the book falls within the educational scope of their program. Books are produced in all major fields of study, including highly specialized technical subjects. RFB records only complete, published, and copyrighted texts but does not produce partial recordings, articles, leaflets, pamphlets, periodicals, magazines, journals, manuscripts, atlases, dictionaries, or other reference materials for the Master Tape Library. Whenever possible, however, a limited amount of such recording will be done for borrowers on a private basis and without commitment to deadlines.

RFB recorded books are provided on 15/16ips, four-track cassettes, each containing four hours of recorded text. The cassettes cannot be played on standard two-track cassette machines. Compatible equipment may be purchased from the American Printing House for the Blind or obtained on free loan by registered borrowers of the National Library Service for the Blind and Physically Handicapped. The NLS equipment must also be used with recorded reading material provided by NLS; otherwise it must be returned to NLS.

A catalog of all RFB titles is available at a charge. A supplement may be obtained free of charge. Requests for the catalog, the supplement, application forms, or other information should be sent to:

Recording for the Blind
215 East 58th Street
New York, NY 10022
(212) 751-0860

American Foundation for the Blind (AFB)

The American Foundation for the Blind (AFB) supplies publications related to the blind and visually impaired, films, posters, aids, and appliances. The M. C. Migel Memorial Library contains over 25,000 items which are available to students and the general public. In addition, AFB publishes two periodicals: *Touch and Go*, a monthly news periodical in braille for deaf-blind persons, and *The New Outlook for the Blind*, a monthly professional journal available in print, braille, and recorded editions. Catalogs and information may be requested from:

American Foundation for the Blind
15 West 16th Street
New York, NY 10011
(212) 924-0420

Choice Magazine Listening (CML)

Choice Magazine Listening (CML) is an audio anthology for those who are blind, visually impaired, or physically disabled. It was created to bring the joy of reading back into the lives of those who are unable to read normal print, and the service is *completely free of charge.* CML selects and records memorable writing from print magazines. Every other month it offers subscribers eight hours of the best articles, fiction, and poetry, chosen from over seventy contemporary periodicals and read by professional voices onto 8rpm phonograph records. Record players with this speed, which are provided free by the National Library Service for the Blind and Physically Handicapped, can be used with CML materials. The recordings include a wide range of unabridged selections from such periodicals as *Smithsonian, Harper's, The New Yorker, Ms., Sports Illustrated, Time, The New Republic, The Wall Street Journal*, and *The New York Times Magazine.* Since the selections are taken from general adult periodicals, the service will be more useful to teenagers rather than elementary school-age children. Special material from other media sources is also made available occasionally. New subscribers are received on a first-come-first-served basis. Subscriptions may be obtained through the regional libraries of the National Library Service or by writing to:

Choice Magazine Listening
P.O. Box 10
Port Washington, NY 11050
(516) 883-8280

Perkins School for the Blind

Perkins School for the Blind, Watertown, Massachusetts 02171, publishes such items as curriculum materials. It also administers the Samuel P. Hayes Research Library, which has the largest collection in the world of print materials on the nonmedical aspects of blindness, and it produces bibliographies on special subjects as well as photocopied bibliographies from its holdings. The Howe Press, part of the Perkins School but now consolidated under the auspices of the National Braille Press in Boston, produces devices and appliances for the blind.

Hadley School for the Blind

The Hadley School for the Blind in Winnetka, Illinois, offers correspondence courses for persons who are visually disabled from fifth-grade through high school, college, vocational, and adult avocational. Discs and tapes are included as a supplement but not as a substitute for braille. Magazines, newspapers, amateur radio, and compressed speech are also used. The school is located at the following address:

Hadley School for the Blind
700 Elm Street
Winnetka, IL 60093
(312) 446-8111

Vision Foundation

For visually impaired persons, the Vision Foundation distributes informational materials in regular print, large print, braille, records and flexible discs, and cassettes, including publications of the National Library Service for the Blind and Physically Handicapped. All materials are free, except for some which have a small cost. There is a handling charge based on the number of items ordered. A copy of the Vision Inventory List, which is also available on cassette tape, may be received by writing:

Vision Foundation
770 Centre Street
Newton, MA 02158
(617) 965-5877
Massachusetts Toll Free Number: (800) 852-3029

National Information Center on Deafness

Established by Gallaudet College, the National Information Center on Deafness serves as a central source of information on deafness for professionals, parents, students, and members of the general public. The center provides specific answers to questions through personal letters, brochures, fact sheets, bibliographies, and, in some cases, a referral to a more appropriate source for an answer. Topics include education, research, demographics, law, technology, barrier-free design, and many others. Address inquiries to:

The National Information Center on Deafness
Gallaudet College
Kendall Green
Washington, DC 20002

Captioned Films for the Deaf (CFD)

Chartered by the U.S. Congress in 1958, Captioned Films for the Deaf (CFD)[14] is a branch of the U.S. Department of Education Bureau of Education for the Handicapped and provides subtitled films to deaf persons free of charge. The subject matter and footage of these films are the same as uncaptioned films. The only difference is that the soundtracks have been slightly altered to synchronize better with the superimposed text. CFD has over 1,000 educational films which are available to schools and programs for the deaf and distributed from sixty regional depositories. Classroom teachers of both deaf and hearing children from public and residential schools participate with librarians and program supervisors in screening, evaluating, selecting, writing captions, and developing study guides. Among the films in the collection are such titles as *Little Engine That Could, Mike Mulligan and His Steamshovel, The Ugly Duckling, Dr. Heidigger's Experiment, Why We Have Elections*, and *John Fitzgerald Kennedy—1917-1963*. The only requirement for the use of these films is that the audience must include a minimum of one deaf student. Applications should be sent to:

Captioned Films for the Deaf
Distribution Center
5034 Wisconsin Avenue, NW
Washington, DC 20016
(202) 363-1308

In addition to the educational films, CFD supplies full-length captioned entertainment films, such as *Sound of Music, Lion in Winter, Bambi, That Darn Cat*, and *Around the World in Eighty Days*. About 1,000 entertainment films are available from only one film depository, located in Indianapolis. Either deaf children or deaf adults may borrow the films as long as there is a minimum audience of six deaf viewers. The entertainment films are restricted to the exclusive enjoyment of deaf viewers because of an agreement with commercial theater exhibitors, designed to protect them from unfair competition. Librarians, however, can act as coordinating agents in programming, scheduling, and screening these film presentations as long as the requirement of the minimum six deaf viewers is met. Information about the films may be obtained from CFD at the above address.

Joyce Media

Joyce Media supplies a variety of materials for deaf persons and about deafness, including sign language books, books about deafness, posters, mini-dictionaries, stickers, cards, stationery, and school supplies. Also available are video specials for cable television, videocassettes for purchase, movies that teach sign language, sign language Bible stories, and sign language practice audiotapes. A catalog may be obtained by writing to:

Joyce Media
8613 Yolanda
P.O. Box 458
Northridge, CA 91328
(213) 885-7181 (Voice or TTY)

Other Sources of Information about Deafness

Several excellent sources supply materials for the deaf, and some of them provide professional materials regarding deaf persons and deafness. Among them are the following:

Alexander Graham Bell Association for the Deaf
3417 Volta Place, NW
Washington, DC 20007
(Oral/Aural Materials)

Association of Specialized and Cooperative Library Agencies
American Library Association
50 East Huron Street
Chicago, IL 60611
(Library Services Materials)

American Speech and Hearing Association
9030 Old Georgetown Road
Washington, DC 20014
(Audiology Materials)

Gallaudet College Bookstore
Gallaudet College
Kendall Green
7th and Florida Avenue, NE
Washington, DC 20002
(General Materials)

John Tracy Clinic
806 West Adams Boulevard
Los Angeles, CA 90007
(Oral/Aural Materials)

National Association of the Deaf
814 Thayer Avenue
Silver Spring, MD 20910
(General Materials)

Registry of Interpreters for the Deaf
P.O. Box 1339
Washington, DC 20013
(Interpreting Directory)

In addition to professional materials, the National Association of the Deaf has books in signed English for children, baby books, and other children's books on sex education and for explaining deafness to hearing children. Gallaudet College also offers some materials for child-use in signed English, pre-primers, and flash cards, and provides films and videotapes to the public.

Video materials by and for deaf persons are distributed by the following sources:

Alexander Graham Bell
Publications
3417 Volta Place, NW
Washington, DC 20007

Gallaudet Media Distribution
Center
Gallaudet College Library
7th and Florida Avenue, NE
Washington, DC 20002

Handicapped Learner
Materials—Special Materials
Project
624 East Walnut Street
Suite 223
Indianapolis, IN 46204

John Tracy Clinic
806 West Adams Boulevard
Los Angeles, CA 90007

Joyce Media
8613 Yolanda
P.O. Box 458
Northridge, CA 91328

National Association of the Deaf
Publishing Division
814 Thayer Avenue
Silver Spring, MD 20910

National Center on Deafness
Instructional Media Center
California State University
18111 Nordhoff Street
Northridge, CA 91330

National Technical Institute for
the Deaf
Media Services
Rochester Institute of
Technology
One Lomb Drive
Rochester, NY 14623

Sign Language Store
9420 Reseda Boulevard
P.O. Box 4440
Northridge, CA 91328

Special Materials Project
814 Thayer Avenue
Silver Spring, MD 20910

T-J Publishers
817 Thayer Avenue, 305-D
Silver Spring, MD 20910

Films in American Sign Language can also be obtained from Joyce Media at the address above.

HANDICAPPED LEARNER MATERIALS—SPECIAL MATERIALS PROJECT (HLM-SMP)

Child-use, teacher-use, and teacher training materials which have been produced as a result of the activity of the Bureau of Education for the Handicapped in the U.S. Department of Education are distributed by the Handicapped Learner Materials—Special Materials Project (HLM-SMP). Now located in Indianapolis, Indiana, this distribution center was formerly headquartered at Indiana University in Bloomington and called the Handicapped Learner Materials Distribution Center and also previously known as the Special Office for Materials Distribution. HLM-SMP has several catalogs of materials. The items in the *Catalog of Instructional Materials for the Handicapped Learner* and the *Catalog of Training Films and Other Media for Special Education* are loaned for a use period of seven calendar days for a small cash-covering usage fee. The *Catalog of Educational Captioned Films for the Deaf* is a list of captioned films on a large variety of subjects which may be borrowed on a free-loan basis. Videotape programs listed in the *Catalog of Video Tape Masters* will be duplicated on an "at-cost" basis according to the length of the tape and the number of copies requested. Information may be obtained from:

Handicapped Learner Materials — Special Materials Project
624 East Walnut Street
Second Floor
Indianapolis, IN 46204
(317) 636-1902 (Office)
(317) 636-1870 (Orders)

INSTRUCTIONAL MEDIA PRODUCTION PROJECT
FOR SEVERELY HANDICAPPED STUDENTS

In October 1980 the Instructional Media Production Project for Severely Handicapped Students[15] began as a continuation of the National Media Materials Center for Severely Handicapped Persons, which ended on September 30, 1980. This project promises to make a contribution to helping librarians select materials for severely disabled children and young people.

The National Media Materials Center for Severely Handicapped Persons, under contract from the Bureau of Education for the Handicapped, conducted Project MORE (Mediated Operational Research for Education). In this project, materials were developed, tested, and produced for teachers, parents, or others to use to teach daily-living skills to severely handicapped people. These materials were distributed by Hubbard, P.O. Box 104, Northbrook, IL 60062. The center was also involved in locating, analyzing, and assessing existing instructional media materials that were designed for training severely disabled persons. Abstracts of the instructional materials that were reviewed were produced in printed form.

The goals of Project MORE and the Instructional Media Production Project are the same, that is, to produce instructional materials for severely disabled children and young people. However, the current project is more limited in scope in two ways: 1) a strong emphasis is placed on producing materials for use *with* and *by* severely disabled students; and 2) two curricular areas are stressed: "age-appropriate response to others" and "job preparation/skills development." This emphasis excludes some of the training packages which were produced by Project MORE for a larger audience and for in-service. The current project is also pursuing a more experimental approach in the designs and formats of the media products. Further information about the project may be obtained from:

Instructional Media Production Project for
  Severely Handicapped Students
George Peabody College of Vanderbilt University
Nashville, TN 37203

NATIONAL REHABILITATION INFORMATION CENTER (NARIC)

Located on the campus of The Catholic University of America, the National Rehabilitation Information Center (NARIC) houses a comprehensive collection of rehabilitation research reports, audiovisual materials, reference books, microfiche, and journals for those interested in the rehabilitation of disabled persons. The collection covers all aspects of the rehabilitation of physically or mentally disabled individuals. Bibliographic information and brief abstracts for each item in the collection are maintained in an on-line computer system which is available for direct access, both nationally and internationally, through standard telecommunication links. NARIC also maintains the ABLEDATA System, a national computerized data bank which contains information about rehabilitation products and a network of information brokers. The system includes more than 10,000 commercially available aids and equipment useful to disabled persons.

NARIC's services are available to anyone but are of particular help to disabled persons and rehabilitation professionals. Duplicate copies of reports are mailed at no charge. If photoduplication is required, there is a nominal fee. Audiovisual materials may be used at the center or obtained for the cost of reproduction. Upon request, the center's computerized data base will be searched for materials on a particular topic, or a search will be made for relevant materials in other commercially available data bases. Publications from the center include:

"The Pathfinder" — a guide to information resources and technology; a newsletter, in both braille and print editions

"NARIC Thesaurus" — a list of descriptors with definitions used in organizing the center's collection

"NARIC Periodical List" — a list of over 200 journal and newsletter titles in the collection

An indexed microfiche set of many research reports in the collection

For further information about NARIC's services, write to:

The National Rehabilitation Information Center
4407 Eighth Street, NE
The Catholic University of America
Washington, DC 20017
(202) 635-5826
(202) 635-5884 (TDD)

CENTER FOR REHABILITATION INFORMATION

Another center which is gathering a multimedia collection for individuals involved in the rehabilitation of persons with physical disabilities is the Center for Rehabilitation Information, established at the Library of the Health Sciences of the University of Illinois. This center has three primary objectives. First, it is creating a comprehensive up-to-date collection of print and nonprint materials dealing with physical disability and rehabilitation. Secondly, it is developing model library instruction materials created with the disabled user in mind. Thirdly, the center conducts educational workshops for library personnel throughout Illinois. The services of the center are available to all who work with the physically disabled in the rehabilitation field and also to those who are disabled. Within its scope are all physical disabilities, including blindness and visual impairment, deafness and hearing impairment, speech disorders, orthopedic and neurological disorders, and disabling conditions which result from cancer and stroke. Disabilities which are not included are mental illness, mental retardation, alcoholism, and aging. Some of the subject areas which the center has identified as important are barrier-free design, independent living, legal issues, mechanical aids and equipment, medical treatments, physical rehabilitation, psychological adjustment, and societal attitudes. Further information can be obtained by writing to:

Center for Rehabilitation Information
Library of the Health Sciences
102 Medical Sciences Building
University of Illinois
Urbana, IL 61801
(217) 333-0183

EDUCATIONAL PRODUCTS INFORMATION EXCHANGE (EPIE)

EPIE gathers and disseminates analytical and descriptive information about instructional materials, systems, and equipment. The candid and objective analyses of materials and equipment assist in making informed decisions about instructional materials and equipment. Several types of membership and subscriber arrangement are offered: 1) a comprehensive member receives eight EPIE Reports a year and thirty-six EPIEgram newsletters; 2) a materials member receives four reports and eighteen materials newsletters; 3) an equipment member receives four equipment reports and eighteen equipment newsletters; 4) a comprehensive subscriber receives thirty-six EPIEgrams; 5) an EPIE material subscriber receives eighteen materials newsletters; and 6) an EPIE equipment subscriber receives eighteen equipment newsletters. A list of publications is available on request. Information about membership and subscription costs may be obtained from:

EPIE Institute
P.O. Box 620
Stony Brook, NY 11790
(516) 751-1457

PERIODICALS

Many periodicals publish articles which give information about materials for disabled children and young people, bibliographies and mediagraphies of useful materials, general articles about disabilities, and articles specifically about library services for disabled children and young people. Regular reading of at least some of these journals is a good way for a librarian to keep up to date in this area. Among the periodicals are the following:

School Library Journal
School Library Media Quarterly
   (formerly *School Media*
   Quarterly)
Top of the News
Instructional Innovator (former-
   ly *Audiovisual Instruction*)
Booklist
The Exceptional Child

Exceptional Children
Teaching Exceptional Children
Exceptional Child Education
   Resources
Instructor
Teacher
Language Arts
Early Years
Rehab Film Newsletter

Two periodicals are available in braille for the use of blind children:

My Weekly Reader
Current Events

Within recent years, a number of journals have devoted entire issues to the subject of disabled children and young people. The following issues have special pertinence and value for librarians:

Audiovisual Instruction 14 (November 1969). Issue theme: "The Role of Media in Special Education"

Audiovisual Instruction 21 (December 1976). Issue theme: "Technology and the Exceptional Student"

The Bookmark 40 (Fall 1981). Issue theme: "Library Service to the Disabled"

Catholic Library World 52 (November 1980). Issue theme: "Library Services for the Disadvantaged"

Drexel Library Quarterly 16 (April 1980). Issue theme: "Information Services to Disabled Individuals"

Emergency Librarian 9 (November-December 1981). Issue theme: "Library Services for Disabled Young People"

Exceptional Children 43 (November 1976). Issue theme: "A Helping Relationship: Federal Programs for Special Children"

Illinois Libraries 57 (September 1975). Issue theme: "Special Library Services"

Illinois Libraries 59 (September 1977). Issue theme: "Media/Information/ Services for Exceptional Children"

Interracial Books for Children Bulletin 8 (Numbers 6 and 7, 1977). Special double issue on "Handicapism in Children's Books"

Interracial Books for Children Bulletin 11 (Numbers 1 and 2, 1980). Entire issue is related to deafness, including "American Sign Language: An Analysis" and "A Review of Deafness in Children's Books"

Ohio Media Spectrum 30 (January 1978). Issue theme: "The Special Child in the Library/Media Center"

School Media Quarterly 6 (Summer 1978). Feature section: "Special Education: A Continuum of Services"

School Media Quarterly 8 (Fall 1979). Feature section: "Special Students — Our Special Challenge"

Top of the News 25 (April 1969). Issue theme: "The Exceptional Child and the Library"

HIGH-INTEREST/LOW-READING-LEVEL MATERIALS

Numerous publishers produce high-interest/low-reading-level materials and can be contacted for information about their latest publications. Their addresses are as follows:

Addison-Wesley Pub. Co.
South Street
Reading, MA 01867

Las Americas Pub. Co.
37 Union Square West
New York, NY 10003

Baker & Taylor Co.
1515 Broadway
New York, NY 10036

Channing L. Bete Co.
200 State Road
South Deerfield, MA 01373

Book-Lab Inc.
1449 37 Street
Brooklyn, NY 11218

Cambridge Book Co.
11th Floor, 888 Seventh Ave.
New York, NY 10019

Center for Literacy
3723 Chestnut Street
Philadelphia, PA 19104

Childrens Press
1224 West Van Buren St.
Chicago, IL 60607

Crestwood House
P.O. Box 3427, Dept. 1024
Highway 66 South
Mankato, MN 56001

Dell Pub. Co.
245 East 47th Street
New York, NY 10017

Doubleday & Co.
501 Franklin Avenue
Garden City, NY 11530

EMC Publishing
Changing Times Ed. Svcs.
180 East Sixth Street
Saint Paul, MN 55101

Fawcett Books Group
Educational Marketing Dept.
1515 Broadway
New York, NY 10036

Finney Company
3350 Gorham Avenue
Minneapolis, MN 55426

Adult Learning Resources
Follett Pub. Co.
1010 West Boulevard
Chicago, IL 60607

Garrard Pub. Co.
1607 N. Market St.
Champaign, IL 61820

Globe Book Co., Inc.
175 5th Avenue
New York, NY 10010

Good Reading Rack Service
Good Reading Communications
505 Eighth Avenue
New York, NY 10018

Grolier Educational Corp.
845 3rd Avenue
New York, NY 10022

Hammond, Inc.
Hammond Building
Maplewood, NJ 07040

Harcourt Brace Jovanovich
757 Third Avenue
New York, NY 10017

Hobbs/Context Corp.
52 Vanderbilt Avenue
New York, NY 10017

Holt, Rinehart & Winston
Adult Basic Ed. Program
383 Madison Avenue
New York, NY 10017

Houghton Mifflin Co.
Pennington-Hopewell Road
Hopewell, NJ 08525

Jamestown Publishers
Box 6743
Providence, RI 02940

Janus Book Publishers
3541 Investment Boulevard
Suite 5
Hayward, CA 94545

Johnson Publishing Co.
1820 South Michigan Avenue
Chicago, IL 60616

King Features
Dept. 134
235 East 45th Street
New York, NY 10017

Lakeshore Co. Headquarters
2695 E. Dominguez Street
P.O. Box 6261
Carson, CA 90749

Lerner Pub. Co.
241 First Avenue, North
Minneapolis, MN 55401

Literacy Volunteers of
America, Inc.
Sixth Floor, Midtown Plaza
700 East Water Street
Syracuse, NY 13210

Longman Inc.
Suite 1012
19 West 44th Street
New York, NY 10036

Macmillan Pub. Co.
866 3rd Avenue
New York, NY 10022

McGraw-Hill Book Co.
1221 Avenue of the Americas
New York, NY 10020

Charles E. Merrill Pub. Co.
1300 Alum Creek Drive
Columbus, OH 43216

Multimedia Servicecenter
Sherwood, OR 97140

New Readers Press
P.O. Box 131
Syracuse, NY 13210

Noble and Noble, Publishers
750 Third Avenue
New York, NY 10017

Pendulum Press, Inc.
The Academic Building
Saw Mill Road
West Haven, CT 06516

Pitman Learning, Inc.
6 Davis Drive
Belmont, CA 94002

Frank E. Richards Co.
215 Church Street
Phoenix, NY 13135

Scholastic Book Svcs.
904 Sylvan Avenue
Englewood Cliffs, NJ 07632

SRA
Science Research Associates
259 E. Erie Street
Chicago, IL 60611

Scott, Foresman & Co.
1900 E. Lake Avenue
Glenview, IL 60025

Steck-Vaughn, Co.
Box 2028
Austin, TX 78767

Troll Associates
320 Rte 17
Mahwah, NJ 07430

U.S. Dept. of Agriculture
Supt. of Documents
U.S. Gov. Printing Office
Washington, DC 20402

Weekly Reader Multimedia
1250 Fairwood Avenue
P.O. Box 16629
Columbus, OH 43216

Xerox Education Publications
1250 Fairwood Avenue
P.O. Box 16618
Columbus, OH 43216

GAMES AND TOYS

Many games and toys are available for disabled children and young people: braille games such as Monopoly®, Scrabble®, Chinese checkers, and dominoes; tactile animal dice; playing cards in braille or with jumbo numbers; king-sized card games such as Old Maid, Queen of Hearts, and Go Fish; and Fisher-Price® toys. Among the sources for such items are the following:

American Foundation for the
   Blind
15 West 16th Street
New York, NY 10011

American Printing House for the
   Blind
1839 Frankfort Avenue
Louisville, KY 40206

Childcraft
964 Third Avenue
New York, NY 10022

Constructive Playthings
1040 East 85th Street
Kansas City, MO 64131

David C. Cook
Elgin, IL 60120

Developmental Learning
   Materials
7440 Natchez Avenue
Niles, IL 60648

Dick Blick
Box 1267
Galesburg, IL 61401

Nasco
901 Janesville Avenue
Fort Atkinson, WI 53538

Howe Press
Perkins School for the Blind
Watertown, MA 02172

Northern School Supply
P.O. Box 2627
Fargo, ND 58102

Independent Living Aids, Inc.
11 Commercial Court
Plainview, NY 11803

Science for the Blind Products
Box 385
Wayne, PA 19087

Instructional Resource Center
Center for the Developmentally
    Disabled
University of South Dakota
Julian Hall
Vermillion, SD 57069

Triangle School Service
1409 "C" Avenue
Sioux Falls, SD 57104

COMPUTER SOFTWARE PROGRAMS

With the rise in the use of computers and microcomputers by and with both disabled and nondisabled children and young people, there has been an increase in the number of catalogs of software as well as centers and sources of information about the uses and applications of computer technology. Among the directories of software are the following:

Appleseed
Software Publications
6 South Street
Milford, NH 03055

Huntington Computing
    Catalogue
P.O. Box 787
Corcoran, CA 93212

Educational Software Directory
Sterling Swift Publishing Co.
P.O. Box 188
Manchaca, TX 78652

International Microcomputer
    Software Directory
Imprint Software
420 South Howes Street
Fort Collins, CO 80521

Educational Software Directory
Libraries Unlimited, Inc.
P.O. Box 263
Littleton, CO 80160

K-12 Micro Media
P.O. Box 17
Valley Cottage, NY 10989

Educator's Handbook and Soft-
    ware Directory
Vital Information, Inc.
350 Union Station
Kansas City, MO 64108

Marck, Inc.
280 Linden Drive
Branford, CT 06082

Microcomputers Corporation
Catalogue
P.O. Box 191
Rye, NY 10580

MicroSIFT
Northwest Regional Educational
Laboratory
710 Second Avenue, SW
Portland, OR 97204

Opportunities for Learning, Inc.
Dept. L-4
8950 Lurline Avenue
Chatsworth, CA 91311

Purser's Atari Magazine
P.O. Box 466
El Dorado, CA 95623

Queue
5 Chapel Hill Drive
Fairfield, CT 06432

School Microware Directory
Dresden Associates
Dept. CCN, P.O. Box 246
Dresden, ME 04342

Skarbeks Software Directory
11990 Dorsett Road
St. Louis, MO 63043

TRS-80 Software Directory
Radio Shack
1600 One Tandy Center
Fort Worth, TX 76102

VanLoves Apple II/III Software Directory
Vital Information, Inc.
350 Union Station
Kansas City, MO 64108

Only a few of the above sources give evaluations of computer software. Most are simply catalogs of available software and give only descriptive information. It would be advisable to obtain further information directly from each source.

In addition, many centers have been established which provide information about the use and applications of computer technology. One of them is specifically dedicated to providing information regarding software for disabled persons — Apple Computer Clearinghouse for the Handicapped — while the others may be of benefit in reference to disabled persons by extension. Information about the activities of each source can be obtained from the addresses below:

Alameda County Office of
Education
224 West Winton Avenue
Hayward, CA 94544
(415) 881-6201

Apple Computer Clearinghouse
for the Handicapped
Prentke Romich Company
R.D. 2, P.O. Box 191
Shreve, OH 44676
(216) 767-2906

Computers in Education as a
Resource (CEDAR)
Exhibition Road
London S.W. 7, United Kingdom
01-589-5111, ext. 1160

Computer Literacy
1466 Grizzly Park Boulevard
Berkeley, CA 94707
(415) 644-2400

CONDUIT
P.O. Box 388
Iowa City, IA 52244
(319) 353-5789

Courseware, Inc.
10075 Carroll Canyon Road
San Diego, CA 92131
(714) 578-1700

DATASPAN
University of Michigan
109 East Madison Street
Ann Arbor, MI 48104
(313) 763-4410

Dresden Associates
P.O. Box 246
Dresden, ME 04342
(207) 737-4466

Educational Technology Center
University of California
Irvine, CA 92717
(714) 883-6945

Educator's Hot Line
Vital Information, Inc.
(913) 384-3860

EPIE Institute
P.O. Box 620
Stony Brook, NY 11790
(516) 246-8664

Florida Educational Computing
    Project
Department of Education
109 Knott Building
Tallahassee, FL 23201
(904) 488-1234

Human Resources Research
    Organization (HumRRO)
300 North Washington Street
Alexandria, VA 22314
(703) 549-3611

Intentional Educations
51 Sprint Street
Watertown, MA 02172
(617) 923-7707

Laboratory for Personal Com-
    puters in Education
State University of New York
Stony Brook, NY 11094
(516) 246-8418

Math City
4040 Palos Verdes Drive North
Rolling Hills Estates, CA 90274
(213) 541-3377

Math/Computer Education
    Project
Lawrence Hall of Science
University of California
Berkeley, CA 94720
(415) 642-3167

Micro Co-op
P.O. Box 432
West Chicago, IL 60185
(312) 231-0912

Microcomputer Center
San Mateo Educational Re-
    sources Center Library
333 Main Street
Redwood City, CA 94063
(415) 363-5469

Microcomputer Resource Center
Teachers College
Columbia University
525 West 121st Street
New York, NY 10027
(212) 678-3740

Microcomputer Education
    Applications Network
    (MEAN)
256 North Washington Street
Falls Church, VA 22046
(703) 536-2310

Minnesota Educational Comput-
    ing Consortium (MECC)
2520 Broadway Drive
St. Paul, MN 55113
(612) 376-1101

National Education Association
1201 16th Street, NW
Washington, DC 20036

Science Teaching Center
International Clearinghouse
University of Maryland
College Park, MD 20742
(301) 454-2024

The North Carolina Instructional Computing Project
116 West Edenton Street
Education Building, Room 58
Raleigh, NC 27611
(919) 733-4695

Technical Education Research
Centers, Inc. (TERC)
Computer Resource Center
8 Eliot Street
Cambridge, MA 02138
(617) 547-3890

Russ Walter
92 St. Botolph Street
Boston, MA 02116
(617) 265-8128

University of Washington Computing Information Center
3737 Brooklyn Avenue, NE
Seattle, WA 98105
(206) 543-5818

SPECIALIZED BIBLIOGRAPHIES AND MEDIAGRAPHIES: A SELECTED LIST

In addition to the comprehensive NICSEM publications and various retrieval systems, a multitude of shorter bibliographies and mediagraphies of materials which can be used by and with disabled children and young people are available. State libraries, state education departments, and the special education offices of school districts produce locally prepared lists of suggested materials. Many listings have been published by various state and national organizations as well as colleges and universities. These are often specialized according to disabling condition, age level, format, or subject matter, such as sex, career and vocational education, physical education, health, leisure time, recreation, and other topics. Following is a highly selected, and by no means exhaustive, listing of bibliographies/mediagraphies which have been published in book form or in library journals and therefore might be readily accessible to librarians. Some of them can be easily obtained by writing to the sponsoring agency. A few such lists have already been discussed in chapter 4 in regard to attitudes.

American Library Association. Association for Library Service to Children and Young Adult Services Division. *Selecting Materials for Children and Young Adults: A Bibliography of Bibliographies and Review Sources.* Chicago: American Library Association, 1980.
    One section of this slim volume is titled "Special Needs" and is subdivided into "Books to Help Face Problems," "For and about the Disabled," and "High Interest, Low Vocabulary." Besides the bibliographic citation, each entry contains a brief descriptive annotation.

American Library Association. Young Adult Services Division. "High-Interest Low-Reading Level Booklist." Chicago: American Library Association, 1980.

This is a selected list of books that have been popular and useful with teenagers. Reading level, as determined by the Fry Readability Formula, is given for each book. The list is divided into two sections: Part I—Very Easy Books, Fry Level 1-3; Part II—Easy-to-Read Books, Fry Level 4-5. Very brief descriptive annotations are included. A directory of the publishers whose books are represented in the list is appended.

Bisshop, Patricia, comp. *Books about Handicaps for Children and Young Adults: The Meeting Street School Annotated Bibliography.* East Providence, RI: The Meeting Street School, Rhode Island Easter Seal Society, 1978.

The compiler presents evaluative annotations for books in eight categories according to types of disability, including nonfiction and different styles of fiction. Two criteria guided the evaluations: 1) a positive, realistic portrayal of disabled persons; and 2) the quality of the books as literature. Some titles are designated as "Recommended" or "Not Recommended," while those without such a designation have both good and bad features and should be read with caution. The grade levels which are indicated refer to interest level rather than reading ability. Another section contains a list of books which were not available for examination or have been reviewed in other sources and therefore are given only brief nonevaluative annotations. In both the annotated and the briefly noted sections, every effort was made to include books that were currently in print at the time of the preparation of the booklet. In addition to the list of titles briefly noted, the appendices contain titles available in paperback editions, publishers' addresses, and resource reading. An Author-Title Index and Titles Indexed by Interest Level complete the volume.

Bliton, Gilbert, and Ash, Paul. *Time Project Report, 1979-80: An Aid in the Selection of Special Education Materials.* Indianapolis: Indiana State Department of Public Instruction, 1979. (ED 184 284)

This booklet identifies effective materials for use with exceptional learners, based on reporting forms from nearly 500 teachers. The entries are divided into various exceptionality areas: educable mentally retarded, trainable mentally retarded, severely and profoundly retarded, communication handicapped, learning disabled, emotionally disturbed, deaf and hearing impaired, blind and visually impaired, physically handicapped, and multiply handicapped. Wherever appropriate, grade level and curricular area are indicated. Materials are listed by title with the publisher in the appropriate section. A directory of selected publishers is also included.

Bopp, Richard E. "Periodicals for the Disabled: Their Importance as Information Sources." *Serials Librarian* 5 (Winter 1980): 61-70.

In this article, the author discusses twenty periodicals which are published for, and often by, disabled persons. A list of the periodicals which are discussed in the text is given at the conclusion of the article and includes full citation, frequency, and publisher's address. Most of the entries are duplicated in Ruth A. Velleman's article, "Library Service to the Disabled: An Annotated Bibliography of Journals and Newsletters" (see below).

Bopp, Richard E., and Anstine, Francesca A. "Rehabilitation Literature: A Guide to Selection Materials." *Library Resources and Technical Services* 25 (July/September 1981): 228-43.

    This article contains two brief lists in the appendices. One is titled "Selected Bibliographies of Rehabilitation Materials," and the other is a list of "Selection Tools for Audiovisuals in the Area of Rehabilitation." Each list includes full bibliographic citation and an annotation which is descriptive and, in some cases, evaluative.

Children's Services Division. Toys, Games, and Realia Committee. "Realia in the Library." *Booklist* 73 (January 1, 1977): 671-74.

    Although not prepared specifically with disabled children in mind, the materials in this bibliography can be used with children who have disabilities. It is a recommended list of realia which have been successfully used in public and school libraries and which can serve as a model for collection building. The list is divided into seven categories: coordination; discrimination: visual, tactile, and auditory; construction; dramatic play; verbal skills; quantitative skills; and strategy skills. For each item, the type of skill or activity for which it can be helpful and suggested age levels are indicated. Most of the materials are for children who are ten years old and younger. A list of distributors is included.

Cooke, Katherine B. *Let's Play Games.* Available from the National Easter Seal Society, 2023 West Ogden Avenue, Chicago, IL 60612.

    This illustrated booklet suggests more than fifty active games for disabled children and young people between the ages of five and eighteen.

Davis, Emmett A., comp. "Mediagraphy on Mainstreaming: Library Service to Disabled Persons." Printed and distributed by the Office of Public Libraries and Interlibrary Cooperation, 301 Hanover Building, 480 Cedar Street, St. Paul, MN 55101.

    This mediagraphy lists materials under the following headings: print materials, films/video, suppliers and publishers of special materials, resources for those with visual impairments, resources for the developmentally disabled, and resources for deaf persons. Entries contain bibliographic citation and a brief annotation. The mediagraphy was not intended to be exhaustive, nor a list of the best, nor a review. The materials are useful for general circulation as well as for professional training.

Davis, Walter. "Physical Education 16 mm Instructional Films for the Handicapped: An Annotated Bibliography." *International Journal of Instructional Media* 4 (No. 3, 1976-77): 185-204.

    This annotated filmography of 104 films was compiled to emphasize the use of 16mm films as an effective teaching technique and to assist teachers of physical education for disabled persons in utilizing this teaching method. A list of university film centers is included.

Dequin, Henry C. "Services and Materials for Disabled Children." *Illinois Libraries* 63 (September 1981): 546-54.

    Two lists are included in this article: 1) Audiovisual Materials about Disabilities for Children and Young People; and 2) Books about Disabilities for Children and Young People, divided according to elementary and junior high/high school.

Dreyer, Sharon Spredemann. *The Bookfinder: A Guide to Children's Literature about the Needs and Problems of Youth Aged 2-15.* 2 vols. Circle Pines, MN: American Guidance Service, 1977 and 1981.

In this reference work, the author describes and categorizes 1,031 (volume one) and 723 (volume two) current children's books according to more than 450 psychological, behavioral, and developmental topics. Subject, author, and title indexes and a publishers' directory are contained in a split-page arrangement, which makes it possible to leave any of the indexes open while referring to the other portion which contains the annotations alphabetically arranged by author. Each annotation includes the bibliographic information, main subject heading, a synopsis, a commentary, general reading level, and information about other forms of the publication, including materials for the blind or physically disabled. Besides the general heading of "Handicaps," twenty-seven other subject headings are related to disabilities and disabled persons.

"Easy Reads for Teens." Included in the "High Interest/Low Reading Level Information Packet" available from the American Library Association, Young Adult Services Division, 50 East Huron Street, Chicago, IL 60611.

This bibliography consists of books which have comparatively low reading levels and a high interest potential for teenagers who are thirteen to eighteen years old. It is divided into three sections:

1. "Easy Reads for Teens-I"—3rd and 4th grade reading levels; 8th through 12th grade interest level

2. "Easy Reads for Teens-II"—5th and 6th grade reading levels; 8th through 12th grade interest level

3. "Easy Reads for Teens-III"—7th and 8th grade reading levels; 8th through 12th grade interest level

Each section is subdivided into broad categories, such as stories about teenagers and young adults; biography, autobiography, history, and adventure, mystery and the occult. The titles in each section were selected on the basis of their easy reading levels and their *recreational* interest potential. Each title was tested for reading difficulty and assigned a grade level according to the Fry Readability Formula.

Elswit, Sharon. "Special Books for Special People." *School Library Journal* 28 (December 1981): 28-29.

The author recommends twenty-nine "first-class" books for children from preschool to the teen years. Grade levels and brief descriptive annotations are included.

"Films for the Deaf and Hearing-Impaired." For information, contact: Honore Francois, Coordinator of Extension and Special Services, Prince George's Memorial Library System, 6532 Adelphi Road, Hyattsville, MD 20782.

This is a catalog which describes approximately 500 films which are available from the Prince George's County Memorial Library System and are suitable for use by those who are deaf and hearing impaired. The catalog lists films ranging from stories for preschoolers to educational and feature films.

Garry, V. V. "Mainstreaming: Children's Books about Children with Disabilities." *The Exceptional Parent* 8 (April 1978): F8-F12.

Evaluative comments on a few books in each of these disability categories: deafness, blindness, mental retardation, physical disabilities, learning disabilities, and physical size.

Gilbert, Laura-Jean. "Materials, Program Suggestions for Hearing-Impaired Children." *School Media Quarterly* 4 (Spring 1976): 263-68.

Several listings are included in this article: 1) four books for parents and teachers; 2) books for very young hearing-impaired children, arranged under the headings Words and Pictures, Simplest Tales, Picture-Story Books, and Books without Words; 3) books for elementary school-age deaf children, in which the pictures can carry the story and including some that are nonverbal books; 4) texts for the study of sign language; 5) books to help hearing children understand deafness or to assist hearing-impaired children gain more self-understanding, listed under the headings Young Children, Children Ages 9-14, and High School; and 6) games.

Good, Margaret. "Stories about Handicapped Children: A Select List." *The School Librarian* 25 (June 1977): 110-16.

In this article is presented an annotated list of forty-one books suitable for children ten years of age and above, either for those children who are disabled to gain perspective on their disability or for those who are not disabled to gain insight into the difficulties that disabled children experience. The list is divided into six areas: Physically Handicapped, Blind, Deaf, Dumb, Mentally Handicapped, and Autistic. Although most of the books are British publications, they can be useful with children in the United States and other English-speaking countries. Included are some books well known in the United States, such as Laura Ingalls Wilder's *By the Shores of Silver Lake* and Marguerite Henry's *King of the Wind*.

High Interest-Low Vocabulary Reading Materials Including Books and Kits: Intermediate, Junior High and Senior High School Level. Austin, TX: Texas Area Learning Resource Center, 1975.

This publication is a listing of series books and audiovisual materials. Bibliographic and descriptive information, including price, are given.

High Interest/Low Reading Level Information Packet. Available from American Library Association, Young Adult Services Division, 50 East Huron Street, Chicago, IL 60611.

The eight items in the packet were distributed at the 1978 Preconference, "Dispelling the High-Low Blues," sponsored by ALA's Association for Library Service to Children and YASD. Although developed to assist those who work with junior and senior high school students who have low reading levels and lack the motivation to read, some of the materials may be equally beneficial in working with disabled young people who have reading difficulties. Of particular note in this regard are the bibliography of "Sources of Materials for Poor Readers," a list of "Easy Reads for Teens," and a list of publishers who publish high/low material.

The High/Low Report. Riverhouse Publications, 20 Waterside Plaza, New York, NY 10010.

Begun in 1979, this publication evaluates high/low books for professionals who are concerned with literature for the teenage reluctant reader. On the basis of evaluative criteria, books are thoroughly reviewed according to design, format, storyline, typesize, and illustrations. Reading level is given according to the Fry Readability Formula, and the reading level indicated by the publisher is also given for most books. The report is published monthly ten times a year.

Hirshberg, Robin. "The Developmentally Disabled in Literature for Young People." *Catholic Library World* 53 (April 1982): 391-94.

The author discusses nine books in this article. Appended is a "Bibliography of Books for Further Reading," which contains thirty-two additional titles without annotations.

Hunt, Abby Campbell, comp. "Annotated Bibliography of Books Depicting the Handicapped." In *Now Upon a Time: A Contemporary View of Children's Literature*, pp. 423-35. By Myra Pollack Sadker and David Miller Sadker. New York: Harper and Row, 1977.

This list of fiction and nonfiction books is divided into picture books and books for the middle and upper grades. Brief descriptive annotations and age levels are given.

Jackson, Clara O., compiler. "Keeping Up to Date with Information about Youth with Special Needs." *Ohio Media Spectrum* 30 (January 1978): 59-63.

A very brief and highly selected list arranged according to bibliographies, books and reference aids, films, sources, sources for captioned films, filmstrips, magazines and newsletters, special issues, services, sources for materials, and videotapes. Short annotations are included for a few of the entries.

Kelly, Jeff. "The Disabled in Fiction: A High School Guide." *The Exceptional Parent* 8 (October 1978): 12-15.

Evaluative comments on a few books in each of these disability categories: emotional problems, mental retardation, blindness, deafness, and physical disabilities.

Lambert, Roger H. *Vocational Education Resource Materials: A Bibliography of Free Loan Materials for Handicapped and Special Education.* 2nd ed. Madison, WI: Center for Studies in Vocational and Technical Education, University of Wisconsin-Madison, 1975.

This list is arranged by a coding system which is a combination of the Department of Education Curriculum Guides and ERIC descriptors. Descriptive notes are included. There is also an annotated list of films dealing with the needs and capabilities of disabled persons.

Large Type Books in Print. 5th edition. New York: R. R. Bowker, 1982.

This volume lists over 5,500 large-type novels, nonfiction books, textbooks, children's books, and periodicals without any attempt at selectivity or evaluation. It includes only materials which have been printed in 14-point type or larger. The volume itself was reproduced in 18-point type for the convenience of users with visual impairments and is divided into two main subject sections, General Reading and Textbooks. Each section is subdivided into more narrowly defined subject and genre areas, arranged alphabetically by title. Also included are separate author, title, and publisher indexes, and separate sections for children's books and literature in foreign languages.

"Library Services to the Exceptional Child." American Library Association, 50 East Huron Street, Chicago, IL 60611.

Twelve items are in this packet, including eight bibliographies. The first four titles were prepared by the Public Library of Cincinnati and Hamilton County in 1969:

"Books for the Deaf and Hard-of-Hearing Children: Primary Grades, Intermediate Grades"

"Books for Mentally Retarded Children"

"Books Used for Discussion with Socially Maladjusted Girls, Ages 12-15"

"Books Used for Discussion with Socially Maladjusted Boys, Ages 12-15"

"The Hostile Child in Books," a reprint from *Exceptional Children*, September 1966.

"Self-Discovery through Books," by William F. Elder and Hilda K. Limper, a reprint from *Child Welfare*, December 1968.

"Books as an Aid in Preventing Dropouts," by Helen F. Faust, a reprint from *Elementary English*.

"Without Whip or Rod," by Hilda K. Limper, a reprint from *Federal Probation Quarterly*, December 1966.

LiBretto, Ellen V., comp. and ed. *High/Low Handbook: Books, Materials, and Services for the Teenage Problem Reader*. Serving Special Populations Series. New York: R. R. Bowker, 1981.

Ten chapters of this book were written by various authors and are divided into two parts: "Identifying and Serving the High/Low Reader" and "Selecting and Evaluating High/Low Materials." The third part, titled "The Core Collection," constitutes about one-half of the book and is divided into three sections. In the first section, LiBretto presents "High/Low Books and Periodicals for the Disabled Reader: A Core Collection" as a selection tool and literature guide to reading materials for teenagers who are seriously disabled in reading. After presenting a checklist of evaluation criteria which were followed in selecting the entries, both fiction and nonfiction titles are listed in one sequence and arranged alphabetically by author. Each entry contains the bibliographic citation, number of pages, price, a designation of fiction or nonfiction, reading level based on the revised Fry Readability

Formula, interest level, and a descriptive annotation. The section is concluded with information on four high-interest/low-reading-level periodicals. In the next section, "Appendix I. Books for the Reluctant Reader: A Supplement to the Core Collection," LiBretto recommends books for *reluctant* teenage readers. These books contain more demanding reading material than the books listed in the core collection for disabled readers. The titles in the list include the bibliographic citation, price, a designation of fiction or nonfiction, and a brief descriptive annotation. The third section, "Appendix II," contains a list of bibliographies and sources of current reviews prepared by Patsy Perritt. Each entry contains the bibliographic citation, price, and a descriptive annotation.

McCarr, Dorothy. *Materials Useful for Deaf/Hearing Impaired; An Annotated Bibliography*. Rev. ed. Lake Oswego, OR: Dormac, 1976.

Not intended to be comprehensive, the book is an annotated list of materials known to be useful with deaf and hearing-impaired children and young people. Eleven areas are covered: career education, driver education, family life and health, language, mathematics, reading—high interest, reading—skills, science, social studies, speech—auditory training, and total communication. Interest level and reading level are indicated for each item. For those children beyond primary age, most of the entries are high-interest/low-reading-level materials. A list of publishers is included.

Mental Health Materials Center. *A Selective Guide to Materials for Mental Health and Family Life Education*. 3rd ed. Detroit: Gale Research Company, 1976.

This book gives details on more than 500 books, pamphlets, films, and audiovisual materials related to mental health.

Metcalf, Mary Jane. "Library Services for the Hearing Impaired." *Illinois Libraries* 63 (October 1981): 626-33.

In this article, the author presents a list of seventy recommended book series which have been found to be helpful for hearing-impaired children. Reading level, interest level, and publisher are noted for each series title. In addition, the article contains annotations on three recommended periodicals (*National Geographic World, Scholastic Action*, and *Silent News*) and a list of five sign language books.

Miller, Hannah Elsas. "Films about 'Special' Young People." *Top of the News* 35 (Fall 1978): 75-80.

The author discusses twenty 16mm films which show what disabled people are like and which can help to overcome stereotyped ideas.

Moore, Coralie B., and Morton, Kathryn Gorham. *A Reader's Guide for Parents of Children with Mental, Physical, or Emotional Disabilities*. Rockville, MD: U.S. Department of Health, Education, and Welfare, Public Health Service, Health Services Administration, Bureau of Community Health Services, 1979.

The authors of this guide are parents who experienced the problems of raising children with disabilities. The volume is divided into four parts. Part I, "Families and Children ... with Disabilities," is relevant to all disabilities and is divided into four categories: 1) basic reading; 2) books that tell how to teach, train, and play at home; 3) books which were written by parents and others who have "lived it"; and 4) books which deal more intensively with particular issues, problems, and solutions to problems. Part II contains books on particular disabilities and is divided into the four categories of basic reading; how to teach, train, and play at home; from those who have lived it; and issues and answers. Part III lists books *for* children *about* children with disabilities. Part IV includes other sources of information, organizations, agencies, directories, and a list of popular journals on various disabilities. Each entry contains the bibliographic citation, price, and a descriptive annotation. The books for children also contain an age-level designation.

Nicholsen, Margaret E. *People in Books.* First Supplement. New York: H. W. Wilson, 1977.

Recommended biographies of disabled persons are identified by vocation, field of activity, country, and century under headings such as "Victims of Blindness," "Victims of Deafness," and "Victims of Epilepsy." The books can be used with various age groups—children, young people, and adults.

Parlato, Salvatore J., Jr. *Films ex Libris: Literature in 16mm and Video.* Jefferson, NC: McFarland and Company, 1980.

This directory describes over 1,000 16mm films, many of which are silent or nonverbal and some of which are accompanied by sign language. Section headings are: The Bible, Biography, Children's Stories, Drama, Fables/Fairy Tales/Folktales, Nonfiction, Novels, Poetry, and Short Stories. With each category, the films are arranged alphabetically by title. In addition to the title, each entry includes a descriptive annotation, producer, length, color or black and white, and date of production. Additional sections are devoted to a producer/distributor directory, an authors-on-film index, and an original title index.

Parlato, Salvatore J., Jr. *Films—Too Good for Words; A Directory of Nonnarrated 16mm Films.* New York: R. R. Bowker, 1973.

Nearly 1,000 16mm films which are nontheatrical and mostly curriculum-oriented "educational" films are included in this directory. The chapters are divided into thirteen subject categories: The Arts, Other Places, Other Customs, Science, Nature, Expression, City and Suburb, Values, Fun, Action, War and Peace, Fantasy, Literature, and More. Each entry includes producer, number of minutes, color or black and white, sound or silent, year produced, and a descriptive annotation. A title index, subject index, and producer/distributor directory are appended.

Parlato, Salvatore J., Jr. *Superfilms: An International Guide to Award-Winning Educational Films.* Metuchen, NJ: Scarecrow Press, 1976.

Almost 1,500 high-quality films on a variety of subjects are included in this directory. Many titles are listed under the categories of children's stories and nonverbal films, and twenty-three are given under the heading "Handicaps." The films are entered alphabetically by title, and each entry includes length, color or black and white, producer, year, awards, description, and age level.

Pick a Title: A Collection of Children's Books and Other Media about the Handicapped. Baltimore: Maryland State Department of Education, 1978.

This brief 20-page publication was designed for librarians, teachers, and parents to assist them in selecting and creatively using books and other media to enhance and promote an understanding of disabled children, young people, and adults. The Children's Book Section is divided into books for preschool and primary grades, books for the middle grades, and books for young adults. The Audiovisual Section contains 16mm films, filmstrips, and slides. Complete bibliographic citations and brief descriptive annotations are included. In addition, there is a Professional Reference Section and a list of publishers and producers.

Pick a Title II: A Collection of Media about the Handicapped. Baltimore: Maryland State Department of Education, 1980.

A companion to the 1978 edition of *Pick a Title*, the second edition is slightly different because it incorporates print and nonprint media in each of the interest-level areas and also includes a section for parents which lists instructional materials for use in the home. The Media Section is again divided by age level: preschool and primary, middle or intermediate, and young adult and adult. The Professional Section contains both print and nonprint media. All titles include full bibliographical citation and a brief descriptive annotation. A list of publishers is appended.

Pokorni, Judith, and Wujcik, Anne. *Audio Visual Guide for Services to the Handicapped*, 1977. (ED 145 616). Available from Head Start Resource and Training Center, 4321 Hartwick Road, Room L-220, College Park, MD 20740.

This 45-page list annotates approximately 110 films, filmstrips (some with cassettes or records), and slides on dealing with various types of disabilities in young children. Listed by title, each entry includes information on length, color or black and white, date, availability, and a brief description. A subject guide lists materials under headings such as exceptional children—general, deaf and hearing impaired, emotionally disturbed, learning disabilities, mentally retarded, speech impaired, and visually handicapped. A list of producers and distributors concludes the document.

Putnam, Rosemary. "Books Can Introduce Your Class to the Mainstreamed Child." *Learning* 7 (October 1978): 118-20.

Thirty books for grades K-8 are included in this bibliography which was compiled for teachers to help children in regular classrooms to form a realistic picture of what an individual with a particular disability can and cannot do. The books can also help to foster an atmosphere of acceptance in the classroom and help to emphasize the similarities between nondisabled and disabled children. Full bibliographic citation, price, a short descriptive annotation, and grade level are given for each book.

Rouleau, Ruth O., and Craig, Helen B. *Looking Ahead: Filmstrips for the Hearing Impaired; An Annotated Bibliography Featuring ... Living Skills, Community Involvement, Vocational Options.* Pittsburgh, PA: Western Pennsylvania School for the Deaf, 1980.

The filmstrips included in this annotated list have been judged acceptable in assisting the deaf and/or language-impaired young person who contemplates the responsibilities and opportunities of career, community, and everyday living. Criteria for acceptance into the list were: technical quality, organization, accuracy, effectiveness, appeal, interest level, correlation with curricula, supportive materials, and captions. The list of individual filmstrips is arranged alphabetically by title. Each citation includes title, distributor or producer, date, and notations regarding color film, captioned, noncaptioned cassette, and supportive material. The annotation includes the subject of the filmstrip, critical comments and special features, and interest level. In addition to the alphabetical listing, there is a list of subject areas included, a list of series titles for filmstrip sets arranged according to captioned and noncaptioned titles, and a list of individual filmstrip titles arranged according to captioned and noncaptioned titles. There is also a list of resources and a directory of distributors and producers. Although this specialized list is no longer available from the Western Pennsylvania School for the Deaf, copies were sent to all state libraries and can be obtained through interlibrary loan.

Ruark, Ardis, and Melby, Carole. *Kangaroo Kapers, or How to Jump into Library Services for the Handicapped.* Pierre, SD: Division of Elementary and Secondary Education, 1978.

Several bibliographies are contained in this booklet: 1) Children's books relating to the hearing impaired, 2) Sign language and interpreting, 3) Wordless books, 4) Hearing impaired — professional or adult reading, 5) Children's books relating to the mentally handicapped, 6) Books to use in storytelling sessions, 7) Children's books relating to other disabling conditions, and 8) Bibliography of special child, professional or adult reading relating to other handicapping conditions.

Sleeman, Linda B. "Mental Retardation ... An Annotated Bibliography of Non-Print Instructional Materials." *International Journal of Instructional Media* 4 (No. 2, 1976-77): 177-44.

Since most bibliographies concerning mental retardation usually include only print material, the author's intent in preparing this annotated bibliography was to present a list of nonprint instructional materials in order to identify a basic core of data which could be used for locating nonprint instructional media. Included are 16mm films, 8mm films, curriculum packages, audiotapes, recordings, videotapes, supply companies, and film rental sources.

"Special Education." Available free from the National Audiovisual Center, National Archives and Records Service, General Services Administration, Order Section RT, Washington, DC 20409. (301) 763-1896.

This free booklet lists selected United States government audiovisuals which may be purchased or rented from the National Audio Visual Center. The materials include both child-use and teacher training materials in the areas of manual communication, the hearing impaired, speech and language development, captioned films, human development, mental retardation, the emotionally disturbed, the physically handicapped, parent education, and the handicapped adult. Entries are arranged alphabetically by title and also include the following: 1) physical description, 2) organization that produced the material, 3) organization that sponsors distribution of the materials, 4) National Audiovisual Center control number, 5) three-day rental fee, 6) sale price, 7) descriptive annotation, 8) series note, and 9) additional notes on use or production. Other services of the center include catalogs, information lists, and brochures on a variety of subjects; "Films Etc.," a monthly newsletter; loan referrals; computer searches; and research regarding film sources.

Special Education Materials Made Available through the Office of Special Education Marketing Program. Available free from LINC Resources, Inc., 1875 Morse Road, Suite 225, Columbus, OH 43229. (614) 263-LINC.

This catalog was prepared as part of the Market Linkage Project for Special Education, a new model for disseminating special education resources developed with federal funds. The products listed in the catalog were developed in projects funded by the U.S. Department of Education's Office of Special Education (OSE). They have passed through OSE's Marketing Program and have been judged appropriate for commercial distribution to the disabled learners, parents, and professionals they were intended to reach. Most of the materials were developed over a period of several years, and many have been field-tested and revised based upon feedback from the intended audience. The materials listed in the catalog include child-use instructional materials, assessment instruments, curriculum guides, multimedia training materials, and equipment items. All entries are listed alphabetically by title of the product with media format and date of publication. Also given are the availability source, price, developer, purpose, audience, descriptors, contents, and supplementary information. Two indexes provide access to the product entries by publisher and descriptor.

Special People, Special Needs, Special Services. Athens, GA: University of Georgia, Bureau of Educational Studies and Department of Educational Media and Librarianship, 1978.

Several highly selected lists are included in this booklet: Publications for the School Media Center Professional Staff, Periodicals, Newsletters, Understanding the Special Child, and Suggested Selection Sources.

Stough, Helen. " 'Let Me Hear Your Hand'—Library Service for Handicapped Children." *Illinois Libraries* 62 (December 1980): 881-82.

A brief list of twenty-three children's books about handicapped individuals is appended to this article. In addition to bibliographic information, a notation is made regarding the type of disability which is presented in the book. A short list of books for professional reading is also included.

Stroud, Janet G. "Characterization of the Emotionally Disturbed in Current Adolescent Fiction." *Top of the News* 37 (Spring 1981): 290-95.

Stroud, Janet G. "Portrayal of Physically Handicapped Characters in Adolescent Fiction." *Top of the News* 36 (Summer 1980): 363-67.

Stroud, Janet G. "Treatment of the Mentally Handicapped in Young Adult Fiction." *Top of the News* 36 (Winter 1980): 208-212.

In the three articles listed above, Stroud analyzes thirty-six books for their portrayal of characters with the disabling conditions indicated in each title.

Thorum, Arden R., and others. *Instructional Materials for the Handicapped: Birth through Early Childhood.* Salt Lake City: Olympus Publishing Company, 1976.

Two sections of this book can be helpful in locating suitable materials for disabled children. One is a general listing of commercial producers of toys, games, education kits, and other instructional aids. The other is a listing of over 270 instructional kits identified and described according to name of kit, manufacturer, cost, recommended age level, developmental skill areas, subject areas, format, and components.

Velleman, Ruth A. "Library Service to the Disabled: An Annotated Bibliography of Journals and Newsletters." *Serials Librarian* 5 (Winter 1980): 49-60.

Fifty journals and newsletters are presented in this list under the following categories: "By and for Disabled People," "Deaf and Hearing Impaired, Blind and Visually Impaired, Deaf/Blind," "Medical Rehabilitation," "Mental Retardation," "Rehabilitation − General," "Rehabilitation Counselling," "Special Education," and "Newsletters." Publisher's address, frequency, cost, and a brief descriptive annotation are given for each title. Some of the titles are also discussed by Richard E. Bopp in his article, "Periodicals for the Disabled: Their Importance as Information Sources" (see above).

Velleman, Ruth A. *Serving Physically Disabled People: An Information Handbook for All Libraries.* New York: R. R. Bowker, 1979.

Three sections of this book contain extensive annotated lists of materials which are suggested to librarians as basic collections. Chapter 8 is a core public library collection with entries listed under the following headings: Rehabilitation, General; Rehabilitation, Medicine; Rehabilitation Counseling; Independent Living; Barrier-Free Design; Travel; Sex and the Disabled; Periodicals; Newsletters; and Directories. In chapter 11 the author presents a model rehabilitation library in the fields of medical and vocational rehabilitation; in addition to the same subdivisions included in chapter 8, there are sections which are headed "Recreation" and "Sources for Audiovisual Materials." In chapter 14 is a core special education collection of materials in the areas of the blind and visually impaired, deaf and hearing impaired, orthopedically disabled, and learning disabled. The areas covered are: Directories, Catalogues, and Bibliographies; Special Education, General Mainstreaming; Medical; Psychology; Parents; Death; Physical Education and Recreation; Deafness and Hearing Impairment; Blind, Deaf-Blind, and Visually Impaired; Periodicals; Newsletters; Sources and Publishers' Catalogues of Instructional Materials; Legislation and Financing; and Audiovisual Materials.

Wilms, Denise. "Children's Books on Disabilities." *Booklist* 78 (November 1981): 395-97.

    Fifty-nine fiction and nonfiction books about disabilities are recommended. Brief descriptive annotations are given, and grade levels are indicated between grade one through grade ten.

Wise, Bernice Kemler. *Teaching Materials for the Learning Disabled: A Selected List for Grades 6-12.* Chicago: American Library Association, 1980.

    This 64-page bibliography was designed for librarians and teachers who work with learning-disabled children and young people in grades six through twelve and is an aid in teaching academic subjects, in reading remediation, and in guiding recreational reading. Titles were chosen on the basis of four criteria: 1) relation of the material to the curriculum, 2) topicality, 3) quality, and 4) format. Separate sections are devoted to professional materials, reading programs, and curricular and noncurricular materials, divided by subject area. Included are a bibliography, a list of publishers, and an author-title index.

Wright, Louise M. "A Look Behind the Wall of Silence." *Ohio Library Association Bulletin* 47 (April 1977): 6-8.

    In this article, the author discusses suggested reading for younger deaf people, books of interest to deaf adults, and books to create an understanding of the deaf by those who can hear.

Young Adult Fiction 1981. Available free from the National Library Service for the Blind and Physically Handicapped, Library of Congress, Washington, DC 20542.

    This annotated bibliography of books is intended for sight-handicapped young people ages twelve to twenty and is available on disc-cassette or in braille. Subject, format, and grade-level guides are included.

Knowledge of sources of information about materials for disabled children and young people and the intelligent use of these sources enables librarians to give better assistance to disabled users themselves and to teachers who seek materials for disabled students. Such knowledge and use will help to achieve the ultimate goal of librarians and other educators: to provide the most suitable educational and recreational materials to each individual child and young person.

NOTES

    [1]Eliza T. Dresang, "There Are No *Other* Children," *School Library Journal* 24 (September 1977): 20.

    [2]Robert R. Lange, Charyl T. Mattson, and James B. Thomann, "Needs for Instructional Media and Materials Services for Handicapped Learners: A Summary of Extant Information" (Columbus, OH: The National Center on Educational Media and Materials for the Handicapped, Ohio State University, 1974), pp. 19-20.

    [3]Ibid., pp. 4-11.

[4]Discussions of the NCEMMH can be found in Victor E. Fuchs, "National Center of Educational Media and Materials for the Handicapped Program," *Illinois Libraries* 59 (September 1977): 525-30; Victor Fuchs and Joyce Ellis, "Service: A Priority with the National Center on Educational Media and Materials for the Handicapped," *Journal of Learning Disabilities* 10 (February 1977): 13-19; Henry C. Dequin, "Selecting Materials for the Handicapped: A Guide to Sources," *Top of the News* 35 (Fall 1978): 57-59; Gabriel D. Ofiesh, "A National Center for Educational Media and Materials for the Handicapped," *Audiovisual Instruction* 14 (November 1969): 28-29; and John C. Belland, "Mission and Services of the National Center on Educational Media and Materials for the Handicapped," in *The Special Child in the Library*, ed. Barbara Holland Baskin and Karen H. Harris (Chicago: American Library Association, 1976), pp. 188-95.

[5]For a discussion of CEC, ECER, and the ERIC Clearinghouse on Handicapped and Gifted Children, see Donald K. Erickson, "Exceptional Child Education Resources: A One-of-a-Kind Data Base," *Illinois Libraries* 59 (September 1977): 519-23. An earlier article was written by Marylane Soeffing, "The CEC Information Center on Exceptional Children," *Audiovisual Instruction* 14 (November 1969): 42-43.

[6]For a discussion of the Educational Patterns, Inc. Retrieval System, see James E. McCormack, Cathy Doyle, and Jody Blieberg, *Guide to Finding Appropriate Instructional Materials: Existing Retrieval Systems* (Medford, MA: Center for Program Development and Evaluation, 1977), pp. 10-11. (ED 141 996).

[7]For a discussion of System FORE, see McCormack, Doyle, and Blieberg, *Guide to Finding Appropriate Instructional Materials*, p. 19; and Alan F. Reeder and Jacqueline M. Bolen, "Match the Materials to the Learner," *Audiovisual Instruction* 21 (December 1976): 24-25.

[8]U.S. Department of Health, Education, and Welfare, Office of Human Development Services, Office for Handicapped Individuals, *Directory of National Information Sources on Handicapping Conditions and Related Services* (Washington, DC: Government Printing Office, 1980).

[9]For discussions of the National Library Service, see the following: Margaret Bush, "Books for Children Who Cannot See the Printed Page," *School Library Journal* 26 (April 1980): 28-31; Henrietta Wexler, "Books That Talk," *American Education* 17 (January/February 1981): 15; Frances M. Peters, "Reading Is for Everyone," *Ohio Media Spectrum* 30 (January 1978): 22-25; Donna Dziedzic, "The Same Only Different Service," *Illinois Libraries* 63 (October 1981): 633-38; Jan Ames, "Libraries Serving Handicapped Users Share Resources," *Catholic Library World* 52 (February 1981): 287-300; and JoEllen Ostendorf, "National Library Services for the Blind and Physically Handicapped," in *School Library Media Services to the Handicapped*, ed. Myra Macon (Westport, CT: Greenwood Press, 1982), pp. 131-65.

[10]American Library Association, Association of Specialized and Cooperative Library Agencies, Standards for Library Service to the Blind and Physically

Handicapped Subcommittee, *Standards of Service for the Library of Congress Network of Libraries for the Blind and Physically Handicapped* (Chicago: American Library Association, 1979), p. 3.

[11]Bush, "Books for Children Who Cannot See the Printed Page," pp. 28-29.

[12]For a description of the NLS music collection, see Eyler Robert Coates, "Music for the Blind and Physically Handicapped from the Library of Congress," *American Music Teacher* 25 (February 1976): 21-24, reprinted in *Meeting the Needs of the Handicapped: A Resource for Teachers and Librarians*, ed. Carol H. Thomas and James L. Thomas (Phoenix: Oryx Press, 1980), pp. 275-82.

[13]For discussions of the services of the American Printing House for the Blind, see the following: Carl W. Lappin, "At Your Service — The Instructional Materials Reference Center for the Visually Handicapped," *Teaching Exceptional Children* 5 (Winter 1973): 74-76; reprinted in *The Special Child in the Library*, ed. Barbara Holland Baskin and Karen H. Harris (Chicago: American Library Association, 1976), pp. 174-75; Carl W. Lappin, "The Instructional Materials Reference Center for the Visually Handicapped," *Education of the Visually Handicapped* 4 (October 1972): 65-70; Carl W. Lappin, "School Books for the Blind and Physically Handicapped Child," *Health and Rehabilitative Library Services Division Journal* 2 (Fall 1976): 5-7; and Carl W. Lappin, "Textbooks for Visually Impaired Students," *Ohio Media Spectrum* 30 (January 1978): 32-34.

[14]For discussions of Captioned Films for the Deaf, see Malcolm J. Norwood, "Captioned Films for the Deaf," *Exceptional Children* 43 (November 1976): 164-66; and Salvatore J. Parlato, "Captioned and Nonverbal Films for the Hearing-Impaired," *Library Trends* 27 (Summer 1978): 59-63. For a more historical perspective, see James J. Kundert, "Media Services and Captioned Films," *Educational Technology* 10 (August 1970): 40-42, reprinted in *The Special Child in the Library*, ed. Barbara Holland Baskin and Karen H. Harris (Chicago: American Library Association, 1976), pp. 179-81.

[15]For a discussion of the Instructional Media Production Project for Severely Handicapped Students, see Karen Hughes, "Exploring 'Direct-Use' Media for Severely Handicapped Students," *Media Management Journal* 1 (Fall 1981): 6-8, 16.

9____Evaluating and Selecting Materials

"Choose an author as you choose a friend."
— Wentworth Dillon, Earl of Roscommon
"Essay on Translated Verse"

INTRODUCTION

The ever-growing quantities of materials that are suitable for use by and with disabled children and young people, as well as the increasing numbers of indexes, bibliographies, and mediagraphies of these materials, is both a bane and a blessing. It is good to have an abundance of materials from which to choose, but the abundance also makes it more difficult to choose. Just as in buying new clothes, an automobile, appliances, or any other product, when there are more options in brands and styles and colors and other factors, the decision can become extremely difficult. So also is the case in selecting materials for disabled children and young people. When there are so many different materials and varieties of formats on a given subject:

— How can a librarian know which materials to select for addition to the library's collection for the general informational and recreational use of disabled children and young people?

— How can librarians and teachers determine which materials would be best for the informational and recreational needs and interests of a particular disabled child or young person on the basis of the individual's abilities and learning style?

Professional education in librarianship, on-the-job experience, and continuous professional growth and development provide librarians with special expertise in locating and selecting suitable materials for the general collection and for individuals. Knowledge of materials, selection principles, and selection tools gives librarians the opportunity and a challenge to assist parents, special education teachers, regular classroom teachers, medical and clinical personnel, and others who work with disabled children and young people. Other professionals usually have not had formal education in selection principles and the utilization of bibliographic selection tools, and therefore they require and frequently desire training and assistance in locating and selecting appropriate materials.[1] Frequently, also, other professionals have a limited amount of time to devote to this important task of selecting materials. In Shotel, Iano, and McGettigan's study on teacher attitudes associated with the integration of disabled children, almost all of the teachers (99%) expressed a need for special methods and materials in teaching disabled children.[2]

Between 1974 and 1976 the Educational Products Information Exchange (EPIE) conducted a National Survey and Assessment of Instructional Materials. Although the survey did not focus on the evaluation and selection of materials either by special education teachers or by regular classroom teachers who had mainstreamed students in their classes, the findings were indicative of teachers in general in relation to the evaluation and selection of materials. The following results of this study were based on returns from 12,389 teachers of mathematics, reading, science, and social studies:

— Instructional materials, print and nonprint, are used during 90 to 95 per cent of all K-12 classroom instructional time. Schools spend about 1 per cent of their budgets on these materials that are used during 90 to 95 per cent of instruction.

— Almost one half (45 per cent) of classroom teachers have no role in choosing the instructional materials they are required to use.

— More than one half of teachers who do have a role in selecting materials (54 per cent) spend less than one hour per year in selecting those materials.

— The average teacher has never been trained to evaluate or to select materials for classroom use.[3]

In view of these findings, the role of librarians is vital and critical. As professional materials specialists, librarians can make a distinct contribution to teachers and other professionals in locating, evaluating, and selecting suitable materials for disabled children and young people. Therefore, this chapter relates the selection process specifically to the evaluation and selection of materials for these library users by discussing 1) *basic selection principles*, including a philosophy of selection, the characteristics of users, and the characteristics of materials; and 2) *specific criteria* to be considered when evaluating and selecting materials for disabled children and young people.

BASIC SELECTION PRINCIPLES

Selection of materials for collection building, for group and individual use, or for library programs is a primary professional task of librarians. Because funds are always limited, it is necessary that the selection process be conducted very carefully. As every librarian knows, selecting appropriate quality materials within the limits of available funds, and keeping the collection balanced according to subject matter and format, is a difficult, demanding, and continuous task. Therefore, the basic principles of selection must apply also to selecting materials for disabled children and young people:

1. Establishing a philosophy of selection which includes disabled users;

2. Analyzing the characteristics of the users and the characteristics of the materials;

3. Locating suitable materials through selection tools and other sources;

4. Evaluating materials on the basis of specific established criteria.

The third point, locating materials, was discussed in chapter 8, while the other three points will be discussed in the following pages.

Selection Philosophy

The selection of materials should always be based on a philosophy of selection, both the philosophy of the selector and the philosophy of the selector's institution in regard to library users and the selection process. What does the *selector* believe about the user of materials and the role of the library in supplying materials for the user? What position or view does the *institution* hold in regard to the library's users?

The literature of librarianship and national standards for various types of libraries stress the importance of having a written materials selection policy which has been adopted by the library and which should be followed by all persons who are involved in the selection of materials.[4] In effect, the selection policy is "a summation of the philosophy, the standards, and the principles which underlie the choice of books and other communication materials that make up the resources of a library."[5] The materials selection policy should state clearly the philosophy of selection which is followed in the library and should include a statement regarding the selection of materials for disabled persons (as well as other special groups). The selection policy should also include selection criteria in relation to specialized materials for those who are disabled.

In an excellent, classic statement, Florence Grannis discussed the philosophical implications of book selection for blind persons. Her statement has equal value in relation to children and young people with all types of disabilities, as well as in regard to all types of media. What is the librarian's philosophy — what does the librarian *believe* — about disabilities and disabled children and young people? Unconsciously, the selector selects or rejects materials on the basis of his or her concept of what disabled children need and want and should have, a concept that is influenced to a great extent by the views held by other individuals regarding disabled children and young people. Attitudes toward disabled persons, whether positive or negative, are therefore inherently involved in the selection process and will determine the subjects and formats and quantities of materials that are selected. If the selector believes that the interests and tastes of disabled children and young people in regard to reading and audiovisual materials are basically the same as the interests and tastes of corresponding groups of nondisabled children and young people, then the selector will provide for those who are disabled the same variety of formats and subject matter which are offered to the nondisabled.[6]

Characteristics of Users

Another basic principle which should be observed in selecting materials for disabled children and young people is to consider the characteristics of the users: age and/or grade level, needs, interests, abilities, learning styles, attitudes, preferences, physical characteristics, and social or cultural background. These characteristics have been discussed in chapter 5 in relation to the similarities and differences which exist between those who are disabled and those who are not disabled, as well as the similarities and differences between children and young people with the same type of disability. In order to meet the materials needs of library users on the basis of their unique characteristics, it is necessary to provide materials in a variety of forms, at different ability levels, and suitable for different needs and interests.

Disabled children and young people are distinctive in regard to needs, experiential background, and learning style. Each individual has informational and recreational needs that are comparable to others of the same chronological age, as well as having special informational and recreational needs that are determined by individual interests. The experiential background of a disabled child, however, is often severely limited and far behind others of the same age. In addition, each disabled child, because of individual ability and personal preference as well as because of the particular disability, has a learning style that determines the modality or modalities through which learning can best be achieved. Materials that utilize these modalities should be used to compensate, as much as possible, for the deprivations that affect the life of a disabled child or young person.

One aspect needs emphasis at this point, however, and that is physical characteristics. While the age, needs, interests, abilities, and other characteristics of disabled children and young people may be similar to other disabled and nondisabled children and young people, there may be important differences in *physical characteristics* caused by the disability. The disability, as a class defect, cannot be ignored because it may have implications for the learning of a disabled child and the child's use of materials. In fact, the disability may automatically impose limitations on the child which affect the selection of appropriate materials for the child.[7] For instance, *informational and subject matter needs* may be identical or comparable whether an individual is disabled or not, but *materials format needs* may vary greatly according to a particular disability. A blind student, because of the blindness, has a need for learning materials that use the auditory and tactile senses. A hearing-impaired student, because of the hearing impairment, has a need for materials that utilize the printed word and pictorial representations. A twelve-year-old mentally retarded child, because of the intellectual impairment, may be reading several grades below age level and require simple reading materials at an interest level which appeals to those of the same chronological age. Tuttle compared three reading media for the blind—braille, normal recording, and compressed speech—and found that compressed speech was the most efficient media to meet the reading demands of blind children and young people. Reading by listening ranked second in effectiveness as a reading medium for the blind. Although braille ranked third, Tuttle remarked that braille is not outmoded because it is the most precise format for reading and writing for the blind.[8]

The characteristics of the slow learner were discussed by Boutwell. The slow learner, he wrote:

1. Has a low capacity for schooling, is a poor reader, and consequently is poor in other academic areas;

2. Has a short attention span;

3. Resists hardcover books because they look long and are heavy;

4. Has not been read to during the preschool years;

5. Needs to experience success in reading;

6. Has a limited acquaintance with the external world;

7. Is limited in oral expression;

8. Is often an alienated child.[9]

Characteristics of Materials

In addition to the characteristics of the user, the characteristics of materials must also be considered as a basic principle in selecting materials. Each type of material has its own characteristics which make it unique from other formats, and each format has particular advantages as well as limitations. A book, for instance, is different in some respects from a magazine or a pamphlet and far different from a filmstrip, 16mm film, videotape, or recorded material.

All types of materials have inherent strengths and weaknesses. For example, *printed materials* are useful as a private individualized tool for examining behavior and allowing time for the reader to reflect, away from peer pressure and the need to perform in a group. The weakness of print is that it can serve as a form of retreat or withdrawal from critical examination, and feedback may be less spontaneous than in other formats.

Film presentations are strong in providing a necessary element of realism in depicting values, beliefs, and attitudes fleshed out in action. They are good for focusing abstract concepts concretely. However, since the film is a total package, there is little chance of deleting those parts which may be irrelevant to learning or program objectives, that is, those parts that might obscure or confuse the emphasis which a person wishes to bring into focus. Also, because of the noninteractive nature of films, feedback regarding impressions is delayed and any follow-up discussion might lack the immediacy of interruption which is possible in other formats.

The weakness of film presentation is the strength of *filmstrips and slides*, which can be advanced or backed up as determined by the needs of the moment. There is also a wide latitude for improvisation, e.g., creating a sound cassette to accompany the visuals, orally discussing the visual and its relationship to the objectives, or staying with the visual as long as is required in order to accommodate feedback. Filmstrips, however, tend to be low in realistic impact and therefore serve best in illustrating points for discussion rather than as a vehicle for exciting response by way of viewer emotional involvement. This can be a plus, however, if viewer distance is preferred.

Through *games/simulations*, role playing, and competition, a sense of immediacy and "rehearsal" are provided directly, involving the players in a "hands-on" confrontation with differing value perspectives. No other format provides such a high level of participation in actualizing the real world within the confines of an artificial environment. Games and simulations are weak, however, because evaluation of the players' ability to maintain a distinction between game and reality is necessary for control. Follow-up debriefings are essential if the experience is to have learning effects, since there is a likelihood that some players may become too invested in the experience. However, instructor modification and game level appropriateness are factors which can temper the intensity level of play.

The following characteristics of materials should be considered in evaluating and selecting either print or nonprint materials for disabled children and young people:

- —What is the difficulty level of the material?

- —What is the interest level?

- —What is the size of the print?

- —How many illustrations are there? What size are they? How concrete are they?

- —How concrete are the pictorial representations, either in books, films, filmstrips, slides, or other pictorial materials?

- —Does the material have high motivational qualities?

- —Does the material have multisensory components?

- —What attention span is required?

- —How is the material related to lifestyles?

- —What is the material like in its organization and presentation of information?

- —Does the learner have to do anything with the materials? If so, how does the learner get feedback and how is performance evaluated?

- —Is anything required of the teacher or librarian?

- —Are any data available which show the effectiveness of the material and whether it is worth the price?[10]

SPECIFIC CRITERIA

Professional evaluation and selection of materials must be based on well-defined criteria in order to determine the appropriateness of materials for disabled children and young people. "What am I looking for? What qualities must a material have?" These are questions that selectors must consider seriously in any search for materials, whether judging on the basis of personal examination and preview or on the basis of an evaluative review.

Materials vary greatly in quality and usefulness. Simply because a material has been published or produced does not, in itself, make the material "good." Every effort needs to be expended to determine quality and usefulness. Unfortunately, however, evaluative information exists for only a relatively low percentage of resource materials. In an analysis of various resource materials which was conducted in 1974, an extensive review of the literature revealed that evaluative information was available for only 24% of the materials.[11] There is still a paucity of evaluative reviews of materials, especially audiovisual materials and realia, despite the recent attempts to fill this need to some extent in *Booklist, School Library Journal, Media Review Digest*, and other reviewing sources. Most frequently, the only information available is a descriptive abstract or annotation which takes on much significance in the evaluation and selection of materials.

Librarians have an important task, therefore, in evaluating materials before they are purchased or used. All materials, either print or nonprint, that are being considered for use with disabled children and young people should be personally examined, previewed, and evaluated on the basis of specific criteria before being selected for purchase and/or use, just as they should be when selecting for nondisabled library users. The library's present collection of books, films, other audiovisual materials, games, and realia should also be re-evaluated on the basis of the same criteria in order to determine their possible usefulness with and by disabled children and young people.

For many years, criteria have been available to guide the evaluation and selection of printed materials — books, magazines, newspapers, and pamphlets. With the phenomenal rise of audiovisual materials within recent years, criteria have also been developed for other kinds of materials. These criteria are readily available in many sources[12] and assist in evaluating and selecting print and audiovisual materials for the general user.

Many materials that are evaluated and selected for nondisabled children and young people on the basis of general criteria, as well as specific format criteria, can also be selected for disabled children and young people on the basis of the same criteria. Consideration of such factors as difficulty level, interest level, technical quality, durability, cost, etc., can be applied to all kinds of materials, whether they will be used by those who are disabled or nondisabled.

Specific criteria, however, need to be considered in regard to the needs of disabled children and young people in general and of particular types of disabilities. For example, the size and weight of a book are important considerations for those who are manually impaired. The type size used in a book is important for the partially sighted. Captions on films, filmstrips, and other pictorial presentations are necessary for the hearing impaired.

Both librarians and special educators have addressed the formulation of specific criteria for the evaluation and selection of materials for disabled persons. Regular and special educators are concerned about individual students and prescribing for each student an Individualized Education Program (IEP) which includes appropriate materials. The concern of school library media professionals and public librarians in evaluating and selecting materials for the disabled is two-pronged. For one thing, this concern is directed toward disabled children and young people *in general*, with consideration for specific disabling conditions, such as the educable mentally retarded, the visually impaired, the hearing impaired, and the orthopedically impaired. Also, the concern is directed toward *specific disabled individuals* and involves the evaluation and selection of appropriate materials for *an individual*. Therefore, librarians need to consider criteria in two ways:

1. Criteria for general materials that are being evaluated with disabled users in mind;

2. Criteria to be used when evaluating materials for use by specific individual disabled users.

Within recent years, specific criteria have been presented for evaluating and selecting materials for children and young people with various types of disabilities. Some of these presentations on criteria, however, although written with disabled persons in mind and published in specialized journals about exceptional children, nevertheless suggest criteria that are very general and are applicable to almost any kind of library user and any kind of material. Such general lists of criteria have been offered by Eash, Boland, Latham, Teter, Bleil, Wiederholt and McNutt, Thorum, and Hart.[13] Criteria which are more specifically pertinent to disabled children and young people have been developed by a number of groups and individuals and are discussed below.

Aserlind[14]

Writing in 1969, Aserlind outlined the research on learning and its implications for materials for disabled persons, claiming that a lag existed between basic research and the action level (a lag which undoubtedly still exists today). He stated that studies which have used disabled children as subjects have indicated that materials should contain some essential elements in order to be effective with disabled children. Aserlind summarized the research on various aspects of learning and demonstrated that these aspects, while applicable to all students, have definite implications also for those who are disabled. Table 5 presents an overview of Aserlind's synthesis of eleven areas of research and the implications of such research in regard to materials for disabled children and young people.

Table 5
Research on Learning and Its Implications
for Materials for the Disabled

Area	Research	Implications for Materials
Attention	Retarded students demonstrate attention deficits	Use color, shape, or other attention facilitator
Comprehension	Retarded students have difficulty with abstractions—greatest in verbal or visual communication	Materials should be simple, free of abstractions and other extraneous elements
Perception	Brain-injured students have perceptual problems in mastering academic concepts and materials	Materials should be free from perceptual and conceptual ambiguities and distortions

Table 5 (cont'd)

Area	Research	Implications for Materials
Progression	Retarded students learn in much the same way as regular students, and they can learn if material is presented in smaller increments than those presented to regular students	Materials should be sequenced in short incremental steps
Motivation	Must be considered in any type of learning involving a handicapped student	Materials should have built-in or adaptive possibilities for immediate and meaningful reinforcement
Reception	Involvement of additional receptors can facilitate the learning of handicapped students	Materials should utilize more than one receptor system: sight, sound, touch, movement
Interaction	Much learning depends on the quality and frequency of adult-child interaction	Materials should provide opportunity for meaningful adult-child (teacher-learner) interactions
Repetition	Retarded students have deficits in retention, which can be aided by overlearning (repeated presentations of the material)	Precise identification of steps required in the acquisition of a concept or skill can provide repetition of these steps until the goal is mastered
Completion	Handicapped students (as also regular students) have the desire to achieve success by satisfactorily completing a task	Materials should be designed so that a learner achieves a sense of mastery by completing a part or all of an assigned task
Identification	Learners identify with the materials of learning and this identification should be positive. Physical, social, and emotional growth of handicapped students frequently outstrips their intellectual growth	Format and design of materials should be geared to the learner's chronological and social age, and the cognitive aspects geared to the approximate mental age (i.e., high interest level-low ability level type of material)
Limitation	Problems arise when the physical, mental, and emotional limitations of handicapped students are not considered in choosing materials	Materials should reflect consideration of physical, neurological, and emotional characteristics of the learner

Association for Library Service to Children[15]

In 1980 the Association for Library Service to Children (ALSC) published a brief pamphlet titled *Selecting Materials for Children with Special Needs*, prepared by the Library Service to Children with Special Needs Committee. Three principles which underlie the evaluation and selection of materials for children with special needs were emphasized: 1) focus on the particular needs, interests, and abilities of the special child and do not overemphasize the disability; 2) look at existing materials and collections in new ways, with a view to adaptations or alternate uses of present resources because it may be more appropriate and less expensive to use existing materials rather than to seek out and purchase new materials, although it is sometimes necessary to select new materials; and 3) consider all forms of materials. The guidelines are intended for selecting materials for the general collection from which the needs and interests of the individual disabled child will be met. Enumerated are the following special groups: the blind or partially sighted, the deaf or hearing impaired, the emotionally disturbed, the learning disabled, the mentally disabled, and the physically disabled. For each of these classifications are listed characteristics and the types of materials that can be used with children who have a particular disability.

Standard Criteria for the Selection and Evaluation of Instructional Materials[16]

An extensive list of criteria, *Standard Criteria for the Selection and Evaluation of Instructional Materials*, was prepared as a response to the contemporary emphasis on disabled children and young people. The criteria are reproduced in their entirety in Appendix A. These criteria are the result of the efforts of former agencies sponsored by the Bureau of Education for the Handicapped (BEH), namely: the Special Education Instructional Materials Centers and Regional Media Centers Program (SEIMC/RMC Program) and the Area Learning Resource Center, Specialized Office, and National Center on Educational Media and Materials for the Handicapped Program (ALRC/SO/NCEMMH Program). The *Standard Criteria* were carefully and thoroughly formulated and can be used in the evaluation and selection of materials for nondisabled as well as disabled children and young people.

The *Standard Criteria* are divided into two levels, the teacher level and the national level, and can assist in evaluating and selecting materials for *individual learners* at the teacher level and for *groups of learners* at the national level. The document itself, however, does not clearly state these distinctions nor define "teacher level" and "national level." Consequently, the use of the latter term is confusing.

The two divisions of teacher level and national level both have the same four subdivisions:

1. Identification of needs
2. Initial selection
3. Review
4. Decision making

The national level has one additional subdivision: Evaluation.

At the *teacher level* the identification of needs includes consideration of criteria on the basis of the characteristics and educational requirements of a specific learner for whom material is sought. Initial selection emphasizes the process of searching materials information sources and screening the materials by means of abstracts and reviews, but not necessarily by actual examination of the material. The review section focuses on an in-depth analysis of an instructional material in order to define the characteristics of the material and to match its characteristics to the learner's characteristics already determined. Decision making involves the final determination of suitable material for use in a specific individualized learning situation.

Identification of needs at the *national level* is directed toward identifying the availability and adequacy of sources of need information before selecting suitable materials. The initial selection criteria direct the seeker of materials to search various potential materials information sources and to screen the materials by means of abstracts and reviews, but not necessarily by personal inspection. In the review stage there should be an in-depth analysis of the material in order to match the material with a specific student on the basis of learner characteristics, teacher requirements, and materials characteristics; this stage involves the actual examination of the material. The decisions stage requires a final determination of suitable material that can be used or adapted in a specific learning situation. Evaluation, the fifth stage at the national level, necessitates a final judgment, either positive, negative, or inconclusive, regarding the usefulness and effectiveness of the material with the learner in a given learning situation.

While these criteria are indeed applicable when evaluating and selecting materials at the *national* level (that is, for the broad range of handicapped students throughout the country), they are equally applicable at the *local* level (that is, for groups of learners in a smaller segment of the nation: school, district, or state). This understanding may help to clarify the question in the minds of librarians: "Where do I fit into these criteria?" The answer is: "At both levels." The criteria statements at the *teacher level* can guide librarians in assisting teachers to evaluate and select materials for *individual learners*. The statements at the *national level* can guide librarians in evaluating and selecting materials for *groups of learners* at whatever level the professional is working: school, district, or state (as well as the nation).

Gallimore[17]

In 1973 Gallimore reviewed the literature up to that time which presented criteria for the evaluation of materials for use by and with the mentally retarded. She summarized her findings in eighteen questions about criteria, which an evaluator should ask when selecting materials for the mentally disabled. Most of the questions are applicable to other types of disabilities also. It should be noted that not all of the questions relate to every library setting. Some of them are obviously more germane for a school library than a public library, that is, those questions which are concerned with the curriculum and the subject studied. The questions are as follows:

1. Are the materials durable, simple, concrete, accurate, colorful, aesthetically appealing, and essential?

2. Are the illustrations appropriate to the chronological age of the user?

3. Is the difficulty level of the material appropriate to the mental age of the user?

4. Are the materials interesting to the chronological age of the user?

5. Are the materials appropriate to the social age of the user?

6. Are the materials related to the learning characteristics of the retarded?

7. Are the materials programmed for a diminishing number of cues as the concept is learned?

8. Are the materials realistic, so that there will be a maximum carry-over of learning?

9. Is there a discernible developmental pattern to the materials as presented?

10. Do the materials involve more than one sense input?

11. Do the materials provide for immediate reinforcement?

12. Do the materials provide an opportunity for self-expression?

13. Are the materials related to the life needs of the retarded?

14. Do the materials implement the curriculum?

15. Are the materials pertinent to the subject studied?

16. Are the materials of high technical, mechanical, and educational quality?

17. Can the effect of the materials be evaluated?

18. Are the materials worth the cost?[18]

Altoona Area Public Library[19]

Criteria for the evaluation and selection of materials for the mentally retarded were developed by Anne-Marie Forer and Mary Zajac as part of a pilot project, "Learning Is For Everyone" (L.I.F.E.), for the Altoona Area (Pennsylvania) Public Library. Although prepared in regard to materials for the mentally retarded, the criteria are applicable also when selecting materials for other disabled persons, as well as for nondisabled children and young people. The criteria were included in the report on the L.I.F.E. project, titled "Library Services to the Mentally Retarded," which also offered suggestions for library services and programs for the retarded. Since these criteria are not available in published form, they are reproduced in Appendix B and include criteria for various kinds of materials: 1) books, 2) multimedia book kits, 3) periodicals, 4) multimedia filmstrip kits, 5) records, 6) toys, 7) puzzles, 8) games, 9) pictures and posters, and 10) librarian-made kits.

Boutwell[20]

Boutwell recommended a list of criteria which should be considered when evaluating materials for slow learners:

1. Length of sentences should range between ten and fifteen words.

2. Dependent clauses and compound sentences should be minimized.

3. Verbs and verb forms should be in the simple tenses of the present and the past.

4. Hard words with affixes or spellings which obscure their true sound should be avoided.

5. Contractions and dialects should be avoided.

6. Conjunctions should be simple and not used too frequently.

7. Conversational style should be used because it is easier for the slow learner to understand.

8. Personal references should be used generously because they make the text more readable.[21]

In addition to the above criteria, Boutwell offered a number of questions which should be asked when considering materials for the slow learner. The questions can be summarized in this way:

1. The material should not be preachy, patronizing, reflect an attitude of "teacher-knows-best," or include injunctions such as "ought" and "must."

2. The material should repeat words.

3. The material should involve the reader as much as possible.

4. The material should relate closely to the lives and personal interests of children and young people.

5. The material should be geared for the child's age and grade level.

6. The material should recognize the different interests of males and females.

7. The material should be humorous.

8. The material should be in tune with the current movies and television programs that are popular with young people because they can promote reading.[22]

Thormann and Rosemont[23]

Learning-disabled children and young people may have auditory and/or visual dysfunctions which interfere with their ability to read. Therefore, in evaluating and selecting books and other reading material for them, certain aspects must be considered. Thormann and Rosemont have suggested the following criteria when evaluating and selecting reading materials for those who have learning disabilities:

1. Since the reader's knowledge of vocabulary is critical, there should be clues in the context which will provide information about the meaning of difficult words.

2. The introduction of new words should be accompanied by some means of vocabulary study, together with pictures. New concepts and terminology should be clearly described.

3. Information should be presented in its simplest written form.

4. Illustrations should organize the material for the reader.

5. Words with many syllables and sentences with many clauses should be avoided. Words and sentences should be simple. The reader should be able to anticipate what will follow without being hindered by complicated sentence structure.

6. Descriptive words which are not necessary should be omitted.

7. Ideas should be presented in a direct way.

8. Pages should not be cluttered with a lot of words, but there should be a minimum number of words on each page.

9. The size of the print should be large enough to read with ease but not too large so that it looks childish.

10. Books should be short so that the reader has a feeling of success and accomplishment and is stimulated to read more.

11. Simple puzzles or games which the reader can master can be challenging and thought-provoking.[24]

Blake[25]

Ruth Blake and her colleagues prepared a set of questions for use as a guide in selecting instructional materials for visually impaired children. The questions were based on responses from over 400 individuals who participated in a study conducted under the sponsorship of the American Printing House for the Blind and the Instructional Materials Reference Center of Louisville, Kentucky. Although based on the responses of persons who were working with multihandicapped visually impaired children, the questions are also applicable to materials for use by and with those who are partially sighted as well as children and young people with other types of disabilities. These questions should be asked about the materials:

1. Is the multisensory approach emphasized? Is the development of the senses, preferably more than one sense modality, promoted?

2. Are the materials multipurpose? Can they be adapted in a number of ways?

3. Is practicality stressed? Is there a focus on everyday situations and prevocational skills?

4. Is simplicity incorporated into the design? Are nonessential elements eliminated?

5. Are the materials highly motivating? Do they have built-in rewards? Do they use a high-interest, low-vocabulary approach?

6. Is the learning of basic skills and knowledge incorporated? Are these materials designed to help teach elementary concepts which may be accomplished by other children through incidental learning?

7. Are the materials structured for sequential learning? Are they programmed from the very simple to the more complex?

8. Is each item sturdy and durable? Can they be used by older children who function on very elementary levels?

9. Do the materials deal more with concrete experiences than with abstract concepts? Is the child involved in learning by doing?

10. Do the materials focus on the development of communication and language? Is the area of listening skills development fostered?

11. Is independent functioning promoted?

12. Can the materials be used by parents?

13. Do the materials provide for repetition? Are they designed to present the same concept in a variety of ways?

14. Do the materials meet the needs of the older child? Are these items of particular value in the light of a limited quantity of instructional materials available for older multihandicapped visually impaired children?[26]

Computer Software

With the current rapid expansion of computer technology, librarians must give attention to the use of microcomputers by disabled and nondisabled children and young people. Consequently, consideration must be given to the evaluation and selection of quality software, and criteria have been developed for this purpose. Two sets of recently published criteria questions are reproduced below. In both instances, the criteria are directed toward educational purposes and the use of the software programs by all students in general, although they can be useful in evaluating programs for the use of disabled students specifically or in regard to noneducational programs.

Kleiman, Humphrey, and Van Buskirk suggested the following guideline questions to ask about computer software which is designed for educational use:

1. Does the program fulfill its purpose?

2. Is the software appropriate for the situation in which it will be used?

3. Is the software suitable for the intended users?

4. Does the software adapt the computer to the user or must the user adapt to the computer?

5. Does the software take advantage of the capabilities of the computer in presenting the lessons?

6. Is the program adaptable to different children and teaching methods?

7. Will the program hold the user's attention?

8. Does the software provide useful feedback to the user?[27]

In *Classroom Computer News*, under the issue theme "The First Annual Compendium of Common and Uncommon Computer Lore," the following criteria were presented:

Description
  Beyond a brief overview of what the program does, consider:
  • Is the program designed for individuals or group use?
  • Is it especially appropriate for remedial, gifted, or special needs students?
  • How long is it?
  • Do any good support materials come readily to mind?

Remarks
  Does the program make good use of the computer?
  • Could a workbook do the same job? If so, is the exercise worth the price of a computerized version?
  • Do the graphics and sound contribute to the program or are they distracting or ancillary?
  • Is information presented in varied formats?
  • Does the program allow for a good deal of interaction?
  • Do management routines really make your job easier?

Is the program easy to use?
  • Does it load correctly and run without errors?
  • Is the documentation clear?
  • Are the instructions clear?
  • Can the user get help by returning to instructions or content material if necessary?
  • Can he or she skip over familiar instructions?
  • Is the program bomb-proof?

Is the program pedagogically sound?
- Is the content correct?
- Is the spelling correct?
- Is the instructional objective clear and appropriate?
- Is the level of presentation consistent?
- Is the treatment of right and wrong answers suitable?
- Are the rewards for right answers more appealing than those for wrong?
- Do the kids like it?
- Do you like it?[28]

Other lists of criteria are available in the growing supply of books and journals which have appeared on this subject.[29] Evaluations of computer software can be found in a number of sources, including *InfoWorld, The Book* (for Apple Software), *Educational Software Directory, VanLoves Software Directory, The Computing Teacher, Creative Computing, MicroSIFT, School Microware Reviews*, and *Software Review*. A list of software directories as well as centers and sources of information about computer software is given in chapter 8. In addition, the National Council of Teachers of Mathematics, 1906 Association Drive, Reston, VA 22091, has produced a booklet, *Guidelines for Evaluating Computerized Instructional Materials*, which gives information on obtaining software, guidelines for review, and an evaluation form.

High-Interest/Low-Reading-Level Books

Since high-interest/low-reading-level books are essential for the reading development of many disabled children and young people, it is also useful to consider specific criteria for the evaluation of these books. Barbara Bates has suggested criteria in three categories:

Appearance: Wide margins, extra leading space between lines, short chapters, a type style that is easy to read, and paper of good quality

Content: Fiction—the author tells what to look for in the narrative line, story line, point of view, characters, cast, situations, emotional appeal, mood, and the opening sentence. Nonfiction—scope, technique, and subject matter

Style: Vocabulary, sentence length, size of paragraphs, concepts, sensory appeal, rhythm, and pace[30]

The Hi/Lo Committee of the American Library Association's Young Adult Services Division prepared an extensive list of evaluation criteria suggested for use in the selection of high-interest/low-reading-level materials for reluctant teenage readers. The criteria are as follows:

Is the appearance of the book suitable to the age intended?

210 / 9—Evaluating and Selecting Materials

Are photographs or pictures of teenagers or of children? Are they geared to the text in terms of the age group intended, story, content, etc.?

Do photos or illustrations move story along? Do they add texture?

Are photos or illustrations a substitute for characterizations? If removed, can the book stand on its own?

Glance at the printed page; is the type in overly large letters, set in wide margins to look like a reader, or is the type set in sentence and paragraph arrangement?

Is the book awkward in shape (i.e., square) using glossy paper, which sets it apart from other books geared to this age group?

Does writing style assume that young people reading on this level are dumb?

Is the story censored?

If it's a biography, are facts about the figure's personal life omitted or brushed off? If the figure is divorced or having problems, is material presented in an understandable fashion?

Is the tone condescending or overly juvenile?

If the book is fiction, how does it compare with some of the better junior novels? Do you see similarities in theme and character?

Do difficult words define themselves in the text?

Does the subject have teenage appeal? Is the topic current or of immediate interest to teenagers (e.g., King Tut, alcoholism, sports figures or popular sport)?

If subject is alien to teenage interest (e.g., historical or scientific), can you still see this as being part of curriculum or a unique addition to one's reading experience? If yes, perhaps this is an ideal book for the reluctant reader for a book report, etc.

Are facts presented clearly and accurately?

Is this a first book on a topic?

Does the book cover its subject with enough depth to stimulate interest for the reluctant reader to want to read further?

Can you see this title as a bridge to something more difficult?

Can young people identify with the premise of the book?

Has the book appeared to promise too much? Does it deliver?

Would a glossary or index add to the overall package or would it make it seem like a school text?

Overall is book readable?[31]

Criteria for Toys

The U.S. Consumer Product Safety Commission has counseled that toys for very young children should be chosen with great care. The commission listed a number of characteristics which should be considered when purchasing a toy. Choose a toy that:

1. Is too large to be swallowed;

2. Does not have detachable small parts that can be lodged in the windpipe, ears, or nostrils;

3. Is not apt to break easily into small pieces or leave jagged edges;

4. Does not have sharp edges or points;

5. Has not been put together with straight pins, sharp wire, nails, and the like that might be easily exposed;

6. Is not made of glass or brittle plastic;

7. Is labeled "non-toxic." Avoid painted toys for infants who put things in their mouths;

8. Does not have parts that can punch fingers or catch hair;

9. Does not have cords or strings over twelve inches in length;

10. Check fabrics for "non-flammable," "flame retardant," or "flame-resistant" labels;

11. Look for "washable" and "hygienic materials" notices on stuffed toys and dolls;

12. Avoid toys with excessive loud noises.

Megan Smith, at the South Dakota School for the Visually Handicapped, has suggested five categories to assist decision-makers in their choice of toys and games. Toys and games should:

1. Meet the requirements of those using them as to size, form, indoor-outdoor possibilities, and the need for both learning and sheer fun.
    a. Interest the children.
    b. Adapt to more than one purpose, more than one child, and more than one age limit.
    c. Withstand hard usage and weather.

      d. Comply with safety and sanitation standards.

      e. Encourage action that can be completed in a relatively short time for younger children, or challenge the ingenuity and perseverance of older ones.

2. Help the child gain some competence for living in the world.
    a. Build variety of understanding with each child level.
    b. Further some of the skills of reading, writing and figuring appropriate to the child's needs, interests, and abilities; contribute toward the child's readiness for the next stage of growth.
    c. Invite exploration of the arts and sciences.
    d. Develop strength and skills together with hand-eye coordination.

3. Strengthen the relationship with other people.
    a. Offer opportunities to consult, converse, or correspond with others.
    b. Provide for both social and independent activities.

4. Arouse wonderment, imagination, or creative thinking.
    a. Promote constructive expression of feelings, thoughts, and ideas.
    b. Please the eye in line, color, proportion, and general appearance; the ear in sound; the hand in feeling.
    c. Suggest experimentation.
    d. Help children relive and clarify their experiences.
    e. Make possible opportunities for children to feel good about themselves when they do their own thinking.

5. Justify their cost in quality rather than quantity.
    a. Compare favorably in price to similar articles by other manufacturers.
    b. Represent exactly what the manufacturer claims, such as ease of assembling for use.[32]

In addition, Smith also suggested the following important considerations when selecting a toy for visually impaired children:

1. Is it clearly marked in large, bold, letters — colors, clear and not too much background "activity"?

2. Can it easily be adapted to the braille reader or visually handicapped student? To outline an area for a braille student, make a line with Elmer's glue or glue a piece of string on the lines. When making braille labels use clear Dymo embossing tape — the braille lasts longer on it than on Labelon tape. For the low vision student, lines may be outlined with black magic marker.

3. Are the instructions easily read and understood? Some students take one look at complex instructions and give up. When the type used is too small — it is necessary to copy them in large type. Keep a copy on file as they are often lost.

4. Consider your client ratio—at present we have more boys than girls; more low vision students than braille. Follow same ratio when making selections.

5. In a residential setting, quality and durability are important as the children use the toys in their dormitory rooms where they are not always closely supervised. The game "Booby Trap" (which is plastic) was broken the first time it was checked out by a student in the dorm.

6. Toys that have a lot of pieces are discouraged by house-parents—Legos, Lincoln Logs, and puzzles. These are hard to supervise although they are popular among students.

7. As we serve pre-school children in the deaf-blind department, it is good to follow the U.S. Consumer Product Safety Commission guidelines.

8. It is advisable to check each item when it is returned to see if all the pieces are there. Chances of finding a missing piece are better if you can check on it immediately.[33]

It has been suggested that toys should have the following characteristics:

Action. The toy must *do* something, that is, be able to perform some movement or pattern of movements with (usually) little or no input from the player.

Sight and Sound. Good toys should be bright and, if possible, shiny. They should make noise, such as music.

Shape. The toy should have holdability, that is, be easily grasped, held to the chest, or manipulated in some fashion. Indentations, bumps, extensions, curves, and handholds contribute to a child's interest in a toy and to its holdability.

Size—neither too small to hold or see, nor too large to hold or manipulate.

Texture—should have a relationship to the other characteristics. Either soft or hard textures have their own interest. Together with other characteristics, texture is good only if it commands focus.

Mobility—ability to get from place to place. The mobility of a toy should be in relation to the child's ability to maintain it within an interesting range so that it does not get away.

Safety in regard to breaking, swallowing, and throwing.[34]

On the basis of these characteristics, toys can be evaluated and a score given to the various elements. Since certain characteristics may be considered more important than others, each characteristic can be weighted accordingly. For instance, in the following example (see table 6, page 214) action and safety are regarded as the most important, sound/sight and mobility are next, and these are followed by size, shape, and texture. Such a scoring procedure provides a general score for the toy and a basis upon which to make a decision regarding selection.[35]

Table 6
Scoring Procedure for Toys

Characteristic	Weight	Superior (3)	Good (2)	Adequate (1)	Inadequate (0)
Action	2 x				
Safety	2 x				
Sound/sight	1.5 x				
Mobility	1.5 x				
Size	1 x				
Shape	1 x				
Texture	1 x				
Score					
Total Score in Range		30	20	10	0

From *The Value of Toys in Institutional Libraries* (Pierre: South Dakota State Library, 1980), p. 42.

Evaluation Forms

In the literature of librarianship and instructional technology are many examples of evaluation forms which can be used in the evaluation of various types of materials which are utilized by library users in general. These forms can be helpful when evaluating materials with disabled children and young people in mind. In addition, some publications specifically related to those who are disabled have included examples of evaluation forms. Only two of these are reproduced here. The first example is usable for the evaluation of general materials, while the second is for the evaluation of toys. A third example is for the evaluation of high-interest/low-reading-level books.

The first example appeared in an article titled "Materials Analysis" in the *Journal of Learning Disabilities*. It is suitable for the evaluation of various types of materials and is not restricted to use with materials for those who have learning disabilities. It can be used in the evaluation of materials which may be used by children and young people with various types of disabilities.

MATERIALS EVALUATION FORM

Title: _____

Author: _____

Publisher: _____

Address: _____

_____

Cost: _____

1. LEARNER CHARACTERISTICS:
   a. Chronological age:
   b. Grade level:

Reprinted by special permission of The Professional Press, Inc. from the *Journal of Learning Disabilities* 9 (August/September 1976): 408-416. © 1976 by The Professional Press, Inc.

c. Mental age:
d. Reading level:
e. Specific population for which material was designed:
f. Developmental age of concepts in instructions and activities:
g. Level of physical development required:

_____ Major factor   _____ Minor factor   _____ Not important

Comment: _____

2. MATERIAL PURPOSE:
   a. What does material say it will do? _____

   b. Objectives:
      _____ Behavioral   _____ Nonbehavioral

3. ORGANIZATION:
   _____ Lessons, explain
   _____ Units, explain
   _____ Chapters, explain
   Other _____

4. MATERIALS FORMAT:
   _____ Live verbal input   _____ Workbooks
   _____ Records   _____ Consumable
   _____ Tapes   _____ Nonconsumable
   _____ Film (bw/color)   _____ Textbook
   _____ Filmstrips (bw/color)   _____ Flashcards (bw/color)
   _____ Posters (bw)   _____ Models
        _____ Consumable   _____ Demonstration
        _____ Nonconsumable   _____ Programmed
   _____ Worksheets

5. PRIMARY SENSORY PATH USED TO TRANSFER INFORMATION:
   _____ Auditory (lectures, tapes, records, etc.)
   _____ Audio-visual (tape & worksheets, sound film, etc.)
   _____ Visual (filmstrips, flashcards, worksheets, workbooks, textbooks, etc.)
   _____ Olfactory (scent bottles)

6. SPACE REQUIREMENTS: _____

7. TIME REQUIREMENTS: _____

8. LEARNER INTERACTION:
   _____ Motor
        _____ Physical activity (dance, jump, etc.)
        _____ Manipulation (beads, puzzles, etc.)
        _____ Write a response
        _____ Mark a response
        _____ Other _____
   _____ Verbal
        _____ Answers questions

(Form continues on page 216)

_____ Repeats information
_____ Spontaneous contribution
_____ Other _____
_____ Visual-Motor
    _____ Copying tasks (bead or block patterns, etc.)
    _____ Tracing
    _____ Other _____
_____ Visual
    _____ Read
    _____ Observe
    _____ Matching
    _____ Other _____
_____ Verbal-Motor
    _____ Dramatization
    _____ Other _____

9. LEARNER KNOWLEDGE OF PROGRESS:
  a. How does teacher and student know response is correct?
    _____ Teacher checks student's work
    _____ Self-checking by student when work is complete
    _____ Immediate feedback process of some kind

Comment: _____
_____

10. EVALUATION AND DATA RECORDING PROCEDURES:
  a. How is starting point of instruction established?
    _____ Written test   _____ Oral test
    _____ Checklist   _____ Criterion test
    _____ Performance test
    _____ Direct & continuous measurement
    _____ Direct & noncontinuous measurement
    _____ Other _____

Comment: _____
_____

  b. How is mastery of content demonstrated and recorded?
    _____ Written test   _____ Oral test
    _____ Checklist   _____ Criterion test
    _____ Performance test
    _____ Direct & continuous measurement
    _____ Direct & noncontinuous measurement
  c. Data forms provided:
    _____ Yes   _____ No
  d. Are criteria for acceptable performance stated?
    _____ Yes, explain _____
    _____ No, explain _____

Comment: _____
_____

11. TEACHER INVOLVEMENT REQUIRED: TEACHER PREPARATION
    (CHECK ONE)
    _____ Extensive   _____ Minimal   _____ Reasonable

Teacher involvement during time in use:

_____ Constant interaction

_____ Teacher introduces & student completes

_____ Supportive help or monitor role

_____ Virtually none or none at all

Teacher responsibility when student is through with material:

_____ Teacher must check & provide feedback

_____ Virtually none or none at all

Comment: _____

12. TEACHER AIDS: IS THERE A TEACHER'S GUIDE OR MANUAL?

_____ Yes _____ No

If yes, what does it include?

_____ Script

_____ Annotated copy of student material

_____ Background information

_____ Extended activities

_____ Follow-up activities

_____ Other _____

Comment: _____

13. POTPOURRI:

General design (describe): Illustrations (describe): Print type and size:

14. EFFICIENCY QUOTIENT:

Cost vs. skills, concepts presented:	How many students can participate at one time?	Required teacher involvement?	How much time is required by the student?

_____ Consumable _____ Reusable

15. FIELD TEST DATA:

_____ In manual or guide _____ Available on request

_____ None given or available

Quality of data:

_____ High

_____ Average

_____ Poor

Comment: _____

16. RESEARCH DATA:

_____ In manual or guide _____ Available on request

_____ None given or available

Quality of data:

_____ High

_____ Average

_____ Poor

Comment: _____

The second example is a very good evaluation form for toys, covering the essential aspects that need to be considered. It is included here because it is for a specific type of material and a form which may not be readily found elsewhere.

Toy Evaluation

Toy_____   Student _____
Manufacturer _____   General Handicaps_____
Where Purchased_____   _____
_____   _____

Toy Section	Student Section

I ACTION

I   1. What motions does the toy make?
_____
_____

I. 2. Will the motions continue when initiated? _____
How long?_____

I. 3. What is required to initiate motion? _____
_____

I. 3a. Can the student initiate the motion? if he is helped _____ Why not?_____
_____

I. 3b. How can motion initiation be modified for this student?_____
_____

II SOUND AND SIGHT

II. 1. Is the toy brightly colored?_____
II. 2. Is the toy shiny?_____

II. 3. Does the toy make noise?_____

II. 4. How is the noise initiated?_____
_____
Will the noise continue after initiation? _____ How long?_____

II. 2a. Does the student watch or reach for the toy?_____
II. 3a. Does the student attend to the noise made by the toy?_____
II. 4a. Can the student initiate the noise?
_____
II. 4b. How can noise initiation be modified for this student?_____
_____

III SHAPE

III. 1. What are the shape features of this toy? _____
_____

From *The Value of Toys in Institutional Libraries* (Pierre: South Dakota State Library, 1980), pp. 47-49.

III. 2. Can this toy be held with one hand? _____ How?_____

III. 2a. for this student, this toy is: Easily manipulated, 1 2 3 4 5 Not manipulable

III. 2b. Can the toy be modified for easier manipulation? _____ How?_____

IV SIZE

IV. 1. What are the general configurations? _____

IV. 1a. Can this student easily see this toy? _____

IV. 1b. Is the toy (too large) (too small) for the student to manipulate?_____

V TEXTURE

V. 1. What textures are present?
_____
_____

V. 1a. Does the student indicate appreciation of this toy's texture?_____
How? _____

VI MOBILITY

VI. 1. What are the toy's mobility features? _____

VI. 2. This toy is: (very mobile) (somewhat mobile) (not mobile)

VI. 2a. Can the student follow the trajectory of the toy?_____

VI. 2b. Can the student retrieve the toy?
_____

VI. 2c. How can mobility be changed if necessary? _____

VII SAFETY

VII. 1. Toy composition_____
_____

VII. 2. Can the toy be swallowed?_____

VII. 2a. Does the student swallow small objects? _____

VII. 3. Can the toy be broken by dropping or pounding? (how much exertion required?)_____

VII. 3a. Can this student exert enough force to break this toy? How?_____
_____

VII. 4. When broken, are there harmful residues? What?_____

VII. 5. Can the student hurt others by throwing?_____ How?_____
_____

VII. 5a. Does this student throw objects?
_____

(Form continues on page 220)

SUMMARY

This toy is, in general: For this student, this toy is:

Characteristic	Superior	Good	Adequate	In-adequate	Superior	Good	Adequate	In-adequate
Action								
Sound & Sight								
Shape								
Size								
Texture								
Mobility								
Safety								

The third example is a form for evaluating high-interest/low-reading-level books which was included in the *High Interest/Low Reading Level Information Packet* distributed by the Young Adult Services Division of the American Library Association. Both librarians and teachers are becoming more concerned about selecting high-interest/low-reading-level books for disabled children and young people as well as for those who are nondisabled but are poor readers. In the evaluation process, it is helpful to use an evaluation form such as the example shown below.

EVALUATION: HI-LOW BOOK

PUBLISHER   AUTHOR   TITLE

Type of Book
Fiction   **Nonfiction**
Adventure   Automotive   Science
Automotive   Biography-General   Sports
Legend-folklore   Biography-Sports   Travel-Geography
Mystery   Career
Social Problems   Health
Sports   History

Rating Factors (Describe in a brief phrase or two)
 1. Size and Shape
 2. Cover art
 3. Title
 4. Subject or content appeal
 5. Inside illustration
 6. Type page
 7. Opening

8. Organization (Nonfiction)
   Time line (fiction)
9. Scope
10. Style
11. Vocabulary—general
12. Special Vocabulary

*Rating for use in your library: D R Ad M NR Sp

*Distinguished
 Recommended
 Additional
 Marginal
 Not Recommended
 Special Reader only

In evaluating materials, it is not only important to know what to look for, but it is also necessary to know what to "watch out for." Bleil has suggested four things to view with caution. First is the *magic solution* offered by the publisher or producer through the use of superlative language. Second are the *diagnostic labels* which may or may not indicate the children or young people for whom the materials are appropriate. Third are fad *words or phrases*, such as "high interest, low vocabulary" and other jargon which implies that the material can be matched to a specific need, but the match may or may not be accurate. Fourth are *grade levels* which can be deceptive because it is not known how the level was determined, who picked the grade level, and whether it can really be relied upon.[36]

NOTES

[1]Robert R. Lange, Charyl T. Mattson, and James B. Thomann, "Needs for Instructional Media and Materials Services for Handicapped Learners: A Summary of Extant Information" (Columbus, OH: The National Center on Educational Media and Materials for the Handicapped, Ohio State University, 1974), pp. 18-22.

[2]Jay R. Shotel, Richard P. Iano, and James F. McGettigan, "Teacher Attitudes Associated with the Integration of Handicapped Children," *Exceptional Children* 38 (May 1972): 681-82.

[3]"NSAIM: Two Years Later," *EPIEgram* 5 (December 1, 1976): 1. From EPIE Institute, PO Box 620, Stony Brook, New York 11790.

[4]Cf., for example, American Association of School Librarians and Association for Educational Communications and Technology, *Media Programs: District and School* (Chicago: American Library Association; and Washington: Association for Educational Communications and Technology, 1975), pp. 64-65.

[5]Ruth Gregory, "Principles Behind a Book Selection Policy," *ILA Record* 10 (October 1956): 23.

[6]Florence Grannis, "Philosophical Implications of Book Selection for the Blind," *Wilson Library Bulletin* 43 (December 1968): 330-33, reprinted in *The Special Child in the Library*, ed. Barbara Holland Baskin and Karen H. Harris (Chicago: American Library Association, 1976), pp. 29-34.

[7]Barbara Holland Baskin and Karen H. Harris, *The Special Child in the Library* (Chicago: American Library Association, 1976), p. 26.

[8]Dean W. Tuttle, "A Comparison of Three Reading Media for the Blind—Braille, Normal Recording, and Compressed Speech," *Education of the Visually Handicapped* 4 (May 1972): 44, reprinted in *The Special Child in the Library*, pp. 45-48.

[9]William D. Boutwell, "Motivating the Slow Learner," *Wilson Library Bulletin* 40 (September 1965): 75-76, reprinted in *The Special Child in the Library*, pp. 39-42.

[10]Some of these characteristics were adapted from Baskin and Harris, *The Special Child in the Library*, p. 25; and "Materials Analysis," *Journal of Learning Disabilities* 9 (August/September 1976): 408-416.

[11]*SRM Manual, Selected Resource Materials: Description and Evaluation* (Edmonton, Alberta, Canada: Alberta Department of Education, Special Educational Services Branch, 1974), p. i.

[12]See, for example, James W. Brown, Kenneth D. Norberg, and Sara K. Srygley, *Administering Educational Media: Instructional Technology and Library Services*, 2nd ed. (New York: McGraw-Hill, 1972), pp. 172-73; Carlton W. H. Erickson, *Administering Instructional Media Programs* (New York: Macmillan, 1968), pp. 71-75; Emanuel T. Prostano and Joyce S. Prostano, *The School Library Media Center*, 3rd ed. (Littleton, CO: Libraries Unlimited, 1982), p. 146; and Robert Heinich, Michael Molenda, and James D. Russell, *Instructional Media and the New Technologies of Instruction* (New York: John Wiley & Sons, 1982), pp. 46-322, passim.

[13]Maurice Eash, *Evaluation of Instructional Materials for Exceptional Children and Youth* (New York: City University of New York, ED 040540, 1969); Sandra K. Boland, "Instructional Materialism—Or How to Select the Things You Need," *Teaching Exceptional Children* 8 (Summer 1976): 156-58; Glenn Latham, *Teacher Use of Instructional Materials and Other Matters Related to Special Education IMC/LRC Collections*, Theoretical Paper No. 59 (Madison: University of Wisconsin, Research and Development Center for Cognitive Learning, ED 126663, 1976); Ralph O. Teter, ed., *Handbook: The Operation of Programs for Language-Handicapped Children* (Austin: Texas Education Agency, Division of Special Education, ED 096791, 1973); Gordon Bleil, "Evaluating Educational Materials," *Journal of Learning Disabilities* 8 (January 1975): 12-19; J. Lee Wiederholt and Gaye McNutt, "Evaluating Materials for

Handicapped Adolescents," *Journal of Learning Disabilities* 10 (March 1977): 132-40; Arden R. Thorum and others, *Instructional Materials for the Handicapped: Birth through Early Childhood* (Salt Lake City: Olympus, 1976); and Verna Hart, *Mainstreaming Children with Special Needs* (New York: Longman, 1981), pp. 171-72.

[14]Leroy Aserlind, "Research: Some Implications for the Classroom," *Teaching Exceptional Children* 1 (Winter 1969): 42-54.

[15]American Library Association, Association for Library Service to Children, Library Service to Children with Special Needs Committee, *Selecting Materials for Children with Special Needs* (Chicago: American Library Association, 1980).

[16]*Standard Criteria for the Selection and Evaluation of Instructional Materials* (Columbus, OH: National Center on Educational Media and Materials for the Handicapped, Ohio State University, 1976), reprinted in *Illinois Libraries* 59 (September 1977): 531-40.

[17]Janet Elizabeth Gallimore, "Criteria for the Selection and Evaluation of Book and Non-Book Materials for Mentally Retarded Adolescents and Adults," (Master's thesis, California State University, San Jose, 1973).

[18]Ibid., pp. 36-37.

[19]Anne-Marie Forer and Mary Zajac in cooperation with the Altoona Area Public Library, "Library Services to the Mentally Retarded," Report on the L.I.F.E. Project (Altoona, PA: Altoona Area Public Library, n.d.).

[20]Boutwell, "Motivating the Slow Learner," pp. 75-77, 100.

[21]Ibid., pp. 76-77.

[22]Ibid., pp. 77 and 100.

[23]Joan Thormann and JoAnn Rosemont, "Criteria for Books for Learning Disabled Children," *Appraisal* 10 (Winter 1977): 1-4.

[24]Ibid., pp. 2-3.

[25]Ruth Blake and others, *Visually Handicapped: An Approach to Program Development* (Indianapolis: West Central Joint Services for the Handicapped, ED 079903, 1972).

[26]Ibid., p. 9.

[27]For further discussion of these guidelines, see Glenn Kleiman, Mary M. Humphrey, and Trudy Van Buskirk, "Evaluating Educational Software," *Creative Computing* 7 (October 1981): 85-90. Reprinted from *Creative Computing Magazine*, copyright © 1981 AHL Computing, Inc.

[28]"A Level-headed Guide to Software Evaluation," *Classroom Computer News* 1 (July-August 1981): 22-23. Reprinted by permission.

[29]See, for example, Susan R. Dyer and Richard C. Forcier, "How to Pick Computer Software," *Instructional Innovator* 27 (September 1982): 38-40.

[30]Barbara S. Bates, "Identifying High Interest/Low Reading Level Books," *School Library Journal* 24 (November 1977): 19-21.

[31]Reprinted by permission of the American Library Association from the *High Interest/Low Reading Level Information Packet*; copyright © 1978 by the American Library Association.

[32]Megan Smith, "South Dakota School for the Visually Handicapped Toy Library," in *The Value of Toys in Institutional Libraries* (Pierre: South Dakota State Library, 1980), pp. 4-5.

[33]Ibid., pp. 6-7.

[34]*The Value of Toys in Institutional Libraries* (Pierre: South Dakota State Library, 1980), pp. 34-41.

[35]Ibid., pp. 41-42.

[36]Bleil, "Evaluating Educational Materials," pp. 21-22.

10_____Equipment and Devices

"I was eyes to the blind,
and feet was I to the lame."
Job 29:15

INTRODUCTION

A multitude of devices and aids are available which can increase the functional abilities of disabled children and young people. Sensory aids, corrective and prosthetic devices, and mobility devices take the form of corrective lenses, hearing aids, long canes, laser canes, guide dogs, wheelchairs, and many others. Such devices and equipment are extremely effective in assisting an individual to see and read printed and visual materials, to hear the spoken word, to move from place to place, and, in general, to function in everyday life.

ABLEDATA, an online computerized data bank of equipment for the disabled, describes some 10,000 aids and devices for disabled persons.[1] In addition, various companies and organizations publish catalogs and listings of such products. Because many of these aids and devices are personal in nature, they must be the personal property of the individual and cannot be supplied in a library. For this reason, they will not be discussed in this chapter, although librarians should be familiar with sources of information about such personal devices in order to refer library users who need and request such information to the proper source.

Many other kinds of equipment and devices, however, are suitable for location in a library for the use of disabled persons. Librarians, teachers, and parents need to be aware of those which are available, and disabled children and young people need to learn how to operate those machines which are suitable for them. This chapter describes some of the pieces of special equipment and devices which can be provided in libraries for the use of disabled children and young people and also indicates some of the sources of information about such equipment and devices. The chapter is divided as follows: 1) utilization of technology for the disabled, 2) equipment for the deaf and hearing impaired, 3) equipment for the blind and visually impaired, 4) devices for the physically disabled, and 5) other sources of information about equipment and devices.

UTILIZATION OF TECHNOLOGY FOR THE DISABLED

For many years, conventional audiovisual technology in the form of film projectors, filmstrip projectors, slide projectors, overhead projectors, tape recorders, and video recorders has been used for educational and recreational purposes. As indicated in previous chapters, this equipment can be effectively used with and by disabled children and young people. Therefore, for the benefit of both nondisabled and disabled persons, audiovisual equipment, along with the accompanying materials, should be provided in all types of libraries for the use of those persons who need and desire them.

More recently, computer technology has revolutionized modern society. The computer has altered the techniques of science and accelerated scientific study. It has made a significant impact on management and business practices, and has exerted an influence on almost every individual and institution in our society. Currently, computers are used almost universally in science, business, and industry; and they are becoming more widely applied in education, libraries, government, medicine, communication, and transportation.[2] With the increasing development and decreasing cost, microcomputers are being increasingly purchased for home and personal use. A survey conducted by Market Data Retrieval, Inc. indicated that in 1980 small businesses were purchasing the most microcomputers, followed in rank order by scientific institutions, homes, offices, and schools. On the basis of the survey, it was predicted that in 1985 the sales of microcomputers would be, in rank order, to small businesses, offices, scientific institutions, homes, and schools.[3]

Computer technology has provided the potential for many new approaches to presenting information and learning materials to disabled children and young people as well as to those who are not disabled. Microcomputers can be used by almost everyone and are now being utilized effectively by those who are impaired physically, mentally, visually, and aurally. They are patient, accurate, nonthreatening, and private. In addition, they have an almost miraculous ability to motivate as well as to give a disabled individual a feeling of independence. Some specialists believe that the use of microcomputers will soon become just as common for all types of disabled persons as the use of wheelchairs is now for those who cannot walk.[4]

Disabled persons can now operate microcomputers on their own. They can control computers through special electronic devices which respond to almost any voluntary body movement, even the twitch of an eyebrow or a puff of breath. Those who cannot use their hands can write electronically on a cathode ray tube screen by means of a light pen. Some computers respond to voice commands, while others reproduce the synthetic sounds of the human voice.[5] Computers can also control other equipment, such as video recorders, videodiscs, audiocassettes, and slide projectors.

In the interests of disabled children and young people, microcomputers that are used in the library should produce large print, use software which has low reading level, and print-out paper should be glare-free. There should be adequate lighting in the area where microcomputers are used, and tables should be high enough to accommodate wheelchairs. Any signage on the equipment or in the area should be adequate for those who are hearing or visually impaired. Equipment should be placed so that it is not dangerous for visually impaired children.[6]

Computer technology can serve disabled children and young people in two ways. First, computers can assist in instruction and the learning process through computer-assisted instruction, computer-managed instruction, games and simulations, tutorial exercises, drill and practice, and other modes. Secondly, computer technology provides prosthetic devices to disabled persons, thereby opening up communication channels between a disabled child and the outside world.[7] Those who cannot talk or use sign language, those who cannot see, those who cannot hear, and those who are immobile are benefiting from such devices. Computer technology is making it possible for them to receive information and communication through various equipment and also to convey their thoughts and express themselves to others. Efforts are continually being made to develop new uses and applications of computer technology for disabled persons. One such endeavor, begun in 1981, was the First National Search for Applications of Personal Computing to Aid the Handicapped, sponsored by Johns Hopkins University's Applied Physics Laboratory. Information about future searches may be obtained by writing to:

Personal Computing to Aid the Handicapped
Johns Hopkins University
P.O. Box 670
Laurel, MD 20810

Selected pieces of equipment which have been developed through computer technology are included among the products discussed in the following pages. All of the items which are described are appropriate for placement in a library for the use of disabled children and young people. Further information about some of the products discussed here, as well as other equipment for disabled persons, is given in a survey of selected equipment published in the November/December 1981 issue of *Library Technology Reports*. That survey provides detailed specifications and descriptions for two closed-captioning decoders, eighteen desks/tables/carrels suitable for use by persons in wheelchairs, eleven low-vision aids, eleven page turners, two reading machines, and nineteen telecommunication devices for the deaf. For each model, the following information is given in *Library Technology Reports*: manufacturer or supplier's name and address, price, description, how it works, warranty, regulatory approval, field tests, and, when available, a list of libraries using it.[8]

EQUIPMENT FOR THE DEAF AND HEARING IMPAIRED

Closed-Captioning Decoders

Reference has already been made in chapter 7 to the television programming which is produced by the National Captioning Institute and aired by the National Broadcasting Company (NBC), American Broadcasting Company (ABC), and Public Broadcasting Service (PBS). A special decoding device receives the electronic closed-captioning code and translates it into subtitles which can be seen only by those who have a decoder. Closed-captioning decoders are sold under the trade name TeleCaption by Sears Roebuck and Company, Sears Tower, Chicago, IL 60684, or the National Captioning Institute, 5203 Leesburg Pike, Falls Church, VA 22041. They are available in two types: 1) the TeleCaption Adapter can be attached to any television set to enable it to display the closed captions, and 2) the TeleCaption TV is a portable color television set which already has the decoding circuitry built into it. Either or both of these can be made available in libraries so disabled children and young people as well as disabled adults can use them in the library or borrow them for use at home.

Telecommunication Devices for the Deaf

Communication by and with deaf and hearing-impaired persons via the telephone is possible through a teletypewriter (TTY) or a telecommunication device for the deaf (TDD). A TTY is a hardcopy teleprinter machine which enables the user to send and receive messages through telephone lines with the aid of a coupler which acts as an interface. A TDD functions similarly to a TTY, but TDDs are all kinds of devices—hardcopy machines, semi-portable devices, and portable devices. The TDD is a new definition, coined a few years ago when semi-portables and portables came on the market.

TDDs are electromechanical devices which have a typewriter-like keyboard, a telephone coupler, and a visual display. Each character on the keyboard has its own tone code. When characters are pressed on the keyboard, a series of tones is generated and transmitted through the coupler over the telephone lines to the TDD at the other end, where the tones are decoded into the appropriate character and visually displayed.

TDDs are being installed in more and more libraries as a means of providing information and reference services to hearing-impaired persons, for example, in the Dallas Public Library. When a deaf person dials the special number for the deaf, an answering mechanism types out the response: "Dallas Public Library. Please type your questions followed by your name and phone number." When the library staff locates the answers to the questions, a staff member returns the call by printing the answers on the teletypewriter.[9]

Since there are many manufacturers of TDDs with different capabilities and a range of prices, it is best to shop around to choose the model which will best suit the needs of the library. Following are some of the suppliers of TDDs:

American Communication Corporation
180 Roberts Street
East Hartford, CT 06108
(203) 289-3491 (TDD and Voice)

Applied Communications Corporation
P.O. Box 555
Belmont, CA 94002
(415) 592-1622 (Voice)
(415) 592-1623 (TDD)

Bell Canada
393 University Avenue, F19
Toronto, Ontario M5G 1W9
(416) 599-6597 (Voice)

C-Phone
553 Wolfner Drive
Southport Commerce Center
Fenton, MO 63026
(314) 343-5883 (TDD and Voice)

Krown Research
6300 Arizona Circle
Los Angeles, CA 90045
(213) 559-6767 (TDD and Voice)

Micon Industries
252 Oak Street
Oakland, CA 94607
(415) 763-6033 (TDD and Voice)

Phone-TTY
14-25 Plaza Road
Fair Lawn, NJ 07410
(201) 796-5414 (TDD and Voice)

Phonics Corporation
814 Thayer Avenue
Silver Spring, MD 20910
(301) 588-8222 (Voice and TVphone)

Plantronics
345 Encinal Street
Santa Cruz, CA 95060
(408) 426-5858 (Voice)

Quadri Netics International
  Technology
3700 Yale Way
Fremont, CA 94538
(415) 651-3252 (Voice)
(415) 651-3253 (TDD)

Specialized Systems
11339 Sorrento Valley Road
Building 7
San Diego, CA 92121
(714) 481-6000 (Voice)
(714) 481-6060 (TDD)

Teleprinter Corporation of America
550 Springfield Avenue
Berkeley Heights, NJ 07922
(201) 464-5310 (Voice)

Teletype Corporation
5555 Touhy Avenue
Skokie, IL 60077
(312) 982-2000 (Voice)

Ultratec
P.O. Box 4062
Madison, WI 53711
(608) 273-0707 (TDD and Voice)

Reconditioned models of TDDs are distributed by the Teleprinter Corporation of America.

Additional information about TDDs can be obtained from:

Telecommunications for the Deaf
814 Thayer Avenue
Silver Spring, MD 20910

EQUIPMENT FOR THE BLIND AND VISUALLY IMPAIRED

A large variety of equipment is available to assist blind and visually impaired persons in the reading process, such as cassette recorders, braille equipment, closed-circuit television, "talking" calculators, print readers, and large-type typewriters. This section discusses only the Kurzweil Reading Machine®, the Optacon Print Reading System®, the VersaBraille System®, the Visualtek®, the Viewscan®, and the Variable Speech Control Recorder-Player.® The National Library Service for the Blind and Physically Handicapped has published a bibliography, *Reading Machines for the Blind*, which is a selected list of books, articles, reports, and other materials on reading machines for the blind. The bibliography is divided into general works, the Optacon, other reading machines, research, and a list of the names and addresses of some organizations involved in research and development in the field of reading machines for the blind.

Kurzweil Reading Machine

The Kurzweil Reading Machine (KRM) for the blind converts printed materials up to 11x14 inches in size—books, magazines, typewritten material—in approximately 300 type styles and sizes of type, to synthetic full-word English speech. Its component parts include a mini-computer, a scanner with internal automatic camera, a keyboard for input of all commands, software cassettes, and cables. The electronic camera scans the printed material which is placed facedown on the glass surface of the scanner, and feeds the images into the mini-computer, which recognizes each letter, groups the letters into words, computes pronunciation and stress, and finally produces synthetic speech. The machine is programmed for 1,000 linguistic rules and 2,000 exceptions.

A user activates the KRM by means of a separate, hand-sized control panel. The machine automatically locates the first line of text and begins scanning the page. Within a few seconds an electronic voice is heard reading the material. The synthetic voice is readily understandable after a short period of familiarization.

The control panel enables users to make a wide range of choices about the manner in which the material is read. The tonality of the voice can be adjusted, and the reading rate can be slowed down or speeded up. A compressed-speech feature produces fully comprehensible reading at up to 250 words a minute, much faster than the normal speaking rate of around 150 words a minute. Through the use of thirty-three controls, the machine can perform many different reading functions according to the immediate personal needs of the user during the actual reading process, such as repeating the previous few lines or words, spelling out words which may be obscure, announcing punctuation and capitalization, and marking certain words or phrases for later reference. The machine can learn to recognize new typefaces while it reads them and also announce the form of the text presented to it, for example, whether it is in columns or frequently indented. A browsing device makes it possible for a user to scan a page quickly without having to start at the top of a page and proceed line by line to the bottom of the page.

The KRM also serves as an advanced talking calculator. A simple change of program tape enables it to perform and announce not only ordinary computations but complex logarithmic, trigonometric, and exponential functions as well. The KRM is also expediting the production of braille material by automatically scanning and converting printed matter into signals used to drive braille printers. As improvements in functioning are achieved through continuing research and field experience, new programs are provided on cassette tape so they can be implemented in any existing model.

Information about the KRM may be obtained by writing:

Kurzweil Computer Products
33 Cambridge Parkway
Cambridge, MA 02142
(617) 864-4700

Optacon Print Reading System

The Optacon is a compact, portable reading system which gives blind and deaf-blind persons immediate independent access to printed materials. Using advanced electronics, the Optacon converts the image of a printed letter or symbol into a tactile form that can be felt with one finger. Different type styles, symbols, and languages can be read with the Optacon because it reproduces exactly what is printed in an enlarged vibrating tactile form.

Three integrated component parts make up the Optacon: a camera, an electronic unit, and a stimulator array. The camera is the size of a pocketknife and contains two tiny lamps and a silicon integrated circuit with 144 light-sensitive phototransistors. The electronics unit consists of solid-state circuitry and miniaturized components which make the Optacon highly portable, reliable, and low in maintenance. The stimulator array is composed of 144 miniature rods, each corresponding to a single phototransistor in the camera module and capable of vibrating to reproduce the image which is "seen" by the camera as it passes across the printed word.

To read with the Optacon, the blind person moves the camera across a line of print with the right hand. The index finger of the left hand is placed on the Optacon's tactile array, which is approximately 1½ inches long and 1 inch wide. As the camera is moved across the letter, the image is simultaneously reproduced on the tactile array by vibrating rods. The reading finger feels the enlarged letter as it passes across the tactile screen. Whatever image is viewed by the camera's lens is thereby felt by the user.

Training is essential in order to read effectively with the Optacon. Training courses have been developed for both Optacon students and blind and sighted Optacon teachers. Courses in a variety of training formats are available from the manufacturer, Telesensory Systems. Students are taught effective Optacon reading techniques and character and word recognition skills as a basis on which to build increased reading speed. Tracking aids and the line scanners, a visual display for sighted teachers, and a set of training manuals have been developed to facilitate the training process. The length of the training programs varies: more than sixty hours may be necessary for young children, while teenagers and adults may require between fifty and sixty hours of training. Reading speed in the beginning may be ten words per minute and increase to an average of thirty to fifty words per minute.

Several lens modules have also been developed for use with the Optacon. A *typewriter lens module* can be attached to a typewriter to allow the Optacon user to proofread, make corrections, locate typing position following interruptions, and fill in information on preprinted forms. The *cathode ray tube (CRT) lens module* enables the user to read many CRT displays directly. As the user moves the lens module across the face of the CRT, the Optacon presents the images on the tactile array. The *calculator lens module* enables the user to read directly the display of many electronic calculators with light emitting displays. The *magnifier lens module* replaces the standard lens module and allows the user to read extremely fine print, providing fixed magnification of 1.4 times the greatest magnification of the standard lens.

For information about the Optacon and its accessories, contact:

Telesensory Systems
3408 Hillview Avenue
P.O. Box 10099
Palo Alto, CA 94304
(415) 493-2626
(800) 227-8418

VersaBraille System

Telesensory Systems has also produced the VersaBraille system, a self-contained braille and audio information center. This electronic braille information system records braille in electronic impulses on cassette tape and displays braille on a twenty-character line of electromechanical cells. It can be used for writing, reading, note-taking, and storing brailled text. It is also an audio tape recorder which can record sound and braille on the same tape and can provide an index and automatic retrieval system for both braille and audio materials. The system is simple to operate and adaptive to a wide variety of applications.

The VersaBrailler is a compact and portable unit with attached handle and weighs approximately ten pounds. It consists of a twenty-character electromechanical display, a keyboard with all keys labeled with tactile symbols, and a place for insertion of a cassette tape. It operates on self-contained rechargeable batteries or AC charger and includes a battery charger, an external microphone, and an earphone. Optional features are a visual braille character display and an input/output connector which allows attachment to typewriters or to computers and teletypewriters for communication with outside communication centers. Controls are easily learned since the VersaBraille system carries on a dialog with the user, and information on the braille display, along with the audio cues, keep the user continually informed about the status of the system.

Using the VersaBraille system, both braille and audio can be recorded on the same tape, with 400 pages of braille stored on a sixty-minute cassette tape (200 pages per side). The tapes can be duplicated on low-cost cassette duplication equipment. The braille information can be organized the same as a book, with a table of contents, chapters, pages, and paragraphs. Each "page" has room for 1,000 braille characters (approximately the same as paper braille pages), giving a single cassette the capacity of 400,000 characters. Up to fifty chapter titles can be assigned to each tape side. Chapter length is at the discretion of the user. Therefore, on one side of a sixty-minute cassette tape, chapter length could be as short as one page or as long as 200 pages. Skimming through text is extremely fast. Chapters, paragraphs, and pages of braille text selected by the user can be located automatically, and chapter titles can be searched instantaneously. Location of information in any random order is automatic. The average time for random access of any page (one complete side of a sixty-minute cassette tape) is sixteen seconds. A "paragraph search" feature permits rapid skimming of the text by paragraphs. A "word search" feature permits instantaneous location of words or character strings within a 1,000-character page, even if misspelled. Recorded audio material can be labeled with braille titles for future retrieval and located randomly and easily. There is a variable audio speed control, and information is automatically protected from loss due to low power and/or low battery.

Editing capabilities permit adding, deleting, or substituting characters, words, phrases, or paragraphs within a 1,000-character page without rebrailling any other text. Chapter titles can be added or changed, and the user can control the automatic deletion of chapters.

Visualtek

A variety of electronic visual aids for the partially sighted are manufactured by Visualtek of Santa Monica, California. Each of them is a video visual aid system using closed-circuit television circuitry, enabling a partially sighted person to read regular printed material by magnifying the material on a display screen. The basic components of the Visualtek products consist of a camera, lens, illumination, movable table, and display screen. The user places the reading material on the movable table, and the camera projects the image onto the display screen.

Visualtek products all include the same features: variable print size, image contrast enhancement, clustered control panel, movable viewing table, and built-in lighting. *Variable print size* permits the user to adjust the magnification of the printed material up to sixty times, according to the needs of the user and regardless of the size of the original print. The brightness and sharpness of the letters can be adjusted through the *image contrast enhancement*, thus making it possible for the reader to read the material more easily. A reader can also select "positive" (black letters on white background) or "negative" (white letters on black background) contrast, according to personal ease and reading comfort. A *clustered control panel* locates all important controls in an easy-to-reach area right in front of the reader, and all controls can be located by touch alone. The *movable viewing table* enables a reader to move even the heaviest book with fingertip control. Through the *built-in lighting*, reading material is illuminated evenly, regardless of room lighting conditions.

Several Visualtek models are available. The RS-10 Video Visual Read/Write System features a nineteen-inch display screen and a separate external camera and lens which provides more flexibility for special uses, such as viewing a wall display, a person's face, or a blackboard. A typewriter accessory is standard equipment and permits use of the camera with most moving-platen typewriters. Special needs have been accommodated through the development of typing aid systems for fixed-platen typewriters, computer terminal viewing aid systems, microviewer systems, and a drafting table viewing system.

Two portable models carry the name Voyager. Voyager XL is a two-piece model which has a separate "reading section" and "display section." The "reading section" contains the camera, lens, and built-in illumination and may be transported easily from place to place. It can be connected with another display screen or with an ordinary television receiver. The Voyager is a one-piece model which is complete with a twelve-inch diagonal display screen and viewing table. It has a handle on top for maximum portability and weighs less than thirty pounds.

Visualtek products are available through many local dealers. The main office may be contacted at the following address:

Visualtek
1610 26th Street
Santa Monica, CA 90404
(213) 829-6841

Other closed-circuit television reading aids are available from the following sources:

Apollo Lasers
E.V.A. Division
6357 Arizona Circle
Los Angeles, CA 90045

EduTrainer
615 North Alfred Street
Alexandria, VA 22314

Pelco Sales
351 East Alondra Boulevard
Gardena, CA 90248

Opaque projection aids are manufactured and supplied by:

Copeland Intra Lenses Service
129 East 61st Street
New York, NY 10021

Best Visual Products Ltd.
65 Earle Avenue
Lynbrook, NY 11563

Viewscan

A unique reading aid for the partially sighted, Viewscan is a self-contained electronic magnifying system consisting of a small hand-held camera, a display screen, two high-speed microcomputers, and an ambient light deflector. Also included are a carrying case with shoulder strap, a power cord, an owner's manual (tape and print), a series of training exercises, a training aid to assist in the development of scanning skills, and a maintenance kit. Compact and portable, the complete unit is small enough to fit into a typical briefcase and weighs approximately ten pounds. Internal rechargeable batteries allow fully portable operation and may be recharged while the unit is in use.

Handwriting, typing, numerals, and different languages can be handled by Viewscan, allowing those who are partially sighted to read normal printed material. The miniature fibre optic camera is on roller guides, enabling the user to scan print accurately. As the camera is moved across the printed or hand-written materials, the high-speed microcomputers process the camera signals and generate a bright, magnified image on a flat, neon matrix, low-resolution display screen which was specially developed for use by the partially sighted. Choice of presentation includes moving or static, positive or negative images which can be magnified up to sixty-four times. The ambient light deflector is a cover which can be used to reduce distracting reflections and glare as well as to protect the screen during transit.

Viewscan is designed and manufactured in New Zealand by Wormald International Sensory Aids. For further information, contact the United States distributor:

Sensory Aids Corporation
Suite 110
White Pines Office Center
205 West Grand Avenue
Bensenville, IL 60106
(312) 766-3935

Variable Speech Control Recorder-Player

Library users can listen to hours of recorded tapes in half the time by means of the Four-Track Variable Speech Control Recorder-Player. A portable audiocassette unit, the machine has a speed range that may be varied from 60% slow-down to 250% speed-up of normal speech, with minimal distortion. The unit can compress or expand recorded sound at 15/16 or 1 ⅞ ips and will play the standard Talking Book cassettes available from the National Library Service for the Blind and Physically Handicapped. Its features include adjustable speed control, variable speech control processing throughout, built-in condenser microphone, audio stop system, automatic level control, automatic bias control, VU meter, automatic pitch control, solid-state components and accessory jacks. It can be powered by ordinary AC current or battery. Available accessories include an on-off remote foot pedal, headphone, separate microphone (including remote), ear plug, auto cigarette lighter attachment, battery pack, and a battery charger. The machine is manufactured by:

Variable Speech Control Company
2088 Union Street
San Francisco, CA 94123

It is also distributed through:

American Foundation for the Blind
15 West 16th Street
New York, NY 10011

Other variable speech devices are available from the following sources:

American Printing House for the Blind
1839 Frankfort Avenue
Louisville, KY 40206

Lexicon
60 Turner Street
Waltham, MA 02154

Visualtek
1610 26th Street
Santa Monica, CA 90404

DEVICES FOR THE PHYSICALLY DISABLED—PAGE TURNERS

Page turners are of a great variety, from the very simple to the very complex, from very inexpensive to very expensive. Although some types of page turners, such as those attached to the head or held in the mouth, might best be considered as the personal property of the user, one or more other types of page turners can appropriately be available in a library for disabled children, young people, and adults who need them. Among the simpler types are the standard baton page turner available from Beil Designs, a hand-held page turner and a mouth-held page turner, both of which are manufactured by Maddak. More complex mechanical types are the Automaddak Page Turner® manufactured by Maddak; the Brussee Page Turner® manufactured by WTB; the Lakeland Automatic Page Turner® manufactured by Lakeland Tool Works and Products; the Puff and Sip/Cushion Page Turner® manufactured by Technical Aids to Independence; the Saltus Reader® manufactured by Dickey Engineering; and the Touch Turner models manufactured by the Touch Turner Company. A more complex and more expensive type is the GEWA BLV-6 Page Turner® manufactured by Zygo Industries, which consists of plane holding reading materials, Plexiglas® sheets holding pages flat, and a friction action rubber grip roller for different page sizes and textures. This turner may be used by a person lying flat in bed and would undoubtedly not be necessary in a library.

Addresses of the manufacturers of page turners referred to above are as follows:

Beil Designs
Easy Reading Devices
5435 North Artesian
Chicago, IL 60625

Dickey Engineering
3 Angel Road
North Reading, MA 01864

Lakeland Tool Works and Products
21 Birnamwood Drive
P.O. Box 1224
Burnsville, MN 55337

Maddak
6 Industrial Road
Pequannock, NJ 07440

Technical Aids to Independence
12 Hyde Road
Bloomfield, NJ 07003

Touch Turner Company
443 View Ridge Drive
Everett, WA 98203

WTB
P.O. Box 566
Warren, OH 44482

Zygo Industries
P.O. Box 1008
Portland, OR 97207

OTHER SOURCES OF INFORMATION ABOUT EQUIPMENT AND DEVICES

Numerous other equipment and devices are available for disabled persons, and many of them are suitable for placement in a library. The National Library Service for the Blind and Physically Handicapped has published a reference circular, *Reading, Writing, and Other Communication Aids for Visually and Physically Handicapped Persons.* Among the items listed in the circular are the following: bookholders, stands, calculators for visually handicapped persons, communication aids for multiply handicapped persons, low-vision aids, page turning devices, radio and television aids, and typewriters and accessories. For each piece of equipment or device, the circular indicates suppliers and lists the addresses of the sources in the back of the booklet. The document can be obtained from the National Library Service free of charge.

The American Foundation for the Blind publishes a catalog, *Products for People with Vision Problems*. Most of the items listed are personal in nature, such as watches, clocks, and timers; canes, tips, and accessories; household and other personal items; recreational games; writing and communication devices; tools and instruments; mathematical aids; and medical devices. Also included, however, are light magnifiers and an adjustable bookstand which could be purchased and kept in a library for the use of blind and visually impaired persons. The address is:

American Foundation for the Blind
Consumer Products Department
15 West 16th Street
New York, NY 10011

Adaptive devices intended for the aid of the blind or visually impaired and, in some cases, the physically disabled can be borrowed from Handicapped Learner Materials—Special Materials Project (HLM-SMP). Many ordinary devices have been altered or modified in various ways—audible signals, braille lettering, raised lines—to make the item more suitable for use by the disabled person. Because of the ingenuity of adaptations as well as the extensive scope of devices—from angle dividers to tire pressure gauges—one can appreciate their necessity and practicality for the disabled user. Many of the devices are intended for personal use in handwriting, health, time telling, homemaking, and orientation and mobility. Others, however, can be useful in libraries, such as pressure-sensitive tape for braille labels, recreational games, and easy-grip scissors. These items are listed in the *Catalog of Instructional Materials for the Handicapped Learner*, which can be obtained from:

Handicapped Learner Materials—Special Materials Project
624 East Walnut Street
Second Floor
Indianapolis, IN 46204
(317) 636-1902 (office)
(317) 636-1870 (orders)

Similarly, Help Yourself Aids supplies many devices in the categories of eating, dressing, wheelchair accessories, reachers, recreation, communication, homemaking, and hygiene. Most of the items in the catalog are useful for disabled persons on a personal basis. Only a few—magnifying readers, bookholders, and page turners—are suitable for a library. A catalog may be requested from:

Help Yourself Aids
P.O. Box 192
Hinsdale, IL 60521

The Sign Language Store distributes materials from various publishers and producers which pertain to deafness, signed English, American Sign Language, total communication, and cued speech. Many of the books, audiocassettes, and videocassettes are suitable for addition to library collections for the use of both hearing impaired and hearing persons. A mini-dictionary of "133 Library Survival Signs" would be helpful to librarians in communicating with deaf persons. A catalog may be obtained from:

Sign Language Store
8613 Yolanda
P.O. Box 4440
Northridge, CA 91328
(213) 993-SIGN (TTY and Voice in California)
(800) 423-5413 (TTY and Voice outside California)

A wholesale hospital gift shop supplier, Benton-Kirby, lists in its catalog some recreational materials for partially sighted persons. These include such items as large-print word search puzzles, word game books, crossword puzzle books, books of sport fun, and giant face playing cards. Write for a catalog to:

Benton-Kirby
332 North Water Street
Milwaukee, WI 53202

NOTES

[1]ABLEDATA was developed by the National Rehabilitation Information Center (NARIC) and was referred to in chapter 8.

[2]Paul Watson, "The Utilization of the Computer with the Hearing Impaired and the Handicapped," *American Annals of the Deaf* 124 (September 1979): 672.

[3]"Market Survey Discovers Where the Micros Are," *Electronic Learning* 1 (March/April 1982): 14.

[4]Andrew L. Ragan, "The Miracle Worker: How Computers Help Handicapped Students," *Electronic Learning* 1 (January/February 1982): 57.

[5]Ibid., p. 58.

[6]Barbara Harvie, "Out of the Arcades and into the Library," *American Libraries* 12 (November 1981): 602.

[7]Watson, "The Utilization of the Computer," p. 671.

[8]Nancy H. Knight, "Library Service to the Disabled: A Survey of Selected Equipment," *Library Technology Reports* 17 (November/December 1981): 497-628.

[9]"Not Loud, but Clear," *Wilson Library Bulletin* 54 (November 1979): 153.

Standard Criteria for the Selection and Evaluation of Instructional Material

The National Center on Educational Media and Materials for the Handicapped (NCEMMH) in cooperation with the national system of learning resource centers, professional associations, various other public and private agencies, and interested individuals provides a comprehensive program of activities to facilitate the use of new educational technology in instructional programs for handicapped persons. NCEMMH provides leadership and service in the development, design, and dissemination of learning resources that are effective for the handicapped. The Center is funded under Contract OEC-300-72-4478 by the Bureau of Education for the Handicapped, U.S. Office of Education, Department of Health, Education, and Welfare. The contract is administered through the College of Education and the Research Foundation of The Ohio State University.

This document was prepared pursuant to a contract with the U.S. Office of Education, Department of Health, Education, and Welfare, Bureau of Education for the Handicapped. Contractors undertaking such projects under government sponsorship are encouraged to express their judgment freely in professional and technical matters. Points of view or opinions do not, therefore, necessarily represent official Office of Education position or policy. Duplication of the criteria, as distributed by NCEMMH, is permitted.

TEACHER LEVEL

I. IDENTIFICATION OF NEEDS

The outcome of stage I will be: a definition of the target learner and the learning environment prior to any selection of suitable instructional materials.

A. Learner Characteristics

(The following outline is intended to serve as a guideline to the selector of instructional materials in identifying the characteristics and educational requirements of the specific learner for whom material is being sought.)

1. Has an assessment of the learner occurred, and does the resulting data specify:
   a. demographic information about the learner, including:

Yes No NA

——— ——— ———   (1) age
——— ——— ———   (2) sex
——— ——— ———   (3) instructional / developmental level
——— ——— ———   (4) language development or preference
——— ——— ———   (5) interest level
——— ——— ———   b. limiting conditions (medical/physical factors, etc.)
——— ——— ———   c. behavioral/affective characteristics
——— ——— ———   d. preferred modalities
——— ——— ———   e. strength areas
——— ——— ———   f. deficit areas

2. Has an educational plan been developed, based on learner assessment data, which specifies:
——— ——— ———   a. needed skill area
——— ——— ———   b. short and long-term instructional objectives
——— ——— ———   c. instructional strategies, including:
——— ——— ———   (1) sequencing

Prepared by the ALRC/SO/NCEMMH Program. Distributed by NCEMMH, The Ohio State University, Columbus, Ohio 43210.

___	___	___	(2) reinforcement
___	___	___	(3) modalities (input/output)
___	___	___	(4) monitoring
			d. recommendations for:
___	___	___	(1) general instructional areas
___	___	___	(2) specific materials
___	___	___	(3) related activities

B. Program Characteristics

(The following outline is intended to serve as a guideline to the selector of instructional materials in identifying the overall program considerations with the specific learner(s) and learning requirements in mind.)

Yes   No   NA

1. Have provisions been made for integration of the individual educational plan into the total instructional program:

___ ___ ___ a. content
___ ___ ___ b. curricular compatibility
___ ___ ___ c. format/alternatives

2. Would implementation of the educational plan be affected by any of the following environmental constraints:

___ ___ ___ a. time/cost/physical considerations
___ ___ ___ b. grouping
___ ___ ___ c. equipment
___ ___ ___ d. personnel
___ ___ ___ e. teacher skill

II. INITIAL SELECTION

The outcome of stage II will be: the identification of at least two pieces of instructional material which, on first screening, appear compatible with learner requirements and which will be considered for further review. Identification of alternative materials for examination will facilitate final selection decisions on a comparative basis.

A. Search

(The items listed below outline the most common information resources available to the selector of instructional materials. The intent of this section is to encourage the user to investigate various potential materials information sources.)

1. Have you located resources which might provide information about materials:

___ a. colleagues
___ b. commercial
___ c. materials bibliographies
___ d. journals
___ e. curriculum libraries and centers (colleges, schools for handicapped, learning resource centers)
___ f. professional organizations
___ g. governmental agencies (national network, audiovisual center, etc.)
___ h. information systems (NIMIS, EPIE, ERIC, etc.)

2. As a result of the above process, have you identified at least two instructional materials which appear to address the learner's needs?

B. Screen

(Under optimal conditions, a written product abstract or review will provide information pertaining to all of the items listed below, so that actual inspection of the product is not necessary. In the absence of thorough and accurate material descriptions, however, scrutiny of the material itself will be required.

A secondary intent of this section is to educate both material users and material abstractors [including commercial publishers] about desirable elements to be included in product reviews.)

    1. Does the material information resource provide information about the identified instructional product(s), such as:

Yes No NA

___ ___ ___   a. instructional level
___ ___ ___   b. language level
___ ___ ___   c. interest level
___ ___ ___   d. sensory input and output modalities
___ ___ ___   e. educational subject/skill content
___ ___ ___   f. format
___ ___ ___   g. cost
___ ___ ___   h. grouping requirement(s)
___ ___ ___   i. required equipment

    2. On the basis of the available information, does the identified instructional material appear compatible with:

___ ___ ___   a. learner characteristics
___ ___ ___   (1) the learner assessment
___ ___ ___   (2) the learner educational plan
___ ___ ___   b. program characteristics
___ ___ ___   (1) the total instructional program considerations
___ ___ ___   (2) the identified environmental constraints

III. REVIEW

The outcome of stage III will be: an in depth analysis of an instructional material in order to define the material's characteristics and match these characteristics to previously defined learner requirements. Implementation of this stage necessitates actual examination of the instructional material.

A. Analysis of Material

(This section includes recommended questions for determining the intrinsic qualities of the material[s] independent of specific learner characteristics and program requirements.)

Yes No NA

___ ___ ___   1. Are objectives in behavioral terms (specifying what the student task is, under what conditions, and level of performance expected)?
___ ___ ___   2. Are techniques of instruction for each lesson either clearly specified or self-evident?
___ ___ ___   3. Are facts, concepts, and principles ordered in a logical manner (e.g., chronologically, easy to difficult, etc.)?
___ ___ ___   4. Does the material contain appropriate supplementary or alternative activities that contribute to or extend proposed learning?
___ ___ ___   5. Is repetition and review of content material systematic and appropriately spaced?
___ ___ ___   6. Does the content appear accurate?
___ ___ ___   7. Does the material avoid content which betrays prejudice, perpetuates stereotypes, or neglects the talents, contributions, or aspirations of any segment of the population?
___ ___ ___   8. Can the material be readily adapted to meet individual learner differences in abilities and interests?
___ ___ ___   9. Can pacing of the material be adapted to variations in learner rate of mastery?
___ ___ ___   10. Is provision made for adapting, altering, or combining input and response modalities according to learner variations?
___ ___ ___   11. Does the material incorporate evaluation items and procedures which are compatible with program objectives?
___ ___ ___   12. Are there sufficient evaluative items to accurately assess student progress?

_____ _____ _____ 13. Is performance assessed frequently enough to allow accurate assessment of student progress and continuous feedback to learner?

_____ _____ _____ 14. Is the format uncluttered, grammatically correct, and free of typographical errors?

_____ _____ _____ 15. Are illustrations and photographs clear, attractive, and appropriate to content?

_____ _____ _____ 16. Are auditory components of adequate clarity and amplification?

_____ _____ _____ 17. Are all necessary components either provided with the material or readily and inexpensively available?

_____ _____ _____ 18. Can consumable portions of material be easily and inexpensively replaced or legally reproduced?

_____ _____ _____ 19. Is cost reasonable in comparison with similar commercial materials or homemade alternatives?

_____ _____ _____ 20. Does the publisher clearly state the rationale for selection of program elements, content, and methodology (e.g., choice may be based on tradition, survey of other materials, logic of subject matter, experimental evidence, unvalidated theory)?

_____ _____ _____ 21. Are testimonials, research, and publisher claims clearly differentiated?

_____ _____ _____ 22. Are reinforcement procedures and schedules clearly indicated?

_____ _____ _____ 23. Is a variety of cuing and prompting techniques used?

B. Matching Material to Learner

(This section involves the integration of the identified learner needs with the analyzed material characteristics to determine compatibility for instructional purposes.)

Yes   No   NA

_____ _____ _____ 1. Are stated objectives and scope of the material compatible with learner's need?

_____ _____ _____ 2. Are prerequisite student skills/abilities needed to work comfortably and successfully with the material specified and compatible with the learner's characteristics?

_____ _____ _____ 3. Are the skills and abilities needed by the instructor to work effectively with the material specified and compatible with instructor's expertise?

_____ _____ _____ 4. Are levels of interest, abstraction, vocabulary, and sentence structure compatible with characteristics of the learner?

_____ _____ _____ 5. Is the degree of required teacher involvement (constant interaction, supportive or monitoring role, largely student directed, variable) compatible with teacher resources and learner characteristics?

_____ _____ _____ 6. Does the material incorporate motivational devices to sustain student interest which are appropriate to the learner's characteristics?

_____ _____ _____ 7. Are input and output modalities (visual, auditory, motor, tactile) compatible with learner characteristics?

_____ _____ _____ 8. Is the demonstration of task mastery (e.g., written test, performance test, oral test) compatible with or adaptable to intended learner's characteristics?

_____ _____ _____ 9. Is the format of the material (e.g., game, book, filmstrip, etc.) compatible with the learner's mental and physical abilities?

_____ _____ _____ 10. Is the durability and safety of the material adequate for the learner?

_____ _____ _____ 11. Is information provided indicating (successful) field testing of the material with students similar in learning characteristics and interests to those of the learner?

IV. DECISION MAKING

The outcome of stage IV will be: a final determination of material suitability for use in a specific learning situation. Individualization of the decision making, based on items of priority concern, is implicit in this process.

A. As a result of the review process, which questions have you identified as (most) critical to you in deciding to utilize the material with the learner?

B. On the basis of those critical priority concerns, is the material appropriate for specified learning requirements?

_____ Yes (Implies accept)

_____ No (implies reject)

_____ Unsure (requires more analysis)

C. If unsure of appropriateness, are there other less critical questions which could be considered in making the decision to utilize the material?

D. On the basis of those additional considerations, is the material now deemed appropriate for specified learning requirements?

_____ Yes

_____ Unsure

E. If still unsure of appropriateness of the material, will comparison with other previewed material(s), in relation to critical questions, help identify the material which most closely approximates the specified learning requirements?

F. If still unsure of the appropriateness of the material, would modifications of the material render it usable?

   1. Do you have access to resources for required modification?

G. If no:

   1. Return to search process. Reexamine sources of material identification and information in locating other potential materials.

   2. Review learner characteristics in an effort to modify requirements for material.

NATIONAL LEVEL

I. IDENTIFICATION OF NEEDS

The outcome of stage I will be: identification of the availability and adequacy of sources of need information prior to any selection of suitable instructional materials.

A. Sources

_____ 1. The National Needs Assessment sponsored by the Bureau of Education for the Handicapped

_____ 2. Consumers who are currently working with handicapped children

_____ 3. Analysis of curriculums and instructional priorities at Learner Level

_____ 4. Analysis of learner characteristics

_____ 5. Availability of appropriate materials for curricular areas

_____ 6. Availability of effective materials for learners

II. INITIAL SELECTION

The outcome of stage II will be: the identification of at least ten pieces of instructional material which, on first screening, appear compatible with learner requirements and which will be considered for further review. Identification of alternate materials for examination will facilitate final selection decisions on a comparative basis.

A. Search

(The items listed below encourage the user to investigate various potential materials information sources and to consider essential points when gathering information about materials.)

Yes No NA

_____ _____ _____ 1. Have you identified resources for materials which have potential use with the handicapped?

_____ _____ _____ 2. Have materials been identified which may be appropriate for the learner characteristics of the handicapped?

_____ _____ _____ 3. Have materials been identified which may be appropriate for the curricular needs of the handicapped?

B. Screen

(Under optimal conditions, a written product abstract or review will provide information pertaining to all of the items listed below, so that actual inspection of the product is not necessary. In the absence of thorough and accurate material descriptions, however, scrutiny of the material itself will be required.)

Yes No NA

___ ___ ___	1.	Is it a learner-use material?
___ ___ ___	2.	Is it an instructor-use material?
___ ___ ___	3.	Are all components of the material available?
___ ___ ___	4.	Does the material have potential for use with the handicapped?
___ ___ ___	5.	Is the material designed for use by the handicapped?
___ ___ ___	6.	Does the material appear to be practical to use with the handicapped?
___ ___ ___	7.	Does the material appear to be easily usable by the handicapped?
___ ___ ___	8.	Is the format of the material appropriate for the target handicapped audience?
___ ___ ___	9.	Is the material of acceptable technical quality?
___ ___ ___	10.	Does the material have instructional objectives?
___ ___ ___	11.	Does the material appear to meet the curricular needs of the handicapped target population?
___ ___ ___	12.	How does the cost of the material affect the accessibility to the material?
___ ___ ___	13.	Does the material appear to present any physical danger to the target handicapped audience?

III. REVIEW

The outcome of stage III will be: an in depth analysis of an instructional material in order to match (section D) the material for use with a specific student based on section A, Learner Characteristics, section B, Teacher Requirements, and section C, Materials Characteristics. Implementation of this stage necessitates actual examination of the instructional material.

A. Learner Characteristics

(The following outline is intended to serve as a guideline to the selector of instructional materials in identifying the characteristics and educational requirements of the specific learner for whom material is being sought.)

1. What are the possible modes of input?
   - ___ auditory
   - ___ visual
   - ___ tactile
   - ___ kinesthetic
2. What are the preferred modes of input?
   - ___ auditory
   - ___ visual
   - ___ tactile
   - ___ kinesthetic
   - ___ multisensory
3. What are the possible modes of response?
   - ___ verbal
   - ___ written
   - ___ gesture
4. ___ What is the learner's instructional level?
5. ___ What is the learner's interest level?
6. ___ What is the learner's reading level?
7. ___ What is the learner's interest areas?
8. What are the learner's interest/motivation requirements?
   - a. ___ use of a game-type format
   - b. ___ use of humor
   - c. ___ use of a variety of stimuli
   - d. ___ use of suspense
   - e. ___ use of novelty

     f. _____ use of an interaction system of instantaneous feedback
     g. _____ use of cartoon format
     h. _____ use of puppets
     i. _____ use of characters
  9. _____ What are the learner's entry level skills?
10. _____ What are the learner's reinforcement requirements?

B. Teacher-Requirements

    (The following outline is intended to serve as a guideline to the selector of instructional materials in identifying the requirements to allow a teacher/instructor to effectively use the material.)

  1. _____ Are a teacher's manual and/or instructions provided?
  2. If a teacher's manual and/or instructions are provided, does it include:
     a. _____ philosophy and rationale
     b. _____ statement of objectives
     c. _____ statement of instructional and interest levels
     d. _____ statement of reading level
     e. _____ statement of prerequisite skills
     f. _____ listing of material/program elements
     g. _____ listing of required materials and equipment
     h. _____ suggestions for teacher/instructor use
     i. _____ suggestions for student/learner use
     j. _____ suggestions for instructional alternatives
     k. _____ suggestions for evaluation
     l. _____ suggestions for additional resources
  3. Instructor time requirements:
     a. _____ training
     b. _____ preparation
     c. _____ use
     d. _____ cleanup
  4. What is the degree of instructor involvement?
     a. _____ full-time teacher involvement is required during instructional period
     b. _____ part-time teacher involvement required
     c. _____ no teacher involvement required
     d. _____ full-time aide involvement required
     e. _____ part-time aide involvement required
     f. _____ no aide involvement required
     g. _____ full-time parent involvement required
     h. _____ part-time parent involvement required
     i. _____ no parent involvement required
     j. _____ full-time peer involvement required
     k. _____ part-time peer involvement required
     l. _____ no peer involvement required
     m. _____ materials can be used independently by learners
  5. Is the material practical?

Yes	No	NA	
___	___	___	a. maneuverability
___	___	___	b. ease of storage
___	___	___	c. number of parts
___	___	___	d. identification of parts
___	___	___	e. size of parts
___	___	___	f. storage/organization of parts
___	___	___	g. durability of product and packaging

    ___ ___ ___   h. replaceability of consumable and nonconsumable parts
    ___ ___ ___.   i. requires use of specialized equipment

6. Is the total cost reasonable?
   Yes No NA

    ___ ___ ___   a. in-service training
    ___ ___ ___   b. initial cost
    ___ ___ ___   c. per use cost (replacement of consumables)
    ___ ___ ___   d. required supplementary materials costs
    ___ ___ ___   e. replacement cost (replacement of nonconsumables)

7. ___ ___ ___ Is the material appropriate for the curriculum?
8. ___ ___ ___ Has this material been field tested?
9. ___ ___ ___ If so, has it been found to be effective?

C. Materials Characteristics

(The following outline is intended to serve as a guideline to the selector of instructional materials in identifying specific characteristics a material requires to allow for communication with a learner.)

1. Technical quality
  a. Quality of auditory presentation:

	Acceptable	Unacceptable
(1) clarity (easily understood, recording quality good)	___	___
(2) amplification	___	___
(3) voice level	___	___
(4) dialect/accent	___	___
(5) voice speed	___	___
(6) voice quality	___	___
(7) sequence	___	___
(8) quality of narration (reader style)	___	___
(9) music/sound/voice mixing	___	___

  b. Quality of visual presentation:

(1) sharpness	___	___
(2) color	___	___
(3) distracting elements	___	___
(4) complexity	___	___
(5) size relationships	___	___
(6) sequence	___	___
(7) subjective angle (learner point of view)	___	___
(8) objective angle (observer point of view)	___	___
(9) composition (visual format, visual arrangement)	___	___
(10) figure-ground definition	___	___

  c. Quality of print and graphic presentation:

(1) legibility (style and size)	___	___
(2) captioning (location and pacing)	___	___
(3) clarity of print (contrast)	___	___
(4) accuracy	___	___

  d. Quality of tactile presentation:

(1) Braille (clear and easily discriminable)	___	___
(2) tactile drawings (clear and easily discriminable)	___	___
(3) texture (clear and easily discriminable	___	___
(4) composition (physical format, physical arrangement)	___	___
(5) manipulables (discriminable, dimension, shape, mass)	___	___

2. Instructional quality
   Yes No NA

    ___ ___ ___   a. Does the selection of subject matter facts adequately represent the content area?

_____ _____ _____ b. Is the content presented in the material accurate?
_____ _____ _____ c. Is the content logically sequenced?
_____ _____ _____ d. Is the content organized for ease of study?
_____ _____ _____ e. Are various points of view, including treatment of minorities, handicapped, ideologies, personal and social values, sex roles, etc., objectively represented?
_____ _____ _____ f. Are the objectives of the material clearly stated?
_____ _____ _____ g. Is the content of the material consistent with the objectives?
_____ _____ _____ h. Are the prerequisite skills for use of the materials stated?
_____ _____ _____ i. Are essential sub-skills required included in the instructional sequence?
_____ _____ _____ j. Is the reading level of the material stated?
_____ _____ _____ k. Is the vocabulary systematically introduced?
_____ _____ _____ l. Is the vocabulary consistent with the stated reading level?
_____ _____ _____ m. Is the instructional level stated?
_____ _____ _____ n. Is the interest level stated?
_____ _____ _____ o. Is the material self-pacing?
_____ _____ _____ p. Does the material provide for frequent reinforcement of major concepts?
_____ _____ _____ q. Does the material summarize and review major points?
_____ _____ _____ r. Does the material provide frequent opportunities for active student involvement and response?
_____ _____ _____ s. Does the material provide for evaluation of user performance?
_____ _____ _____ t. Does the material provide criterion-referenced assessment?
_____ _____ _____ u. Are all of the supplementary materials needed for instruction included in the materials package?

D. Matching Material to Learner

(The following questions require a synthesis of information gained from stage III, Review. The synthesis is essential before proceeding to stage IV, Decision.)

Yes No NA
_____ _____ _____ 1. Are the characteristics of the material compatible with perceived learner characteristics?
_____ _____ _____ 2. Are the characteristics of the material compatible with perceived teacher requirements?
_____ _____ _____ 3. Have you checked the list of criteria in the TEACHER LEVEL, stage III, Review, section B, Matching Material to Learner?

IV. DECISIONS

The outcome of stage IV will be: a final determination of material suitability for use in a specific learning situation. Individualization of the decision making, based on items of priority concern, is implicit in this process.

After the review process, it was found that the material was:

Yes No NI
_____ _____ _____ needed by the learner
_____ _____ _____ usable with the learner
_____ _____ _____ usable by the instructor
_____ _____ _____ effective

Decisions to:

A. Use

B. Adapt

C. Field Test

can be made by identifying from the review data responsiveness of the material to learner need, usability with the learner, usability by the instructor, and effectiveness.

Directions: For each criterion met, place a "+" in the appropriate box. For each criterion not met, place a "—" in the appropriate box. If no information is available, place an "NI" in the appropriate box.

Needed	Usable with Learner	Usable by Teacher	Effective

Match your review summary with the decision matrix below:

D. Recommendations

N	UL	UT	E	Recommend for:
+	+	+	+	U = Use/make available for use/information dissemination
+	+	+	—	A = Adapt
+	+	+	NI	U/FT = Use/Field Test
+	+	—	+	R/A/D = Reject/Adapt/Develop
+	+	—	—	R/A/D = Reject/Adapt/Develop
+	—	—	—	R/A/D = Reject/Adapt/Develop
+	—	+	—	R/A/D = Reject/Adapt/Develop
+	—	+	+	R/A/D = Reject/Adapt/Develop
+	—	+	NI	R/A/D = Reject/Adapt/Develop
—	+	+	+	R = Reject/not acceptable
—	—	+	+	R = Reject/not acceptable
—	—	—	+	R = Reject/not acceptable
—	—	—	—	R = Reject/not acceptable
—	—	—	NI	R = Reject/not acceptable

V. EVALUATION

The outcome of stage V will be: a final judgment, either positive, negative, or inconclusive, as to the usefulness and effectiveness of the material with the learner in a given learning situation.

Yes No NA

____ ____ ____ 1. Does this material meet the requirements of the teacher? (see teacher requirement section in review instrument)

____ ____ ____ 2. Does this material meet the requirements of the learner? (see learner characteristics section in review instrument)

____ ____ ____ 3. Does this material lead to the attainment of the specified objectives? (see instructional quality section in the review instrument)

____ ____ ____ 4. Does the technical quality of the material meet the requirements of the learner? (see technical quality section in review instrument)

____ ____ ____ 5. Do the instructional qualities of the material meet the requirements of the learner? (see instructional quality section of review instrument)

Criteria for Media Selection*

The most effective service a library can provide for the retarded is access to multi-media materials which have been selected to meet their special needs. Establishing a special collection exclusively for the retarded is not the goal however. The more practical and philosophically sound goal is to include materials for the retarded in the regular collection. Inclusion of special materials is philosophically sound because it encourages mainstreaming. Everyone can select from these things, and the retarded are not singled out. Inclusion is practical since everyone can use and enjoy the materials. The game which is instructive for the retarded child can be equally instructive for the average child. The lacing boards, double handled scissors, and other specialized materials can be used to teach the older trainable child as well as the preschool child. The books, records, media kits, etc. can be universally used by all. So the cost of selecting materials using the specific criteria developed for the retarded can be justified because more than one type of patron can use it. This cannot always be said of materials selected for the general public. Often, not only are the retarded excluded from their use due to their handicap, but so are other handicapped and low-functioning individuals.

Another consideration for adding special materials to your existing collections, particularly high-interest, low-vocabulary books, is the fact that the special needs of the retarded are often shared by other handicapped groups such as the learning disabled and those with speech and language problems. Poor readers and unmotivated readers who are reading significantly below grade level can profit from many of the same things selected for the retarded as long as those things are not separated from the regular collection. So providing special multi-media materials will help make it possible for libraries to serve many more non-users.

In general, material selection is based upon the same considerations as program planning, i.e.: age, ability, level of functioning, length of attention span, special learning problems which interfere with reception of visual or auditory information, and other complicating factors such as an additional physical handicap. As mentioned earlier, teachers and therapists are the best sources of advice on what materials are appropriate.

---

*From: Anne-Marie Forer and Mary Zajac, "Library Services to the Mentally Retarded." Report on the L.I.F.E. Project of the Altoona Area Public Library, Altoona, Pennsylvania, n.d.

The most important criterion for developing a collection for the retarded is its multi-media nature. Although books should be the heart of the collection, most libraries undoubtedly have many books in their existing collections which are suitable for the retarded. Therefore, we advise spending more at the outset on multi-media materials, especially book and record kits and manipulative materials such as games and educational toys or devices. The retarded individual learns and comprehends more easily if a concept is presented in several different modes so that he/she is required to respond visually, auditorially and experientially.

Selection Criteria

Books

Easy or picture books:

1. Pictures should be simple and uncluttered.

2. Pictures should be as realistic as possible. Photographs are preferred.

3. Text should not be very long since the retarded child's attention span may be shorter than average.

4. Color drawings are more effective than black and white.

5. Storyline or plot should be simple. Many young retarded children have difficulty following a storyline. They like to point out and name different things in the pictures. Older retarded children often enjoy hearing the stories in picture books.

Fiction and non-fiction:

1. Reading level should not exceed 5.0. The majority of books should be at the 3.5 and below levels of readability.

2. Pictures should be numerous but not babyish.

3. Print should be fairly large and evenly spaced so that an overwhelming amount of text per page is avoided.

4. Books should be quite short and thin. Books of very low readability (3.0 and below) should not exceed 100 pages and include a good number of pictures. The shorter book is more apt to be finished by the retarded reader and therefore, give him a sense of satisfaction and completion.

5. Subjects of interest in the non-fiction area: Cars, racing, motorcycles, horses, dogs, cooking, nature, animals, biographies of sports heroes or movie stars (biographies of other types of successful and famous people are generally not popular with the retarded). Generally, retarded people have the same interests as their average peers.

6. Subjects of interest in the fiction area: mysteries, ghost stories, romance, adventure, social type novels which involve teenagers dealing with personal problems and family conflicts.

Multi-Media Book Kits

1. Follow the same criteria for selecting books.

2. If a record or cassette accompanies a book, choose the record version since more patrons have record players at home to use. It is also easier for them to operate a record player than a cassette player.

3. Clear signals or instructions should be given on the recording to indicate when to turn pages of the book.

4. Be careful of some publishers' packaging. They often include multiple copies of the same title. If we order a title which has multiple copies, we put the extras on the book shelf so that a retarded reader can borrow and read the same title which he has learned to read from the record version.

Periodicals

1. High interest easy reading are desirable.

2. Lots of pictures. If the readability level of a magazine is high, but it contains many pictures, it will be used.

3. Areas of interest: beauty and fashion, nature, cars, sports, crafts, and comic books.

Some suggested special titles: *Sesame Street, Electric Company, News for You* (New Readers Press), *National Geographics World, Spidey*, a high-interest, low-vocabulary comic book (Marvel Comics).

Multi-Media Filmstrip Kits

1. Captioned (silent) filmstrips should not be purchased since most retarded patrons will have difficulty reading the captions.

2. Color is much more effective than black and white.

3. Cassettes are probably more convenient than records. The program should be repeated on both sides, one side with audible signals and the other with automatic inaudible signals. The automatic signal is most necessary since many retarded patrons may have difficulty following directions for advancing the filmstrip at the proper time.

4. Emphasis should be placed upon selecting non-fiction subjects, especially in the areas of social studies and elementary science. We have found that retarded individuals more easily comprehend and

Multi-Media Filmstrip Kits (cont'd)

understand difficult concepts which are presented in an audio-visual format than those in a print format.

5. Fables, legends, folk tales and other more high level stories that are too difficult in book format are most suitable for selection in the fiction area.

Records

1. Albums are better than 45 rpm discs.

2. Most children's records which are song and/or game type are preferable. More capable children do like to listen to stories on records which have no accompanying pictures. However, such stories require higher listening comprehension skills than most retarded children have acquired.

3. Adults prefer music, especially country-western, current popular songs of singers like Tony Orlando, the Carpenters, Neil Diamond, etc.

   "Oldies but goodies" are moderately popular. Classical and hard rock are not recommended.

4. Special education records should be carefully selected. Some are too instruction oriented, and without a teacher to provide direction, these do not make good records for the children to listen to alone. Parents and teachers, on the other hand, can make great use of this media.

Toys

1. No sharp edges.

2. Made with non-toxic paints and dyes.

3. Sturdy construction with few moving parts which are easily broken.

4. Few accompanying pieces or parts. They get lost too easily.

5. Large parts or pieces which cannot be swallowed easily.

6. Washable.

7. Educational, i.e.: Teach a concept or encourage development of coordination or language.

8. Puppets can be included, but ordinary dolls and stuffed animals should be avoided. Children usually have these at home.

9. Included in this category are teaching devices such as lacing boards, double handled scissors, etc. Although they require some direction, we found that the children like to practice with these things unassisted.

Puzzles

Primary puzzles:

1. Knobbed, wooden puzzles with pieces which fit into a contained space are the best for young educable and older trainable children.

2. Wooden puzzles with adjacent pieces should not exceed 10 large pieces.

3. Puzzles with pictures beneath the pieces provide clues so that re-assembling the puzzle is easier.

4. Crepe or rubber puzzles are also very good since these materials have more give and make it easier for the child to succeed.

Intermediate puzzles:

1. Heavy pressboard or cardboard pieces should be large with 25-50 per puzzle.

2. Wooden puzzles with more than 10 pieces are good for this level also.

3. Since trainable adults use these puzzles, select those with pictures which are not too childish.

Advanced puzzles:

1. 75-100 pieces are best, although a few retarded patrons may be able to handle a 250-500 piece puzzle.

2. Pictures of lakes, forests and the like which contain many pieces of the same color and few distinguishing marks should be avoided.

Games

1. Should be primarily educational. Colors, numbers, letters, money, time, etc. are concepts which should be emphasized. Following directions and playing fairly are also concepts which are taught through games.

2. Clear and uncomplicated rules and directions.

3. Minimum of playing pieces.

Games (cont'd)

4. Sturdy construction of game boards and spinners.

5. Uncluttered game boards with large spaces to make counting out easier.

6. Playing time short since a retarded child's attention span is usually short.

7. Outdoor type games can be included if they encourage development of large muscle coordination, can be easily carried and conveniently used at home.

Pictures and Posters

1. Pictures should be appealing to the retarded patron. They do not necessarily have to be great art.

2. Modernistic or psychedelic posters are not recommended. Realistic pictures or photographs are more readily understood.

3. Inexpensive.

4. Posters seem to be more popular than art reproductions.

5. 8-1/2" x 11" or larger are recommended.

Selected Bibliography

Chapter 1

American Association of School Librarians and Association for Educational Communications and Technology. *Media Programs: District and School.* Chicago: American Library Association; and Washington: Association for Educational Communications and Technology, 1975.

American Library Association. Association of Specialized and Cooperative Library Agencies. Standards for Libraries at Institutions for the Mentally Retarded Subcommittee. *Standards for Libraries at Institutions for the Mentally Retarded.* Chicago: American Library Association, 1981.

American Library Association. Association of Specialized and Cooperative Library Agencies. Standards for Library Service to the Blind and Physically Handicapped Subcommittee. *Standards of Service for the Library of Congress Network of Libraries for the Blind and Physically Handicapped.* Chicago: American Library Association, 1979.

American Library Association. Public Library Association. *Minimum Standards for Public Library Systems, 1966.* Chicago: American Library Association, 1967.

Commission on Standards and Accreditation of Services for the Blind. *The COMSTAC Report: Standards for Strengthened Services.* New York: National Accreditation Council for Agencies Serving the Blind and Visually Handicapped, 1966.

Duplica, Moya Martin. "The Librarian and the Exceptional Child." *Rehabilitation Literature* 33 (July 1972): 198-203.

"Illinois White House Conference Recommendations." *Illinois Libraries* 61 (April 1979): 333-42.

National Commission on Libraries and Information Science. *Information for the 1980's: Final Report of the White House Conference on Library and Information Services, 1979.* Washington, DC: U.S. Government Printing Office, 1980.

National Commission on Libraries and Information Science. *Toward a National Program for Library and Information Services: Goals for Action.* Washington, DC: U.S. Government Printing Office, 1975.

Standards for Library Services for the Blind and Visually Handicapped. Chicago: American Library Association, 1967.

Stough, Helen. " 'Let Me Hear Your Hand'—Library Service for Handicapped Children." *Illinois Libraries* 62 (December 1980): 878-83.

"The WHCLIS Resolutions." *American Libraries* 11 (January 1980): 22-23.

Wright, Kieth C. "Funding Media Services for Handicapped Children." In *School Library Media Services to the Handicapped*, edited by Myra Macon, pp. 117-29. Westport, CT: Greenwood Press, 1982.

Chapter 2

Abeson, Alan, and Zettel, Jeffrey. "The End of the Quiet Revolution: The Education for All Handicapped Children Act of 1975." *Exceptional Children* 44 (October 1977): 114-28.

American Library Association. Association for Library Service to Children. Library Service to Children with Special Needs Committee. *Selecting Materials for Children with Special Needs.* Chicago: American Library Association, 1980.

Biklen, Douglas, and Bogdan, Robert. "Media Portrayals of Disabled People: A Study in Stereotypes." *Interracial Books for Children Bulletin* 8 (Numbers 6 and 7, 1977): 4-9.

Bowe, Frank. *Handicapping America: Barriers to Disabled People.* New York: Harper and Row, 1978.

Brace, Michele J. "Who Needs Special Attention?" *Audiovisual Instruction* 21 (December 1976): 13.

Brewer, Garry D., and Kakalik, James S. *Handicapped Children: Strategies for Improving Services.* New York: McGraw-Hill, 1979.

Coet, Larry J. "Defining the Term 'Handicap': A Function of Sex, Race, Religion, and Geographic Location." *Psychological Reports* 41 (1977): 783-87.

Congressional Quarterly Almanac; 94th Congress, 1st Session ... 1975. Vol. 31. Washington: Congressional Quarterly, 1976.

Coombs, Ronald H., and Harper, Jerry L. "Effects of Labels on Attitudes of Educators toward Handicapped Children." *Exceptional Children* 33 (February 1967): 399-403.

Davis, Emmett A., and Davis, Catherine M. *Mainstreaming Library Service for Disabled People.* Metuchen, NJ: Scarecrow Press, 1980.

Dimond, Paul R. "The Constitutional Right to Education: The Quiet Revolution." *The Hastings Law Journal* 24 (May 1973): 1087-1127.

"Disabled People in the U.S.: Facts and Figures." *Interracial Books for Children Bulletin* 8 (Numbers 6 and 7, 1977): 20-21.

"Disabled — Yes; Handicapped — No: The Language of Disability." *Interracial Books for Children Bulletin* 8 (Numbers 6 and 7, 1977): 5.

Education for All Handicapped Children Act. Statutes at Large. Vol. 89 (1975).

Gillung, Tom B., and Rucker, Chauncy N. "Labels and Teacher Expectations." *Exceptional Children* 43 (April 1977): 464-65.

Gliedman, John, and Roth, William, for the Carnegie Council on Children. *The Unexpected Minority: Handicapped Children in America.* New York: Harcourt Brace Jovanovich, 1980.

Henne, John F. "Serving Visually Handicapped Children." *School Library Journal* 25 (December 1978): 36-37.

Jacobs, William R. "The Effect of the Learning Disability Label on Classroom Teacher's Ability Objectively to Observe and Interpret Child Behaviors." *Learning Disability Quarterly* 1 (Winter 1978): 50-55.

Kirk, Samuel A., and Gallagher, James J. *Educating Exceptional Children.* 3rd ed. Boston: Houghton Mifflin, 1979.

Lippman, Leopold, and Goldberg, I. Ignacy. *Right to Education: Anatomy of the Pennsylvania Case and Its Implications for Exceptional Children.* Teachers College Series in Special Education. New York: Teachers College Press, Teachers College, Columbia University, 1973.

McCracken, Sarah. "Selecting Materials for Individual Handicapped Learners." In *Services and Materials for the Handicapped; Proceedings of an Institute for School Library Media Professionals, August 12-17, 1979,* edited by Henry C. Dequin, pp. 109-121. DeKalb, IL: Northern Illinois University, 1979.

Meers, Gary D., editor. *Handbook of Special Vocational Needs Education.* Rockville, MD: Aspen Systems Corporation, 1980.

Pennsylvania Association for Retarded Children v. Commonwealth of Pennsylvania, 334 F. Supp. 1257 (E.D. Pa. 1971).

Smith, I. Leon, and Greenberg, Sandra. "Teacher Attitudes and the Labeling Process." *Exceptional Children* 41 (February 1975): 319-24.

Special People, Special Needs, Special Services. Athens, GA: University of Georgia, Bureau of Educational Studies and Department of Educational Media and Librarianship, 1978.

ten Broek, Jacobus, and Matson, Floyd W. "The Disabled and the Law of Welfare." *California Law Review* 54 (May 1966): 809-840.

Tollifson, Joan. "An Open Letter ..." *Interracial Books for Children Bulletin* 8 (Numbers 6 and 7, 1977): 19.

Turnbull, H. Rutherford III. "The Past and Future Impact of Court Decisions in Special Education." *Phi Delta Kappan* 59 (April 1978): 523-27.

U.S. Department of Health, Education, and Welfare. "Nondiscrimination on the Basis of Handicap." *Federal Register* 42 (May 4, 1977): 22676-22694.

U.S. Department of Health, Education, and Welfare. Office of Education. "Education of Handicapped Children: Implementation of Part B of the Education of the Handicapped Act." *Federal Register* 42, no. 163, August 23, 1977, 42474-42518.

U.S. Department of Health, Education, and Welfare. Office of Education. Bureau of Education for the Handicapped. *Progress toward a Free Appropriate Public Education; A Report to Congress on the Implementation of Public Law 94-142: The Education for All Handicapped Children Act*, prepared by the State Program Implementation Studies Branch. HEW Publication No. (OE) 79-05003, January 1979.

U.S. Department of Health, Education and Welfare. Office of Education. National Advisory Committee on the Handicapped. "Education of the Handicapped Today." *American Education* 12 (June 1976): 6-8.

U.S. Department of Health, Education and Welfare. Office of Education. National Advisory Committee on the Handicapped. *The Unfinished Revolution: Education for the Handicapped; 1976 Annual Report.* Washington, DC: Government Printing Office, 1976.

Velleman, Ruth A. *Serving Physically Disabled People: An Information Handbook for All Libraries.* New York: R. R. Bowker, 1979.

Wright, Kieth C. "Characteristics of the Handicapped." In *School Library Media Services to the Handicapped*, edited by Myra Macon, pp. 43-74. Westport, CT: Greenwood Press, 1982.

Wright, Kieth C. "Handicapping Conditions and the Needs of Handicapped Children." In *Services and Materials for the Handicapped; Proceedings of an Institute for School Library Media Professionals, August 12-17, 1979*, edited by Henry C. Dequin, pp. 14-34. DeKalb, IL: Northern Illinois University, 1979.

Wright, Kieth C. "Introduction to and Interpretation of PL 94-142." In *Services and Materials for the Handicapped; Proceedings of an Institute for School Library Media Professionals, August 12-17, 1979*, edited by Henry C. Dequin, pp. 1-13. DeKalb, IL: Northern Illinois University, 1979.

Wright, Kieth C. *Library and Information Services for Handicapped Individuals.* Littleton, CO: Libraries Unlimited, 1979.

Zames, Frieda. "The Disability Rights Movement — A Progress Report." *Interracial Books for Children Bulletin* 8 (Numbers 6 and 7, 1977): 16-18.

Zettel, Jeffrey J., and Abeson, Alan. "Litigation, Law, and the Handicapped." *School Media Quarterly* 6 (Summer 1978): 234-45.

Chapter 3

Abeson, Alan. "Movement and Momentum: Government and the Education of Handicapped Children." *Exceptional Children* 39 (September 1972): 63-66.

Abeson, Alan, and Zettel, Jeffrey. "The End of the Quiet Revolution: The Education for All Handicapped Children Act of 1975." *Exceptional Children* 44 (October 1977): 114-28.

Ashcroft, Samuel C. "Learning Resources in Special Education: The Quiet Evolution." *Education and Training of the Mentally Retarded* 12 (April 1977): 132-36.

Ballard, Joseph, and Zettel, Jeffrey. "Public Law 94-142 and Section 504; What They Say about Rights and Protections." *Exceptional Children* 44 (November 1977): 177-85.

Barbacovi, Don R., and Clelland, Richard W. *Public Law 94-142: Special Education in Transition.* Arlington, VA: American Association of School Administrators, n.d.

Beatty, L. F. "Impact of Public Law 94-142 on the Preparation of School Media Coordinators." *Educational Technology* 18 (November 1978): 44-46.

Bolick, Nancy, ed. *Digest of State and Federal Laws: Education of Handicapped Children.* 3rd ed. Reston, VA: The Council for Exceptional Children, 1975.

Bowe, Frank. *Handicapping America: Barriers to Disabled People.* New York: Harper and Row, 1978.

Bunch, Austin W. "A History of the Education of the Handicapped." In *School Library Media Services to the Handicapped*, edited by Myra Macon, pp. 3-23. Westport, CT: Greenwood Press, 1982.

Calovini, Gloria. "Implications of Public Law 94-142." *Illinois Libraries* 59 (September 1977): 468-69.

Congressional Quarterly Almanac; 94th Congress, 1st Session ... 1975. Vol. 31. Washington, DC: Congressional Quarterly, 1976.

Dimond, Paul R. "The Constitutional Right to Education: The Quiet Revolution." *The Hastings Law Journal* 24 (May 1973): 1087-1127.

Education for All Handicapped Children Act. Statutes at Large, vol. 89 (1975).

Gliedman, John, and Roth, William, for the Carnegie Council on Children. *The Unexpected Minority: Handicapped Children in America.* New York: Harcourt Brace Jovanovich, 1980.

Goodman, Leroy V. "A Bill of Rights for the Handicapped." *American Education* 12 (July 1976): 6-8.

Kirk, Samuel A., and Gallagher, James J. *Educating Exceptional Children.* 3rd ed. Boston: Houghton Mifflin, 1979.

Kundert, James J. "Media Services and Captioned Films." *Educational Technology* 10 (August 1970): 40-42.

Kuriloff, Peter, and others. "Legal Reform and Educational Change: The Pennsylvania Case." *Exceptional Children* 41 (September 1974): 35-42.

Lance, Wayne D. "Who *Are* All the Children?" *Exceptional Children* 43 (October 1976): 66-76.

"Latest in Dealing with Handicapped Pupils." *U.S. News and World Report,* February 27, 1978, pp. 49-50.

Lippman, Leopold, and Goldberg, I. Ignacy. *Right to Education: Anatomy of the Pennsylvania Case and Its Implications for Exceptional Children.* Teachers College Series in Special Education. New York: Teachers College, Columbia University, 1973.

Melcher, John W. "Law, Litigation, and Handicapped Children." *Exceptional Children* 43 (November 1976): 126-30.

National Conference on Human and Civil Rights in Education. *Education of All Handicapped Children and PL 94-142; Report of the Sixteenth National Conference on Human and Civil Rights in Education, March 17-19, 1978, Sheraton Park Hotel, Washington, D.C.* Washington, DC: National Education Association, 1978.

O'Donnell, Tom. "Sources of Law: Right to an Equal Educational Opportunity." *Amicus* 2 (April 1977): 22-25.

Orelove, Fred P. "Administering Education for the Severely Handicapped after P.L. 94-142." *Phi Delta Kappan* 59 (June 1978): 699-702.

Postlewaite, Jean. "*Mattie T. v. Holladay*: Denial of Equal Education." *Amicus* 2 (April 1977): 38-44.

Roubinek, Darrell L. "Will Mainstreaming Fit?" *Educational Leadership* 35 (February 1978): 410-12.

Ryor, J. "Integrating the Handicapped; Education for All Handicapped Children, Act of 1975." *Today's Education* 66 (September/October 1977): 24-26.

Schipper, William. "Overview of the Legislation — P.L. 94-142." *School Media Quarterly* 8 (Fall 1979): 17-21.

Semmel, Melvyn I., and Heinmiller, Joseph L. "The Education for All Handicapped Children Act of 1975: National Perspectives and Long Range Implications." *Viewpoints; Bulletin of the School of Education, Indiana University* 53 (March 1977): 1-16.

Shapiro, Siglinda. "Public Law 93-112: A Bill of Rights for the Disabled." *The Exceptional Parent* 8 (August 1978): L11-L13.

Stowell, L. James, and Terry, Cindy. "Mainstreaming — Present Shock." *Illinois Libraries* 59 (September 1977): 475-77.

Turnbull, H. Rutherford III. "The Past and Future Impact of Court Decisions in Special Education." *Phi Delta Kappan* 59 (April 1978): 523-27.

U.S. Department of Education. Office of Special Education and Rehabilitative Services. Office for Handicapped Individuals. *Summary of Existing Legislation Relating to the Handicapped.* Pubn. E.80-22014. Washington, DC: Government Printing Office, 1980.

U.S. Department of Health, Education, and Welfare. Office of Education. Bureau of Education for the Handicapped. *Progress toward a Free Appropriate Public Education; A Report to Congress on the Implementation of Public Law 94-142: The Education for All Handicapped Children Act*, prepared by the State Program Implementation Studies Branch. HEW Publication No. (OE) 79-05003, January 1979.

U.S. Department of Health, Education, and Welfare. Office of Education. National Advisory Committee on the Handicapped. *The Unfinished Revolution: Education for the Handicapped, 1975 Annual Report.* Washington, DC: Government Printing Office, 1976.

Vocational Rehabilitation Act. Statutes at Large, vol. 87 (1973).

Weintraub, Frederick J. Editorial Comment to "The End of the Quiet Revolution: The Education for All Handicapped Children Act of 1975," by Alan Abeson and Jeffrey Zettel. *Exceptional Children* 44 (October 1977): 114.

Weintraub, Frederick J., and Abeson, Alan. "New Education Policies for the Handicapped: The Quiet Revolution." *Phi Delta Kappan* 55 (April 1974):

526-29, 569. Reprinted in *Public Policy and the Education of Exceptional Children*, edited by Frederick J. Weintraub, Alan Abeson, Joseph Ballard, and Martin L. LaVor, pp. 7-13. Reston, VA: The Council for Exceptional Children, 1976.

Weintraub, Frederick J.; Abeson, Alan; Ballard, Joseph; and LaVor, Martin L., editors. *Public Policy and the Education of Exceptional Children.* Reston, VA: The Council for Exceptional Children, 1976.

Wright, Kieth C. "Federal Legislation." In *School Library Media Services to the Handicapped*, edited by Myra Macon, pp. 25-42. Westport, CT: Greenwood Press, 1982.

Wright, Kieth C. "Introduction to and Interpretation of PL 94-142." In *Services and Materials for the Handicapped; Proceedings of an Institute for School Library Media Professionals, August 12-17, 1979*, edited by Henry C. Dequin, pp. 1-13. DeKalb, IL: Northern Illinois University, 1979.

Wright, Kieth C. *Library and Information Services for Handicapped Individuals.* Littleton, CO: Libraries Unlimited, 1979.

Zames, Frieda. "The Disability Rights Movement — A Progress Report." *Interracial Books for Children Bulletin* 8 (Numbers 6 and 7, 1977): 16-18.

Zettel, Jeffrey J., and Abeson, Alan. "Litigation, Law, and the Handicapped." *School Media Quarterly* 6 (Summer 1978): 234-45.

Chapter 4

Ashcroft, Samuel C. "This Issue." *Theory into Practice* 14 (April 1975): 59-60.

Baldwin, Willie Kate. "The Social Position of the Educable Mentally Retarded Child in the Regular Grades in the Public Schools." *Exceptional Children* 25 (November 1958): 106-108, 112.

Baskin, Barbara H., and Harris, Karen H. *Notes from a Different Drummer: A Guide to Juvenile Fiction Portraying the Handicapped.* New York: R. R. Bowker, 1977.

Batson, Trenton. "The Deaf Person in Fiction — From Sainthood to Rorschach Blot." *Interracial Books for Children Bulletin* 11 (Numbers 1 and 2, 1980): 16-18.

Begg, Robert T. "Disabled Libraries: An Examination of Physical and Attitudinal Barriers to Handicapped Library Users." *Law Library Journal* 72 (Summer 1979): 513-25.

Biklen, Douglas, and Bogdan, Robert. "Media Portrayals of Disabled People: A Study in Stereotypes." *Interracial Books for Children Bulletin* 8 (Numbers 6 and 7, 1977): 4-9.

Billings, Helen K. "An Exploratory Study of the Attitudes of Noncrippled Children toward Crippled Children in Three Selected Elementary Schools." *Journal of Experimental Education* 31 (Summer 1963): 381-87.

Bobbitt, W. Leslie. "When Schools Change." *Educational Leadership* 34 (March 1977): 439-43.

Bowe, Frank. *Handicapping America: Barriers to Disabled People.* New York: Harper and Row, 1978.

Bruininks, Virginia L. "Actual and Perceived Peer Status of Learning-Disabled Students in Mainstream Programs." *Journal of Special Education* 12 (Spring 1978): 51-58.

Bryan, Tanis H. "Peer Popularity of Learning Disabled Children." *Journal of Learning Disabilities* 7 (December 1974): 621-25.

Bryan, Tanis H., and Bryan, James H. "Social Interactions of Learning Disabled Children." *Learning Disability Quarterly* 1 (Winter 1978): 33-38.

Bunch, Austin W. "A History of the Education of the Handicapped." In *School Library Media Services to the Handicapped*, edited by Myra Macon, pp. 3-23. Westport, CT: Greenwood Press, 1982.

Case v. State of California. Civil No. 13127, Court of Appeals, Fourth District. California, filed December 14, 1973.

Centers, Louise, and Centers, Richard. "Peer Group Attitudes toward the Amputee Child." *Journal of Social Psychology* 61 (October 1963): 127-32.

Chalfant, James C., and Foster, Georgiana E. "Helping Teachers Understand the Needs of Learning Disabled Children." *Journal of Learning Disabilities* 10 (February 1977): 79-85.

Clore, Gerald L., and Jeffrey, Katherine McMillam. "Emotional Role Playing, Attitude Change, and Attraction toward a Disabled Person." *Journal of Personality and Social Psychology* 23 (July 1972): 105-111.

Cohen, Shirley. "Fostering Positive Attitudes toward the Handicapped: A New Curriculum." *Children Today* 6 (November/December 1977): 7-12.

Cohen, Shirley. "Improving Attitudes toward the Handicapped." *Educational Forum* 42 (November 1977): 9-20.

Cohen, Shirley. *Special People: A Bright Future for Everyone with Physical, Mental, and Emotional Disabilities.* Englewood Cliffs, NJ: Prentice-Hall, 1977.

Cohen, Shirley, and Koehler, Nancy. *Fostering Positive Attitudes toward the Handicapped: A Selected Bibliography of Multimedia Materials.* New York: City University of New York, Graduate School and University Center, 1975.

Cohen, Shirley, and Koehler, Nancy. *A Selected Bibliography on Attitudes toward the Handicapped.* New York: City University of New York, Graduate School and University Center, 1975.

Conine, Tali A. "Acceptance or Rejection of Disabled Persons by Teachers." *Journal of School Health* 39 (April 1969): 278-81.

Coombs, Ronald H., and Harper, Jerry L. "Effects of Labels on Attitudes of Educators toward Handicapped Children." *Exceptional Children* 33 (February 1967): 399-403.

Crandell, John M., Jr. "The Genesis and Modification of Attitudes toward the Child Who Is Different." *Training School Bulletin* 66 (1969): 72-79.

Cummins, Thomas Randolph. "Attitudes: An Essential Ingredient of Service." *Texas Library Journal* 55 (Winter 1979): 8.

Dequin, Henry C., and Faibisoff, Sylvia G. "Results of an Attitudinal Survey." In *Summary Proceedings of a Symposium on Educating Librarians and Information Scientists to Provide Information and Library Services to Blind and Physically Handicapped Individuals, San Francisco, California, July 2-4, 1981*, pp. 6-9. Washington, DC: The Library of Congress, National Library Service for the Blind and Physically Handicapped, 1981.

Donaldson, Joy. "Channel Variations and Effects on Attitudes toward Physically Disabled Individuals." *AV Communication Review* 24 (Summer 1976): 135-44.

Donaldson, Joy, and Martinson, Melton C. "Modifying Attitudes toward Physically Disabled Persons." *Exceptional Children* 43 (March 1977): 337-41.

Duplica, Moya Martin. "Mainstreaming Exceptional Children." *Health and Rehabilitative Library Services Division Journal* 3 (Spring 1977): 8-10.

Evans, Joseph H. "Changing Attitudes toward Disabled Persons." *Rehabilitative Counseling Bulletin* 19 (June 1976): 572-79.

Fix, Colleen, and Rohrbacher, Jo Anne. "What Is a Handicap? The Impact of Attitudes." *Personnel and Guidance Journal* 56 (November 1977): 176-78.

Gellman, William. "Roots of Prejudice against the Handicapped." *Journal of Rehabilitation* 25 (January-February 1959): 4-6, 25.

Gerber, Paul J., and Harris, Karen. "Into the Mainstream: Using Books to Develop Social Skills in Perceptually Impaired Children." *Top of the News* 35 (Summer 1979): 379-84.

Gillung, Tom B., and Rucker, Chauncy N. "Labels and Teacher Expectations." *Exceptional Children* 43 (April 1977): 464-65.

Gliedman, John, and Roth, William, for the Carnegie Council on Children. *The Unexpected Minority: Handicapped Children in America.* New York: Harcourt Brace Jovanovich, 1980.

Goodman, Hollace; Gottlieb, Jay; and Harrison, Robert H. "Social Acceptance of EMRs Integrated into a Nongraded Elementary School." *American Journal of Mental Deficiency* 76 (January 1972): 412-17.

Gottlieb, Jay, and Budoff, M. "Social Acceptability of Retarded Children in Non-graded Schools Differing in Architecture." *Studies in Learning Potential* 2 (1972): 1-17.

Gottlieb, Jay, and Gottlieb, Barbara W. "Stereotypic Attitudes and Behavioral Intentions toward Handicapped Children." *American Journal of Mental Deficiency* 82 (July 1977): 65-71.

Groff, Patrick. "The Child's World of the Fictional Deaf." *Top of the News* 32 (April 1976): 261-67.

Hafer, Marilyn, and Narcus, Margery. "Information and Attitudes toward Disability." *Rehabilitation Counseling Bulletin* 23 (December 1979): 95-102.

Hall, Candace Catlin. "Introducing Sighted Children to Visual Handicaps: A Short Program Description." *Education of the Visually Handicapped* 8 (Fall 1976): 91-94.

Harasymiw, Stefan J., and Horne, Marcia D. "Integration of Handicapped Children: Its Effect on Teacher Attitudes." *Education* 96 (Winter 1975): 153-58.

Haring, Norris Grover. "A Study of Classroom Teacher's Attitudes toward Exceptional Children." Ed.D. dissertation, Syracuse University, 1956.

Haring, Norris G.; Stern, George G.; and Cruickshank, William M. *Attitudes of Educators toward Exceptional Children.* Syracuse, NY: Syracuse University Press, 1958.

Harris, Karen; Banbury, Mary; and Litton, Freddie. "The Library Media Specialist as a Mainstreaming Facilitator." *School Media Quarterly* 9 (Fall 1980): 40, 49-53.

Haynes, John. "No Child Is an Island." *Children's Literature in Education* 15 (1974): 3-18.

Higgs, Reginald W. "Attitude Formation—Contact or Information?" *Exceptional Children* 41 (April 1975): 496-97.

Higgs, Reginald W. "Attitudes toward Persons with Physical Disabilities as a Function of Information Level and Degree of Contact." *Dissertation Abstracts International* 32 (8-A) (February 1972): 4450.

Hollander, Edwin P. *Principles and Methods of Social Psychology.* New York: Oxford University Press, 1967.

Hopkins, Carol J. "Developing Positive Attitudes toward the Handicapped through Children's Books." *Elementary School Journal* 81 (September 1980): 34-39.

Hughes, James H. "Attitude Is Keystone to Success." *School Shop* 37 (April 1978): 76-80.

Iano, Richard P., and others. "Sociometric Status of Retarded Children in an Integrative Program." *Exceptional Children* 40 (January 1974): 267-71.

Interracial Books for Children Bulletin 11 (Numbers 1 and 2, 1980): 10-24.

Jacobs, William R. "The Effect of the Learning Disability Label on Classroom Teacher's Ability Objectively to Observe and Interpret Child Behaviors." *Learning Disability Quarterly* 1 (Winter 1978): 50-55.

Jones, G. Orville. "A Study of the Social Position of Mentally-Handicapped Children in the Regular Grades." *American Journal of Mental Deficiency* 55 (July 1950): 60-69.

Jones, Reginald L.; Lavine, Karen; and Shell, Joan. "Blind Children Integrated in Classrooms with Sighted Children: A Sociometric Study." *New Outlook for the Blind* 66 (March 1972): 75-80.

Jones, Reginald L., and Sisk, Dorothy D. "Early Perceptions of Orthopedic Disability: A Developmental Study." *Rehabilitation Literature* 31 (February 1970): 34-38.

Kennedy, Patricia, and Bruininks, Robert H. "Social Status of Hearing Impaired Children in Regular Classrooms." *Exceptional Children* 40 (February 1974): 336-42.

Kirk, Samuel A., and Gallagher, James J. *Educating Exceptional Children.* 3rd ed. Boston: Houghton Mifflin, 1979.

Lazar, Alfred L.; Gensley, Juliana T.; and Orpet, Russel E. "Changing Attitudes of Young Mentally Gifted Children toward Handicapped Persons." *Exceptional Children* 37 (April 1971): 600-602.

Lazar, Alfred L.; Orpet, Russell; and Demos, George. "The Impact of Class Instruction on Changing Student Attitudes." *Rehabilitation Counseling Bulletin* 20 (September 1976): 66-68.

Lippman, Leopold D. *Attitudes toward the Handicapped: A Comparison between Europe and the United States.* Springfield, IL: Charles C. Thomas, 1972.

Lombana, Judy H. "Fostering Positive Attitudes toward Handicapped Students: A Guidance Challenge." *The School Counselor* 27 (January 1980): 176-82.

McCarthy, Richard M., and Stodden, Robert A. "Mainstreaming Secondary Students: A Peer Tutoring Model." *Teaching Exceptional Children* 11 (Summer 1979): 162-63.

March, Velma, and Friedman, Robert. "Changing Public Attitudes toward Blindness." *Exceptional Children* 38 (January 1972): 426-28.

Monroe, J. Donald, and Howe, Clifford E. "The Effects of Integration and Social Class on the Acceptance of Retarded Adolescents." *Education and Training of the Mentally Retarded* 6 (February 1971): 20-24.

Monson, Dianne, and Shurtleff, Cynthia. "Altering Attitudes toward the Physically Handicapped through Print and Non-Print Media." *Language Arts* 56 (February 1979): 163-70.

Mosley, James L. "Integration: The Need for a Systematic Evaluation of the Socio-Adaptive Aspect." *Education and Training of the Mentally Retarded* 13 (February 1978): 4-8.

National Conference on Human and Civil Rights in Education. *Education of All Handicapped Children and PL 94-142; Report of the Sixteenth National Conference on Human and Civil Rights in Education, March 17-19, 1978, Sheraton Park Hotel, Washington, D.C.* Washington, DC: National Education Association, 1978.

Newman, J. "Faculty Attitudes toward Handicapped Students." *Rehabilitation Literature* 37 (July 1976): 194-97.

Orlansky, Michael D. "Active Learning and Student Attitudes toward Exceptional Children." *Exceptional Children* 46 (September 1979): 49-52.

Panieczko, Sophia, compiler. *Attitudes and Disability: A Selected Annotated Bibliography, January 1975-August 1977.* Washington, DC: Regional Rehabilitation Research Institute on Attitudinal, Legal and Leisure Barriers, The George Washington University, n.d.

Pieper, Elizabeth J. "Preparing Children for a Handicapped Classmate." *The Instructor* 84 (August 1974): 128-29.

Rucker, Chauncy N.; Howe, Clifford E.; and Snider, Bill. "The Participation of Retarded Children in Junior High Academic and Nonacademic Regular Classes." *Exceptional Children* 35 (April 1969): 617-23.

Rusalem, Herbert. "Engineering Changes in Public Attitudes toward a Severely Disabled Group." *Journal of Rehabilitation* 33 (June 1967): 26-27.

Schaefer, F. M. "The Social Traits of the Blind." Master's thesis, Loyola University, 1930.

Schilling, Irene Normark. "A Survey of the Attitudes of Academic Librarians in Illinois toward Disabled Persons." Study conducted in the Department of Library Science, Northern Illinois University, DeKalb, IL, December 1981.

Schwartz, Albert V. "Books Mirror Society: A Study of Children's Materials." *Interracial Books for Children Bulletin* 11 (Numbers 1 and 2, 1980): 19-24.

Schwartz, Albert V. "Disability in Children's Books: Is Visibility Enough?" *Interracial Books for Children Bulletin* 9 (Numbers 6 and 7, 1977): 10-15.

Shaw, Marvin E., and Wright, Jack M. *Scales for the Measurement of Attitudes.* New York: McGraw-Hill, 1967.

Shotel, Jay R.; Iano, Richard P.; and McGettigan, James F. "Teacher Attitudes Associated with the Integration of Handicapped Children." *Exceptional Children* 38 (May 1972): 677-83.

Smith, I. Leon, and Greenberg, Sandra. "Teacher Attitudes and the Labeling Process." *Exceptional Children* 41 (February 1975): 319-24.

Steinhebel, Jennie Pamela. "An Evaluation of Institute Participants in Providing Library Media Services for the Handicapped." DeKalb, IL: Northern Illinois University, Department of Library Science, 1980. (Typewritten)

Strong, Edward K., Jr. *Change of Interests with Age; Based on Examination of More than Two Thousand Men between the Ages of Twenty and Sixty Representing Eight Occupations.* Palo Alto, CA: Stanford University Press, 1931.

Stroud, Janet G. "Characterization of the Emotionally Disturbed in Current Adolescent Fiction." *Top of the News* 37 (Spring 1981): 290-95.

Stroud, Janet G. "Portrayal of Physically Handicapped Characters in Adolescent Fiction." *Top of the News* 36 (Summer 1980): 363-67.

Stroud, Janet G. "Treatment of the Mentally Handicapped in Young Adult Fiction." *Top of the News* 36 (Winter 1980): 208-212.

"Teaching about Handicapism." *Interracial Books for Children Bulletin* 8 (Numbers 6 and 7, 1977): 22-26.

Triandis, H. C. *Attitude and Attitude Change.* New York: John Wiley, 1971.

Tringo, John L. "The Hierarchy of Preference toward Disability Groups." *Journal of Special Education* 4 (Summer/Fall 1970): 295-306.

U.S. Committee for UNICEF. *News of the World's Children* 28 (December 1980): 1-2.

U.S. Department of Health, Education, and Welfare. Office of Education. National Advisory Committee on the Handicapped. *The Unfinished*

Revolution: Education for the Handicapped; 1976 Annual Report. Washington, DC: Government Printing Office, 1976.

Velleman, Ruth A. *Serving Physically Disabled People: An Information Handbook for All Libraries.* New York: R. R. Bowker, 1979.

Warnock, Nancy J. "Making General Education 'Special'." *Education and Training of the Mentally Retarded* 11 (December 1976): 304-308.

Warren, Sue Allen, and Turner, Dale Robert. "Attitudes of Professionals and Students toward Exceptional Children." *Training School Bulletin* 62 (February 1966): 136-44.

Weintraub, Frederick J., and Abeson, Alan. "New Education Policies for the Handicapped: The Quiet Revolution." *Phi Delta Kappan* 55 (April 1974): 526-29, 569. Reprinted in *Public Policy and the Education of Exceptional Children*, edited by Frederick J. Weintraub, Alan Abeson, Joseph Ballard, and Martin L. LaVor, pp. 7-13. Reston, VA: The Council for Exceptional Children, 1976.

Wright, Beatrice A. "An Analysis of Attitudes — Dynamics and Effects." *New Outlook for the Blind* 68 (March 1974): 108-118.

Wright, Beatrice A. "Changes in Attitudes toward People with Handicaps." *Rehabilitation Literature* 34 (December 1973): 354-57, 368.

Wright, Kieth C. *Library and Information Services for Handicapped Individuals.* Littleton, CO: Libraries Unlimited, 1979.

Yuker, Harold E. "Attitudes of the General Public toward Handicapped Indivisuals." In *The White House Conference on Handicapped Indivisuals.* Vol. 1: *Awareness Papers*, pp. 89-105. Washington, DC: Government Printing Office, 1977.

Yuker, Harold E.; Block, J. R.; and Younng, Janet H. *The Measurement of Attitudes toward Disabled Persons.* Albertson, NY: Human Resources Center, 1966.

Chapter 5

Abbott, Robert E. "Materials Components of Individualized Education Programs." In *Services and Materials for the Handicapped; Proceedings of an Institute for School Library Media Professionals, August 12-17, 1979*, edited by Henry C. Dequin, pp. 45-56. DeKalb, IL: Northern Illinois University, 1979.

Abeson, Alan, and Zettel, Jeffrey. "The End of the Quiet Revolution: The Education for All Handicapped Children Act of 1975." *Exceptional Children* 44 (October 1977): 114-28.

Alexander, Elnora. "All Students Are Exceptional." *Learning Today* 6 (Spring 1973): 30-35.

American Association of School Librarians. *Standards for School Library Program*. Chicago: American Library Association, 1960.

American Association of School Librarians and Association for Educational Communications and Technology. *Media Programs: District and School*. Chicago: American Library Association; and Washington, DC: Association for Educational Communications and Technology, 1975.

American Association of School Librarians and Department of Audiovisual Instruction. *Standards for School Media Programs*. Chicago: American Library Association; and Washington, DC: National Education Association, 1969.

American Library Association. Association for Library Service to Children. Library Service to Children with Special Needs Committee. *Selecting Materials for Children with Special Needs*. Chicago: American Library Association, 1980.

Ashcroft, Samuel C. "Learning Resources in Special Education: The Quiet Evolution." *Education and Training of the Mentally Retarded* 12 (April 1977): 132-36.

Ballard, Joseph, and Zettel, Jeffrey. "Public Law 94-142 and Section 504; What They Say about Rights and Protections." *Exceptional Children* 44 (November 1977): 177-85.

Barbacovi, Don R., and Clelland, Richard W. *Public Law 94-142: Special Education in Transition*. Arlington, VA: American Association of School Administrators, n.d.

Bateman, Barbara D. "Prescriptive Teaching and Individualized Education Programs." In *Educating All Handicapped Children*, edited by Robert Heinich, pp. 39-61. Englewood Cliffs, NJ: Educational Technology Publications, 1979.

Beatty, L. F. "Impact of Public Law 94-142 on the Preparation of School Media Coordinators." *Educational Technology* 18 (November 1978): 44-46.

Blankenship, Colleen S. *Interim Resource Manual for Preparing Individualized Education Programs*. Springfield, IL: Department of Specialized Educational Services, State Board of Education, Illinois Office of Education, 1977.

Blankenship, Colleen S. "The Role of the Library Media Specialist in the IEP Process." In *Services and Materials for the Handicapped; Proceedings of an Institute for School Library Media Professionals, August 12-17, 1979*, edited by Henry C. Dequin, pp. 35-44. DeKalb, IL: Northern Illinois University, 1979.

Brewer, Garry D., and Kakalik, James S. *Handicapped Children: Strategies for Improving Services.* New York: McGraw-Hill, 1979.

Calovini, Gloria. "Implications of Public Law 94-142." *Illinois Libraries* 59 (September 1977): 468-69.

Connolly, John A., and Hoaglund, Mary L. "Adapting Instruction to School Objectives and Student Needs." *Educational Technology* 12 (April 1972): 31-34.

Dewey, Melvil. "The Profession." *The American Library Journal* 1 (September 30, 1876): 5-6.

Diehl, Sue. "Making the Media Center Special to the Special Child." *School Media Quarterly* 6 (Summer 1978): 273-74.

Dunn, Rita Stafford. "Individualizing Instruction—Teaming Teachers and Media Specialists to Meet Individual Needs." *Audiovisual Instruction* 16 (May 1971): 27-28.

Dunn, Rita, and Dunn, Kenneth. *Teaching Students through Their Individual Learning Styles: A Practical Approach.* Reston, VA: Reston, 1978.

Ehlinger, Clifford J., and Fleig, Gail Sullivan. "Media Specialist and Special Educator—A Partnership That Works." *Audiovisual Instruction* 21 (December 1976): 20-22.

Fagan, Ellen C. "Developing and Implementing an Individualized Educational Program for the Handicapped Child." In *School Library Media Services to the Handicapped,* edited by Myra Macon, pp. 89-116. Westport, CT: Greenwood Press, 1982.

Green, Kerry. "Service for the Handicapped: What the AV Professional Can Do." *Media and Methods* 16 (March 1980): 39-40.

Heinich, Robert, editor. *Educating All Handicapped Children.* Englewood Cliffs, NJ: Educational Technology Publications, 1979.

Kaye, Nancy L., and Aserlind, Roy. "The IEP: The Ultimate Process." *The Journal of Special Education* 13 (Summer 1979): 137-43.

Kirk, Samuel A., and Gallagher, James J. *Educating Exceptional Children.* 3rd ed. Boston: Houghton Mifflin, 1979.

Lance, Wayne D. "Learning Resource Systems for Special Education." *Theory into Practice* 14 (April 1975): 90-98.

Lance, Wayne D. "Technology and Media for Exceptional Learners: Looking Ahead." *Exceptional Children* 44 (October 1977): 92-97.

Lance, Wayne D. "What You Should Know about P.L. 94-142." *Audiovisual Instruction* 21 (December 1976): 14-15.

McCain, Floyd, Jr., and Brown, Laurence D. *The Effect of Cognitive Style in Verbal and Pictorial Concept Formation Tasks.* Bloomington, IN: Indiana University, 1969.

McCracken, Sarah. "Selecting Materials for Individual Handicapped Learners." In *Services and Materials for the Handicapped; Proceedings of an Institute for School Library Media Professionals, August 12-17, 1979,* edited by Henry C. Dequin, pp. 109-121. DeKalb, IL: Northern Illinois University, 1979.

McIntyre, Kenneth. "Media Systems and the Handicapped Child." *Audiovisual Instruction* 14 (November 1969): 21-23.

Maslow, A. H. 'A Theory of Human Motivation." *Psychological Review* 50 (July 1943): 370-96.

Metcalf, Mary Jane. "Helping Hearing Impaired Students." *School Library Journal* 25 (January 1979): 27-29.

Paroz, Jo Anne; Siegenthaler, Loy Sue; and Tatum, Verlene H. "A Model for a Middle-School Resource Room." *Journal of Learning Disabilities* 10 (January 1977): 7-15.

Robertson, Patricia. "Impact of the Physical Environment on the Emotionally Disturbed and Socially Maladjusted Student." In *The Special Child in the Library,* edited by Barbara Holland Baskin and Karen H. Harris, pp. 7-10. Chicago: American Library Association, 1976.

Stolovich, Harold. "A Pocket Calculator Never Loses Patience." *Audiovisual Instruction* 21 (December 1976): 19-20.

Stracener, Loyce. "The Library/Media Center in Adaptive Education." *School Media Quarterly* 6 (Summer 1978): 276-77.

Tickton, Sidney G., ed. *To Improve Learning: An Evaluation of Instructional Technology.* 2 vols. New York: R. R. Bowker, 1970. Vol. 1.

Turnbull, Ann P.; Strickland, Bonnie; and Brantley, John C. *Developing and Implementing Individualized Education Programs.* Columbus, OH: Charles E. Merrill, 1978.

U.S. Department of Health, Education, and Welfare. Office of Education. "Education of Handicapped Children: Implementation of Part B of the Education of the Handicapped Act." *Federal Register* 42, no. 163, August 23, 1977, 42474-42518.

U.S. Department of Health, Education, and Welfare. Office of Education. National Advisory Committee on the Handicapped. *The Individualized*

Education Program: Key to an Appropriate Education for the Handicapped Child; 1977 Annual Report. Washington, DC: Government Printing Office, 1977.

Vocational Rehabilitation Act. Statutes at Large, vol. 87 (1973).

Warnock, Nancy J. "Making General Education 'Special'." *Education and Training of the Mentally Retarded* 11 (December 1976): 304-308.

Weintraub, Frederick J. "Understanding the Individualized Education Program (IEP)." *Amicus* 2 (April 1977): 26-30.

Wood, Frances, and Hirshoren, Alfred. "The Hearing Impaired in the Mainstream: The Problem and Some Successful Practices." *Journal for Special Educators* 17 (Spring 1981): 291-301.

Zettel, Jeffrey J., and Abeson, Alan. "Litigation, Law, and the Handicapped." *School Media Quarterly* 6 (Summer 1978): 234-45.

Chapter 6

Acevedo, Pedro. "It's Hearing People Who Make Problems for Deaf People." *Interracial Books for Children Bulletin* 11 (Numbers 1 and 2, 1980): 10-11.

Adcock, Donald C. "Media Services for Exceptional Children: Some Practices in Illinois." *Illinois Libraries* 59 (September 1977): 477-79.

Barrow, John. "Library Service for the Deaf." *Wisconsin Library Bulletin* 74 (September-October 1978): 215-16.

Baskin, Barbara Holland, and Harris, Karen H., eds. *The Special Child in the Library.* Chicago: American Library Association, 1976.

Begg, Robert T. "Disabled Libraries: An Examination of Physical and Attitudinal Barriers to Handicapped Library Users." *Law Library Journal* 72 (Summer 1979): 513-25.

Bell, Lorna. "Think Big! Look Again!" *Library Association Record* 81 (May 1979): 235-37.

Bennett, Janet M. "The Library: The Retarded Person's Alternative." *Catholic Library World* 45 (April 1974): 420-22.

Bodart, Joni. "Bibliotherapy: The Right Book for the Right Person at the Right Time — and More!" *Top of the News* 36 (Winter 1980): 183-87.

Buckley, Cozetta White. "Media Services for Exceptional Students: An Exploratory Study of the Practices and Perceptions of Library Media Specialists in Selected Southern States." Ph.D. dissertation, University of Michigan, 1978.

Carpenter, Myra. "Task Card Instruction." *Ohio Media Spectrum* 30 (January 1978): 52-54.

Cory, Patricia Blair. *School Library Services for Deaf Children.* Washington, DC: Alexander Graham Bell Association for the Deaf, 1960.

Dain, Pat. "Coping with the Disruptive." *Library Association Record* 81 (May 1979): 237-38.

Daniell, Winifred G. "School Library Service to the Visually Handicapped." *School Media Quarterly* 3 (Summer 1975): 347-48.

Dequin, Henry C. "Services and Materials for Disabled Children." *Illinois Libraries* 63 (September 1981): 546-54.

Dequin, Henry C., and Smith, Jane. "Learning Disabled Students Can Be Tutors in Library Media Skills." *Top of the News* 36 (Summer 1980): 352-56.

Diehl, Sue. "Making the Media Center Special to the Special Child." *School Media Quarterly* 6 (Summer 1978): 273-74.

Donahoe, Barbara. "The Mentally Retarded Enjoy Libraries Too." *Illinois Libraries* 56 (March 1974): 209-212.

Dresang, Eliza T. "Mainstreaming All Children: Exceptional Children Use School and Public Libraries." *Wisconsin Library Bulletin* 74 (March-April 1978): 68-70.

Dresang, Eliza T. "There Are No *Other* Children." *School Library Journal* 24 (September 1977): 19-23.

Fast, Betty. "Mediacentric." *Wilson Library Bulletin* 52 (October 1977): 133-35.

Forer, Anne-Marie, and Zajac, Mary, in cooperation with the Altoona Area Public Library. "Library Services to the Mentally Retarded." Report on the L.I.F.E. Project. Altoona, PA: Altoona Area Public Library, n.d.

Hagemeyer, Alice. *Deaf Awareness Handbook for Public Librarians.* Washington, DC: Public Library of the District of Columbia, 1975.

Hall, Candace Catlin. "Use of a Type Size Transparency in School Libraries and Media Centers." *Education of the Visually Handicapped* 11 (Winter 1979-80): 112-17.

Hammer, Sharon. "Radio Reading—A Logical Form of Library Service." *Health and Rehabilitative Library Services Division Journal* 2 (Fall 1976): 17-19.

Harris, Karen H. "Selecting Library Materials for Exceptional Children." *School Media Quarterly* 8 (Fall 1979): 22-28.

Harris, Karen, and Baskin, Barbara. "The Exceptional Child — A Challenge for Librarians." *Louisiana Library Association Bulletin* 37 (Spring 1974): 21-24.

Harris, Karen, and Baskin, Barbara. "Library Service to the Handicapped Child." *Texas Library Journal* 56 (Fall 1980): 193-95.

Hunsicker, Marya. "When the Blind Begin to Read; Selected Reading List for Legally Blind Children." *Library Journal* 97 (November 15, 1972): 3817-18.

Hunsucker, Coy Kate. "Public Library Service to Blind and Physically Handicapped Children." *Health and Rehabilitative Library Services Division Journal* 2 (Fall 1976): 3-5.

Iffland, Carol C. "Mainstreaming." *Illinois Libraries* 58 (December 1976): 906-909.

Imholt, K. S. "Special Children — Special Libraries." *Connecticut Libraries* 19 (No. 3, 1977): 4-6.

Interracial Books for Children Bulletin 8 (Numbers 6 and 7, 1977): 18.

Jensen, Joanne C. "The Library and the Deaf Child." *Catholic Library World* 45 (April 1974): 426-28.

Jerrolds, Bob W. "Preparing Librarians to Help the Disabled Reader." *Wilson Library Bulletin* 50 (May 1976): 719-21.

Jeske, Dale. "New Library Patrons — The Mentally Retarded." *Connecticut Libraries* 19 (No. 1, 1977): 24-26.

Kessler, Beverly. "Books at Your Finger Tips." *Ohio Media Spectrum* 30 (January 1978): 25-29.

Kobax, Dorothy, and Nisenson, Estelle. "Poetry Therapy." In *Meeting the Needs of the Handicapped: A Resource for Teachers and Librarians*, edited by Carol H. Thomas and James L. Thomas, pp. 169-71. Phoenix: Oryx Press, 1980. (Also ED 133 957).

Lenkowsky, Barbara E., and Lenkowsky, Ronald S. "Bibliotherapy for the LD Adolescent." *Academic Therapy* 14 (November 1978): 179-85. Reprinted in *Meeting the Needs of the Handicapped: A Resource for Teachers and Librarians*, edited by Carol H. Thomas and James L. Thomas, pp. 122-27. Phoenix: Oryx Press, 1980.

"Libraries Are for Everyone." *Exceptional Parent* 6 (June 1976): 43-46.

"Libraries for People with Handicaps." *Ohio Media Spectrum* 30 (January 1978): 12-13.

Limper, Hilda. "Library Services to Deaf Children." *AHIL Quarterly* 7 (Fall 1966): 7-10.

Limper, Hilda K. "Serving Mentally Retarded Children in Our Libraries." *Catholic Library World* 45 (April 1974): 423-25. Reprinted in *Library Services to the Blind and Physically Handicapped*, edited by Maryalls G. Strom, pp. 91-95. Metuchen, NJ: Scarecrow Press, 1977.

Mahoney, Sally M., and Stokes, Lisslotte Z. "A School Library Program for the Blind." *Wilson Library Bulletin* 40 (May 1966): 829 + .

Marshall, Margaret R. *Libraries and the Handicapped Child*. Boulder, CO: Westview Press, 1981.

Mattern, Russell H. "Detecting Visual Problems." *Ohio Media Spectrum* 30 (January 1978): 35-36.

Metcalf, Mary Jane. "Helping Hearing Impaired Students." *School Library Journal* 25 (January 1979): 27-29. Reprinted in *Meeting the Needs of the Handicapped: A Resource for Teachers and Librarians*, edited by Carol H. Thomas and James L. Thomas, pp. 197-203. Phoenix: Oryx Press, 1980.

Metcalf, Mary Jane. "Library Services for the Hearing Impaired." *Illinois Libraries* 63 (October 1981): 626-33.

Meyers, Sister Edna Marie. "Teaching Library Skills to Deaf Children." *Catholic Library World* 51 (September 1979): 58-60.

Newberry, William F. "The Last Unserved: Are Public Libraries Ready to Mainstream Mentally Retarded Patrons?" *American Libraries* 11 (April 1980): 218-20.

Parlato, Salvatore J., Jr. "Read Any Good Films Lately?" *Audiovisual Instruction* 22 (September 1977): 30-31.

Philippoff, M. "Serving the Deaf Child." *Georgia Librarian* 14 (November 1977): 39-40.

Posell, Elsa Z. "Libraries and the Deaf Patron." *Wilson Library Bulletin* 51 (January 1977): 402-404.

Putman, Lee. "Information Needs of Hearing Impaired People." *Health and Rehabilitative Library Services Division Journal* 2 (Spring 1976): 2-14.

Rosemeyer, Martha, and Sundheimer, Marian. "Canton City Works with Visually Impaired Students." *Ohio Media Spectrum* 30 (January 1978): 29-32.

Rubin, Rhea J. "Uses of Bibliotherapy in Response to the 1970s." *Library Trends* 28 (Fall 1979): 239-52.

Sadoski, Michael J., and Sadoski, Doris C. "Building Libraries to Serve the Deaf." *Library Journal* (LJ Special Report #6, 1978): 29-34.

Sadoski, Michael J., and Sadoski, Doris C. "Sign Language Films for Library Users." *California Librarian* 39 (April 1978): 56-58.

Sangster, Collette. "Library Service to the Deaf." *The Bookmark* 38 (Winter 1979): 59-63.

Schultz, Jane, and Posner, Rita. "The Library/Media Center in a Children's Hospital." *School Media Quarterly* 6 (Summer 1978): 274-76.

Special People, Special Needs, Special Services. Athens, GA: University of Georgia, Bureau of Educational Studies and Department of Educational Media and Librarianship, 1978.

Stark, Bill. " 'Meanwhile ...': A Look at Comic Books at Illinois School for the Deaf." *American Annals of the Deaf* 121 (October 1976): 470-77. Reprinted in *Meeting the Needs of the Handicapped: A Resource for Teachers and Librarians*, edited by Carol H. Thomas and James L. Thomas, pp. 208-213. Phoenix: Oryx Press, 1980.

Stoneburg, Mary Rita. "Bibliotherapy and Its Use with Exceptional Children." *Illinois Libraries* 62 (October 1980): 665-71.

Stough, Helen. " 'Let Me Hear Your Hand' — Library Service for Handicapped Children." *Illinois Libraries* 62 (December 1980): 878-83.

Stracener, Loyce. "The Library/Media Center in Adaptive Education." *School Media Quarterly* 6 (Summer 1978): 276-77.

Strom, Maryalls G., ed. *Library Services to the Blind and Physically Handicapped.* Metuchen, NJ: Scarecrow Press, 1977.

Sykes, K. C. "Print Reading for Visually Handicapped Children." *Education of the Visually Handicapped* 4 (October 1972): 71-75.

"Teaching about Handicapism." *Interracial Books for Children Bulletin* 8 (Numbers 6 and 7, 1977): 22-26.

Tepe, Ann. "We're Goin' to the Library!" *Ohio Media Spectrum* 30 (January 1978): 50-51.

Thomas, Carol H., and Thomas, James L., eds. *Meeting the Needs of the Handicapped: A Resource for Teachers and Librarians.* Phoenix: Oryx Press, 1980.

Truquet, Monique. "The Blind, From Braille to the Present." *Impact of Science on Society* 30 (April-June 1980): 133-41.

Turner, Dorothy B. "Where It All Begins." *Learning Today* 6 (Summer 1973): 88-90.

Velleman, Ruth. "Serving Exceptional Children." *School Libraries* 20 (Summer 1971): 27-30.

Velleman, Ruth. *Serving Physically Disabled People: An Information Handbook for All Libraries.* New York: R. R. Bowker, 1979.

Warner, Lucy. "The Myth of Bibliotherapy." *School Library Journal* 27 (October 1980): 107-111.

Wright, Kieth C. "Handicapping Conditions and the Needs of Handicapped Children." In *Services and Materials for the Handicapped; Proceedings of an Institute for School Library Media Professionals, August 12-17, 1979,* edited by Henry C. Dequin, pp. 14-34. DeKalb, IL: Northern Illinois University, 1979.

Wright, Kieth C. *Library and Information Services for Handicapped Individuals.* Littleton, CO: Libraries Unlimited, 1979.

Wright, Louise M. "Library at Ohio School for the Deaf." *Ohio Media Spectrum* 30 (January 1978): 37-42.

Zajac, Mary. "Learning Is for Everyone." *RQ* 18 (Spring 1979): 248-50.

Chapter 7

Abbye, Sonya. "The Learning-Disabled Child ... Films for Social, Emotional, Language and Sensory Needs." *Film Library Quarterly* 9 (No. 3, 1976): 37-43. Reprinted in *Meeting the Needs of the Handicapped: A Resource for Teachers and Librarians,* edited by Carol H. Thomas and James L. Thomas, pp. 128-35. Phoenix: Oryx Press, 1980.

American Alliance for Health, Physical Education, Recreation, and Dance. "Creative Dramatics." *Practical Pointers* 1 (September 1977): 1-9. Reprinted in *Meeting the Needs of the Handicapped: A Resource for Teachers and Librarians,* edited by Carol H. Thomas and James L. Thomas, pp. 73-80. Phoenix: Oryx Press, 1980.

American Library Association. Association for Library Service to Children. Library Service to Children with Special Needs Committee. *Programming for Children with Special Needs.* Chicago: American Library Association, 1981.

Aserlind, Leroy. "Audiovisual Instruction for the Mentally Retarded." *Audiovisual Instruction* 11 (November 1966): 727-30. Reprinted in *The Special Child in the Library,* edited by Barbara Holland Baskin and Karen H. Harris, pp. 65-68. Chicago: American Library Association, 1976.

Baker, D. Philip, and Bender, David R. *Library Media Programs and the Special Learner.* Hamden, CT: Shoe String Press, 1981.

Baskin, Barbara H., and Harris, Karen H. "Storytelling for the Young Mentally Retarded Child." In *The Special Child in the Library*, edited by Barbara Holland Baskin and Karen H. Harris, pp. 114-17. Chicago: American Library Association, 1976.

Batt, Sister Doris. "The Hearing Impaired Child in the Library." In *The Special Child in the Library*, edited by Barbara Holland Baskin and Karen H. Harris, pp. 14-15. Chicago: American Library Association, 1976.

Biehl, Jane. "Storyhours for the Deaf." *Ohio Media Spectrum* 30 (January 1978): 43-46.

Brown, Jean D. "Storytelling and the Blind Child." *The New Outlook* 66 (December 1972): 356-60. Reprinted in *The Special Child in the Library*, edited by Barbara Holland Baskin and Karen H. Harris, pp. 109-112. Chicago: American Library Association, 1976.

Dardig, Jill C. "A Visual Literacy Program for Deaf Students." *Audiovisual Instruction* 19 (October 1974): 24-27.

Dempsey, Angeline. "A Junior High School Program for Retarded Readers." *School Libraries* 16 (Spring 1967): 9-15. Reprinted in *The Special Child in the Library*, edited by Barbara Holland Baskin and Karen H. Harris, pp. 119-23. Chicago: American Library Association, 1976.

Elwyn Institute. "Using the Library to Enhance Awareness of Life's Realities in Handicapped Children Residing in an Institution." Harrisburg: Pennsylvania State Library, 1978. (ED 167 140).

Esteves, Roberto. "Video Opens Libraries to the Deaf." *American Libraries* 13 (January 1982): 36, 38.

Genensky, S. M., and others. "A Second-Generation Interactive Classroom Television System for the Partially Sighted." *Journal of Visual Impairment and Blindness* 72 (February 1978): 41-45.

Glazzard, Peggy H. "Simulation of Handicaps as a Teaching Strategy for Preservice and Inservice Training." *Teaching Exceptional Children* 11 (Spring 1979): 101-104.

Goldberg, Leonard M. "Interactive Computer-Controlled TV for the Deaf." *Audiovisual Instruction* 23 (January 1978): 16-17.

Hall, Candace Catlin, and Yarmal, Ann. "Libraries and P.L. 94-142; Awareness Planning Makes a Difference." *Top of the News* 35 (Fall 1978): 67-73.

Harris, Karen H. "Selecting Library Materials for Exceptional Children." *School Media Quarterly* 8 (Fall 1979): 22-28.

Henne, John F. "Serving Visually Handicapped Children." *School Library Journal* 25 (December 1978): 363-67. Reprinted in *Meeting the Needs of the*

Handicapped: A Resource for Teachers and Librarians, edited by Carol H. Thomas and James L. Thomas, pp. 234-37. Phoenix: Oryx Press, 1980.

Horn, William A. "To See and to Touch." *American Education* 6 (August-September 1970): 35-36. Reprinted in *The Special Child in the Library*, edited by Barbara Holland Baskin and Karen H. Harris, pp. 81-82. Chicago: American Library Association, 1976.

Hunsucker, Coy Kate. "Public Library Service to Blind and Physically Handicapped Children." *Health and Rehabilitative Library Services Division Journal* 2 (Fall 1976): 3-5.

Huston, Patrick. "Storytelling." *The Volta Review* 74 (February 1972): 200-204. Reprinted in *The Special Child in the Library*, edited by Barbara Holland Baskin and Karen H. Harris, pp. 112-14. Chicago: American Library Association, 1976.

Irwin, Michael. "Media, the Arts, and the Handicapped." *Audiovisual Instruction* 24 (November 1979): 33-36.

Jackson, William D. "Educational Media in Teaching the Deaf Child." *Audiovisual Instruction* 11 (November 1966): 715-18. Reprinted in *The Special Child in the Library*, edited by Barbara Holland Baskin and Karen H. Harris, pp. 63-65. Chicago: American Library Association, 1976.

Johnson, Diane. "Handicapped Awareness Day." *Library Journal* 105 (February 1, 1980): 360.

Johnson, Elizabeth, and Merriweather, Thelma. "Blind Children Learn to Relate." *American Libraries* 1 (February 1970): 168-69.

Johnson, Shirley A. "A Toy Library for Developmentally Disabled Children." *Teaching Exceptional Children* 11 (Fall 1978): 26-28. Reprinted in *Meeting the Needs of the Handicapped: A Resource for Teachers and Librarians*, edited by Carol H. Thomas and James L. Thomas, pp. 66-72. Phoenix: Oryx Press, 1980.

Knight, John J. "Teacher-Produced Slides Aid Reading for Low Vision Children." *Teaching Exceptional Children* 3 (Summer 1971): 203-208. Reprinted in *The Special Child in the Library*, edited by Barbara Holland Baskin and Karen H. Harris, pp. 75-77. Chicago: American Library Association, 1976.

Kreis, Max. "Project Video Language: A Successful Experiment." *American Annals of the Deaf* 124 (September 1979): 542-48.

Leavitt, Glenn. "Time, Money, and Students with Visual Limitations." *The New Outlook* 65 (October 1971): 271-75. Reprinted in *The Special Child in the Library*, edited by Barbara Holland Baskin and Karen H. Harris, pp. 82-84. Chicago: American Library Association, 1976.

Limper, Hilda K. "Serving Mentally Retarded Children in Our Libraries." *Catholic Library World* 45 (April 1974): 423-25. Reprinted in *Library Services to the Blind and Physically Handicapped*, edited by Maryalls G. Strom, pp. 91-95. Metuchen, NJ: Scarecrow Press, 1977.

McClanahan, Fay D. "Toys for Learning." In *The Value of Toys in Institutional Libraries*, pp. 14-23. Pierre, SD: South Dakota State Library, 1980.

McKay, Richard J.; Schwartz, Linda; and Willis, Kathy. "The Instructional Media Center's Function in Programs for Special Needs of Children at the Middle School Level." *International Journal of Instructional Media* 4 (No. 1, 1976-1977): 1-6.

Mahaffy, Carolyn T. "Expanding Limited Lives with Media." *Audiovisual Instruction* 14 (November 1969): 34-35.

Maillard, E. C.; Barkin, M.; and Brathwaite, E. "A Very Special Arts Festival." *Instructor* 86 (March 1977): 134-38.

Marcoux, J. Paul. "Helping Emotionally Disturbed Children through Creative Dramatics." *Communication Education* 25 (March 1976): 174-77. Reprinted in *Meeting the Needs of the Handicapped: A Resource for Teachers and Librarians*, edited by Carol H. Thomas and James L. Thomas, pp. 164-68. Phoenix: Oryx Press, 1980.

Metcalf, Mary Jane. "Helping Hearing Impaired Students." *School Library Journal* 25 (January 1979): 27-29. Reprinted in *Meeting the Needs of the Handicapped: A Resource for Teachers and Librarians*, edited by Carol H. Thomas and James L. Thomas, pp. 197-203. Phoenix: Oryx Press, 1980.

Molhoek, Leslie. "A Special Place for Special Children." *Catholic Library World* 52 (November 1980): 158-59.

Morgan, Ken. "The School Library and Children with Learning and Behavior Problems." *Utah Libraries* 13 (Spring 1970): 20-24. Reprinted in *The Special Child in the Library*, edited by Barbara Holland Baskin and Karen H. Harris, pp. 117-19. Chicago: American Library Association, 1976.

Mullen, Frances A., and Peterson, Miriam. "Special Education and the School Librarian." *Illinois Libraries* 47 (May 1965): 407-416. Reprinted in *The Special Child in the Library*, edited by Barbara Holland Baskin and Karen H. Harris, pp. 95-97. Chicago: American Library Association, 1976.

National Library Service for the Blind and Physically Handicapped. *Reaching People: A Manual on Public Education for Libraries Serving Blind and Physically Handicapped Individuals.* Washington, DC: Library of Congress, 1980.

Parlato, Salvatore J., Jr. "Captioned and Nonverbal Films for the Hearing-Impaired." *Library Trends* 27 (Summer 1978): 59-63.

Parlato, Salvatore J., Jr. *Films—Too Good for Words; A Directory of Non-narrated 16mm Films*. New York: R. R. Bowker, 1973.

Parlato, Salvatore J., Jr. "Films without Words: Benefits and Caveats." *International Development Review* 17 (Winter 1975): 33-34.

Parlato, Salvatore J., Jr. "Using Non-Verbal Films with the Deaf and Language-Impaired." *Sightlines* 10 (Winter 1976/77): 10-11. Reprinted in *Meeting the Needs of the Handicapped: A Resource for Teachers and Librarians*, edited by Carol H. Thomas and James L. Thomas, pp. 223-27. Phoenix: Oryx Press, 1980.

Pfau, Glenn S. "Programed Instruction: An Exploration into Its Effectiveness with the Handicapped Child." *Audiovisual Instruction* 14 (November 1969): 24-27.

Pfau, Glenn S. "Programmed Movies—A Supplemental Medium for Language Development." *American Annals of the Deaf* 115 (October 1970): 569-72. Reprinted in *The Special Child in the Library*, edited by Barbara Holland Baskin and Karen H. Harris, pp. 70-72. Chicago: American Library Association, 1976.

Pieper, Elizabeth J. "Preparing Children for a Handicapped Classmate." *Instructor* 84 (August 1974): 128-29.

Schaefer, Florence, and others. "Project 'ME': A New Approach to Media in the Education of Learning Disabled Children." *Journal of Learning Disabilities* 7 (February 1974): 18-28.

Schisgall, Jane. "The Creative Use of Multimedia (or The Shape of Strings to Come)." *Teaching Exceptional Children* 5 (Summer 1973): 162-69.

Sharapan, Hedda B. "Misterogers' Neighborhood: A Resource for Exceptional Children." *Audiovisual Instruction* 18 (February 1973): 18-20.

Smith, Harry. "Games and Simulation Studies for the Deaf." *American Annals of the Deaf* 124 (September 1979): 611-15.

Stark, Bill. " 'Meanwhile ...': A Look at Comic Books at Illinois School for the Deaf." *American Annals of the Deaf* 121 (October 1976): 470-77. Reprinted in *Meeting the Needs of the Handicapped: A Resource for Teachers and Librarians*, edited by Carol H. Thomas and James L. Thomas, pp. 208-213. Phoenix: Oryx Press, 1980.

"Storytellers Visit Homebound Children." *School Library Journal* 23 (November 1976): 14.

Strom, Maryalls G., ed. *Library Services to the Blind and Physically Handicapped*. Metuchen, NJ: Scarecrow Press, 1977.

Thomas, Carol H., and Thomas, James L., eds. *Meeting the Needs of the Handicapped: A Resource for Teachers and Librarians.* Phoenix: Oryx Press, 1980.

Uldrich, Bette Claire. "The Little Red Hen." *Ohio Media Spectrum* 30 (January 1978): 54-56.

Velleman, Ruth A. *Serving Physically Disabled People: An Information Handbook for All Libraries.* New York: R. R. Bowker, 1979.

Vidler, Virginia. "Use Puppets to Reach the Emotionally Disturbed." *Instructor* 81 (May 1972): 68. Reprinted in *The Special Child in the Library*, edited by Barbara Holland Baskin and Karen H. Harris, pp. 149-50. Chicago: American Library Association, 1976.

Vincent, Ruth. "A Library Program to Educate Students in Understanding the Handicapped." *The Bookmark* 38 (Winter 1980): 308-310.

Walter, John, and Long, Sarah. "Story Hours for Children with Learning Disabilities." *Top of the News* 35 (Summer 1979): 385-88.

Chapter 8

Abbye, Sonya. "The Learning-Disabled Child ... Films for Social, Emotional, Language and Sensory Needs." *Film Library Quarterly* 9 (No. 3, 1976): 37-43. Reprinted in *Meeting the Needs of the Handicapped: A Resource for Teachers and Librarians*, edited by Carol H. Thomas and James L. Thomas, pp. 128-35. Phoenix: Oryx Press, 1980.

Ames, Jan. "Libraries Serving Handicapped Users Share Resources." *Catholic Library World* 52 (February 1981): 297-300.

Ashcroft, Samuel C. "Learning Resources in Special Education: The Quiet Evolution." *Education and Training of the Mentally Retarded* 12 (April 1977): 132-36.

Ashcroft, Samuel C. "NCEMMH: A Network of Media/Material Resources." *Audiovisual Instruction* 21 (December 1976): 46-47.

Audiovisual Guide for Services to Handicapped. College Park, MD: Head Start Resource and Training Center, 1977. (ED 145 616).

Belland, John C. "Mission and Services of the National Center on Educational Media and Materials for the Handicapped." In *The Special Child in the Library*, edited by Barbara Holland Baskin and Karen H. Harris, pp. 188-95. Chicago: American Library Association, 1976.

Belland, John C. "The National Center on Educational Media and Materials for the Handicapped." *Audiovisual Instruction* 18 (February 1973): 7-9.

Berger, Allen, and Kautz, Constance R. "Sources of Information and Materials for Blind and Visually Limited Pupils." *Elementary English* 47 (December 1970): 1097-1105. Reprinted in *The Special Child in the Library*, edited by Barbara Holland Baskin and Karen H. Harris, pp. 168-74. Chicago: American Library Association, 1976.

Bland, Elwood L. "Learning Resources for the Handicapped." *Exceptional Children* 43 (November 1976): 161-63.

Boland, Sandra K. "Materials and Resources for Career Development of Retarded Individuals." *Education and Training of the Mentally Retarded* 12 (April 1977): 163-65.

Bush, Margaret. "Books for Children Who Cannot See the Printed Page." *School Library Journal* 26 (April 1980): 28-31.

Carl, Elizabeth. "The National Library Service for the Blind and Physically Handicapped." In *Services and Materials for the Handicapped; Proceedings of an Institute for School Library Media Professionals, August 12-17, 1979*, edited by Henry C. Dequin, pp. 122-25. DeKalb, IL: Northern Illinois University, 1979.

Coates, Eyler Robert. "Music for the Blind and Physically Handicapped from the Library of Congress." *American Music Teacher* 25 (February 1976): 21-24. Reprinted in *Meeting the Needs of the Handicapped: A Resource for Teachers and Librarians*, edited by Carol H. Thomas and James L. Thomas, pp. 275-82. Phoenix: Oryx Press, 1980.

Dequin, Henry C. "Bibliographic Sources of Materials for Handicapped Learners." In *Services and Materials for the Handicapped; Proceedings of an Institute for School Library Media Professionals, August 12-17, 1979*, edited by Henry C. Dequin, pp. 57-76. DeKalb, IL: Northern Illinois University, 1979.

Dequin, Henry C. "Resources for Disabled Learners." *Media Management Journal* 1 (Fall 1981): 4-5, 18.

Dequin, Henry C. "Selecting Materials for the Handicapped: A Guide to Sources." *Top of the News* 35 (Fall 1978): 57-66.

Dequin, Henry C. "Services and Materials for Disabled Children." *Illinois Libraries* 63 (September 1981): 546-54.

Dequin, Henry C. "Sources of Information about the Handicapped." *School Library Journal* 26 (November 1979): 38-41.

Dresang, Eliza T. "There Are No *Other* Children." *School Library Journal* 24 (September 1977): 19-23.

Dziedzic, Donna. "The Same Only Different Service." *Illinois Libraries* 63 (October 1981): 633-38.

Erickson, Donald K. "Exceptional Child Education Resources: A One-of-a-Kind Data Base." *Illinois Libraries* 59 (September 1977): 519-23.

Fuchs, Victor E. "National Center of Educational Media and Materials for the Handicapped Program." *Illinois Libraries* 59 (September 1977): 525-30.

Fuchs, Victor, and Ellis, Joyce. "Service: A Priority with the National Center on Educational Media and Materials for the Handicapped." *Journal of Learning Disabilities* 10 (February 1977): 13-19.

Gearreald, Karen. "A World of Knowledge through Sound: The Audio Program of the Hadley School." *Audiovisual Instruction* 14 (November 1969): 31-33. Reprinted in *The Special Child in the Library*, edited by Barbara Holland Baskin and Karen H. Harris, pp. 175-77. Chicago: American Library Association, 1976.

Gray, Karen, and Altgilbers, Cynthia. "Serving the Exceptional Child—A System Response." *Illinois Libraries* 59 (September 1977): 513-15.

Hughes, Karen. "Exploring 'Direct-Use' Media for Severely Handicapped Students." *Media Management Journal* 1 (Fall 1981): 6-8, 16.

Kundert, James J. "Media Services and Captioned Films." *Educational Technology* 10 (August 1970): 40-42. Reprinted in *The Special Child in the Library*, edited by Barbara Holland Baskin and Karen H. Harris, pp. 179-81. Chicago: American Library Association, 1976.

Lange, Robert R.; Mattson, Charyl T.; and Thomann, James B. "Needs for Instructional Media and Materials Services for Handicapped Learners: A Summary of Extant Information." Columbus, OH: The National Center on Educational Media and Materials for the Handicapped, Ohio State University, 1974.

Lappin, Carl W. "At Your Service—The Instructional Materials Reference Center for the Visually Handicapped." *Teaching Exceptional Children* 5 (Winter 1973): 74-76. Reprinted in *The Special Child in the Library*, edited by Barbara Holland Baskin and Karen H. Harris, pp. 174-75. Chicago: American Library Association, 1976.

Lappin, Carl W. "The Instructional Materials Reference Center for the Visually Handicapped." *Education of the Visually Handicapped* 4 (October 1972): 65-70.

Lappin, Carl W. "School Books for the Blind and Physically Handicapped Child." *Health and Rehabilitative Library Services Division Journal* 2 (Fall 1976): 5-7.

Lappin, Carl W. "Textbooks for Visually Impaired Students." *Ohio Media Spectrum* 30 (January 1978): 32-34.

McCormack, James E.; Doyle, Cathy; and Blieberg, Jody. *Guide to Finding Appropriate Instructional Materials: Existing Retrieval Systems.* Medford, MA: Center for Program Development and Evaluation, 1977. (ED 141 996).

Niederer, Margaret, and Reguly, Bobby. "A Program to Enable Visually Impaired Students in Illinois to Realize Their Full Potential." *Illinois Libraries* 59 (September 1977): 495-98.

Norwood, Malcolm J. "Captioned Films for the Deaf." *Exceptional Children* 43 (November 1976): 164-66.

Ofiesh, Gabriel D. "A National Center for Educational Media and Materials for the Handicapped." *Audiovisual Instruction* 14 (November 1969): 28-29.

Oldsen, Carl F. "The National Instructional Materials Information System." *Audiovisual Instruction* 21 (December 1976): 48-50.

Oldsen, Carl F. "National Instructional Materials Information System (NIMIS)." *Illinois Libraries* 59 (September 1977): 516-19.

Ostendorf, JoEllen. "National Library Services for the Blind and Physically Handicapped." In *School Library Media Services to the Handicapped*, edited by Myra Macon, pp. 131-65. Westport, CT: Greenwood Press, 1982.

Parlato, Salvatore J. "Captioned and Nonverbal Films for the Hearing-Impaired." *Library Trends* 27 (Summer 1978): 59-63.

Peters, Frances M. "Reading Is for Everyone." *Ohio Media Spectrum* 30 (January 1978): 22-25.

"Producers of Materials for Exceptional Children." *Teacher* 94 (May 1977): 119-22.

Reeder, Alan F., and Bolen, Jacqueline M. "Match the Materials to the Learner." *Audiovisual Instruction* 21 (December 1976): 24-25.

Reisinger, Carol. "Illinois Resource and Dissemination Network: Datamation, Dissemination, Determination." *Illinois Libraries* 59 (September 1977): 470-75.

Sadoski, Michael J., and Sadoski, Doris C. "Sign Language Films for Library Users." *California Librarian* 39 (April 1978): 56-58.

Soeffing, Marylane. "The CEC Information Center on Exceptional Children." *Audiovisual Instruction* 14 (November 1969): 42-43.

Stowitschek, Joseph J.; Gable, Robert A.; and Hendrickson, Jo Mary. *Instructional Materials for Exceptional Children: Selection, Management, and Adaption.* Germantown, MD: Aspen Publications, 1980.

U.S. Department of Health, Education, and Welfare. Office of Human Development Services. Office for Handicapped Individuals. *Directory of National Information Sources on Handicapping Conditions and Related Services.* Washington, DC: Government Printing Office, 1980. DHEW Publication Number (OHDS) 80-22007.

Velleman, Ruth A. *Serving Physically Disabled People: An Information Handbook for All Libraries.* New York: R. R. Bowker, 1979.

Wexler, Henrietta. "Books That Talk." *American Education* 17 (January/ February 1981): 15-17.

Wright, Kieth C. *Library and Information Services for Handicapped Individuals.* Littleton, CO: Libraries Unlimited, 1979.

Young, Diana, and Simmons, Beverley J. "We Can Grow!" *School Library Journal* 23 (May 1977): 44.

Chapter 9

American Library Association. Association for Library Service to Children. Library Service to Children with Special Needs Committee. *Selecting Materials for Children with Special Needs.* Chicago: American Library Association, 1980.

American Library Association. Young Adult Services Division. *High Interest/ Low Reading Level Information Packet.* Chicago: American Library Association, 1978.

Aserlind, Leroy. "Research: Some Implications for the Classroom." *Teaching Exceptional Children* 1 (Winter 1969): 42-54.

Baskin, Barbara H., and Harris, Karen H. "Selecting Materials for the Mainstreamed Library." In *School Library Media Services to the Handicapped*, edited by Myra Macon, pp. 75-88. Westport, CT: Greenwood Press, 1982.

Baskin, Barbara H., and Harris, Karen H., eds. *The Special Child in the Library.* Chicago: American Library Association, 1976.

Bates, Barbara S. "Identifying High Interest/Low Reading Level Books." *School Library Journal* 24 (November 1977): 19-21.

Berdine, William Harry. "A Comparison of Retrieval Systems to Prescriptively Select Materials." *Exceptional Children* 41 (November 1974): 195-97.

Blake, Ruth, and others. *Visually Handicapped: An Approach to Program Development.* Indianapolis: West Central Joint Services for the Handicapped, 1972. (ED 079 903).

Bleil, Gordon. "Evaluating Educational Materials." *Journal of Learning Disabilities* 8 (January 1975): 12-19.

Boland, Sandra K. "Instructional Materialism—Or How to Select the Things You Need." *Teaching Exceptional Children* 8 (Summer 1976): 156-58.

Boland, Sandra K. "Managing Your Instructional Material Dollar." *Teaching Exceptional Children* 6 (Spring 1974): 134-39.

Boutwell, William D. "Motivating the Slow Learner." *Wilson Library Bulletin* 40 (September 1965): 75-77, 100. Reprinted in *The Special Child in the Library*, edited by Barbara Holland Baskin and Karen H. Harris, pp. 39-42. Chicago: American Library Association, 1976.

Cohen, Shirley, and Koehler, Nancy. *Instructional Materials: A Bibliography for Their Selection, Evaluation and Use.* New York: City University of New York, Graduate School and University Center, 1975.

Davis, Emmett A., and Davis, Catherine M. *Mainstreaming Library Service for Disabled People.* Metuchen, NJ: Scarecrow Press, 1980.

Dequin, Henry C. "Criteria for the Selection of Materials for Handicapped Learners." In *Services and Materials for the Handicapped; Proceedings of an Institute for School Library Media Professionals, August 12-17, 1979,* edited by Henry C. Dequin, pp. 77-108. DeKalb, IL: Northern Illinois University, 1979.

Dyer, Susan R., and Forcier, Richard C. "How to Pick Computer Software." *Instructional Innovator* 27 (September 1982): 38-40.

Eash, Maurice. *Evaluation of Instructional Materials for Exceptional Children and Youth.* New York: City University of New York, 1969. (ED 040 540).

Forer, Anne-Marie, and Zajac, Mary, in cooperation with the Altoona Area Public Library. "Library Services to the Mentally Retarded." Report on the L.I.F.E. Project. Altoona, PA: Altoona Area Public Library, n.d.

Fuchs, Victor. "National Center of Educational Media and Materials for the Handicapped Program." *Illinois Libraries* 59 (September 1977): 525-30.

Gallimore, Janet Elizabeth. "Criteria for the Selection and Evaluation of Book and Non-Book Materials for Mentally Retarded Adolescents and Adults." Master's thesis, California State University, San Jose, 1973.

Grannis, Florence. "Book Selection for the Blind." *Catholic Library World* 40 (April 1969): 491-96. Reprinted in *Library Services to the Blind and Physically Handicapped*, edited by Maryalls G. Strom, pp. 111-23. Metuchen, NJ: Scarecrow Press, 1977.

Grannis, Florence. "Philosophical Implications of Book Selection for the Blind." *Wilson Library Bulletin* 43 (December 1968): 330-39. Reprinted in

The Special Child in the Library, edited by Barbara Holland Baskin and Karen H. Harris, pp. 29-34. Chicago: American Library Association, 1976.

Hall, Candace Catlin. "Using Realia with the Visually Handicapped Child." *Connecticut Libraries* 19 (Number 4, 1977): 21-22.

Harris, Karen H. "Selecting Library Materials for Exceptional Children." *School Media Quarterly* 8 (Fall 1979): 22-28. Reprinted in *Meeting the Needs of the Handicapped: A Resource for Teachers and Librarians*, edited by Carol H. Thomas and James L. Thomas, pp. 388-97. Phoenix: Oryx Press, 1980.

Hart, Verna. *Mainstreaming Children with Special Needs.* New York: Longman, 1981.

Heinich, Robert, ed. *Educating All Handicapped Children.* Englewood Cliffs, NJ: Educational Technology Publications, 1979.

Hickman, Maribeth R., and Anderson, Carol R. "Evaluating Instructional Materials for Learning Disabled Children." *Journal of Learning Disabilities* 12 (May 1979): 355-59.

Johnson, Shirley A. "A Toy Library for Developmentally Disabled Children." *Teaching Exceptional Children* 11 (Fall 1978): 26-28. Reprinted in *Meeting the Needs of the Handicapped: A Resource for Teachers and Librarians*, edited by Carol H. Thomas and James L. Thomas, pp. 66-72. Phoenix: Oryx Press, 1980.

Kleiman, Glenn; Humphrey, Mary M.; and Van Buskirk, Trudy. "Evaluating Educational Software." *Creative Computing* 7 (October 1981): 84-90.

Lange, Robert R.; Mattson, Charyl T.; and Thomann, James B. "Needs for Instructional Media and Materials Services for Handicapped Learners: A Summary of Extant Information." Columbus, OH: The National Center on Educational Media and Materials for the Handicapped, Ohio State University, 1974.

Lankford, Mary D., comp. "Microcomputers." *Booklist* 78 (October 1, 1981): 242-44.

Latham, Glenn. *Teacher Use of Instructional Materials and Other Matters Related to Special Education IMC/LRC Collections.* Theoretical Paper No. 59. Madison: University of Wisconsin, Research and Development Center for Cognitive Learning, 1976. (ED 126 663).

"A Level-headed Guide to Software Evaluation." *Classroom Computer News* 1 (July-August 1981): 22-23.

Luchow, Jed F. "Selecting Picture Storybooks for Young Children with Learning Disabilities." *Teaching Exceptional Children* 4 (Summer 1972): 161-64. Reprinted in *The Special Child in the Library*, edited by Barbara Holland

Baskin and Karen H. Harris, pp. 39-42. Chicago: American Library Association, 1976.

McClanahan, Fay D. "Toys for Learning." In *The Value of Toys in Institutional Libraries*, pp. 14-23. Pierre, SD: South Dakota State Library, 1980.

McCormack, James E.; Doyle, Cathy; and Blieberg, Jody. *Guide to Finding Appropriate Instructional Materials: Existing Retrieval Systems*. Medford, MA: Center for Program Development and Evaluation, 1977. (ED 141 996).

"Materials Analysis." *Journal of Learning Disabilities* 9 (August/September 1976): 408-416.

Metcalf, Mary Jane. "Helping Hearing Impaired Students." *School Library Journal* 25 (January 1979): 27-29. Reprinted in *Meeting the Needs of the Handicapped: A Resource for Teachers and Librarians*, edited by Carol H. Thomas and James L. Thomas, pp. 197-203. Phoenix: Oryx Press, 1980.

Moll, Joy K., and Hermann, Patricia. "Evaluation and Selection of Toys, Games, and Puzzles: Manipulative Materials in Library Collections." *Top of the News* 31 (November 1974): 86-89.

"NSAIM: Two Years Later." *EPIEgram* 5 (December 1, 1976): 1-3.

Parlato, Salvatore J., Jr. "Those Other Captioned Films ... Captioned Educational Films." *American Annals of the Deaf* 122 (February 1977): 33-37.

Quisenberry, Nancy L.; Shepherd, Terry R.; and Williams-Burns, Winona. "Criteria for the Selection of Records, Filmstrips and Films for Young Children." *Audiovisual Instruction* 18 (April 1973): 36, 38.

SRM Manual, Selected Resource Materials: Description and Evaluation. Edmonton, Alberta, Canada: Alberta Department of Education, Special Educational Services Branch, 1974. (ED 128 995).

"Selecting Instructional Materials." *EPIEgram* 5 (December 15, 1976): 1-2.

Shotel, Jay R.; Iano, Richard P.; and McGettigan, James F. "Teacher Attitudes Associated with the Integration of Handicapped Children." *Exceptional Children* 38 (May 1972): 677-83.

Smith, Megan. "South Dakota School for the Visually Handicapped Toy Library." In *The Value of Toys in Institutional Libraries*, pp. 1-13. Pierre, SD: South Dakota State Library, 1980.

Standard Criteria for the Selection and Evaluation of Instructional Materials. Columbus, OH: National Center on Educational Media and Materials for the Handicapped, Ohio State University, 1976. Reprinted in *Illinois Libraries* 59 (September 1977): 531-40.

Teter, Ralph O., ed. *Handbook: The Operation of Programs for Language-Handicapped Children.* Austin: Texas Education Agency, Division of Special Education, 1973. (ED 096 791).

Thormann, Joan, and Rosemont, JoAnn. "Criteria for Books for Learning Disabled Children." *Appraisal* 10 (Winter 1977): 1-4.

Thorum, Arden R., and others. *Instructional Materials for the Handicapped: Birth through Early Childhood.* Salt Lake City: Olympus, 1976.

Tuttle, Dean W. "A Comparison of Three Reading Media for the Blind—Braille, Normal Recording, and Compressed Speech." *Education of the Visually Handicapped* 4 (May 1972): 40-44. Reprinted in *The Special Child in the Library*, edited by Barbara Holland Baskin and Karen H. Harris, pp. 45-48. Chicago: American Library Association, 1976.

The Value of Toys in Institutional Libraries. Pierre, SD: South Dakota State Library, 1980.

Wiederholt, J. Lee, and McNutt, Gaye. "Evaluating Materials for Handicapped Adolescents." *Journal of Learning Disabilities* 10 (March 1977): 132-40.

Chapter 10

Bitzer, Donald. "Uses of CBE for the Handicapped." *American Annals of the Deaf* 124 (September 1979): 553-58.

"Blind and Physically Handicapped Individuals Will Soon Have the Same Access as Sighted People to the Library of Congress Book and Periodical Collections." *College and Research Library News* 8 (September 1977): 241.

"Breakthrough for the Blind." *Wilson Library Bulletin* 52 (June 1978): 762.

Champion, Richard R. "The Talking Calculator Used with Blind Youth." *Education of the Visually Handicapped* 8 (Winter 1976/77): 102-106. Reprinted in *Meeting the Needs of the Handicapped: A Resource for Teachers and Librarians*, edited by Carol H. Thomas and James L. Thomas, pp. 259-64. Phoenix: Oryx Press, 1980.

Cronin, Barry. "The DAVID System: The Development of an Interactive Video System at the National Technical Institute for the Deaf." *American Annals of the Deaf* 124 (September 1979): 616-18.

Cushman, Ruth-Carol. "The Kurzweil Reading Machine." *Wilson Library Bulletin* 54 (January 1980): 311-15.

Cylke, Frank Kurt, and Deschere, Allen R. "Information and Communication Devices for Blind and Physically Handicapped Readers." *Bulletin of the American Society for Information Science* 5 (April 1979): 9-11.

Genesky, S. M., and others. "A Second-Generation Interactive Classroom Television System for the Partially Sighted." *Journal of Visual Impairment and Blindness* 72 (February 1978): 41-45.

Goldberg, Leonard M. "Communications Technology for the Hearing Impaired." *Bulletin of the American Society for Information Science* 5 (April 1979): 12-13.

Goldberg, Leonard M. "Creative Use of Media in Schools and Programs for the Hearing Impaired." *The Volta Review* 82 (October/November 1980): 440-46.

Goldberg, Leonard M. "Interactive Computer-Controlled TV for the Deaf." *Audiovisual Instruction* 23 (January 1978): 16-17.

Goldenberg, E. Paul. *Special Technology for Special Children: Computers to Serve Communication and Autonomy in the Education of Handicapped Children.* Baltimore: University Park Press, 1979.

Green, Kerry. "Services for the Handicapped: What the AV Professional Can Do." *Media and Methods* 16 (March 1980): 39-40.

Gutknecht, Karl S. "Optacon—A Tool for Independence." *American Education* 16 (January-February 1980): 8-13.

Harris, Karen, and Baskin, Barbara. "The Exceptional Child—A Challenge for Librarians." *Louisiana Library Association Bulletin* 37 (Spring 1974): 21-24.

Harvie, Barbara. "Out of the Arcades and into the Library." *American Libraries* 12 (November 1981): 602-605.

Kirk, Samuel A., and Gallagher, James J. *Educating Exceptional Children.* 3rd ed. Boston: Houghton Mifflin, 1979.

Knight, Nancy H. "Library Service to the Disabled: A Survey of Selected Equipment." *Library Technology Reports* 17 (November/December 1981): 497-628.

Lance, Wayne D. "Technology and Media for Exceptional Learners: Looking Ahead." *Exceptional Children* 44 (October 1977): 92-97.

"Landmark Legislation Funds Reading Machines." *School Library Journal* 26 (September 1979): 18.

"A Level-headed Guide to Software Evaluation." *Classroom Computer News* 1 (July-August 1981): 22-23.

"Library Acquires New Aid for Visually Handicapped Readers." *Library of Congress Information Bulletin* 39 (January 11, 1980): 9-10.

Marinoff, Shirley Likach. "When Words Are Not Enough — Videotape." *Teaching Exceptional Children* 5 (Winter 1973): 66-73.

Nolan, Carson Y. "Audio Visual Materials for the Blind." *Audiovisual Instruction* 11 (November 1966): 724-26.

"Not Loud, but Clear." *Wilson Library Bulletin* 54 (November 1979): 153.

Pfau, Glenn S. "Educating the Deaf Child." *Audiovisual Instruction* 15 (September 1970): 24-29.

Pfau, Glenn S. "Programmed Instruction: An Exploration into Its Effectiveness with the Handicapped Child." *Audiovisual Instruction* 14 (November 1969): 24-27.

Pfau, Glenn S. "Project L.I.F.E.: Developing High Interest Programmed Materials for Handicapped Children." *Educational Technology* 10 (August 1970): 13-18.

"Quick! Tell Me How to Buy Audiovisual Products for Teaching Handicapped Children." *American School Board Journal* 164 (September 1977): 8.

Ragan, Andrew L. "The Miracle Worker: How Computers Help Handicapped Students." *Electronic Learning* 1 (January/February 1982): 56-58, 83.

"Reading Machine for the Blind Tested in Virginia Beach." *Library Journal* 104 (May 1, 1979): 995.

"Revolutionary Machine Can Read Aloud to Library Users; Blind Are First to Benefit." *American Libraries* 9 (May 1978): 256.

Ryan, Paul. "Videotape and Special Education." *Audiovisual Instruction* 14 (November 1969): 30.

Schisgall, Jane. "The Creative Use of Multimedia (Or the Shape of Strings to Come)." *Teaching Exceptional Children* 5 (Summer 1973): 162-69.

"School Library Utilizes Variable Speech Control." *School Library Journal* 25 (November 1978): 13.

Sims, Donald, and others. "A Pilot Experiment in Computer Assisted Speechreading Instruction Utilizing the Data Analysis Video Interactive Device (DAVID)." *American Annals of the Deaf* 124 (September 1979): 618-23.

Stolovich, Harold. "A Pocket Calculator Never Loses Patience." *Audiovisual Instruction* 21 (December 1976): 19-20.

Torr, Donald. "Computer-Supported Braille Applications." *American Annals of the Deaf* 124 (September 1979): 691-95.

Watson, Paul. "The Utilization of the Computer with the Hearing Impaired and the Handicapped." *American Annals of the Deaf* 124 (September 1979): 670-80.

Weinberg, Belle. "The Kurzweil Machine: Half a Miracle." *American Libraries* 11 (November 1980): 603-604, 627.

Index